Born Again Bodies

CALIFORNIA STUDIES IN FOOD AND CULTURE

Darra Goldstein, Editor

Born Again Bodies

Flesh and Spirit in American Christianity

R. MARIE GRIFFITH

University of California Press

BERKELEY   LOS ANGELES   LONDON

University of California Press
Berkeley and Los Angeles, California

University of California Press, Ltd.
London, England

© 2004 by the Regents of the University of California

The following publishers have generously given permission to reprint
excerpts from copyrighted works in chapter 3: "Apostles of Abstinence:
Fasting and Masculinity During the Progressive Era," *American
Quarterly* 52, no. 4 (December 2000): 599–638; and "Body Salvation:
New Thought, Father Divine, and the Feast of Material Pleasures,"
Religion and American Culture 11, no. 2 (Summer 2001): 119–53.

Library of Congress Cataloging-in-Publication Data

Griffith, R. Marie (Ruth Marie), 1967–
    Born again bodies : flesh and spirit in American Christianity /
R. Marie Griffith.
        p.   cm.—(California studies in food and culture ; 12)
    Includes bibliographical references and index.
    ISBN 978-0-520-24240-1 (pbk. : alk. paper)
    1. Body, Human—Religious aspects—Christianity—History of doc-
trines.   2. Body, Human—Social aspects—United States—History.
3. United States—Religious life and customs.   4. Protestantism—
United States—History.   I. Title.   II. Series.
    BT741.3.G75   2004
    233'.5—dc22   2004005272

Manufactured in the United States of America

14   13   12   11   10   09   08
10   9   8   7   6   5   4   3   2

For Leigh, Zachary, and Ella

Contents

207

✓ 4. PRAY THE WEIGHT AWAY:
SHAPING DEVOTIONAL FITNESS CULTURE 160

Shedd-ing Pounds: Scripture and Devotional Practice
in Service to Weight Loss

The Burgeoning Christian Diet Culture

From Empathy to Authority: Shifting Models of Expertise

Religious Devotion to Thinness Outside Mainstream Protestantism

207

✓ 5. "DON'T EAT THAT": DENIAL, INDULGENCE,
AND EXCLUSION IN CHRISTIAN DIET CULTURE 206

Poisoned Bodies, Blemished Souls: Food as Taint and Transgression

Loved on a Smaller Scale: Women, Weight, and the Divine
Lover Above

The Power of Perfection: Purified Bodies and Racialized Worlds

Illustrations

Acknowledgments

This is a study of Christianity's powerful role in the shaping of American bodies and varied forms of embodiment. It aims to analyze both historical and present-day contexts, by examining a great deal of popular literature as well as probing encounters with people actively involved in religious fitness culture. While not focused solely on current American life, it responds to enduring societal preoccupations and sustains my long-term ethnographic commitments.

The project has undergone several periods of revision, and I owe considerable thanks. It seems proper to begin with the undergraduate and graduate students enrolling in my assorted courses on religion and the body at Princeton University, Princeton Theological Seminary, and Harvard Divinity School. From a diverse array of intellectual and practical commitments, these scholars tenaciously confronted the big questions linking up the inquiry's source material rather than opting for the sheltered comfort of small points. I hope a measure of their inspiring audacity abides in these pages.

I obtained valuable research assistance from Bernadette Arellano, Katy Attanasi, Tammy Brown, Alyson Dickson, Lexi Gelperin, Lauren Teichner, Eric Lyons Thomas, and Jane Yager. Jane also supplied perceptive editorial assistance in the final writing phase. Princeton and Harvard Universities provided necessary funds to pay these enterprising investigators and support other research services. The project received generous financial support, and two cohorts of exceptional colleagues, from the Material History of American Religion Project, directed by James Hudnut-Beumler and funded by the Lilly Endowment; and the Women's Studies in Religion Program at Harvard Divinity School. Natalie Searl transcribed numerous interviews, while Jana Riess kept me informed of new literature relevant to my study.

Thoughtful friends and associates too plentiful to name have shared a range of useful materials with me, and it is a pleasure to thank all of them here.

The Interlibrary Loan staff at Princeton University's Firestone Library helped make my research local when pregnancy and child care deterred travel plans, and I want especially to acknowledge Lois Nase, Patty Ponzoli, and Mark Santangelo. More thanks are due to David Tambo at the American Religions Collection at the University of California at Santa Barbara; C. Alan Anderson of the International New Thought Alliance; Jeannie Sklar at the National Anthropological Archives; and the staff at several libraries: the New York Public Library, including the Schomburg Center for Research in Black Culture; the Library of Congress; the Mary Baker Eddy Library for the Betterment of Humanity; and the Harvard University Libraries, including the Harry Elkins Widener Memorial Library, Andover-Harvard Theological Library, Houghton Library, and the Arthur and Elizabeth Schlesinger Library on the History of Women in America. Special thanks go to the photographer John Blazejewski.

Insightful discussions occurred among lecture-hall audiences at Oregon State University, the University of Tennessee at Chattanooga, the University of North Carolina, Loyola University, Northwestern University, Point Loma University, Berea College, Montclair State University, Rutgers University, Harvard Divinity School, and the University of Southern California. Colleagues at the American Academy of Religion, American Historical Association, and Society for the Anthropology of Religion annual meetings furnished valuable suggestions, particularly commentators Janet Jakobsen, J. Terry Todd, David Morgan, and Linda Barnes. In less formal venues, I received excellent feedback from the Religion and Culture Workshop at Princeton, the American Religion Colloquium at Harvard, and Material Religion Project meetings, as well as from my Harvard cohort of research associates—Paola Bacchetta, Kelly Pemberton, Brigid Sackey, and Elina Vuola—and our facilitator, Clarissa Atkinson. Dynamic and challenging exchanges with Anthea Butler, Claudia Highbaugh, and Monique Moultrie were indispensable for expanding my awareness of the complex factors that influence African American women's relationship to food and their bodies.

In addition to anonymous reviewers of journal articles and the full manuscript, helpful critics and conversation partners have included Gail Bederman, Ann Braude, Tom Bremer, Wendy Cadge, John Corrigan, Heather Curtis, Cynthia Eller, Marla Frederick, Stephanie Fysh, Heather Hendershot, Grace Hong, Kathryn Jay, Kimerer LaMothe, Laura Levitt, Melani McAlister, Colleen McDannell, Robert Orsi, Stephen Prothero, Noliwe Rooks, Dan Sack, Beryl Satter, Leigh Schmidt, Tim Watson, David

Watt, Judith Weisenfeld, Diane Winston, and Alan Wolfe. Cordial gratitude goes especially to those colleagues who read fledgling draft chapters and encouraged me to widen my scope.

The project has vastly benefited from the plethora of formal interviews, phone and e-mail exchanges, and casual discussions I have had with scores of women (and some men) who have participated in Christian diet programs or have had other relevant life experience. As with my previous book, *God's Daughters,* I have learned much from multiple interactions with persons holding worldviews quite different from my own. Some of these took place in formal weight-loss groups, others emerged in semi-anonymous seminar or conference encounters, more from student connections, and still others from online chat groups and e-mail communication. Many authors and influential public figures in the Christian fitness movement have been generous with their time and interest in this project; Carol Showalter and Neva Coyle were especially gracious in welcoming differences of opinion and perspective. Well do I realize that some will not fully agree with my rendering of their multi-faceted religious convictions. Their dissent may be especially sharp since I have grown increasingly troubled by certain social consequences (from the calculated to the inadvertent) of the flesh-conscious devotion many esteem.

I continue to uphold the ethnographic model of critical empathy described more fully in *God's Daughters* and so have endeavored to convey the humanity of complex persons and the subtlety of their religious practices. At the same time, I affirm the prerogative to appraise these, including discrepancies and unintended repercussions, in words that these subjects may not use or find flattering. This book, in fact, comments much more strongly than my earlier work upon social realities that some religious individuals have seemed to deny, ignore, or absolve from faith-based culpability. Such a collective refusal to acknowledge, say, religion's contributing role in the cultural exaltation of slender white bodies over other kinds has many sources—no one person or institution carries unique blame—but it would be wrong to collude in this process by portraying Christianity and its many well-meaning adherents as wholly innocent or blameless. I nonetheless hope that those interviewed took pleasure, as I did, from our exchanges and that they trust the earnestness compelling me to reflect frankly about matters they and I mutually consider of utmost importance. To the women in the mid-Atlantic region who so enthusiastically welcomed me to their devotional weight-loss classes and spent time and energy talking with me outside those spaces, my warmest thanks. I welcome confrontation and ongoing conversation about these vital and complex subjects.

Reed Malcolm, Dore Brown, Edith Gladstone, Patricia Deminna, and other members of the University of California Press editorial team have blended enthusiasm, patience, and professional expertise. I am grateful to them for helping bring this book to fruition.

For reasons each will recognize, my fullest appreciation extends to colleagues, friends, and family who have supported me in different ways throughout: Jennifer Lewis Gess, Becky Gould, Nannelle and Charles Griffith, David Hall, William Hutchison, Anita Kline, Courtney Bickel Lamberth, Robert Orsi, Barbara Savage, Ann and Roger Schmidt, Leigh Schmidt, Jeffrey Stout, and Robert Wuthnow. Leigh lived closest to this book and aided me through it; his encouragement has been imperative. Zachary and Ella have daily reminded me to stop working and start playing, while also embodying in their own passionate humanity the stakes claimed by this project. The book is for them.

No single work could treat anything approaching a total history of the body in American Christianity, and I do not purport to do so here. My aim, rather, has been to deal evenly with some influential episodes in ways that may illumine pressing, socially consequential themes. I admire the many teachers who have taught me to explore religious worlds inhabited by the living and the dead and to cherish connections forged among both. For remaining deficiencies, I remain wholly accountable.

Introduction

Perilous Body Gospels

"Fat People Don't Go To Heaven!" screamed a boldface headline inside the *Globe,* a national weekly tabloid circulated to millions of American readers. The story beneath this lurid caption in November 2000 recounted the rise of Gwen Shamblin, founder and CEO of the nation's largest Christian diet company and recent subject of extensive press coverage from *Larry King Live* and *20/20* to the *New Yorker.* While this media flurry fed on controversies then swirling around Shamblin—including a series of lawsuits filed by former employees whom Shamblin allegedly fired for refusing to join her newly founded church—reporters reacted more to her stringent guidelines for proper Christian body size and their widespread popular reception. "I am not a savvy businessperson," Shamblin had lately pronounced in a front-page *Wall Street Journal* feature. "I'm just a dumb blonde with a genuine heart for God, who found the golden product that everyone wanted." That coveted discovery, a spiritual route to guaranteed weight loss, was marketed in the Weigh Down Workshop, whose Shamblin-packed videos, audiotapes, books, conferences, and twelve-week seminars taught restrained eating as a divine command. The eternal costs of overeating were markedly severe: "Grace," in Shamblin's words, "does not go down into the pigpen."[1]

Though forecasts for the future of Shamblin's enterprise remain mixed, the culture of Christian fitness that she represents appears secure. Today hundreds of thousands of Americans are enrolled in programs like Shamblin's, and millions of American Christians have made a religious duty out of diet. Certain that God desires believers to partake sparingly of Fritos and brownies in order to enter "the Promised Land of thinness" or committed to the view that the divine diet consists only of raw fruits and vegetables—preaching calorie counts, prepackaged foods, and tearful prayers of

1

1. "Fat People Don't
Go To Heaven!" *Globe,*
November 21, 2000, 5. This
sensationalized tabloid image
marked Gwen Shamblin's rise
to moderate celebrity status.

surrender or promoting perfect health with a creationist diet of distilled
water and green leaves of barley—the devout theologize about food and fat
as never before. Disregard what goes into your body, many suggest, and you
will not only gain weight, look ugly, and feel awful but you will also doom
yourself to a lifetime and likely an eternity of divine disfavor. The body is a
hazard to the soul, able to demolish the hardest won spiritual gains merely
through ingesting the wrong material. While women have been major purveyors as well as consumers of this far-reaching genre, men have played
powerful roles as well. If the guidance of a particular authority such as
Shamblin seems distasteful, there are myriad other Christian diet plans from
which to choose, all warning of the perilous yet arduously redeemable body.

Christian diet vendors have plainly hit upon a painful but highly lucra-
tive theme. Today, books categorized as Christian life and spirituality make
up about 40 percent of all self-help books, and a sizeable proportion of the
genre is devoted to weight loss. According to the sociologist Kenneth
Ferraro, religious practice in the United States correlates positively with

2. Front cover of Gwen Shamblin, *Rise Above.* The sequel to Shamblin's popular *Weigh Down Diet*, this book vanished from bookshelves after controversy arose around Shamblin's theology. The earlier book, published by Doubleday, remained in print at least into 2004.

obesity, as Christians generally (and Southern Baptists in particular) are the heaviest of all. Despite the increasing theological attention given to weight since the 1970s and evident as far back as the 1950s, Ferraro cautions, "There is no evidence . . . that religion plays a major role in aiding the management of body weight in the United States. Instead, people who are more active in practicing their religion are also more likely to be overweight. In other words, many 'firm believers' do not have 'firm bodies.'"[2]

The sheer force with which fitness merchants have seized upon this apparent reality elicits wonder: why has such a phenomenon appeared now? Which aspects of it seem new amid much older impulses? What relationship, if any, exists between contemporary Christian fitness culture and the health reform movements of earlier eras? And what religious messages might also be playing out in so-called secular American diet culture? Surveying the past uncovers the tortuous modes by which American Christians have conceptualized, enacted, and practiced the relationship between body and soul, offering distinct insights for understanding not only the particular history of American diet obsessions but much broader social, cultural, and political realities as well.

At the outset, however, I need to qualify the descriptor "Christian." In fact, as this study contends, questions raised about the body in American culture have not been straightforwardly or generically "Christian" at all but rather contextually grounded in white, middle-class Protestantism. My argument is not narrowly occupied with Protestantism as a point of origin (origins of bodily fixations being multifarious and endlessly debatable); instead, I view Protestantism as an influential source of a syncretic matrix of practices that have shaped and continuously reshaped absorption with the body in definite, clearly discernible ways. From the colonial period onward, Protestants in America have wrestled with the dilemmas provoked by human embodiment in ways that would, to all appearances, look increasingly divorced from patristic and medieval models. While both Protestant and Catholic critics of abundance from Cotton Mather to Sylvester Graham to Dorothy Day recall earlier ascetic Christian themes, the evolving fixation on bodily health and perfection departs from older emphases on corporeal acts of penitence aimed at subjugating the flesh or achieving identification with the suffering, crucified Christ. Modern-day obsessions with lean, tight bodies and the equation of extreme thinness with sensual beauty bear only a faint resemblance to the intense rituals of purification and self-denial that occupied Christians in earlier periods.

Hence the term "Christian," which like other general terms such as "religious" or even "American" I uneasily but inescapably employ, here refers foremost to specific strands of influence birthed in white, middle-class Protestant groups from different regions of the United States. Catholics, Jews, and many more certainly participate vigorously in their own distinctive (and some similar) somatic disciplines and devotions. And intentional body regimens cross lines of class and race in very interesting ways. Notwithstanding all the possible crisscrossings and nuances, these practices draw their source and momentum from specific Protestant patterns, even as their most avid participants broadly describe themselves as Christians in ways that totalize and tighten the boundaries around this term. As observers have long verified, collective identities require an "other" against which to define themselves: thus difference expresses relationships of power and exclusion. It is notable that just as the white Protestant imagination, which has historically presumed its own superiority to all other faith systems, expunges Catholics and other non-Protestant Christians from its purview through jealous custody of the term "Christian," so too it defends this select position through practices of abstinence and fitness that comprise this book's subject.[3]

Practices of exclusion serve to fortify other connections, however, and it is important to clarify a few of the most salient in this context. Participants in devotional diet culture rarely imagine health and thinness as final ends; rather, they pursue bodily fitness as a vehicle for developing close, satisfying relationships with a beloved whom they aim to please through obedient self-discipline. These intimate hopes may be equally prominent for nonreligious dieters as well: enthusiasts concentrate on improving connections with family members—"I want to be good-looking so that you will love me again," says a partner in a troubled marriage—or with persons in social circles who appear ever ready to exclude the deficient—"I must be gorgeous for this party so that they will accept me." Dieting also recurrently serves the optimistic end of establishing new relationships with some desired but as yet inaccessible or unknown other: unmarried female dieters, along with their single male counterparts, commonly anticipate attracting a lover or spouse, while unhappy children may starve themselves into anorexic wisps out of loneliness and need for empathic connection. Such relationships deeply matter within secular no less than devotional diet culture, and plainly there are not always clear lines of demarcation between dietary motivations deemed secular and those felt to be religious or spiritual, contentious and elusive categories in this as in other domains. Persons who aspire to ideal bodies conceptualize their relationships in diverse ways, but in any case it is impossible to recognize the full range of meanings underlying these pursuits for perfectibility without realizing, perhaps even identifying with, the aspirations for intimacy and approval that propel them.

What marks religious diet culture as *devotional* is the addition of expressive relationships with sacred figures such as God or Jesus, accompanied by the belief that the human body's fitness affects such relationships in direct and indirect ways. Devotionalism, in one theorist's formulation, is "religious experience at the limits," in the sense that prayerful appeals to divine figures are so often suffused with sickness, suffering, fear, and loss; and yet devotional experience materializes in deceptively mundane forms.[4] Devotional dieters, the following chapters show, deeply care about food intake and physical health because they sense that the able-bodied—those who restrain their bodily desires and seek some degree of health—may more easily establish familiar, loving relations with the divine powers controlling the world. Fitness has taken different forms over the course of American history, and the contours of divine-human intimacy have been equally variable; but one link among such seemingly disparate American groups as seventeenth-century New England Puritans, Progressive Era New Thought physical culturists, and late twentieth-century evangelical diet preachers is a general conviction about the devotional logic of physical discipline. Fit bodies ostensibly signify fitter souls, whose prayers appear particularly, perhaps exclusively, suffused with wonder-working power. An appreciation of the emotional as well as the political intricacy of these coveted connections is vital if we are to discern why so many Americans have literally made a devotion out of the pursuit of health and thinness.[5]

This book pursues a winding passage through distinct American paradigms of religious embodiment, describing briefly some resonant strands in the colonial period and early Republic but focusing on the post–Civil War period through the twentieth century. While by no means a conventional linear account that purports to include all Protestant body practices (or all Protestants) in America during this lengthy stretch, it categorically presumes changing ideals over time. The risks of sweeping generalization here are daunting, but in a qualified sense we may conceptualize such change as an uneven shift, more of memory and desire than evident reality, from ideal norms of Christian devotional practice and civic life guided by asceticism and meek repentance to ones openly typified by obsession with perfect health and slenderness as physical signs of regeneration. That quasi-mythic trajectory has by no means been a straight and easy one, nor does this story follow a tidy chronological sequence of events so much as a series of specific, highly charged cultural moments and episodes: modulated echoes upon common devotional themes. Tropes on the order of purity and peril, virtue and vulnerability, for instance, have recurrently surfaced as Christians— along with the cultures they have helped to shape—wrestle with competing prototypes of the body. Within that tradition the flesh serves as a conduit of grace and temple of the Holy Spirit as well as an unruly repository of sin, temptation, and defilement.

Nor have such warring impulses been at work only within the sacrosanct environs of the churches and homes that have nurtured practices of piety. Indeed, as the magnitude of literature devoted to the histories of public health and American medicine, dietetics and food production, sports and exercise, body image and bariatrics only begins to attest, these themes long ago seeped out into the wider society. They have saturated the national consciousness with anxiety regarding bodily health while remolding each generation's beliefs about fitness and beauty to fit their rigorous and near-compulsory standards. Beyond obvious affinities, then, I also attend to the particular relationship between Christian fitness culture and the wider American obsession with diet and fitness. Religion may be more than a mere "aberration of the digestive function," as William James wryly quipped, but the effects of theological suppositions upon the stomachs of believers and heathens alike have been extraordinary.[6]

A second historical development delineated in this book is the intensifying belief in physical appearance—coded prominently by body shape—as a key, even chief, indicator of individual character and value. The search for external somatic indicators of internal states of being is age-old; and yet the peculiarly modern forms taken by this pursuit for body-soul correspondences have rarely been identified, much less analyzed. In documenting the shift in Christian paradigms of embodiment, this account further illumines the underpinnings of contemporary beauty and slimness ideals as well as the bigotry against fat people. Current movements to halt the perceived epidemic of fat in America aim to improve the health of the general populace, notably those of low socioeconomic status who are obesity's most likely prey. This is surely a worthy project, and investigative studies such as Greg Critser's *Fat Land: How Americans Became the Fattest People in the World* usefully delineate the many adverse factors engorging the public to injurious extremes. Yet it is not difficult to see how high-minded motives on this score coalesce with scorn for persons deemed fat, who allegedly drive up medical costs they cannot pay—parasitic guzzlers not only of food but of the cash guarded by their thinner, generally more affluent fellow citizens. Suffused by a particular form of social class conflict, tensions run high. At the heart of this book's investigation is a concern for the multiple ways in which body type, among assorted possible signifiers, has come to seem a virtually infallible touchstone of the worth of persons about whom one knows nothing else, as well as the value—indeed, the deepest truths—of one's own self: a vital component of subjectivity. While the two themes or histories detailed here are by no means identical, nor solely to blame for the body obsessions that characterize our time, they are paramount, deeply intertwined features of the body's extended social history.

Shoring up the boundaries of American fitness culture appears increasingly natural and quintessentially virtuous as Protestants find themselves living in a more religiously and ethnically diverse world. The link between Christian bodywork and changing American populations is not incidental: new models for health and beauty have stoked larger religious and social agendas by bolstering distinctions between visualized types of human physique—branding and then classifying these dynamic mounds of flesh on a comparatively static spectrum of sin and virtue, bodies worthy of neglect and bodies worth saving. Rather than being subsidiary or epiphenomenal, reflective of supposedly deeper secular realities, religion in this sense has been central to the historical creation of American bodies. Protestant Christians, that is, have neither merely participated in ostensibly secular dieting idioms nor put a religious spin on an inherently irreligious practice (as many critics have resigned themselves to suppose); instead, they have helped establish these material idioms from the start.

Put differently, religious concerns link physical fitness disciplines in the United States to historical patterns of fear and desire, part of our cultural substrata. Venerable Christian questions about the path to salvation have created anxieties anew for generations seeking to believe and behave rightly in order to please God and enter eternal paradise. We need not resort to reductivist explanations of religion or renounce any religious faith of our own to see how these concerns have contributed to a repertoire of robust and potentially divisive social categories that measure persons and groups against specific Protestant norms. The passion for perfect or at least perfectible bodies draws on this selfsame need to divide the world into good and evil, holy and demonic, Christians and infidels. Yet the benign, even altruistic intentions for slimming expressed by devotional diet writers—getting healthy, looking good in order to serve as a witness to God's transformative power, gaining the stamina to live a full and long Christian life—fail to express the less munificent motives and detrimental outcomes of this pursuit. If Ferraro is right that conservative religious Americans—who also produce the majority of Christian diet literature—are fatter than other populations, then dread and self-hatred surely prompt and feed such uneasy vigilance of other bodies. Observers know this to be true in other contexts: the writer Caroline Knapp, for instance, analyzes how the fat butt of many jokes provides "a tangible focus of female anxiety," representing "the shame and humiliation that will be visited upon a woman if her hunger is allowed to go unchecked." Likewise, figurations of "proper" form, whether patrician physiognomy, sinuous muscularity, or leggy leanness have implied supremacy over other bodies viewed as "out of bounds" while yet compelling proponents of such standards to scrutinize, ever more ruthlessly, their own flesh.[7] The faithful may balk at this proposition that many of their own have upheld stringent bodily standards, but the data bear witness to this reality time and again.

Given all that we know, or think we know, about American bodily fixations, it should be no surprise that one of this project's key analytic categories is gender; and I am especially interested in the means by which conceptualizations of maleness and femaleness, femininity and masculinity, have been produced over time through specialized corporeal practices. But gender is not the only attribute stressed here; as a great many theorists, including the historian Joan Scott, have noted, gender is "only one of several equally relevant axes of difference." Sex does not trump all other categories—race, ethnicity, and sexuality, for instance. Rather, gender identity mutually intersects with these other attributes in distinct ways, and throughout I have sought to be clear about such patterns of intersection.[8] This narrative is also more explicit than previous readings of American fitness culture about the role of that culture in restoring and sustaining the powerful ideology of whiteness, a sociocultural system that intermixes suspicions about both race and class. In cultivating a history of the creation of white, middle-class bodies and bodily ideals (with some revealing counters to that storyline, such as Father Divine's Peace Mission movement and Elijah Muhammad's Nation of Islam), I have become ever more mindful of the role played by these classification schemes in American fitness culture, particularly the ways in which that culture aids in bolstering hierarchies of ethnic superiority and difference.

The sheer scale—economics, time investment, and participant numbers—of today's devotional fitness culture is plainly unprecedented. Yet that culture has deep historical roots, some of which are well known while many others have rarely come under extended scrutiny. The familiar tale of the nineteenth-century health reform movements, spearheaded by William Andrus Alcott and Sylvester Graham and extensively documented by American historians, is one episode in the larger narrative of Christianity and the body in American culture. In *Born Again Bodies*, I have embarked upon a more expansive story, one that commences long before the health reformers with the Puritans and early evangelicals but whose center lies later, in the late nineteenth and especially the twentieth centuries. It may be foolhardy to attempt such a broad account, particularly in a climate of still accelerating academic specialization, tight periodization, and general suspicion of historical narratives that dare trail into contemporary times; the twin charges of "presentist" and "generalist" quickly chasten investigators of lived religion. Nevertheless, the profound crises that confront living bodies in the twenty-first century, along with the rapid intensity with which changing western conceptions of embodiment are revolutionizing all aspects of perceived selfhood, necessitate wide-ranging critical reflection and contestation—a need to which I hope this project, whatever its shortcomings, may contribute.

This book is not solely a historical narrative about religion but also an effort, albeit partial and specific, to expose and appraise the body ideology underpinning American consumer culture.[9] From this approach, it is possible to shift away from stale queries about origination—for example, did religion *cause* contemporary body obsessions?—toward analysis of religious and cultural intersections, and of religion's complex utility in the ongoing reproduction of dominant body ideologies. I am ultimately less concerned to prove Protestantism's consistent causal role in the making of American bodies than to analyze specific moments during which religion has helped to incarnate broader cultural desires. Few if any can claim to stand outside the ideology of their time, and conventional scholarly emphasis on causation may work against awareness of multiple sources and forms of complicity in that ideology's social groundwork. In the case of fitness dogma, such generative sources include not simply alliances between so-called religious and secular proponents but, still more, our widespread collusion as readers, writers, and culture makers. Hence, this book's claims are perhaps rudely inclusive: I am implicated in the body ideologies analyzed herein, and so are most people likely to engage this text. The investigation does not culminate in a predicament merely of white, middle-class girls and women—typecast as those most prone to recognized eating disorders—but a syndrome that is more encompassing and insidious, less subject to neat boundaries and simple definitions.

The body, whatever else it is, is the fundamental matter upon which diverse politics of exclusion operate. As countless scholars influenced by feminist, postcolonial, and other subaltern theories have long noted, bodies are not "natural" in any simple sense but are made, through extensive cultural work, to seem that way: that is, they are "naturalized." What, then, of your body? What of mine? What do our senses tell us, how do they communicate, distort, and deceive us when we encounter one another? What work do you perform to make your body express particular messages, and how do you then read and interpret other bodies? In an elemental sense, this book connects its readership to the account of a repetitive process by which bodies signify powerful cultural meanings and carry sizeable political weight. Subtly and not so subtly, we often associate sex and death with female bodies, immigrant bodies, and dark-skinned bodies both domestic and foreign: this is a crucial plot line, though religion has also been a powerful resource for questioning and undermining these same patterns.[10] *Born Again Bodies* aims to illuminate some of these overlapping themes in the ideological mapping of American bodies, adored and despised.

"Fitness is religion." So proclaims the popular 1997 book sporting this title by Ray Kybartas, the personal trainer to Hollywood celebrities and onetime manager of the original Gold's Gym in Venice Beach, California. Kybartas's own narrative is typical of fitness gurus: he was, in his words, an "overweight underachiever" who experienced a thoroughgoing conversion to the gospel of fitness and dedicated his life to spreading the faith far and wide. He saturates his text and accompanying images with religious allusions and slogans such as "keep the faith," while his most famous client, the pop singer Madonna, joins him in calling their personal workouts "church." Though seemingly worlds apart from the devotional traditions that have imparted this lexicon, fitness regimens such as those retailed in Kybartas's book bear basic characteristics of religion for growing numbers of affluent North Americans.[11]

But perhaps such comparisons surface all too easily. They assume—inaccurately—that any activity, pursued with sufficient zeal and time, is usefully classifiable as "religion," a term laden with intricate analytic debris, contradictory meanings, and a high potential for mystification. However evocative such loose comparisons, they are most often devoid of concrete substance and definitional precision, suggesting instead a pastime or distraction. Nonetheless, American popular culture appears devoted to pietistic evocations of fervor and commitment when it comes to fitness culture. Kybartas is hardly alone in his representation of body conditioning as religion; contemporary diet and fitness jargon is glutted with religious metaphors, conversion narratives, testimonials, and a vocabulary that tirelessly invokes the rubric of "spirituality," often as a cure for the supposed emotional hungers of our time.[12]

Nor is this fitness-as-religion presumption limited to the popular merchants of physical health. To the contrary, observers and analysts predictably imbue these anxieties, desires, and convictions about the perfectible body with the whiff of religious fervor. Hence, a plethora of interpretive writings, both journalistic and academic, has described modern fitness and diet practices as evangelical or conversionist in tone; analyzed eating disorders as being, at base, spiritual crises; and even traced out the whole modern history of dieting in religious terms, as a quest for salvation.[13] The tone of twentieth-century fitness promoters and disconsolate seekers alike has easily lent itself to such associations, which are less outright erroneous from a historical point of view than they are elusive and ultimately too imprecise to hold much analytic credence. Few studies of this kind, in fact, have paid more than passing attention to the concrete role of religious emotions, rituals, or communities in American alimentary and fitness practices, an elision all the more conspicuous in the wake of incisive studies of the religious significance of food and body in European history.[14]

Yet the scholarly literature devoted to food, fitness, and the body in American life is vast. Over the past two decades, observers and critics have paid increasing attention to American food fixations, along with embodied practices such as eating, cooking, feeding others, and dieting. The volume of literature that has been produced in this area is remarkable, encompassing several broad social histories of American eating patterns, more concentrated studies of diet and health reform in specific periods, sweeping chronicles of weight loss and "reducing" practices, explorations of women's work as food providers, and accounts of the emergence of clinically designated eating disorders in the twentieth century. In all, historians, anthropologists, sociologists, psychologists, and cultural critics have developed a still expanding array of creative frameworks for interpreting the complex meanings of food and fitness to Americans of various shapes, ethnicities, and social locations.

The story catalogued in *Born Again Bodies* draws from and builds on these prior endeavors yet differs from the standard literature on American diet culture on a number of crucial points. The most important is that, whereas most works presume American diet history to be a secularization tale whereby scientific authority and consumer capitalism joined sometime in the late nineteenth century to displace religion (but co-opted a Protestant "ethic of world mastery" to regulate American food habits), my account highlights the indispensable role of religious belief and practice all along the way.[15] Religion is far too significant in the history of American embodiment to sidestep uneasily, as happens in the otherwise exemplary work of such historians as Joan Jacobs Brumberg (on eating disorders), Hillel Schwartz (on prescriptive diet literature), and Peter N. Stearns (on fat history).[16] There religion crops up chiefly as a metaphorical descriptor to denote such supposed American habits as the fervent belief in the "salvation of slimness" and the "need for guilt" that, while stemming from anxiety over consumerism, surfaces as the secularized "sin" of overeating.

Elsewhere in these same writings, though, religion ambiguously reappears as a causative factor: the "age-old puritanism" that "could generate extremes of self-discipline"—in Stearns's words, "a secular version of Calvinist salvation."[17] Conditions such as anorexia nervosa become, in Brumberg's view, secular forms of older religious disciplines such as fasting. Contemporary practices surrounding diet and exercise, Schwartz argues, comprise identifiable *rituals* in the modern religion of the perfect body. The psychoreligious explanation—American body fixations compensate for sublimated puritan guilt through the creation of a morality-driven diet culture—is evocative and sometimes compelling; yet it favors vague tropes over sustained, complex analysis of lived religion and thus ultimately distorts the social and cultural landscape. More thorough, accurate accounts depend foremost on a richer understanding of religion itself, one that would pass beyond hackneyed formulations of "puritanism" and loose therapeutic paradigms. Such a formulation would likewise develop beyond institutional models of "church," a benchmark that once stalled observers from probing extraecclesial religious experience such as devotionalism.

Rather than a logical outgrowth of religion's supposed dislodgment, American fitness culture is an end that Protestantism's specific American forms boldly pursued: a devotional project aimed at bodily perfectibility. No mere protesters or reluctant bystanders, Christians themselves helped generate the historical shift in religious concern from spirit to body, joined by scientific and medical advances they eagerly cited as proof that the flesh could and should be divinely refined in this life and not merely the eternal world to come. Hence, rather than focus on secular developments within American diet history or underscore a spiritual need's pathological form in latter-day eating disorders, my portrayal delineates ongoing confluences and intersections between religious practice (of distinct yet interrelated groups of American Protestants) and the habits and customs of modern body-obsessed culture. It looks for the concrete relation of presumably secular bodily compulsions to religious pursuits, a link that varied and often hasty attempts at conjoining these two have not clearly demarcated.[18]

While probing associations and themes that have interested previous authors, then, this book frames the investigation in a distinctive way by taking seriously the social and cultural history of religion and positioning that history at center stage. Doing so, it opens up fresh ways of asking about the precise relationship between religion and the American body obsessions of our time. Though people frequently use the language of sin and guilt to talk about what they eat or how much they exercise, this lexicon can easily divert us from religion's complex role in the history of "perfect"—and deviant—American bodies. Keeping this complexity in mind, I analyze some of the most powerful gospels of the body to have flourished in recent memory, ones that remain fundamental preoccupations for growing numbers in the populace. In modern America, the kinship between body and soul has become dramatically reconceptualized, with significant help from men and women professing Christianity but focusing as much on a "promised land of weight loss" as on an eternal kingdom of God. This book's interests lie in discerning how such mutations have occurred, allowing believers' religious preoccupations with celestial (and quasi-celestial) affairs to metamorphose into a multibillion-dollar Christian fitness industry.

Two derivatives of the Protestant tradition assume essential roles in this process: broadly speaking, these are New Thought and evangelicalism, whose pertinent varieties will be more precisely elucidated in the chapters that follow. Worshipers of many kinds could certainly be prone to longings for embodied religion, but these developments proved especially attuned to growing cultural concerns with bodily health, some constituents advocating vegetarianism and physical culture, others meditative disciplines and spiritual attunement, still others an assortment of faith-healing procedures. Like heirs feuding over the legacy of an imposing patriarch, different groups of believers have laid claim to the riches of the Protestant heritage while bitterly disputing its ultimate meaning. Though some differences appear irreconcilable—the import of the historical Jesus, for instance, or the wages of sin—the evangelical and metaphysical strands of the faith entered an unlikely yet inexorable kinship in their formulations of human embodiment.

Even as many modern social institutions have progressively divested themselves of explicit Christian content, metaphysical and evangelical beliefs have thrived in the therapeutic culture they helped create. Within this milieu relentlessly exhorting mind over matter, gospels of wealth and health, and unshakeable optimism in the self, bodily preoccupations have ever risen to the fore, infiltrating contemporary notions of subjectivity while penetrating and intensifying the activities of everyday life. These mutations not only are evident in such popular forms as American gym culture but also appear in proliferating regimens crossing a vast spectrum of political persuasions on the so-called left and right, whether generated by concerns about technology and global capitalism or by anxieties over aging and death. Consider the spreading outrage against smoking, escalating alarm over environmental toxins, and moralizing advocacy of breast-feeding infants into early childhood, for instance, not to mention dramatic rises in plastic surgery, extensive spa treatments, and numerous sex therapies of the pharmacological as well as surgical variety. More acute bodily fixations reside in maladies such as bulimia and anorexia nervosa, along with multiplying expectations and anxieties about physical health and life extension. These diverse, seemingly incongruous yet paradoxically linked practices begin to reveal how religious concerns for fitness can reshape modern vocabularies for evaluating bodies and their newly minted illnesses.

The modern edict to "create" our own bodies is nowhere more apparent than in the fashion industry, where the dream of somatic perfectibility extends an imperial reign. The history of women's fashion, most notably, reveals the intensification of this fantasy since the turn of the twentieth century and particularly since the 1960s. "As women have gained more power in education, politics, and the workplace," writes the fashion historian Rebecca Arnold, "they have also learnt to fight the female body, to present a firm, toned exterior that conforms to sexual stereotypes while resisting the maternal silhouette that had been the defining feature of femininity in the previous century." Far from being a means to accentuate the mundane contours of everyday figures, fashion lures buyers with fanciful bodies, its aim not to celebrate the so-called natural but to "test . . . women's ability to defy it." Like the devotional fitness culture, fashion is "a form of seductive and beautiful coercion into believing in the miracle of perfection that awaits those faithful to its decrees." Never mind that the hyperreal bodies of models are often surgically altered and more frequently manipulated by computer software that removes facial lines, smoothes and brightens the skin, and erases excess rippling flesh. But perhaps enough blame has been heaped upon fashion, which is, as Arnold notes, "always the product of the culture that spawns it, embodying the concerns of the wider society in its myriad styles."[19] Elucidating some of the pietistic derivations of these socially grounded concerns—anxieties about perfectibility and mortality, authenticity and subversion, eroticism and excess, for instance, not to say the brutality of exclusion—is the end toward which *Born Again Bodies* aims.

In setting out to chart the modern historical course of particular linkages between bodily and religious affairs, I begin with some of the initial expressions of Christianity—Reformed Calvinism and early evangelicalism—on American land. Both traditions relied to varying extents on somatic indicators of true faith, each steadfastly promoting corporeal acts of devotion such as fasting while affirming that signs of authentic spiritual renewal were essentially grounded in the body. Extant scholarship on early modern fasting has largely focused on its ostensible trajectory from a devotional act to a politicized simulation of humility, and while much of that literature provides crucial background material, I have returned to many primary sources as well as examining later ones, which together substantiate a somewhat different history of austere eating as an embodied practice. I have also returned to the history of medicine, sexuality, and constitutional studies in physiognomy and phrenology during the eighteenth and nineteenth centuries, to assess other areas relating to physical and spiritual health that helped reorient beliefs about appetite and desire. Following this trajectory, chapter 1 rereads and draws attention to these overlapping histories, construing anew what has more typically been perceived as disgust toward the body, the sign of a severe Protestant asceticism.[20] It asks whether early modern Protestant attitudes toward the flesh, as the outer indicator of the interior soul, may not be more fruitfully read as a heady engrossment in the body's regenerative possibilities, a view that seems all the more illuminating in light of the bodily practices and anxieties that grew out of that context.

If some segments of nineteenth-century Protestantism reputedly forsook concern for the body in favor of the soul, the body continued to matter deeply to many Christians willing to stomach neither a purely otherworldly religion nor a drastic break between the realms of science and theology. Worshipers from all strands of the faith could certainly be prone to such longings for embodied religion, but the most radical were those who energetically developed new procedures of bodily healing or reshaped older ones: notably the health reformers, but also holiness and Pentecostal believers, Christian Scientists, and adherents to the restyled mind-over-matter worldview termed New Thought. While attentiveness to bodily matters was by no means absent outside these assorted circles, it was most enthusiastically expressed within them, whether displayed through practices such as vegetarianism, the laying on of hands for healing, or techniques such as mesmerism, meditative disciplines, and physical culture. In fact the New Thought movement, chronicled in chapter 2, happens to be a fruitful turning point in this history, for that movement's Progressive Era proponents were acutely preoccupied with the correlations of mind and matter, the soul and the body. Their musings would mightily influence American culture and propel the body to the center of popular interest. Dogged optimism in a kind of mechanized etherealization of the flesh—as in the typical affirmation, "I am growing lighter and lighter each day. . . . My food is assimilating properly, all waste is being carried off and I am growing better in every way"—represents one of the most unshakable themes running through American diet culture. This methodic hopefulness has, moreover, blended well with scattered appropriations of medical science: thinking away the fat, Americans well know, has never precluded calorie counting, gym workouts, or even more drastic procedures such as surgery. Mental and physiological techniques for manufacturing slimness have steadily appeared harmonious if not inseparable at least since Progressive Era authors intermixed them.[21]

One of the many interesting developments to emerge in relation to New Thought at the turn of the century was the health craze of fasting, a practice that was promoted as a means of masculine accomplishment and rejuvenation but that also correlated usefully with other concerns of the time, from worries over immigration, race, and eugenics to the efficiency doctrine promoted in relation to business, homemaking, and the burgeoning market economy. In tracking some of the divergent paths taken by New Thought perfectionism, chapter 3 explores the fasting masters of that period along with two subsequent developments. These are, first, the midcentury work of the metaphysical psychologist and physician William Sheldon, whose popular taxonomy of bodies sought to reveal deep, even mystical truths about the flesh; and, second, the notions about body salvation that arose in the religious movements headed by two African American leaders, Father Divine and Elijah Muhammad. Advancing distinctive versions of bodily care that also differed starkly from those of their white counterparts, the theologies of Divine and Muhammad illustrate how New Thought and black nationalism combined to create multiple versions of an ethic of bodily care. Like the fasting masters of the prior generation, Divine and Muhammad purposefully centered their attention on food, yet eating was put to very different and, for many, far more appealing ends.

Other gospels of bodily perfection rose to enormous popularity after the Second World War and, especially, during the final third of the twentieth century. A manifest example of these developments in the conceptualization of ideal bodies, influenced by New Thought while embedded in older but just as optimistic forms of evangelical Protestantism, is the devotional diet movement that materialized in the late 1950s, accelerated during the 1970s, and continued to thrive in multiple adaptations into the early twenty-first century. Chapter 4 scrutinizes the systems and purveyors of this movement, relating them to the enveloping American culture of diet, weight loss, and fitness that escalated dramatically in the twentieth century's latter half. Here I also focus on how religious persons have consumed and contested this body ideology, drawing upon my fieldwork with a diverse array of diet group participants and my interviews with others positioned at the edge of that culture. I attend as well to a few ways in which food regimens and concerns about body image enter the routines of other groups, namely Seventh-day Adventists, Latter-day Saints, Jews, Catholics, and members of Eastern-inspired New Age communities.

Chapter 5 analyzes elemental themes guiding Christian diet culture into the early twenty-first century, themes that go a long way toward disclosing the anxieties driving the modern obsession with bodily perfection: mixed attitudes toward food and feeding practices, a steady panic over shifting gender roles, and the perceived dissolution of shared discourse about racial categories. Contemporary gospels of bodily discipline are surely not restricted to the devotional diet culture, however richly expressed they are there. Hence, the epilogue recounts a smattering of other somatic regulatory practices prominent in the early twenty-first century, from the resurgence of fasting as a highly therapeutic, conflictual practice to the growing appeal of bodily modification procedures, ongoing obsessions over sexuality and fitness, and the mounting incidence of eating disorders. Here, as in earlier chapters, the sheer vastness of available data forces me at times to be more suggestive than exhaustive, and careful readers may imagine far more examples than I have been able to include.

Latter-day American bodily disciplines hardly represent some leftover version of alleged Puritan or Victorian prudery; such would be a simplistic, not to say tedious, argument. Rather, the decisive legacy of early modern and modern forms of religion, and the New Thought movement that arose out of them, is passion for the flesh at the core of the mind-over-matter scheme of causation: the craving for a perfectible, eternal, living, breathing, disciplined yet sensual body, along with its obverse, the sinister repugnance toward deficient, impoverished, or languishing bodies. Particular historical manifestations of Protestantism in America, from the prim to the whimsical, together helped create a bewildering milieu in which older hierarchies of flesh and spirit were upended, carnal aversions masking not only terror and anxiety but also rapt adoration. That innumerable religious Americans in the early twenty-first century—Protestants now cheerfully joined by Catholics, Mormons, and many others—participate vigorously in somatic devotions is neither historical irony nor theological paradox. Surely the more prodigious wonder is that anyone at all continues to resist the call to a born-again body.

A Note on Reading the Images

During the numerous slide and video presentations I delivered while working on this project, audiences typically responded to the images with laughter. Visual depictions of men and women engaged in devotional bodily regimens provoked grins and some rowdy guffaws from academic researchers no less than undergraduates, seminary students and contented secularists, cultural critics along with church historians. No doubt I abetted this reaction by showing particular book covers that sport cheeky titles (*Slim for Him* and *More of Jesus, Less of Me* always reap chuckles) or by displaying illustrations of the most extreme examples of contemporary Christian diet culture and its precedents (whether the Weigh Down Workshop's brassy promotional videos or Bernarr Macfadden's flamboyant muscle-man photographs). This conspicuous imagery helped verify that, like the humorist Dave Barry, I am *not* making this up.

But drawing such laughter serves only a provisional goal, in pursuit of exposing the ambivalent, sometimes unbearably intense emotions toward human desire that trigger this reaction. Much of the startled amusement at before/after photographs of overweight women and men surely refers to the "happily ever after" fantasy embedded in follow-up images, rather than the pain of being fat in America, where obesity is often presumed to be symptomatic of laziness, greed, or lack of control. Indeed, the laughter typically comes loudest from audience members appearing to have swallowed, however uneasily, the same far-fetched promise kindled by these photographic depictions. Are we laughing, then, primarily at ourselves, represented in some exaggerated and safely distant other? Many who chortle at the posed nudes of pious body builders, or the cartoons of gluttonous eaters at church potlucks, surely feel their own wishes and furtive habits are on view. But insofar as the laughter endeavors to conceal the anxiety that prompts these ritualized body practices, even self-mockery sustains the wider cultural vilification of fat bodies. There are undoubtedly additional, intriguing reasons for the titters greeting so many of these figures on public display, from nervous empathy to voyeurism or even outright disgust, and I will not undertake further dissection. Suffice to say that the spectrum of emotional response toward these images deserves mention as a meaningful clue to powerful sentiments, shaped by culture, that in turn mold our ongoing attitudes and experiences relating to human, and explicitly American, embodiment.

Readers' responses to the images, when first viewed in private study rather than public exhibition, are bound to be different and perhaps more dynamic than the uneasy responses incurred in the lecture hall. A concise, explicatory addendum thus seems useful to include here. No one should infer that by publishing and analyzing before/after snapshots, or retelling stories of Christians adamant to fashion born-again bodies, I mean to stir up unkind feelings toward fat people in American society or to deepen the shame felt by many who already suffer derision. It would be a failure if this book, like the Farrelly brothers' 2001 film *Shallow Hal*, ultimately just endorsed the same standards of beauty and personal worth whose promotion and preservation this book probes with definite suspicion. My intent is to press readers to acknowledge the desires evoked by these images, including the enigmatic impulse to laugh. In this way, we may begin to assess their elemental complexity, including hunger for emotional closeness and intimacy: attributes that aid in sustaining the paradigms of what individuals look like and how we wish to be seen. To deny personal reactions under the circumstances—the conditions leading me to expect that the vast majority of my readers long, however surreptitiously, to be thinner and fitter than they are—would be further to accede to the systemic worship of particular somatic types, and condemnation of others, in our time. An assumed political correctness is of no use here.

If possible, then, I would ask readers to take a kind of tender (even if melancholic) pleasure in the visual representations contained in these pages, recognizing the multilayered influences that facilitate such responses. Those who digest such a book as this one constitute together a curious, presumably mixed group of potential informants, each of whose moods and impressions while gazing at the pictures reveals something both general and particular about how bodies have been socially fabricated in recent history. As an author, separated from readers by space and time, I can neither dictate nor inspect all of these reactions, however much they pique my ethnographic appetite; instead, I hope to persuade readers to contemplate such inward sentiments, from humor to revulsion, as they become perceptible. I am no stranger to many of the wishful aspirations represented here; nor, I suspect, are you.

Just as private feelings evoked by these visual images ought to be acknowledged, seeing as they comprise meaningful relics of lived worlds, so too perhaps should readers endeavor to find grounds for responsive engagement with the real people depicted (however quixotically) in the illustrations. There are varied reasons to attempt this de-othering, not least of which is that writing off Christian fitness advocates denies their ascendancy in shaping both contemporary religion and American culture more generally. More to the point, to discount anyone involved in devotional dieting— leaders, participants, infomercial viewers, and occasional readers alike— blinds us to vital processes that aid and intensify more general cultural fixations with purity, power, perfect health, and immortality. The visual depictions included in this book are today arguably more American than old-fashioned apple pie, too fattening to longer serve as an emblem for a health-obsessed society whose inhabitants dream rosy promises of fat's ultimate annihilation. If somehow you have never been tempted to consume such dreams nor felt the dread and delight of seeking a born-again body, then savor the pictures of those poor folks who have, smiling serenely all the while. Eventually, though, their reflection may be mirrored in your flesh.

1 Gluttons for Regimen

*Anglo-Protestant Culture
and the Reorientation of Appetite*

Monks wasting away in the desert, saints beating their bodies and sleeping on nails, apostles renouncing all pleasures and subsisting on the charity of benefactors, pious men and women starving their senses in emulation of Christ: it is by now a truism to note that devout Christians of earlier eras displayed profound ambivalence about the flesh. Both patristic and medieval followers of the faith, women and men, felt the body to be a burden that must be suffered resignedly during earthly life while yet remaining the crucial material out of which devotional practice and spiritual progress were forged. Cultivated as an instrument for salvation, the body necessitated particular forms of control, its appetites subjected to the scrutiny of the spirit and strenuously disciplined.

Such discipline would take many forms across varied eras, but of lasting concern was the complex relationship between the visible body and the invisible soul. Assorted views held currency in different times, at both elite and popular levels, and a range of strategies served to utilize external indicators as signs of sin and purity, so that the flesh could be scoured for indications of damnation or salvation. Historians have paid close attention to the ambiguities and ambivalent attitudes toward the flesh in the Christian imagination. Caroline Walker Bynum, exploring medieval views of resurrection, assesses Thomas Aquinas's conceptualization in terms that have repeatedly played themselves out: "The concept of body implicit here," she writes, "is not entirely coherent or consistent. . . . Aquinas is ambivalent about body itself. Body is the expression, the completion, and the retardation of soul." The focused reverence bestowed upon saintly bodies and body parts opens up one way that Christians deemed human physicality to express profound meanings about the self, even as they imagined the body to be contained by the soul.[1] In the early modern era, Protestant discourse about corporeality shifted as the result of Enlightenment and American attempts to perfect the mind through regulation of the body, as numerous devotional writers promoted the holy possibilities of flesh over its execrable desires—a trajectory that topples stereotyped notions of a supposedly disembodied religion. This chapter treats three sets of devotional practices whose modern enactment both reflected and generated broad cultural variations in the meaning of human embodiment.

One of the most enduring and elastic devotional practices aiming at bodily discipline was food abstinence. The discipline of fasting, well established in the Mediterranean world long before Christianity emerged, became especially important in Christian communal practice during the early fourth century CE, as it was variously used as a method of baptismal preparation, a means of purification, a sign of grief, a work of charity, or an expression of penitence and the desire for God's mercy. Over the next several centuries, as Bynum has documented, both the meaning and the practice of Christian fasting changed significantly, so that by the thirteenth and fourteenth centuries preachers and theologians urged "spiritual more than physical abstinence," meaning general restraint or moderation in all areas of life. Yet many Christians of the later Middle Ages, particularly women, decried this perspective as a dangerous compromise with the world and chose the path of extreme asceticism, imitating and deeply identifying with the broken flesh of Christ on the cross through rigorous renunciation of the flesh. For those such as Catherine of Siena, who died of self-induced starvation at the age of thirty-three, true nourishment came only from Christ, and to rely too heavily on earthly food was to commit the terrible sin of gluttony.[2]

Prescriptions and practices of nutritive abstinence fluctuated in subsequent periods, and scattered examples of intense food refusal among Christians, again mostly though not exclusively women, have continued to dot the historical record.[3] Since the transformative religious revolutions of the sixteenth and seventeenth centuries, Catholics and Protestants alike have participated in the ascetic tradition, though always in very particular, localized ways. Martin Luther condemned extravagant forms of self-denial that destroyed the body; yet he urged moderated fasting both to curb distracting physical desires and to take care of the body so that it might minister to others' needs. John Calvin held more strictly to fasting as a necessary discipline for appeasing God's wrath, a view echoed in later groups like the English Puritans. The churches of England, Rome, and the Orthodox world followed fixed calendrical times for fasting—such as Lent, Ember Days, Rogation Days, Fridays, and vigils prior to certain holy festivals—but varied in the precise meaning given to fasting per se. The first section of this chapter treats the sundry ways in which early American Christians reworked fasting as a vital devotional arena for shaping human appetites, while the next explores the related discussions of restrained eating as a therapeutic instrument of good health. From these practices emerged an array of historically influential and resonant modes for enacting spiritual control over bodily desire.

A second set of disciplinary practices in Christian history with lasting durability, albeit shifting form, pertains to sexual restraint. Like other appetites, sexuality—a capacious category meant here to include the discursive and material contours of desire, the boundaries of purity and transgression, and the means of private discipline and public punishment—operates at the juncture of intersecting cultural concerns. Saint Paul's elevation of celibacy over conjugality received wide-ranging attention and debate, and various historical models emerged to enjoin both temporary renunciation and permanent virginity. Late antique medical science bolstered injunctions to male continence, as physicians objected to frequent intercourse for supposedly diminishing male fertility and physical strength. Early Christian radicals held much stronger views, however; through sexual self-denial, as Peter Brown has shown, they believed that "the human body could join in Christ's victory: it could turn back the inexorable. The body could wrench itself free from the grip of the animal world."[4] In the second-century Mediterranean world, the practice of repudiating sexual appetite signified a dramatic alternative to the moral values and social order of the time, a measure for bringing about the new age promised by the narrative retelling of Jesus' life.

Clerical celibacy had gained increasing support in different parts of the western world by the end of the fourth century, though it was not decisively enacted until the First and Second Lateran Councils (1123, 1139). The ideal of virginity flourished, however, in Christian monastic and ascetic circles among both women and men. As with fasting, later Protestant reformers contested Catholic modes of sexual renunciation, insisting upon the religious appropriateness of a married, child-bearing clergy; and yet Protestants of many kinds placed strict bounds around sexual practice. Put more strongly, sexuality, like eating and not-eating, has comprised a vital symbolic and discursive arena for conceptualizing, enacting, and practicing the relationship between body and soul. Sexual regimentation and experimentation developed into some surprising patterns in America, hence serving as a second set of practices for understanding the modern history of American Protestant embodiment.

A third and final set of practices addressed in this chapter center on body parts—the face and skull, in particular—as external windows upon the inner soul. Ever controversial, pursuits such as physiognomy and phrenology gained widespread credibility in the eighteenth and nineteenth centuries as procedures for discerning somatic authenticity. Not surprisingly, they flourished on American soil during an era when anxieties over sincerity and transparency were high. As with practices focused on disciplined eating and sexuality, however, flesh-reading practices were anything but new to the modern Protestant context. Physiognomy was widely practiced in the ancient world, where its Greek and Latin nomenclature materialized to mean the art of judging character from the outward appearance, particularly the face. Just as beauty and ugliness have long carried significant ethical weight as evidence of others' goodness or depravity, so have diverse historical periods witnessed the rise of methods for defining, measuring, and interpreting aesthetic categories for women and men.

Christians have held diverse and ambivalent attitudes toward human beauty, establishing distinctive types to set apart purity and holiness from deceptive facsimiles. The repertoire of meanings in which medieval Christians operated, for instance, included options for the emaciated ascetic female body to convey the truest loveliness, even as many European artists created softer, fuller figures of Mary and female saints whose peaceful countenances and pliant fleshiness signaled their pious submission to God. Hagiographical accounts often illuminated the godliness of the meekest, homeliest girls, whose inner sanctity escaped the notice of small-minded neighbors and cruel family members. Others emphasized the intense physical beauty of virtuous women and recounted instances of self-disfigurement (such as nose amputations) as measures for debasing the self before God. Often enough, even if those closest to God held a kind of mythic power to detect saintliness in others, the signs of holy beauty were very different from ordinary models of physical comeliness: an inner spiritual purity that shone forth from within to imbue the body with a radiant, all-encompassing aura. As the history of devotional art vividly reveals, however, the beautiful harmony of facial features and physical form continued to signify beautiful souls. Reformed beliefs about the body-soul relationship drew from this ambiguous set of beliefs in both the primary role of interiority and the revelatory power of physical beauty. Protestant ideals shifted dramatically over time, moreover, as scientific and popular procedures were newly developed for reading character in flesh itself. Protestants cleaved to embodiment in multiple ways that, as later chapters show, would have lasting effects on American regimens surrounding beauty, sexuality, and diet.

THE DIET OF ANGELS: FASTING IN EARLY MODERN
ANGLO-AMERICAN PROTESTANTISM

For late sixteenth- and early seventeenth-century reformers in the Church of England, fasting posed a series of dilemmas. Chief among them was the reality that while various kinds of fasting (such as avoiding meat on Fridays) had long been central to Christian devotion, scriptural references to fasting were perplexingly ambiguous. Among various passages on fasting in the Old and New Testaments, the ninth chapter of the book of Matthew seemed to provide the surest evidence that fasting was a practice enjoined, if indirectly, by God: "Then came to him the disciples of John, saying, Why do we and the Pharisees fast oft, but thy disciples fast not? And Jesus said unto them, Can the children of the bridechamber mourn, as long as the bridegroom is with them? But the days will come, when the bridegroom shall be taken from them, and then shall they fast" (Matt. 9:14–15 [KJV]). Early Anglican guides such as Henry Holland's *Christian Exercise of Fasting, Private and Publicke* (1596) and George Buddle's *Short and Plaine Discourse Fully Containing the Whole Doctrine of Evangelicall Fastes* (1609) repeatedly emphasized fasting's necessity, calling for those who breached the command to fast to be grievously punished. Yet the vexed issue of how and when to fast—to separate fasting practices that were absolutely necessary from those merely recommended, and both from those that were superstitious—long remained contested.[5]

Such questions derived their significance from the competing paradigms of body-spirit interaction that underlay Christian devotional practice in this period. Throughout the long reaches of the Christian tradition, various models of corporeality had been proposed, from the Gnostic conviction that all matter was evil, with the spirit sorely trapped within the prison of the body, to views that focused on humankind's creation in God's image and the body as temple for the holy spirit. Those deemed heretics by church authorities had, in fact, consisted regularly of those who dissented from officially sanctioned tenets about corporality. Beset with inconsistencies and lack of theological consensus, sixteenth-century Protestant reformers called Christians to what they considered a more scriptural, more carefully wrought attitude of detachment toward the flesh than that of their Catholic rivals. The Protestant Reformation itself, as Philip Mellor and Chris Shilling have argued, represented a profound re-formation of bodily ideals, of "embodiment" writ large.[6] As they publicly denounced fleshly mortifications such as celibacy and bestowed marriage and family life with new significance,

Reformed thinkers shifted the value of the body in such a way as to make it a lesser instrument of salvation than, in their view, had been advocated by the Roman church hierarchy. Rather than renounce older traditions of mortification, they reshaped doctrines of fleshly denunciation for different ends. Hence practices such as fasting had also to be reconfigured and depicted anew, not as acts that took precedence over other spiritual devotions but as their mild or subtle accompaniment.

Holland, for instance, distinguished a religious fast from several other kinds of "good fasts," such as the physician-prescribed fast "to dissolve and consume raw humours, and to expell superfluous excrements out of the bodie"; the fasting of civil servants so engrossed in a particular task that they forget all food and drink; the general "Christian sobrietie" commanded by scripture for daily living; the forced fasts occurring in times of famine; and the miraculous fasting of figures like Moses and Jesus, whose forty-day fasts were not to be imitated but, rather, used for instruction and confirmation of faith. All these kinds of fasting were subsidiary to the religious fast, with which Holland was primarily concerned:

> A religious fast is an abstinence, more than ordinarie, not only from all meates and drinkes, but also from all other things which may cherish the bodie, so farre as nature will give leave, and civill honestie, for one whole day at the least: proceeding from a true faith, and a cheerfull willing minde, principally to testifie our repentance, and to worke in us a greater humiliation, that our prayers may be more effectuall and better prevaile with God, to obtaine such blessings as concerne our own wants privatly, and the publique state of the Church and people of God.[7]

Privately, Holland explained, one might fast out of sorrow or repentance or use fasting as an instrument for curing the sick, fighting against sin, stirring the heart in preparation for prayer, enduring persecution in the name of Christ, preparing to hear the scriptures and participate in the Eucharist, or protecting church and society from harm. Public fasts could be called by the church in order that God would bless "some special enterprise in warres and peace, or worke which is taken in hand"; in this way, proper fasting should bring about "a happy end to all calamities and miseries (famines, warres, pestilence) so far as expedient in this life and salvation in the next."[8]

Buddle's discourse on fasting, published thirteen years after Holland's, aimed less at drawing up a comprehensive catalog of fasting options than at establishing which practices were absolute and which simply advised. Buddle also took care to distinguish between "ordinary" public fasts prescribed by the Christian calendar (Ember Days, Rogation Days, fasting before communion, and so forth) and "extraordinary" days of fasting precipitated by more than ordinary sins. Such extreme wickedness, whether private or public, "cannot easily be forgiven unto men, unlesse they doe Repent extraordinarily, and Fast extraordinarily, either in private, for their private extraordinary sinnes, or in publicke, and in private also, for their publicke extraordinary sinnes." Fasting in such cases was an "Absolute Commande" of God, and Buddle's vision for such events was severe:

> The Extraordinary Publick Fast, must be a separation of all persons whatsoever, from all worldly businesse; which separation, is to be imployed as it were in sackcloth and ashes, and dust cast upon their heads, necks, loines, in the lowest both inward and outward humiliation, by lying upon the ground, before the Lord, in some publicke place of the assemblie, without all meat and sustenance, for the space of 24 houres at the least, after the example and demeanor of those true Penitents, Joshua and his people.[9]

Those failing to keep the ordinary public fasts could be excused, but those who broke the extraordinary public fasts should be severely punished by means of the confiscation of all their earthly goods and excommunication from the church.

Ministers attempting to instruct the people on proper methods of fasting had also to contend with the problem posed by centuries of "high and hyperbolicall commendations of fasting" issued by Roman church authorities. Convinced that fasting had been erroneously promoted by "papists" as "a work to purchase and merite grace, pardon of sinnes, reconciliation with God, and a speciall worke to purchase heaven," Reformed leaders sought to negate superstition without thwarting the correct enactment of fasting. In addressing a whole section of his text to the abuse of fasting, Holland was especially concerned to guard against the "popish fast," which "hath no more affinity with the religious fast . . . than light with darkness, or Christ with Beliall."[10] Of course, fasting had been abused by non-Christians as well, and Holland gave examples of Egyptian priests' taking pride in their abstinence, Persian and Indian devotion to permanent vegetarianism, and Muslim food refusal on holy days. A far graver problem, however, was the increasing Hebrew and Christian abuse of fasting, evident even in scripture and early church history: the Essenes, Pharisees, Montanists, and Manichees all contributed to a tradition of "wil-worship," which used fasting as a tool for cleansing oneself of sin, attaining righteousness and pardon, rescuing other souls from purgatory, and achieving reconciliation and eternal life. Such blasphemous corruptions, still actively promoted by the "Antichrist" in Rome, had to be stripped from fasting in order that its proper uses be restored. Then and only then could fasting truly embody the "diet of angels," as Jeremy Taylor termed it in 1650, and nourish souls with the holiest of hungers.[11]

Dissenters on both sides of the Atlantic Ocean were similarly concerned to purge fasting of magical accretions and restore to it a purity of purpose. Most agreed with John Calvin that two extremes ought to be avoided: undervaluing the necessity of fasting and rejecting it as "almost superfluous," on the one hand, and turning fasting into an idolatrous superstition, on the other. In the *Institutes,* Calvin had spelled out fasting's purpose in terms that his Reformed followers generally accepted: "Holy and legitimate fasting is directed to three ends; for we practise it either as a restraint on the flesh, to preserve it from licentiousness, or as a preparation for prayers and pious meditations, or as a testimony of our humiliation in the presence of God when we are desirous of confessing our guilt before him." Calvin's focus on the private devotional ends of fasting would continue to be emphasized by seventeenth-century Puritans, even as upheavals in government expanded and politicized its public uses.[12]

As in England, public fast days were held among the migrants to New England upon "extraordinary occasions" or solemn adversities, sometimes proclaimed by civil functionaries for the whole population and other times by church leaders for their members. In fact, fast days were one of the most common ritual events in colonial New England, second only to regular Sunday worship services. During public fasts, ministers and churchgoers abstained from food for twenty-four hours, from evening to evening, and attended special services of morning and afternoon prayers and sermons. All labor was prohibited, as were fancy dress, sexual relations, and, of course, eating. Private fasting was equally central to Puritan devotion and could be undertaken on virtually any occasion of personal failure, wrongdoing, or perceived disfavor with God. Fasts were times for "due examination of our wayes towards God, and consideration of Gods wayes towards us," opportunities to "make a solemn and real profession that we justifie God and judge ourselves." Recapitulating the cycle of conversion, fasting "carried people out of ordinary time—or out of time's decay—back to that moment when all things were 'new,' when time was everlasting, when the ideal coincided with reality." Indeed, fasting was defined primarily in terms of humiliation, or heartfelt sorrow for personal sins; without this authentic emotion, as Calvin and later dissenters concurred, fasting was not only meaningless but, in its hubris and hypocrisy, "the greatest abomination."[13]

Though authentic humiliation was the chief aim of this event, abstinence from food was its most visible sign and a critical necessity for fulfilling the ritual's purpose. The bodily hunger that accompanied abstinence carried important symbolic and instrumental weight, recapitulating the suffering of Christ at the same time that it acted as an aid to prayer. Praying on a full stomach, groggy with surfeit, one could not pray so fervently nor persevere so long in one's devotions as when praying while empty, a condition associated with alertness, concentration, and an urgency of feeling. Fasting raised prayer to higher levels of zeal and also of power, according to believers: God would more readily answer prayers that were accompanied by sincere and rigorous abstinence. Hunger was also intended to remind individuals of their fragile humanity and dependence on God, yet it could easily be transformed into a source of pride. Puritans avoided tying salvation itself to fasting, as they accused corrupt churchmen and Catholics of doing, but the linkage to prosperity persisted in both oblique and vivid ways, suggesting that one skilled at abstinence or humility could attain greater blessings than one who was not. Ever on guard against conceit, Puritan ministers warned of this particular danger in no uncertain terms, admonishing that if fasting incited one to the sin of pride, then abstinence from food turned God's medicine into "our bane and poyson."[14]

The meaning of fasts too was open to dispute; as in England, fasting often had political import and signaled division. Ministers usually initiated the call for a fast day but were required to receive consent from church members for congregational fasts.[15] Refusing to fast was also an option, as when the New England colonists, united in their loathing of the rigid government represented by Sir Edmund Andros, ignored a civil order to fast on the anniversary of the beheading of Charles I. Fasting was no less serviceable as a tool for inducing guilt or for coercing obedience, as when congregations fasted in order to spur wayward members to confess sins such as adultery or witchcraft. Fasting's multiple uses confirm that humility and aggression could mix in more than one way.[16]

In both England and America, ministers and doctors also regularly prescribed fasting as therapy for melancholy and all types of madness. Michael MacDonald, following Keith Thomas, has argued that the abandonment of Catholic methods of mental healing, especially exorcism, compelled Protestants to develop their own methods for curing sick souls. Puritan clerics were especially eager to engage in healing regimens, and they held therapeutic fasts for the insane as well as those possessed by demons. In England these curative rituals led to intense conflict with the Anglican clergy, who were angered by their parishioners' resort to these patently superstitious activities and the "frauds" who conducted them. Still, lay men and women on both sides of the ocean continued to believe in the healing power of fasting and prayer. The English Richard Dugdale, known as the "Surey Demoniack," received treatment from a doctor, a cunning man, and two Roman Catholic priests until finally being cured through prayer and fasting. In Salem Village, Massachusetts, the "possessed" Elizabeth Knapp was prescribed prayer and fasting for her fits, just as several fasts were called to relieve Knapp and the village's other possessed women and children. Hardly marginal, such practices illuminate the persistent belief in fasting's healing efficacy; prayer alone did not suffice.[17]

Just as fasting remained central to Puritan devotion in both communal and private forms, it served similar purposes elsewhere. "Have I been simple and recollected in everything I said or did?" This query helped John Wesley and his fellow members of the Oxford Holy Club lead a disciplined life of meticulous routine and self-denial, including avoidance of sumptuous food.[18] Besides prayer and public worship, studious reading, early rising, and visiting the poor and sick, the group emphasized the importance of fasting. Following the Anglican practice, these early Methodists fasted weekly, as Wesley's journal entry from August 17, 1739, clarifies: "[It was] agreed that all the members of our Society should obey the Church to which we belong by observing all Fridays in the year as days of fasting or abstinence."[19] But fasting was not only a Friday ordinance for Wesley. In a sermon on Matthew 6:16–18, Wesley sought to resolve the conflict between "faith" and "works," or inward versus outward religion, that had been at the heart of earlier controversies over fasting (especially between Catholics and Reformed Protestants). Echoing Calvin, Wesley railed against the two extremes to which fasting had historically been prone: zealous overemphasis and rash disregard. Taking a middle way, he described fasting as a divinely ordained activity that should be practiced at set as well as special times, publicly and communally as well as privately and in secret, and with varying degrees of abstemious self-denial. Wesley added nothing new to the doctrine of fasting, though his discourse explicitly emphasized the importance of bodily health to a degree rarely seen in earlier treatments. Like the Puritans, Wesley outlined the proper aims of fasting as praising God, repenting for sin, averting divine wrath, and obtaining "all the great and precious promises which [God] hath made to us in Christ Jesus." And like Protestant divines before him, Wesley also cautioned severely against imagining that he who fasts merits God's grace and blessings, even as he assured his audience that fasting was a means "wherein, without any desert of ours, he hath promised *freely* to give us his blessing."[20]

Even as fasting continued to be put to patriotic uses in postrevolutionary America, devotional fasting persisted among the Methodists, who followed Wesley's model of avid fasting well into the nineteenth century. Having shifted away from the liturgical uses of fasting as a weekly communal practice, evangelicals retained and intensified the personal meanings of food abstinence as an act of repentance and attentiveness to God. While the venerable institution of civil fast days was gradually transformed into an occasion more for social leisure, the devotional use of fasting among evangelicals lent it renewed seriousness and perhaps extended its corporeal meanings as well. Fasting in private had always been the occasion for evangelicals' most severe prostrations and humiliations before God; hungering silently without the mitigating effects of community kept a body in painfully close touch with its own appetites while making possible the sweetest delights of a fast's conclusion.[21]

Fast days persisted as well among the more liturgical groups of Protestants in America, such as Lutherans and Anglicans. Evangelical Presbyterians in the Middle Colonies, bringing the sacramental traditions of Scotland and Ulster to America, observed days of solemn fasting at the start of annual communion feasts well into the nineteenth century before abandoning the practice for the sake of liturgical reform. Here, as among seventeenth-century Puritans, devotional abstinence centered on physical hunger and the hope for fulfillment: "Empty stomachs symbolized empty souls longing to be filled with the bread of life and the cup of salvation," writes one historian. Fasting also signified shame and penitence; it was meant to be an act of "holy Revenge upon the Flesh or Body for its former Excesses," as John Willison's sacramental catechism put it. Fasting mortified body and soul together, preparing them for the worthy reception of Christ's broken body and blood.[22] But whereas penitential, preparatory fasting would increasingly be divorced from the Eucharist in the American Presbyterian tradition, Christians hardly ceased to discipline their flesh via abstinence. Private devotional fasting persisted, joined by the "dietick gospel" freshly articulated by a Scottish physician and popularized by pietistic reformers and revivalists for whom abstemious living was long a holy habit.

Devotional fasting is not as closely associated with nineteenth-century Protestantism as with seventeenth-century Puritans or eighteenth-century Methodists. Yet Reformed disciples on both sides of the ocean in the period made vigorous defenses of fasting, most notably as a tool of religious revival. The "diet of angels" held vast implications for the evangelization of the world, as the English Baptist James Hargreaves made clear in 1828: "We believe that the various remarkable revivals of religion in America, and elsewhere . . . owe their origin, under God, to the humble fastings, and fervent, constant prayers of some of the Lord's people."[23] A typical article in the Presbyterians' *Congregational Magazine*, also during 1828, cited days of fasting, along with concerts of private prayer and pastoral visitations, as having been "owned and blessed of God, to the quickening and encouragement of his people, and the conversion of sinners."[24] W. C. Walton's *Preparation for Special Efforts to Promote the Work of God* (1833) recommended fasting as a help to the efficacy of prayer and a useful tool in promoting evangelical Christianity.[25] This compelled the physician Amariah Brigham, in his *Observations on the Influence of Religion Upon the Health and Physical Welfare of Mankind* (1835), to mention the recent surge of interest in fasting as a religious duty among the clergy, especially the "new measure clergy." As a critic of penitential austerities, among many other "absurd forms" and fanaticisms adopted by religious persons through the ages that he censured, Brigham undermined the scriptural foundations upon which Christians had long depended for fasting's justification, arguing that fasting, "is hardly reconcilable with the care which Christ had for the bodies of men, as evidenced by his numerous miracles wrought for its welfare, and even a miracle to feed the multitude."[26] For evangelicals, however, fasting's biblical ambiguity hardly precluded its role as an ordinance and aid to prayerful piety. Historians of southern evangelicalism have noted the widespread belief in fasting's efficacy, as a means of bringing revival and gaining God's favor, from the formative years of southern religion into the early years of the nineteenth century.[27]

The writings of the period's foremost revivalist leader, Charles Grandison Finney (1792–1875), placed less emphasis on fasting as a tool for stirring revival; the subject is not even mentioned in the 1835 *Lectures on Revivals of Religion*, though his *Memoirs* contain scattered references to private fasting and praying "in order to retain that communion with God, and that hold upon the divine strength, that would enable me efficiently to labor for the promotion of revivals of religion." Finney considered private fasting an important devotional practice and wrote of it frequently in his memoirs. He also explored the errors one could make in fasting, particularly in attending too closely to personal "feelings," "motives," and "states of mind" rather than meditating solely on Christ (this criticism of "self-examination" suggests how far evangelicals of Finney's sort had traveled from their Puritan forebears). Like prayer, with which it had long been deeply interwoven, fasting was an act of the will paradoxically intended to erase the will altogether. Fasting represented an attempt to empty the self and allow God to fill and overtake one, body and soul; and since the proper approach was surrender, one erred in trying to maintain control. But while outlining the fasts as a surrender to divine power, Finney's writings do not link fasting with repentance, humiliation, or extended submission. Rather, they tie fasting very directly to the receipt of divine blessings, as when God apparently rewarded Finney's strenuous fasting with successful revivals. Neither an instrument for discerning his sins nor mortifying his flesh in shame and sorrow, fasting was a tool for intensifying prayer, obtaining heavenly approval, and inducing God to pour blessings of success upon Finney himself.[28]

More conservative Presbyterians, those who resisted Finneyite revivalism and New School notions of immediate conversion, were traditionalists about devotional fasting. Samuel Miller (1769–1850), a professor of ecclesiastical history and church government at Princeton Theological Seminary for thirty-six years and one of the most respected denominational leaders of his time, published "The Duty, the Benefits, and the Proper Method of Religious Fasting," two sermons based on Daniel 9:3, in 1831.[29] There, Miller focused on the importance of occasional fasting, the frequency and extent of which should be decided only by individual conscience. Unlike the foreboding volumes generated by earlier Reformed leaders, Miller focused much less attention upon the potential perversions and abuses of fasting than upon fasting's spiritual, physical, and intellectual benefits. The spiritual benefits described by Miller were entirely conventional: humility, mortification, and intensified prayer.

Miller's fourth benefit of fasting went well beyond earlier texts authored by Reformed churchmen, however, making central a function that had heretofore been mentioned as a mere peripheral issue: fasting's positive impact on bodily health. Invoking an American statesman and philosopher (probably Benjamin Franklin), Miller noted that the man, "distinguished at once for his talents, his practical character, his vigorous health, and his long life," fasted one day out of every week, not out of religious conviction but for his bodily health and "to give nature a holyday."

> The practice, I am persuaded, was founded in the clearest and soundest principles of physiology. Truly our nature needs such a "holyday" much oftener than we are willing to yield it. The most enlightened physicians have given it as their opinion, that thousands accounted temperate, and really so in the popular sense of the term, are bringing themselves to premature graves for want of such a frequent respite from the burden of aliment as an occasional day of fasting would furnish. It is plain, then, that any sacred religious habit which secures such a respite; which tends, in the course of each month and week, to preserve us from the effects of habitual indulgence and repletion, cannot fail of contributing to the preservation and vigor of our bodily health, as well as preparing our minds for prompt and active application to the most important of all objects.

Christian writers of the past had emphasized the importance of bodily health to one's earthly spiritual pursuits, but Miller, beneficiary of more recent medical critiques of overeating, most forcefully advocated fasting as a healthful, salutary practice. His more famous compatriot, the erstwhile Presbyterian preacher Sylvester Graham, was just beginning his own crusade for restraint in eating and drinking, but Miller alone set such restraint within the context of devotional fasting.[30]

Miller and his Old-School Presbyterian colleagues at Princeton (Charles Hodge, Archibald Alexander, and Miller referred to themselves as an "Association of Gentlemen") may have indeed lived "primarily from the neck up," as one historian later quipped.[31] Miller's sermons surely suggest the extent to which fasting had already fallen into disuse, at least among the educated Protestants of Miller's circle. Yet whereas few of his colleagues may have been concerned by the decline of what was perceived as a primitive, superstitious asceticism now associated with Methodist excesses, for Miller the shift was an ominous one. As he lamented the widespread neglect of the "unfashionable duty" of true fasting in his own time, Miller enjoined fasting not for its own sake but rather "because, when properly conducted, it tends to promote the benefit of both our souls and our bodies." Favorable to health, to the intellect, to the spirit, and above all to happiness, fasting ought to attract reverential gratitude for its wondrous benefits, rather than fretful discontent or disdain.[32]

It had not been so long ago that fasting had been central to Presbyterian devotion, not only prior to the sacramental occasions noted earlier but also in ordinary, private life. The Scottish-born Isabella Graham (1742–1814), a highly influential reformer among widows, orphans, and poor immigrant women in New York City around the turn of the nineteenth century, recorded many occasions when she set aside a private fast and time for humiliation, grief, and repentance, to inventory and confess her iniquities and to ponder mournfully her baseness as a sinner. The vile sins she had to enumerate and confess during a fast were bitter, she wrote, but her meditations on God's forgiveness brought joyous relief.[33] The onetime cleric George Bush's frequent fasting, recorded in his diary, followed a similar pattern. Bush, a graduate of Princeton Seminary and a Presbyterian before he became a Swedenborgian and joined the Church of the New Jerusalem, set apart private days for fasting and prayer when he felt his spiritual state to be "thriftless and languishing." On these days Bush strove for confession and repentance, yet he also emphasized the great hope to which his devotional self-examinations led him. Like Isabella Graham, Bush envisioned days of fasting as a journey through shame, humiliation, mourning, and penitence to a more joyous peace in God's promises. Such occasions were so reviving that Bush could conclude, "God has graciously received my prayer, and . . . everything I have sought agreeable to his will shall be granted sooner or later."[34]

Miller, Graham, and Bush illustrate the devotion to private fasting that endured in Presbyterian circles during the first third of the nineteenth century. As the century wore on, however, fasting among Presbyterians became more and more associated with an older tradition of self-denying asceticism to which many younger Christians no longer felt bound. The popular Presbyterian novelist Elizabeth Prentiss (1818–78) created many female characters who, like Graham, advocated temperance in eating and drinking and strove to achieve high levels of self-sacrifice. Absent among their practices, however, was fasting, which Prentiss explicitly relegated to the dour religion of prior generations. In *Stepping Heavenward*, first published in 1869, the only character who fasts is the female narrator's gloomy, hypochondriacal father-in-law: "Father has been fasting to-day, and is so worn out and so nervous in consequence, that he could not bear the sound of the children's voices. I wish, if he must fast, he would do it moderately, and do it all the time. Now he goes without food until he is ready to sink, and now he eats quantities of improper food." Prentiss's cheerless characterization of an outmoded practice was apt: indeed, Miller's 1831 text appears to be one of private devotional fasting's last wholehearted defenses of its kind from an influential American Protestant leader for nearly a century and a half.[35] As America's well heeled white Christians yoked their faith ever more firmly to Victorian gentility, the austerity of devotional fasting came to seem like a quaint relic of their Puritan past, a practice with little utility in an age of divinely blessed abundance and comfortable, republican religion.

Fasting's demise was little mourned, perhaps because of the derision heaped on health reformers who called for reduced food intake. Physicians such as the neurologist George Miller Beard (1839–83) associated food abstinence with a condition of depleted strength and energy that seemed particularly prevalent among well-to-do professionals in the urban, industrialized classes. Ten years before publishing his classic text on neurasthenia, *American Nervousness, Its Causes and Consequences* (1881), Beard published a manual on diet entitled *Eating and Drinking*, where he lamented the increased incidence of "undereating" and sought to combat it with a freshened heartiness toward food. He dryly reproved promoters of abstinence, vegetarianism, and fasting for their effects on the nation's overall health. "Prolonged fasting," even the kind that allowed for two meals per day, was "the prerogative of savages" and would result not in fruitful Christian virtue but only in sickness. "Dyspepsia in all its phases, nervous diseases of all kinds, and death itself, are the rewards that nature is continually bestowing on those who thus refuse her bounties," Beard warned.

"Abstinence from regular meals in health is a vice which only professed gluttons should indulge. . . . It is far better to overeat at lunch than not to eat at all." Beard's concern was to boost the appetite of the cultivated classes so as to elevate their happiness and morale, and his work fit well into a context of increasing distaste for religious forms of fasting.[36]

Occasionally, elite Protestants did lament the lapse in fasting, as in an 1862 article in the *Princeton Review* titled "The Human Body as Related to Sanctification." Like Miller's earlier text, this essay attempted a thorough-going overhaul of contemporary religious attitudes toward the body and moderated between the poles of overattention to the body in religion ("rit-ualism" associated with Roman Catholicism, the Oxford Movement, and the Mercersburg school of theology) and bodily estrangement from religion ("rationalism" associated with Platonism as well as some modern Protestant currents). As part of his project to redeem bodily habits in service to devo-tional piety, the author praised fasting as a practice to facilitate affliction and repentance, thus fulfilling "that wondrous implication of the states of the body with the states of the soul, which we have been considering." As the urgent tone of this piece clearly indicates, fasting appeared moribund among the era's Protestants.[37]

Devotional fasting continued to thrive in other circles. An "Old cove-nanting and true Presbyterian layman" published a deeply traditional defense of fasting in 1875 that Cotton Mather himself might have penned. Mormons, Mennonites, and Millerites (later Seventh-day Adventists) per-sistently fasted well into the twentieth century.[38] Mormons were especially fervent fasters, in obedience to Joseph Smith's 1832 revelation that the Latter-day Saints "continue in prayer and fasting from this time forth."[39] A practice apparently unique to Mormons, but one that Samuel Miller could have approved, was Smith's institution in the 1830s of fast offerings, money that would otherwise have been used to buy food that was instead collected for the poor; this practice has persisted among the Latter-day Saints into the twenty-first century. Miller and Smith had less in common with other aspects of fasting, however. Since the earliest days of Smith's new church, fasting's traditional emphasis on humiliation and repentance was dimin-ished in exchange for a focus on spiritual strength, power, and perfection—not the journey from grief to peace recorded by Isabella Graham and George Bush but a less arduous resting in the latter.[40] For later Mormons, fasting would be indelibly associated not only with helping the poor but with wor-shipful, inspirational accounts of God's blessings in their lives in monthly fast and testimony meetings. Joseph Smith's doctrine of fasting, dressed up as social activism and therapeutic cheer, established what has been the most lasting and, at least until very recently, most vigorous model of regular Christian fasting in the Anglo-American world.

Christian fasting endured among circles that included some American Anabaptists, Seventh-day Adventists, and scattered holiness adherents, especially those who would later join the fold of Pentecostalism, a tradition where fasting long remained dear. Holiness testimonies repeatedly invoked bodily discipline, as illustrated in the following examples, compiled by Phoebe Palmer in 1868. "Wherein am I in bondage to appetite, or to any of my propensities," asked Asa Mahan, the president of Oberlin College. The Methodist minister F. G. Hibbard wrote in typical fashion of setting apart "weeks of prayer, fasting, watching, and special labor" to attain the blessing of sanctification. The Reverend Henry Belden spoke of his hunger for God that was satiated only by "a special season of fasting" and later "frequent days of fasting and prayer." Many others followed Wesley in belonging to bands of believers who met regularly and fasted every Friday. "I thirsted and hungered that I might be filled," wrote the minister John Scarlett, and those appetites necessitated ever more thorough fasting and prayer. Another recounted knowing that "if I would retain the favor of God I must seek purity," and so, "I resolved never to eat, drink, or sleep until I was fully saved," a joyous event that occurred soon after.[41] These experiential narratives testify to the abiding place of fasting within the doggedly experiential wings of American Protestantism. Among more conservative sectors, however, fasting was not a vital practice in American Christianity by the latter decades of the nineteenth century. As the crusade against alcohol gained force, words like "temperance" and "abstinence" came to be associated almost solely with liquor, not with both drinking *and* eating as before, while calls to moderate food intake were associated with the "faddism" of William Andrus Alcott, Sylvester Graham, John Harvey Kellogg, and other advocates of a simple vegetable diet. In place of earlier advocates like Miller, a fresh crop of health reformers emerged, managing to capitalize on fasting's consumerist attractions while discarding its harsher doctrinal associations. But fasting was not the only indicator of attitudes toward corporeality; even as fasting's interest waned for the era's established Protestants, the body's uses as a visual indicator of piety steadily mounted.

GOSPELS OF PHYSICK: MEDICINE, METHODISM, AND MORTIFICATION

Discourses on fasting had long referred, at least in passing, to fasting's attendant health benefits. Writers' knowledge of Hippocratic and Galenic medicine enabled them to expand the appeal of temperance beyond its role in maintaining spiritual meekness to its supposed ability to increase well-being and longevity. "He that undertakes to enumerate the benefits of fasting, may in the next page also reckon all the benefits of physick," the Anglican minister Jeremy Taylor noted in his most widely read devotional text, in which he had already given thorough attention to "temperance in eating and drinking."[42] Another Anglican cleric and widely read devotional writer, William Law (1686–1761), in *A Serious Call to a Devout and Holy Life* (1728) commended his model character, Miranda, for regularly eating as little as possible, only so much as was necessary for health:

> She eats and drinks only for the sake of living, and with so regular an abstinence, that every meal is an exercise of self-denial, and she humbles her body every time that she is forced to feed it. If Miranda was to run a race for her life, she would submit to a diet that was proper for it. But as the race which is set before her is a race of holiness, purity, and heavenly affection, which she is to finish in a corrupt, disordered body of earthly passions, so her everyday diet has only this one end, to make her body fitter for this spiritual race. She does not weigh her meat in a pair of scales; but she weighs it in a much better balance; so much as gives a proper strength to her body, and renders it able and willing to obey the soul, to join in psalms and prayers, and lift up eyes and hands towards heaven with greater readiness: so much is Miranda's meal. So that Miranda will never have her eyes swell with fatness, or pant under a heavy load of flesh, until she has changed her religion.[43]

The image of eyes swollen with fatness was horrifying indeed, for it at once signified both vice and ill health, evils that had been loosely joined in Puritan thought but that fresh condemnations of indulgence and obesity more severely equated in the eighteenth century. Numerous English editions of Law's influential text were joined by the first American edition in 1793, and by 1835 at least eighteen American editions had already appeared. Eight more American reprints appeared during the nineteenth century (and at least nineteen more thereafter).[44]

Aside from abstinence as a practice of spiritual mortification, dietary restraint received increasing attention on both sides of the Atlantic during the eighteenth century and beyond. As historians have noted, it was during this time that fat (and not simply gluttony itself) became increasingly associated with sin and corruption.[45] Medical and devotional writers alike were influenced by the autobiographical tale of Luigi Cornaro, a sixteenth-century Italian nobleman whose critique of that old Christian foe "gluttony" would be cited for centuries thereafter. The obese Cornaro, tottering toward an early grave before the age of forty, had given up gourmandizing for simplicity, lived sixty more years, and crafted the first conversionist account of weight loss in an ongoing tradition, the "I once was fat but now am thin" genre. Cornaro's *Trattato de la vita sobria* (1558) was later republished, with additions, as *Discorsi della vita sobria*, and the first English edition appeared in 1634, translated by George Herbert. By 1737 a fifth English edition had appeared, and by 1777, a twenty-fifth. The well-known text would be a persistent seller in Anglo-American circles well into the nineteenth century and would continue to receive mention in health literature of the twentieth, its publication often accompanied—even in a 1998 reprint edition—by seventeenth-century paeans to Cornaro penned by Francis Bacon, Joseph Addison, and Sir William Temple.[46]

An influential convert to the body of bodily reduction was the Scottish-born physician George Cheyne (1671–1743), who decried the luxurious living, gluttony, and dyspeptic heft of other upper-class gentlemen and ladies in his best-selling books *An Essay of Health and Long Life* (1724), *The English Malady* (1733), and *The Natural Method of Cureing the Diseases of the Body and the Disorders of the Mind* (1742). The mystically oriented Cheyne was a voracious reader of Law, Taylor, Thomas à Kempis, Jacob Boehme, and Jeanne Guyon—all of whom wrote of suppressing the appetite so that the spirit could rise—and he apparently knew whereof he spoke.[47] His indulgent youth had left him "excessively fat, short-breath'd, lethargick and listless," a condition that only a milk and vegetable diet relieved. Twice afterward Cheyne had returned to meat and other delicacies and grown corpulent again (once tipping the scale at 32 stone, or nearly 450 pounds) before returning to vigorous health by means of abstemious eating and exercise.[48] Reduced to a healthier weight and rid of the many illnesses that had accompanied his obesity, Cheyne focused on the physical and spiritual benefits of "diaetetick management" and corporeal leanness, now conceiving of health as a religious obligation.

As a well-known professional in Bath, highly touted for its therapeutic hot springs, Cheyne attracted many aristocratic clients to whom he taught the spiritual benefits of abstinence. "Crudely put," notes the historian Anita Guerrini, "he posited an inverse relationship between weight and spirituality: the less matter, the more spirit."[49] His wealthy readership, Guerrini further documents, also learned about the pious Miranda in Law's *Serious Call*, to judge by the memoirs and biographies of contemporary English aristocrats. This audience included not only wealthy patrons such as Archibald and Elizabeth Hutcheson (who became a rich widow on the death of her husband, an MP) and philanthropic ascetics descended from the earl of

Huntingdon but also such towering revivalist preachers as George White-field and John Wesley (both of whom also benefited from aristocratic patrons). David E. Shuttleton, who has closely traced out these latter revivalist links, records a letter from Whitefield to Wesley in April 1735, describing Whitefield's use of Cheyne's *Essay of Health;* Whitefield, in poor health at the time, noted that he had "resolved some time agone . . . to consult nothing as to my eating or drinking yet but what should be essentially necessary for the preserving of my body in a fit Condition to serve my Master and fellow Christians." To cure his distemper, Whitefield turned to Cheyne's prescription for "Herbs, Milk etc., for Spring which I would very readily come in with, having little or no appetite and hoping such a way would be a means of mortifying me to sensual pleasures and greatly to promote Christian Purity." It was only very shortly after adopting this regimen that Whitefield's own conversion occurred.[50]

Wesley studied at least three of Cheyne's books during his early years in Oxford, and historians have traced his subsequent lifelong interest in an austere diet to this period. At the age of sixty-eight, he cited his adoption of Cheyne's principles as the source of his longevity; indeed, the abstemious diet that Wesley followed throughout his life had been taken from Cheyne (who had encouraged Wesley personally in this pursuit). In 1747 Wesley published his own guide to medicine and health, *Primitive Physick, or an Easy and Natural Method of Curing Most Diseases,* where he acknowledged his debt to Cheyne and summarized his own position on diet: "The great rule of eating and drinking is, To suit the quality and quantity of the food to the strength of our digestion; to take always such a sort and such a measure of food as fits light and easy to the stomach."[51] As the most widely read medical book of the late eighteenth century—the book went through twenty-three editions in his lifetime and was reprinted long after his death—Wesley's text made Cheyne's "dietick gospel" accessible to a broad audience of ordinary, unlettered men and women while also helping to fuel the equation between dietary faddism and Methodist enthusiasm commonly articulated then and later. In Richard Graves's fictional satire, *The Spiritual Quixote,* for instance, a wide-eyed Methodist rector tells his guests of the wondrous Francis Hongo Hyppazoli (a spoof of Cornaro), whose legendary abstemiousness turned his white hair black again at the age of hundred and caused him to cut two new teeth at a hundred and ten.[52]

Wesley and his early followers feasted on Cheyne's dietetic regimen in large part because it fit so well with their own devotional austerities. Like the Scottish Presbyterian John Willison, along with the mystical writers who so deeply influenced him, Wesley made an explicit connection between fasting and the sin of overeating:

> Many of those who now fear God are deeply sensible how often they have sinned against him by the abuse of these lawful things. They know how much they have sinned by excess of food; how long they have transgressed the holy law of God with regard to temperance, if not sobriety too; how they have indulged their sensual appetites, perhaps to the impairing even their bodily health, certainly to the no small hurt of their soul. . . . To remove therefore the effect they remove the cause; they keep at a distance from all excess. They abstain, as far as is possible, from what had wellnigh plunged them in everlasting perdition. They often wholly refrain; always take care to be sparing and temperate in all things.

Wesley's American followers echoed these teachings; in a watch-night sermon delivered in 1785 and later printed in Baltimore, Jesse Lee warned his hearers of the many worldly lusts against which they must guard themselves: "Many persons by eating too much, and overcharging their stomachs, become so heavy, dull, and sleepy, that they are neither fit for their daily vocations, nor for the service of God. . . . Their spirits are sunk in excess in eating, and sermon after sermon is lost upon them." With a message indebted as much to George Cheyne as Jeremy Taylor or William Law, these pious teachers brought humiliation and health together as grounds for austere eating, in a potent combination that would echo resoundingly long after Wesley's death.[53]

The literary influence of Cornaro, Cheyne, and Wesley pervaded the nineteenth-century popular and medical literature on diet, in North America as much as and soon more than in Britain. Temperance advocates, homeopaths, hydropaths, exercise boosters, vegetarians, and mastication enthusiasts alike quoted copiously from Cornaro ("Luigi" anglicized to "Lewis" or "Louis") and Cheyne in recommending an abstemious diet. In 1796 and again in 1809 and 1810, Philadelphia publishers printed Cornaro's treatise with Benjamin Franklin's *Way to Wealth*, while later American editions appeared in 1814, 1815, 1833, 1842, 1847, and thereafter.[54] The 1833 edition of Cornaro appeared with an introduction and notes by Sylvester Graham, the well known Presbyterian temperance advocate and health reformer. Graham used the opportunity to damn Cornaro with faint praise, noting that his dietary improvement was one not of quality but of mere quantity— since, for instance, Cornaro continued to drink fourteen ounces of wine per day. "Had that oppression been entirely thrown off," Graham railed, "had no portion of the wine been retained, and had the *qualities* of his food been in all respects more consistent with sound physiological principles, he would not only have recovered a more perfect state of health, and, beyond all question, have lived many years longer, but he would entirely have escaped those yearly depressions of health and strength, in which he almost sunk into the grave." Cornaro's writings could do, he concluded, "far more mischief than good to mankind" if read without corrective notes. Graham's need to publish the text with his own commentary signifies its much wider contemporary usage—otherwise, he easily could have ignored Cornaro altogether— and its enduring resonance with health reform literature. George Cheyne was likewise published repeatedly in the United States. According to Guerrini, his *Essay of Health and Long Life,* first published in 1724, went through nine English editions during his own lifetime, with American editions appeared in 1813, 1815, and 1843 (and reprints well beyond).[55]

Benjamin Rush (1745–1813), a prominent Philadelphia physician and signer of the Declaration of Independence, has received more notice for his republican thinking and temperance activism than for his interest in dietary reform, but health reformers in subsequent eras knew well his writings on the latter. His *Sermons to Gentlemen Upon Temperance and Exercise* (1772) decried the social effects of luxurious living, and in fact the first sermon concerned sobriety in eating. While Rush did not go so far as to advocate vegetarianism, he did call for a higher proportion of vegetable food to meat. In fact he believed quality of food to be far less important than its quantity, and his strategies for conquering gluttony included eating only one dish at a time ("Few men, I believe, ever eat to excess more than once of one plain dish") and eating only "one hearty meal a day," preferably in the evening. More than this amount would "oppress nature, and keep her constantly fatigued, in concocting the immense supplies of food which are thrown into the stomach." Countless diseases could be attributed to intemperate eating, Rush contended, and as for the glutton himself: "Better, far better, would it have been for him, had he (in the words of our text) 'put a knife to his throat,' or even plunged a dagger into his heart the first day he gave himself up to his appetite, than lived to endure such aggravated misery." Love of self, family, posterity, and nation demanded strict regulation of the appetite.[56]

The year after Andrew Jackson was elected president of the United States in 1828, an anonymous group of optimistic physicians in Philadelphia began publishing the *Journal of Health,* and the stage was set for exhortations in favor of vegetarianism, unbolted wheat flour, and ongoing debate over the supposed superiority of particular regimens. Best known are the accounts of reformers such as the aforementioned Sylvester Graham (1794–1851) and William Alcott (1798–1859), who crusaded for a revolution in American eating habits and portrayed dietary inhibition in redemptive terms. Like Rush, both men advocated simplicity, and both also viewed physical health as a matter of national, even cosmic significance. James Whorton, the premier historian of the American health reform movement launched at that time, has described in detail the dietary teachings of these "Christian physiologists," whose personal narrative echoed Cornaro and Cheyne (often explicitly) in their assertions of gluttonous decadence, conversion to austerity, and subsequent glorious health. In the decades prior to the Civil War, Graham and Alcott crusaded against "that fatalism which took disease as it came, accepting it as an unpredictable act of Providence beyond human control." Good health was no mere matter of luck, both repeatedly averred, but rather a choice that could be fulfilled by attention to the scientific principles of diet and related regimens of bodily care. The messianic undertones of their ministry left no audience member uncertain that what health reformers believed to be at stake was the salvation of the world. Or, to invoke the language used by the historian Robert Abzug, the health reformers promoted the "sacralization" of both social and personal life, calling for "nothing less than a radical change in the conception of individual holiness."[57]

Most scholarly attention has focused on these familiar Protestant health reformers, but dietary instructions appeared liberally in works by other religious authors as well. The Philadelphia minister Joseph Jones, another Presbyterian, directed his readers to a plain vegetarian diet in *The Influence of Physical Causes on Religious Experience* (1846), though he carefully cited Benjamin Rush rather than Graham or Alcott. While he conceded that Christians might be wary of the "excessive abstinence" practiced by those "under the influence of superstition" (i.e., Roman Catholicism), he cautioned, "the more common and dangerous error by far, is the opposite, or that of indulging the appetite too freely." Hence, Jones affirmed several precepts: "that intemperate eating is almost a universal fault; that it is begun in the cradle and continued till we go down to the grave; that it is far more common than intemperance in drinking; and the aggregate of mischief that it does, is greater." These were important rules for any person wishing for good health, but for Christians they were essential, noted Jones, since scripture taught strict regulation of the appetites. "The spiritual man," more even than all others, "should learn, with the apostle Paul, to keep his body under. He should live in that elevated state of communion with God, that he will not be tempted to descend from the higher and purer enjoyments of his religion, to seek happiness in the gratifications of the epicurean and sensualist."[58]

A few years later the prominent liberal minister Horace Bushnell (1802–76) addressed similar concerns in his widely read *Christian Nurture,* where he emphasized the shaping power of the body upon the soul and its appetites in the ongoing warfare between soul and body. "So important a thing, for the religious life of the soul, is the feeding of the body," he mused. "Vast multitudes of disciples have no conception of the fact. Living in a swine's body, regularly over-loaded and oppressed every day of their lives, they wonder that so great difficulties and discouragements rise up to hinder the Christian clearness of their soul." Bushnell's distress pertained chiefly here to the effects of ignorant parents upon children, as he saw generations growing up with a distorted view of the relation between body and soul. "It is a great mistake to suppose that men and women, such as are to be fathers and mothers, are affected only in their souls by religious experience, and not in their bodies," he wrote. Persons who underwent "a genuine sanctification" were "penetrated bodily, all through, by the work of the Spirit in their life. Their appetites are more nearly in heaven's order, their passions more tempered by reason, their irritabilities more sweetened and calmed, and so far they are entered bodily into the condition of health." The body itself, Bushnell instructed, could undergo with the soul "a remedial process in its tempers and humors," prospering "even as the soul prospereth." But this relationship was not one of sweetness and light. Fasting itself proved an excellent example for Bushnell, as "the soul rising up, in God's name, to assert herself over the body; over its appetites, passions, tempers, and, if possible, distempers. And how often," he noted, "the poor, coarse, stupid, sensual, fast-bound slaves of the body, calling themselves disciples, need this kind of war, and a regular campaign of it, to get their souls uppermost and trim themselves for the race."[59]

While the hygienic reforms of the period may have appeared somewhat less revolutionary than the social overhauls promoted by the temperance, abolitionist, and woman's rights movements, the advance of dietary restraint was palpable. Moreover its success built upon these other broad crusades. In 1858, when the Harvard Divinity School graduate Thomas Wentworth Higginson's essay "Saints and Their Bodies" appeared in the *Atlantic Monthly,* Higginson was already known for his radical abolitionism, and he had been ousted from a Unitarian pulpit in Newburyport, Massachusetts, for expressing his views on slavery, factory labor, and women's rights. In his widely read essay, Higginson lamented Protestant physical decline: "It is to be reluctantly recorded, in fact, that the Protestant saints have not ordinarily had much to boast of, in physical stamina, as compared with the Roman Catholic." Calvin and Luther provided hopeless examples of health, Higginson noted drolly, and "nothing this side of ancient Greece, we fear, will afford adequate examples of the union of saintly souls and strong bodies." Against his alleged foes who promoted pure intellect and feeble bodies, Higginson strongly advocated physical exercise and the cultivation of more robust health, for women no less than for men. The nation's strength depended foremost on a fit population, he urged: "Physical health is a necessary condition of all permanent success." As the "only attribute of power" in which Americans were "losing ground," health was of particular importance. "Guaranty us against physical degeneracy, and we can risk all other perils—financial crises, Slavery, Romanism, Mormonism, Border Ruffians, and New York assassins; 'domestic malice, foreign levy, nothing' can daunt us." National security, to use much later parlance, was Higginson's definitive reason for individuals to commit themselves to good health.[60]

Examples could be endlessly multiplied here to illustrate a broad spectrum of American thinkers and religious groups, including upstarts such as Latter-day Saints (Mormons), Seventh-day Adventists, and Pentecostals, who blended their own sense of spiritual discipline with material concerns about health and longevity. Suffice to note that by the end of the nineteenth century hardly any middle-class American sector had been unaffected by endlessly reinvented versions of older Christian disciplinary practices. Their "secular" and "religious" content was virtually interchangeable; indeed, within most settings the pious and impious alike could altogether agree on the importance of bridled eating habits. For the pious, however, restrained ingestion resonated especially well with biblical injunctions to simplicity, and Protestant reformers repeatedly urged bodily discipline for the sake of God's kingdom. Eventually, an increasingly moralistic pursuit of extreme slimness would vie with the focus on health as a supreme religious value, a notion aided by the accelerating belief in spirit-body correspondence that steadily advanced the body as an expressive language revealing the interior soul.

RAREFIED FLESH: SEXUAL REGULATION, BODILY PLEASURE, AND PERFECTION

Just as devotional fasting ebbed during an era when health reform advanced, marking an important shift in the role of food within religious and medical practice, other projects of bodily discipline also underwent considerable flux between American colonial and post–Civil War periods. These changes were by no means perfectly synchronized with shifts in eating behavior, nor were such discrete adjustments in somatic practice traceable to a singular cause or identical set of implications. Whatever else the recent scholarly upsurge of embodiment studies reveals about its own immediate cultural context, this oeuvre surely demonstrates the prolific multiplicity of meanings produced by distinct ways of attending to the body. Without oversimplifying intricate historical developments, we can identify particular features of a larger cultural process of reorienting desire and appetite to changing ends, with the body in a central and contested role.

In no venue did the Protestant reorientation of desire entail more avid exertion than the American bedchamber. Since the colonial period and escalating in the new republic, allied systems to regulate sex and keep it within heterosexual marriage had vied against divers forms of sexual experimentation, much of these within Christian utopian, millenarian, and perfectionist communities. The various practices also carried significant symbolic weight, addressing anxieties about sexual discipline and the propagation of virtuous citizens. Attending to a few highly charged episodes in this divisive history illuminates another conceptual framework for exploring unstable ideas about the body's potential as an instrument of salvation as well as damnation.

The role of sexuality in Puritan New England has been a topic of extensive scrutiny and debate. Older interpretations of Puritans as sexually repressed and, in turn, repressive accelerated the ongoing use of the term "puritanical" in American popular culture, along with the pervasive trope of the scheming, voyeuristic colonial community that produced such stock literary figures as Nathaniel Hawthorne's hypocritical Reverend Dimmesdale in *The Scarlet Letter* and Arthur Miller's strident version of Samuel Parris in *The Crucible*. Since the 1940s, however, scholarly attention has shifted toward the ways in which Puritans thought more approvingly about sexuality within the context of marriage, despite the rather precarious social situation of women (who were believed, among other things, to be dangerously oversexed) within early New England culture. Since the early sixteenth century, Protestant reformers had argued that celibacy was an unnatural state more liable to trigger sexual sin than holiness. Homosexuality, masturbation, and fornication were vices attributed to Catholic priests and others who forced their bodies to refrain from conjugal relations within a state of monogamous matrimony. Martin Luther, among others, promoted marriage as a "hospital for incurables which prevents inmates from falling into graver sin."[61] Later English Protestants generally tolerated and sometimes actively condoned celibacy (Erik Seeman argues that "supposedly hypersexual religious radicals" like the Ranters and the Seekers posed a greater problem to seventeenth-century Anglicans than any group of religious celibates), whereas their New England counterparts echoed earlier European Reformers in condemning celibacy and promoting marital relations.[62]

The heightened centrality of the patriarchal family, which New Englanders more than the English considered a primary site of social authority, helps to account for this matrimonial drive. The concern for social order did not merely deem marriage a dreary obligation, however, nor did it render bedroom activity a degrading-albeit-compulsory enterprise. Sexuality was clearly vital to Puritan marriage ideals in New England for more than procreative reasons. Clergy stressed the importance of frequent sexual activity between husband and wife, arguing that God's creation of sexual desire deemed it a natural good. Thomas A. Foster, examining seventeenth-century New England attitudes toward male sexual incapacity in marriage, summarizes the prevailing view of the time as one in which "procreative aims and sexual pleasure were compatible; indeed, within the confines of legitimate unions, sexual pleasure could reinforce the bonds upon which the stability of the Puritans' male-headed households rested."[63] Bodies and desires were, in this sense anyway, fundamental to Puritan understandings of domestic and social order.

Else K. Hambleton has scoured court documents, including divorce records, to show how Puritans considered "mutually satisfying sexual intercourse" to be vital to a marriage, not only because the Bible instructed them to "be fruitful and multiply" but also because sex increased affection between a husband and wife.[64] While warning Puritan readers not to allow pleasure to distract them from their religion, marital advice literature taught that sex—properly prioritized—would serve as a delightful cementing of marital bonds. Legal statutes in towns such as New Haven further decreed conditions such as male impotence to be legitimate grounds for divorce, in no small part because this condition denied women the enjoyment they could rightly expect from marriage. Authors such as the rector William Gouge argued, moreover, that female barrenness did not legitimate divorce, since sexual fulfillment was still possible despite infertility. Godly wives were strongly enjoined to give their husbands pleasure; as Cotton Mather wrote, in *Ornaments for the Daughters of Zion,* "A *Vertuous Wife* is one that *pleaseth* God, as much as if she were cloistered up in the strictest and closest *Nunnery;* and therewith, yea, there-*in* she pleases a *Vertuous Husband* also."[65] Because Puritan understandings of biology taught that conception could occur only if both partners reached orgasm, procreation itself actually depended upon bodily pleasure. Sex, then, was considered a positive benefit of matrimonial life and not merely a necessary evil.

Nonetheless, Puritans also worried about the dangers of sexuality and sought to limit its expression for the sake of reining in sinful appetites. Women, considered the more lustful sex in the early modern world, often invited suspicion (and at certain times worse, as during outbreaks of witchcraft accusations) if they were spinsters, widows, or simply postmenopausal; and though men were believed to possess greater self-control than women, unmarried men also encountered mistrust. As Hambleton has shown in her study of Puritan prosecution of women and men accused of fornication, New England Puritans "successfully repressed extramarital sexual intercourse using a combination of criminal prosecutions and cultural conditioning. . . . Ministers and magistrates, working in combination from pulpits and benches, exhorted their parishioners to refrain from sin and administered humiliating public punishments to those who failed." Single women living in the Massachusetts Bay Colony were forbidden by law to have sex, and those who bore bastard children, even in cases of rape, were sometimes prosecuted (including sentences of being fined or whipped) until after the American Revolution. Religious and cultural rules worked together to uphold the importance of premarital chastity for men as well as women; for while sex in marriage was a "comfort" and "delight," extramarital intercourse was "filthiness," "incontinence," and "uncleanness."[66]

Nor was this anxiety only aimed outward; indeed, tremendous intensity was self-directed toward the inmost, private core: Puritan diaries, for instance, vividly illustrate the ways in which personal introspection came to bear upon seemingly uncontrolled desires. A recent analysis of homoerotic pinings in the Puritan minister and poet Michael Wigglesworth's diary reveals a powerful undercurrent of anxiety and shame over the man's desire for his students. That humiliation had nothing whatever to do with the fact that the students were male—"homosexual" was not part of any available lexicon of the time—but only with Wigglesworth's felt lack of control to stem the "filthy lust flowing from my fond affection to my pupils," the "much distracted thoughts I find arising from too much doting affection to some of my pupils."[67] The instability of human desire was worrisome, and the only solution seemed to be to stem its tides altogether through severe self-discipline. Puritan *eros* found other channels as well, such as the voyeuristic public executions of female fornicators and criminals, who were forced to broadcast their sins and proclaim repentance in execution narratives.[68] Such evidence of the ways that Puritans and their offspring defined iniquity, reoriented desire, and, in so doing, rarefied the flesh into a visible symbol of a supremely spiritual reality gives pause to the modern Protestant history of sexual sin. Even without invoking fashionable theories of repression and power, we may infer that the harsh legal sanctions leveled against extramarital sexual infractions in America have sprung from long-standing fears about the chaos of bodily desire.

A common current in early Anglo-Protestant sexual regulation and subsequent modes of bodily management, of course, has been the entrenched aspiration to contain appetites perceived as wayward and aberrant (as changing generations define these attributes). One enduring dimension of Puritan sexuality is the reality of its collective (and not merely private) nature; as the literary critic Ed Ingebretsen has contended, "sex is what a community does together in public."[69] Indictments of sexual perversion and vice have shored up the bounds of American propriety even while stirring polite society to leer at suspected offenders, a mode of scrutiny typifying a thinly veiled impulse to condemn nonconformists and assorted others. Palpably, in our collective memory of the Puritans, but by no means only there, sex in America has always seemed to be everyone's business. Whether policing others' behavior or telling stories of their own, Americans have shown sex to be, at its core, a social event. Hence those who have sought to establish innovations in orthodox Protestant heterosexual monogamy have so often faced vehement opposition, persecution, and even criminalization.[70]

During the eighteenth and nineteenth centuries many such innovators arose to reject heterosexual marriage in favor of other, ostensibly higher forms of sexual practice. Some of the most radical were millenarian, perfectionist groups who sought to hasten the coming of the kingdom of God and to lead lives of Christian perfection, a state that entailed dramatically altered forms of practical embodiment. Such groups did not always, however, agree on what those forms should be. The Massachusetts resident Sarah Prentice (b. 1716) was one of a number of New England Immortalists who believed, first, that their bodies had become incorruptible and would not die and, second, that true marriage should be a spiritual rather than a physical union in which all parties should remain celibate. To the itinerant revivalist Isaac Backus, Prentice noted in 1753 "that this night 2 months ago She passed thro' a change in her Body equivalent to Death, so that She had ben intirely free from any disorder in her Body or Corruption in her soul ever Since; and expected she should be So: and that her Body would never see Corruption, but would Live here 'till Christs personal coming."[71] As Erik Seeman has argued, Prentice and her followers "sought to create a new sort of family, one shorn of its reproductive functions but still organized like traditional families in that a dominant figure inculcated proper religious beliefs and practices." For Prentice and other mid-eighteenth-century Anglo-Protestants who adopted celibacy, restraining human appetites opened clearer pathways for spiritual receptivity and propelled the individual onto a holy journey toward immortality.[72]

Like the Immortalists, the Shakers (the United Society of Believers in Christ's Second Appearing), headed by Mother Ann Lee (1736–84), believed that scripture enjoined them not to be fruitful and multiply but to embody perfection and adopt celibacy. Biblical passages such as Matthew 22:30 (KJV)—"For in the resurrection they neither marry nor are given in marriage, but are like angels in heaven"—provided the foundation for this belief, that to live a saved life meant to refrain completely from sexual intercourse and thus live in complete freedom from carnality.[73] Having arrived in North America in 1774 after fleeing persecution in England, Shakers believed that Lee was the second incarnation of the Christ spirit— a female embodiment, after Jesus' male embodiment—such that physicality played an important if highly ambivalent role within Shakerism. As with Puritans, the body itself played a crucial role in Shaker practice—"an arena of mystical religious experience," in Jean Humez's words, that was a vehicle of spiritual ecstasy.[74] Shakers earned their name, in fact, from using their bodies to dance feverishly during worship, even as they were called upon to "crucify" the flesh; indeed, the very point of their dancing was to overcome carnality through the "purifying fire" of heat-producing physical movement. But even as they understood the body as vital to both worship and to their salvation, Shakers could claim "that the flesh is a clog to the spirit, . . . the body is a clog to the soul." Suzanne Thurman further points out how Shakers (like many other Christian groups) regularly "spiritualiz[ed] the body so as to detract from its corporeality and, hence, from its corruptibility."[75]

The Shakers' repudiation of sexual intercourse as wholly sinful served as a counterclaim to Protestant ideals of marriage and family, while also dramatically shifting participants' own concept of body. Renouncing blood ties for union with likeminded believers, members separated themselves from the rest of the world in order to live in close community with one another. Shakers lived in buildings that were segregated by sex, and most of their daily activities were also separated along gender lines, even to the doors through which they entered into worship spaces. There would be, in that way, no unwanted mixing of the sexes. Many of the Shakers' American critics refused, however, to believe that celibacy—which they considered abnormal—could truly prevail in a religious community. Popular literature on the Shakers, including ostensible autobiographical accounts from former members, promoted the belief that orgiastic sexual activity frequently occurred in Shaker gatherings—thus creating what Thurman has described as "a Shaker body that was doubly deviant." Deemed hypocrites, perverts, and fornicators, Shaker bodies appeared morally depraved precisely because their supposed sexual appetites did not sustain reproduction, or the production of "normal" American citizens.[76]

Beginning in the 1840s, female mediums, or "spirit instruments," in various Shaker societies began receiving spiritual messages from Holy Mother Wisdom, an aspect of the godhead that had been embodied in Lee. By 1841, as Humez has documented, Shaker communities were holding formal visitation ceremonies where Holy Mother Wisdom would speak through living believers, while messages also arrived in writing. Some, received by Paulina Bates of Watervliet, were eventually published as *The Divine Book of Holy and Eternal Wisdom* (1849), where some passages instructed married women how to avoid carnality: "Listen and understand: Ye are not called to become defiled and polluted and to wallow in fleshly gratifications as a sow walloweth in the mire in order to fulfill the marriage covenant and rear up an offspring to him [man] and become a crown of glory to his existence. Nay, in no wise. I, Wisdom, will teach you a far better way to act the part of a mother and a bosom friend to your companion." Non-Shaker women were further urged to "use all your influence to suppress the haunts of iniquity and debauchery" and "to do good to those of [your] sex, that lie buried in ruinous habits." The call to women was clear: control your own sexuality and work to ensure that other members of society control theirs as well.[77] As for men, Louis Kern has noted the prominence of castration imagery in Shaker writings and argues for the presence of a great deal of male sexual anxiety in Shaker theology. Less dramatically, Stephen Stein writes of Shakers' sexual taboos, like their "fixation on cleanliness" and occasional experiments with dietary reform, as "mirror[ing] their fears of disorder."[78]

The rise of celibate female leaders signaled an innovative solution to such disquiet and to the paramount tension within Protestant theology more generally over women's true nature. For the Puritans, the figure of the lustful, oversexed, dangerous woman loomed large, even as newer ideas about virtuous wives began to take hold. Promoting female virtue had the salutary effect of reinforcing the institutions of marriage and the patriarchal family, and yet Protestants remained fearful that female virtue could be faked: that, beneath the surface of a virtuous wife lay a wicked daughter of Eve. Celibate female leaders such as Prentice and Lee frequently had to undergo humiliating physical examinations to prove their womanliness (and to make sure they were not witches); to their followers, however, their purity and holiness comprised unquestionable religious tenets. As later chapters suggest, Protestant chastity movements—no less than their dietary counterparts—

have frequently aimed at resolving such conflicting beliefs about corporeal desire, pleasure, and discipline.

But repudiation of sexual intercourse was not the only solution to uneasiness about sexuality, the body, and the institution of marriage. Another radical perfectionist group, the Oneida Community, also believed in relational ideals radically different than those of the Puritans. But rather than adopt celibacy as the Immortalists or Shakers did, its founder John Humphrey Noyes taught a system that he termed "complex marriage." This meant that all members of the community belonged to all others and should be free to engage in sexual intercourse with multiple partners, since sex reflected the love of Christ to be shared within the community. Individuals within Oneida could select sexual mates based upon love and attraction rather than traditional bonds, though it is dubious whether women felt completely free in those choices: memoirs suggest a strong undercurrent of religious obligation to fulfill the desires of male community members, as well as to follow the rules laid down by the authoritarian Noyes. Complex marriage was not a state that Noyes and his followers believed could or should be adopted by all persons outside their community; rather, it was a sign of the sinless perfection that Oneida members believed they had achieved. This perspective rejected the Calvinist doctrine of inherent human depravity and asserted that sinless perfection was possible under God's grace, though what it suggested was perfection of the attitude and motivation, not an absence from all error. The radical nature of Oneida's reorientation of desire, and its resonance with some later currents in American sexual history, make it worth examining in some depth here.

In order to avoid multiple and random pregnancies within the community, Noyes advocated the practice of "male continence," whereby men were taught to refrain from orgasm except in cases where procreation was desired. Noyes's teaching suggested that uncontrolled ejaculation was a shameful lapse on men's part, not only because it revealed the mind's inability to restrain the body but also because it curtailed the communion between partners along with lessening the woman's pleasure. (As Hilda Herrick Noyes, a grandniece of Noyes, supposedly said, "the men prided themselves on giving the women their orgasm.")[79] Male continence also conveyed important meanings about the future progress of the race:

> The practice which we propose will give new speed to the advance of civilization and refinement. The self-control, retention of life, and ascent out of sensualism, which must result from making freedom of love a bounty on the chastening of physical indulgence, will raise the race to new vigor and beauty, moral and physical. And the refining effects of

sexual love (which are recognized more or less in the world) will be increased a thousand-fold, when sexual intercourse becomes an honored method of innocent and useful communion, and each is married to all.[80]

Explaining their sexual practice as its own form of strict discipline whose adherence would further the civilizing process enabled Noyes and his followers to counter the charges of their critics that they indulged in debasing, hedonistic behavior.

An important rule girding complex marriage was the avoidance of "special loves" that might distract a person from the true Christlike love that should flow to all. Crucial distinctions between "good" and "bad" sex—along with "good" and "bad" ways of practicing complex marriage—appeared recurrently not only in Noyes's own writings but in the writings of other community members, such as Noyes's niece, Tirzah Miller. Miller's memoir, begun in 1867 when she was twenty-four years old and the community was at the peak of its success, recounted her passionate encounters with male community members and vividly evoked her struggle to give up her special loves in order to fully embody the community's perfectionist ideals. This remarkable document illuminates Miller's conflict between allegiance to Noyes (who held tremendous power over the sexual relationships that occurred within the community) and her attachment to men such as Edward Inslee, her onetime lover and the father of her son.

On April 7, 1874, Miller wrote:

> I am now passing through the greatest trial of my faith I was ever called to endure. I wrote to J.H.N. Sunday telling him of my wish to communicate with Edward before the child is born. I had got over the heartache about it, and felt resigned to God. He answered he would not hesitate an instant on my account, but E. had behaved so that he should have to consider the matter. . . . On his way to the train he caught me by the hand, and took me into a room alone, and told me not to worry about the matter, and not to let E. know that I was asking for him, as he thought that would be very disastrous. My God! It seemed as though my heart would break for a while. It is even worse than I feared. I had not supposed that J.H.N. intended to keep us separated all the way through; but I think he did. . . . I told J.H.N. that I would abide by his decision, and feel good about it, and *I will*, though the trials of this winter have caused me the acutest suffering I have ever known. Though E. tortures me so, I love him still perhaps far too much. I pray God to make my heart right about him.[81]

Oneida ideals forced residents such as Tirzah Miller and Edward Inslee to expose their desires for special intimacy to the authority of Noyes and to redirect them elsewhere if such desires proved too potent and exclusive. Whatever else Miller's memoir reveals, it makes plain the heartache entailed by the Oneida system when persons indulged their physical and emotional desires to the brink of propriety. As with the Puritans, desire was a dangerous force that, if left unchecked, threatened to topple the whole community.

Nor was sexual desire the only danger, but any form of desire that distracted one's thoughts away from the good of the community could be subject to restraint. Miller, an accomplished pianist and lover of music, was periodically reprimanded to give up music for the sake of other tasks that would benefit the community. On May 7, 1877, she wrote: "Mr. Noyes asked me to give up music, and become a writer. I was almost paralyzed at first. Then I told him he could ask me nothing that would hurt me so much, and we had some pretty plain talk—perfectly respectful and good-natured, for I told him I should obey him at any rate, though it was like turning the world upside down." Two days afterward, Noyes commented on how pleased he was to have "got at the real root of the difficulty" with Miller, saying to her, "You are too big a woman to be thumping the piano; leave that to the small fools."[82] As with sex, there was no sin in the act of playing piano per se; the sin lay in loving any pursuit or person at the expense of the larger good of the community (as that was singularly interpreted by Noyes himself).

Over time, when the community began engaging in eugenic experiments under the term "stirpiculture" in 1868, Noyes taught that sinless parents could breed in order to produce sinless children. A scientifically selected couple (whom Noyes himself would choose) would reproduce in order to create perfectly formed children. Again, Tirzah Miller's memoir poignantly indicates the constraints imposed by this system upon Oneida inhabitants. Infatuated with Henry Hunter, she was told that she needed to stop seeing him and refrain from speaking with him, so that she could breed with one of the other men in the community with whom Noyes believed her to be better suited. Miller acceded to Noyes's demands, while yet confiding her inner turmoil in the pages of her diary. Noyes could direct the actions of community members—those who went against him simply left Oneida— but the regulation of desire itself proved far more difficult. Still, obedient community members such as Tirzah Miller did their best to reorient their inward desires toward outer objects that were considered appropriate, and— as this memoir makes clear—the discipline involved in that endeavor was considerable.

One of the most revealing episodes about the Oneidan understanding of sexuality was Noyes's desire to have sexual intercourse performed in front of a live audience. As Miller records in March 1869, Noyes noted, "We shall never have heaven till we can conquer shame, and make a beautiful exhibition on the stage." A letter from Miller elaborated Noyes's plan as the random selection of a man and woman from the audience, who would ascend the stage, disrobe, dance "or perform other evolutions" until the man was sufficiently aroused, then proceed with the natural exercise of sexual desire. Such a sight would "purify the whole Community," while also giving pleasure to the older members of the audience who were no longer sexually active.[83] This hopeful application did not apparently come to pass, but the fantasy of performing sexual intercourse in public for purposes of purification testifies to the radically harmonious relationship between body and soul that Christian perfectionists such as Noyes sought urgently to apply.

Puritans, Shakers, and Oneida community members held markedly different views of sexuality, but all three believed that sexual practice was a highly public matter, one subject to religious authority, supervision, and, when necessary, punishment. Bodily discipline suggested far more for these (and other) groups than a private preference for moderation; rather, the ability to restrain and re*train* bodily appetites was a vital sign of the soul's preeminence over lower-order somatic functions. Desires, even when they were believed to be "natural," should not be freely indulged in animalistic fashion but reoriented toward fulfillment of the highest religious and socially harmonious ideals. Whether sexual intercourse was limited to monogamous heterosexual marriage, checked by the ideals of male continence and stirpiculture, or forbidden altogether, its regulation was a matter of deep concern among American Protestants. Only the Oneidans, who dreamed of staging sex in a ritual of shared sanitization, advocated its communal enactment; but all groups agreed that what was an ostensibly private, hidden practice carried highly visible meanings.

PHRENOLOGY AND SOMATIC AUTHENTICITY

The modern histories of fasting and sexuality offer intriguing evidence of fluctuating attitudes and practices pertaining to bodily discipline. Yet these were not the only habits contributing to modern ideals of somatic perfectibility and manipulation. Other technical, scientifically based procedures for reading the signs of physical health gained attention and credibility. Scientific revolutions in eighteenth- and nineteenth-century Europe interested American intellectuals, and popular science flowed, not surprisingly, in several different directions at once. The broad health reform initiatives associated with figures such as William Alcott, Sylvester Graham, and John Harvey Kellogg are well known and have received broad scholarly as well as popular treatment. Other movements, while having an enormous impact in the years of fasting's decline and sexuality's radical redefinition, are less well known. Most pertinent for us here is the experimental system called phrenology, a system that profoundly influenced the movement that would come to be known as New Thought and whose notions of corporeal and spiritual equivalence have had, in turn, a conspicuous impact on American body culture.

The body's enduring power in devotional life received early American testimony in the writings of Jonathan Edwards, the noted theologian whose *Treatise Concerning the Religious Affections* was published just one year before Wesley's *Primitive Physick*. Body and soul effected a "union" of such strength, "that there never is in any case whatsoever, any lively and vigorous exercise of the will or inclination of the soul, without some effect upon the body"; likewise, "the constitution of the body, and the motion of its fluids, may promote the exercise of the affections." While Edwards cautioned against viewing bodily effects as "sure evidences" of true religious affections, he was just as careful to uphold the bodily responses to God's glory that were then on display at evangelical revivals.[84] Later in the century the Swiss Protestant theologian Johann Caspar Lavater published his widely influential corpus on physiognomy, where he argued that virtue and vice, in specific no less than general form, could be read on the body. While his physiognomic reflections centered on the face, or "countenance," Lavater took care to note that *all* body parts acted as sources of knowledge for inner character. Referring to the animal, moral, and intellectual lives that each person was believed to inhabit, he wrote: "These three lives, by their intimate connection with each other, are all, and each, expressed in every part of the body."[85] Far more than Edwards, Lavater believed that the soul carried somatic evidences, a belief that would take increasingly empirical form amid nineteenth-century developments in health reform.

What united seemingly disparate systems of popular physiology during their American heyday in the nineteenth century was unshakeable faith in the bodily indicators of mental and spiritual states: a belief that the art historian Charles Colbert has aptly termed "physical metaphysics." Inspired by Lavater's rendering of physiognomy, and buttressed by the work of the Viennese physician Franz Joseph Gall (1757–1828) and his student Johann Gaspar Spurzheim (1776–1832), Protestants in the new republic seized upon the theory of body-soul correspondences known as phrenology: a system that supposedly proved that the character of any individual could be read in the anatomical details of the skull (later adherents, we shall see, ex-

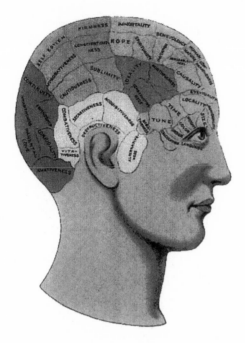

3. Phrenological map. This simulation of Gall and Spurzheim's phrenological chart comes from Renato M. E. Sabbatini, "Phrenology, the History of Brain Localization," in *Brain and Mind: Electronic Magazine on Neuroscience* (1997), www .epub.org.br/cm/no1/frenolog /frenmapO.gif.

tended this precept to other parts of the body). The precept was logical enough: as the organ of the mind, the brain wrought the shape of the skull, such that there was a perfect correspondence between the skull's geography and human character. One needed only the suitable training and sensory capacity to discern the various mental faculties exhibited upon the skin covering an individual's cerebral structure. Possessing this kind of knowledge further enabled persons to learn which of their faculties required "exercise" for growth and which should be inhibited because of overdevelopment. Gall and Spurzheim ultimately identified thirty-seven mental and moral faculties in the surfaces of the skull.[86]

Phrenology made its first major inroads into the United States during the early 1820s, burgeoning in the 1830s among the most prominent literary figures: Ralph Waldo Emerson (who described Spurzheim as one of the world's greatest minds), Walt Whitman, Edgar Allan Poe, Henry Ward Beecher, Horace Greeley, Horace Mann, and Samuel Gridley Howe were among them. When Spurzheim's two-month visit to America in 1832 ended with his sudden death, his brain was preserved at Harvard Medical School. Phrenological doctrines were most vigorously and lastingly popularized— some complained they were vitiated—by Orson Squire Fowler (1809–87), who was headed to the Protestant ministry before discovering a career as an itinerant phrenologist. Working with his brother, Lorenzo Niles Fowler (1811–96), Orson especially emphasized the practical reformist applications of this science: the self-knowledge provided by phrenology would beget a world of opportunity, its fulfillment grounded in freedom of choice and the attainability of reform. For New England audiences in the heady period of antebellum reform, this was a potent message indeed. By insisting upon phrenology's optimistic, millennial implications and by applying the science to such pressing social problems as children's education, the penal system, the treatment of insanity, public health, and female dress reform, the Fowlers managed thoroughly to Americanize the system. Roger Cooter notes that as phrenology increasingly became "one of the 'characteristics of the age'" in the Anglo-American world at midcentury, "it adjusted to the practical needs, amusements, aspirations, and comprehensions of ordinary working people," creating a so-called "bourgeois phrenology" suitable for mass culture.[87]

Still, many remained persuaded of phrenology's respectability, and a diverse array of literary figures, ministers, and reformers sought head readings from the Fowlers along with other known experts. Phrenological readings appeared in popular journals such as the *American Phrenological Journal*, founded by a medical student in 1838 and sold to the Fowlers three years later. Many individual readings, marked by a cheery optimism, have also survived in personal and family papers housed in archival repositories. Moses Austin Cartland (1805–63), a New Hampshire Quaker, educator, and journalist, retained possession of his 1839 reading by Orson Squire Fowler, part of a collection that made its way to the Harvard University Library in 1942. In Fowler's hands, Cartland's head revealed a great deal:

> This gentleman is a real *worker*—does with his might what he does at all—is spirited, resolute—& will accomplish a good deal—is sincere & candid. . . . Is a most devoted & whole souled friend, very fond of society & has one of the largest developments of friendship that I have ever seen on a man. . . . Has a very investigative, inquisitive mind & a superior talent for the study of natural science—also an arithmetic & geometrical mind. . . . Is cheerful—has the highest sense of justice & will take the high moral ground & especially espouse the cause of the oppressed. . . . Maintains an unblemished moral character—has strong domestic feelings & would make a most devoted father & husband— lacks concentration, yet on this very account can attend to many things in a short time—has much patriotism—loves debate & never shrinks from duty to avoid censure but is bold & much obliging in a good case so gladly. His talents show to his advantage.

Such a positive reading, with only a few slight notes of possible improvements thrown in, would be sure to generate good advertising for Fowler's work among the white northeasterners who were his primary clientele.[88]

Behind the broad belief in physical metaphysics (or "spiritual science") in this period was the towering figure of the Swedish natural philosopher and mystic Emanuel Swedenborg (1688–1772). Swedenborg's theory of physiological and spiritual correspondences, elaborated throughout his copious writings, taught that the various components of the natural world were reflected in the spiritual world. In developing this worldview, he suggested that human facial features had at one time been so endowed with expressiveness and authenticity that they—rather than oral or written language—served as the dominant mode of communication. Charles Colbert has noted Swedenborg's belief that as human selfishness replaced innocence, the face came to be a mask of deception rather than a mirror of truth. Yet while Swedenborg postulated the eventual decline, through sin, of somatic-spiritual equivalences, his concern for restoring physiognomic authenticity resonated with Lavater and was a significant source of inspiration for later phrenologists.[89]

Phrenology has usually been interpreted as one more subspecialty within the broader nineteenth-century health reform movement (and often a minor one at that), yet its pronounced popular influence was distinctive. The terminology employed by phrenologists to describe faculties and character traits—a vocabulary they considered to be based on rigorously empirical methods—was based on specialized categorizations, mappings, and techniques whose influence extended beyond parlor games and carnival amusements to penetrate the high echelons of the fine arts. Literature, sculpture, painting, and architecture were steeped in phrenological imagery and associations in ways that demonstrate not only phrenology's broad appeal and cultural impact but, more important, its accepted status as a reputable (if debatable, and emphatically corruptible) scientific hypothesis.[90] Perhaps more than any other physiological system of the time, phrenology promised to satisfy Christian hopes for authenticity and transparency, teaching that physical traits—not merely facial features or expressions but above all skeletal protrusions—perfectly disclosed the inner worlds of their bearers. To persuade audiences that they were not being guided by their subjects, nor merely reading the facial lines forged from habitual smiling or frowning, popular phrenologists such as the Fowlers frequently allowed themselves to be blindfolded while performing evaluations.

One of the results of phrenology's widespread popular appeal was the increasing public interest in human anatomy, documented by Michael Sappol in his historical account of popular anatomy in nineteenth-century

America, *A Traffic of Dead Bodies*. As Sappol notes, phrenology's claim to scientific authority stemmed from practitioners' insistence that their doctrine derived from anatomy, in particular the craniological dissections of Gall, Spurzheim, Combe, and others. Phrenologists concerned about their scientific authority recurrently invoked the vocabulary of anatomico-physiological science: the phrenological lecturer Nelson Sizer, for instance, "asserted that the science did not lie in the reading of bumps, but rather in the assessment of the 'radial distance from the *medulla oblongata*, or capital of the spinal marrow, to the surface of the brain.'" A few Protestants took issue with the implications of such scientific assertions, and some denounced phrenology as an "ignoble doctrine" and "carnal philosophy" that distorted the spiritual truths of God's workings in the world.[91] Still, its emphasis on physiological laws that would display inner goodness—as well as wickedness—on the external flesh, whether in terms of skull bumps, physiognomic indicators, or varying degrees of health and disease, would become sustaining themes within American religion and culture.

The associations between inner and outer worlds, the spiritual and the physical, made headway in the sciences as well as other intellectual arenas. The Austrian poet, philosopher, and physician Baron Ernst von Feuchtersleben (1806–49), in his oft published and translated *Zur Diätetik der Seele* (1838; first English edition published as *The Dietetics of the Soul*, 1854), praised Lavater while clarifying the broader medical and religious significance of his work: "What, then, is beauty, but the spirit glorifying its earthly tabernacle; and what is health but the beauty of its various functions?" Feuchtersleben's book was, in essence, a treatise on how "to direct the body by the force of the mind," an aim very much in vogue in both Europe and America. Quoting Goethe and Schlegel, Kant and Herder, Feuchtersleben promised his reader that, having attained this high self-knowledge, "nothing remains for him but to be and remain what his being prompts him to be—pure and truthful as the incorruptible word of God." His words of wisdom on health would be prescient for later generations of health-seekers no less than those drawn to techniques for character formation, as he promised his own cohort, "Health is nothing but beauty, morality and truth."[92]

Tracking the body's role in forming character several decades later in an American climate, John B. DeMotte, the first full-time professor of physics at Indiana Asbury College (which became DePauw University during his tenure), published *The Secret of Character Building* in 1893, where he vigorously asserted the "physical basis" of character, illustrated both physiognomically and musically. Taking the analogy of nerve passageways for external stimuli that acted upon the body, DeMotte described the "trunk lines" of the body that were formed by habituated activities and responses to daily life experiences, including the experience of Christian conversion.

> The Physical Basis of a vicious life is a network of such Trunk Lines, in which the incarrying waves of stimulation waken in the soul a host of accustomed activities, such as vile memories, alluring imaginations, craving appetites, and their like, having well worn routes through the outcarrying nerves to whatever lines of conduct have been followed in their development. The Physical Basis of a virtuous life is a network of Trunk Lines . . . leading to the God-given higher possessions of the Soul—holy memories, pure imaginations, consecrated ambitions, [and] righteous judgments. . . . Here we stand face to face with a tremendous physical fact. Every voluntary act, whether of good or evil, beats its own path a little smoother, so to speak, for another of like character, and renders it just that much more difficult for one of opposite nature to get the right of way.[93]

DeMotte had left behind traditional physics (and DePauw) in 1891 so as to explicate these broader applications of scientific theory to audiences along the Chautauqua Lyceum circuit. Steeped in the Methodist Episcopal Church, in which he was an ordained minister (and son of the prominent churchman Daniel DeMotte), he perceived his mission as teaching Christian parents and educators the truth of this material, embodied basis for the Christian life, which he felt was neglected in the tolerance of Christian authorities for the wild follies of young men. Seemingly harmless activities actually strengthened physical passageways that, he warned, "shall presently bind us, body and soul, wretched slaves to passions and appetites of our own nurturing."[94]

The permanence of habits, whether virtuous or vicious, was one of DeMotte's major themes, and he traced the physiological evidence of their intransience through a military metaphor that evoked the embodied discipline of the soldier.

> Character is a sort of body-guard to the spirit, always on duty in part or in full as occasion requires. But the service is for life. The forces can not be mustered out and re-enlisted at pleasure; neither may veterans be displaced by raw recruits with any guarantee of valorous behavior under fire. As every private in the Queen's Guard is the embodiment of years of faithful drill and discipline, so every fixed rule of action in a worthy character has back of it a long catalogue of tributary regulations—self-ordered and self-obeyed.[95]

Carrying this teaching to the Protestants who would hear him, DeMotte denied that he was, as at least one minister accused him, "limiting God's power" to transform the human heart via conversion but merely educating citizens as to the limitations of body and character that God had set. The physiognomic and phrenological implications of DeMotte's own neurological analysis were evidenced in the frontispiece of his work, which rendered the facial progression of a male infant, reckless youth, and dissolute old man, under the ignorant gazes of two women, presumably mothers. Character's physical basis was plainly not only neurological but also outwardly manifest upon the body.

Phrenology and its manifold kin, such as DeMotte's formulations, appealed to persons across a wide spectrum of social classes and political views, since they elevated a notion of the self that was at once both constant (attributing basic character to heredity) and at least moderately variable (teaching parents how to bestow particular dispositions upon their children even prior to their birth, so that each generation could more closely approximate perfection of both body and soul). Much like astrology, phrenology's aim of discerning basic inclinations left some room for self-improvement. Indeed, believers imagined that the possibilities for perfecting the self would increase by the bluntly accurate self-portraits supposedly revealed by phrenological means. With one's best and worst characteristics revealed under the faultless light of empirical science, self-development could become a systematic and feasible project with clear goals, reliable techniques, and virtually guaranteed results. Its success displayed itself unerringly in the body's changing landscape. Though historians tracing the prehistory of modern body obsessions have rarely looked closely at phrenology, it was here, perhaps even more than in the contemporaneous realms of fasting and diet reform, that a broad swath of Americans grew accustomed to reading skin and bones as literal maps to the human beings who inhabited them.

The social implications of this teaching—bodies as visible and highly accurate diagrams of inner character—could hardly be greater. American phrenologists participated in a much broader undertaking to chart normalcy and deviance along a narrowing spectrum of corporeal signs, helping turn individuals into typological examples of particular characteristics.[96] The *American Phrenological Journal,* edited by Samuel R. Wells and published in New York by Fowler and Wells, frequently thematized biological, social, and so-called ethnological distinctions. In an 1865 piece on "The Best Indian," Wells claimed to have been approached by "a family of Indians" who wished their characters delineated. Unlike civilized Christians, Wells mused, these "braves of the forest" valued cruelty and physical aggressiveness over intellect, invention, art, music, and devotion. While naming a few groups as "among the more docile and industrious Indians whom we have met," most were "lazy, indolent, quarrelsome, thievish, barbarous tribes, who rob and murder each other for the very love of it." This "savage" type was truly "untamable," and its members could perhaps be left alone to kill off one another. "This may be the course Providence has taken to wipe out these apparently useless barbarians."[97]

A "Correspondents" column later in the same issue carried the following alleged question from a reader: "Do you think all men would be equally good, benevolent, high-minded, and experience all the finer feelings, if they were educated, brought into society, and treated as equals by the so-styled aristocrats?" Wells hypothesized: "*Ans.* If all were organized alike that would be the case, but never until they are. The wide differences now existing between the cultivated and the uncultivated could be very much narrowed by a course of proper and persistent education, but it would take three or four generations to bring up to a high point the children of boors who for several generations have had no culture."[98] Texts like Wells's popular *How to Read Character* (1870) further clarified these implications:

> The skulls of races and nations also differ widely in form, and these differences are found to correspond with known differences of character. In the Caucasian it will be seen that the forehead is prominent and high, the coronal region elevated, and the back-head moderately projected. . . . It indicates great intellectual power, strong moral or spiritual sentiments, and a comparatively moderate development of the propensities. . . . See what a contrast between the Caucasian skull and those of the North American Indian and the Negro here represented!

These members of "savage and barbarous tribes" had skulls demonstrating the predominance of the "animal feelings" over "both the intellectual and the moral sentiments." Like its cousin, popular anatomy, phrenology provided a perfect instrument for promoting a hierarchical typology of race.[99]

But how did ordinary people live with and appropriate phrenological teachings? Yellowed head readings from the nineteenth century rest in countless archives across the United States, but only rarely do personal reflections (from those analyzed) accompany them. One set of diaries filled with annotated transcriptions of prescriptive health and beauty literature does reveal, though, a few of the interpretive possibilities open to phrenology's hopeful enthusiasts. Hattie A. Harlow, a spinster seamstress and piano teacher in Brockton, Massachusetts, was ardently devoted to phrenology. A resolute woman who incurred the ire of her neighbors for her independent ways, Harlow's leisure time during the 1870s and 1880s consisted of a rigorous course of cultivating the highest standards of womanly perfection. Along with measuring her own skull, mapping out the geography of its bumps, and assessing the character traits revealed there—positive ones such as

Sublimity or Agreeableness were usually "Full" or "Very Large," while more troublesome characteristics such as destructiveness were much smaller— Harlow recorded copious details about personal health and beauty, including diet, hygiene, exercise, cosmetics, clothing, foot care, and like topics. The number of notebook passages that she recorded as "authored by Hattie A. Harlow" indicates her intention—never fulfilled—to publish her own works in this field, while her many library book lists show how deeply she drank from the wells of popular literature. Since she did not always note the sources that she copied, it is difficult to discern her own writing from that of published sources, or to sort out precisely which authorities she considered most relevant. But the vast amounts of text she left vividly specify the positions she deemed credible.

Harlow's writings show her to be committed both to self-knowledge and self-improvement. In one notebook she recorded a phrenological excerpt on "The Face and Expression" that began by giving measurement rules for what faces should look like, then offered solace to those who did not meet these standards:

> It is easy to lay down these rules one after another, but how are we to conform to them? What aid can cosmetic art (science) here offer to one not gifted by nature with a handsome face? Directly, perhaps, there is little to be done, but indirectly there is a great deal. For, after all, it is not these mathematical diagrams which we have been describing that make up beauty. It is expression, the soul, if you will, shining through its mortal coil. And here we have no longer to do with unyielding bone and solid flesh, but with material infinitely more plastic than even the tempered clay in which the sculptor forms his model.

A few pages later Harlow wrote, "It should be the aim of every one thus to become 'the lords and owners of their faces,' and it is in the power of every one, not irrecoverably wedded to some grimace, to do so." In the words of another writer, she remonstrated against "tics" such as winking, frowning, sniffing, grinning, and other gestures that would "contort the features." Conveying both beauty and good breeding was the end to which such advice aimed.[100]

Phrenology was one of Harlow's favorite subjects, perhaps because it seemed to offer a viable resolution to the tensions between divine determinism and earthly self-improvement. Yes, the writings suggested, one can cultivate qualities of character and improve, perhaps even perfect, the self; at the same time, these texts promised that the world was governed by inflexible laws of cause and effect that could never be breached, so that everyone would be duly rewarded or punished in a fair and just way. Quoting Samuel

Wells's *New Physiognomy, or Signs of Character*, Harlow recorded this remarkable passage that upheld such a blending:

> We know how widely mankind differ in looks, in opinion, and in character, and it has been our study to discover the causes of these differences. We find them in organization. As we look, so we feel, so we act, and so we are. But we may direct and control even our thoughts, our feelings, and our acts, and thus, to some extent—by the aid of grace—become what we will. We can be temperate or intemperate; virtuous or vicious; hopeful or desponding; generous or selfish; believing or skeptical; prayerful or profane. We are free to choose what course we will pursue, and our bodies, our brains, and our features readily adapt themselves and clearly indicate the lives we lead and the characters we form.

Phrenological teachings provided abundant support to people such as Hattie Harlow who wanted to know that her hard work to care for her physical self truly mattered and that she could improve herself in this world, trusting that she would be rewarded both by people who could observe her beauty and cultivation *and* by the events that would occur in life to bring her happiness.[101]

An undercurrent of worry nevertheless underlay these texts, a sense that character might somehow be "set" in ultimately irrevocable and unchangeable ways. These could be somewhat allayed by the "artifices" of cosmetics (including cosmetic surgery) and other "aids to beauty provided by chemistry and pharmacy," but Harlow's frequent self-assurances that these techniques were neither vain nor deceitful sounded a desperate tone. "If form corresponds with and indicates character," she transcribed, "it must change with the latter, and be, like that, measurably under our control. If the soul builds up, molds, and remolds the body, it must do it in accordance with its own organization and to suit its changing disposition and wants." There was nothing wrong with whitening the skin and making one's body a work of art, since these procedures only made visible what was happening to the invisible soul. "Physical comeliness, then, may be acquired (as well as inherited) like health, or good manners, or correct morals. It is no more difficult to become beautiful than to become good—in fact, physical beauty is closely allied to moral beauty." Beauty in women could take many forms, Harlow's notebooks reiterated, "but in all there must necessarily be the large, clear, eloquent eyes; the shapely nose, indicative of developed faculties, culture, and taste; the full lips, which speak of sweetness of temper, warmth of affection, and womanly dignity; and the well-formed and ample but not heavy chin, which betokens an active circulation and a warm, loving heart." Everyday regimens—diet, exercise, and improved hygienic habits—would aid those not born with such features to acquire them in short order. Authenticity and artifice, for Harlow and other readers of phrenological beauty literature, could mix in many ways.[102]

As the nineteenth century proceeded, developments in both science and philosophy increasingly challenged phrenology.[103] Such challenges were aided by the obscenity charges persistently leveled against Orson Squire Fowler, dubbed "the foulest man on earth" for his graphic writings on sex and his serial marriages. As the phrenological system lost its hold on elite intellectual circles, proponents persistently utilized Lavater's physiognomy and Swedenborg's correspondence theory to shore up phrenology's status, a move that Colbert notes "transformed the study of anatomy from the plane of scientific investigation to that of metaphysical speculation while blurring the distinction between the two."[104] To seek harmony between science and religion was no new thing, but phrenology had captured the popular imagination by reuniting body and soul in a way that seemed at once divinely inspired and coolly sensible. For a nation devoted to the myth of the self-made individual, phrenology's appeal lay in its hopefulness for individual and social perfection. But concern about the limits imposed by heredity—the fixed conditions of birth—remained.

A further purge of limits upon the self was yet ahead, to reinvest the body with grander prophetic transparency. Intent on revamping phrenology's premises but similarly committed to the foundational work of Swedenborg, this worldview brought new urgency to its task of harnessing the spirit in service to the body. It was the religion of New Thought, holding a vision of the human being as a spiritual reality with the nearly limitless capacity to alter the illusions of personal fate. In fact New Thought drew heavily from phrenology but perhaps helped hasten the latter's decline by promising far more: a method to channel, harmonize, and yoke all the powers of the universe in exalted service to health, wealth, and immortality. With the emergence of New Thought, the body's indispensable role in the era's progressive schemas would swell even as fleshly models of perfection steadily shrank in range.

2 Sculptors of Our Own Exterior
New Thought Physiques

If phrenology's far-reaching popularity diminished in the waning decades of the nineteenth century, it remained a companion and source of inspiration for one of the era's most influential, fluid, and enduring movements. When the popular New Thought writer William Walker Atkinson (1862–1932) published *Human Nature: Its Inner States and Outer Forms* in 1910, for instance, he promoted phrenological teachings as the essential foundation of current intellectual and spiritual advances. Even as it fervently defended phrenological categories, however, *Human Nature* updated them to fit the times. Scientific refutations of phrenology's empirical basis had already blended with public skepticism and fatigue to thrust its categories to the margins of popular culture; rather than vanishing, however, assumptions about the correspondence between internal states and external form simply shifted away from the skull to other parts of the head and to the body as a whole. To the usual phrenological skull maps, Atkinson added physiognomic analyses of facial features (chins, mouths, eyes, ears, and noses), along with chapters on the characteristics revealed in hand and finger patterns as well as bodily functions such as walking. This amalgamation of phrenology, physiognomy, and more general theories of correspondence epitomizes both the tenacity and the suppleness with which generations of New Thought writers and their heirs regarded the links between mind and matter, the body deemed not only the soul's mirror but, often enough, the elemental ground of spiritual progress and perfectibility.[1]

Though a later development than phrenology, New Thought was hardly "new," even in 1910. Its roots lay in the heady nineteenth-century world that mixed and matched mystical Swedenborgianism, mesmerism, spiritualism, holiness evangelicalism, and—above all—mind cure: a system that attributed cures of physical illness to the mental or spiritual faculties. Mental treatments for bodily disease were widely practiced in the nineteenth century, inspired by healers like Phineas Parkhurst Quimby and his student Mary Baker Eddy, the founder of Christian Science. These figures and their spiritual heirs adopted the mission of mind cure as an accurate, if perhaps oversimplified, designation for their movement. Though holding diverse opinions on physical and metaphysical questions, mind cure believers adhered to a faith in the power of mind to affect matter, particularly the physical body.

Historians have tended to neglect New Thought, as a kind of embarrassing blip in American culture: the debasement of Emersonian idealism into cheerful gospels of health and wealth, and (still worse) the precursor to New Age spiritual sensibilities alien to many scholars of religion. This swift dismissal of New Thought has obscured a great deal about the movement and its historical influence, including the complexities of its "mind over matter" avowals. In fact, many of its major proponents believed physical health to be a product of physical self-discipline, bodily manipulation, and exhaustive scrutiny of the flesh as well as thought power. Their absorption echoed New Thought's inspirational predecessors, including Eddy, whose private interests in matters material and visual are reflected in her personal correspondence (opened to the public in 2002). The common suspiciousness toward medical means then fashionably deployed did not necessarily make for a matter-denying world. To the contrary, the majority of even the most strenuously spirit-minded participants in the burgeoning mind cure movement were unwilling to stake everything on mental force alone: instead, the New Thought body, as a source of endless techniques, remedies, calculations and quantifications, was itself a fount of healing power.

As for American fitness history, numerous accounts have noted that roughly between 1890 and 1910 white middle-class worship of thinness took the relentless hold that would last into the 2000s.[2] There is no firm consensus as to why this period witnessed the apparent end of older fluctuations in fashionable body types, but the standard argument describes this occurrence as a secularized symptom of puritanical anxieties toward growing American abundance and shifting models of consumption, which rerouted older disciplines of frugality to the appetite. In these same decades New Thought teachers met their greatest popular success, often by promoting similar notions of abundance, though recent observers have also noted a powerful ambivalence toward desire that often underlay New Thought teachings. While by no means did all its proponents write extensively about physical fitness, enough of them did to affirm this as a chief concern within the movement, albeit one often overlooked by its historians. Rereading New

Thought in this way illustrates its vital centrality in the wider American story of dietary and body obsessions.

Offering discrete and intricate models of the body-soul relationship, mind cure proponents divided themselves along contentious lines that, if sometimes opaque to us now, seemed quite clear and of paramount importance to them. Their popular literature—canonical books and periodicals consisting of earnest yet ambiguous, often astonishingly contradictory treatises—testifies to the bundled aspirations that discovered a common refuge in New Thought modes of reasoning. However instructive the differences in these theories, together they reveal a lively fixation on bodily processes; a horror that neglect or misunderstanding of these functions would lead humanity to ruin; and an attendant conviction that material embodiment, correctly practiced, was essential for the journey toward perfection. Even a natural scientist and philosopher like Albert B. Olston could marvel at the body's revelatory promises: "May we not become sculptors working upon our own exterior, and reveal the ideal held in desire and in mind?"[3] That view, tied as it was to other popular mental and corporeal therapeutic systems of the time, from psychology to physical culture, would blossom and proliferate with the passage of the century, swiftly seeping beyond its organizational moorings to infuse varied sectors of American culture with a zeal for body salvation.

"NOTHING BUT A DENSE SHADOW": THE BODY AS DELUSION?

After decades of health reform movements, cautious but fertile alliances between physicians and clerics, and theological treatises about the care of the body, American Protestants may have assumed that an ethic of bodily care was secure. Not all Protestant-derived metaphysical groups in the nineteenth century held what might be called a "high" view of the body, however: indeed, therapeutic systems like animal magnetism, mesmerism, and spiritualism all worked on the principle of the passivity of the flesh. Still, nothing in these systems maintained that the body was inconsequential; to the contrary, they paid close attention to corporeality. They believed that thought power entirely molded the body, health resulting as one tuned the mind to Infinite Spirit and channeled cosmic energy into utterly malleable physical matter.

The most influential figure in this milieu was Phineas Parkhurst Quimby (1802–66), a New Hampshire-born inventor and mesmerist who eventually rejected mesmerism's concentration on the influence of human minds upon one another and focused more intently upon the power of Universal Spirit or

Wisdom. Quimby's students included not only Eddy but also the influential Swedenborgian Warren Felt Evans as well as Julius and Annetta Dresser, all key figures in the history of New Thought. Quimby variously labeled his system of thought the Science of Life and Happiness and the Science of Health and Happiness, and at least once he referred to it as Christian Science, the name Eddy later procured for her teachings.

As a major figure behind the emergence of both Christian Science and New Thought, Quimby would later be reputed a pure idealist—if not as well read in philosophy as his student Evans, still a thoughtful promoter of the unreality of matter. Some of his writings seem to corroborate this view, as when he characterized the body as "nothing but a dense shadow, condensed into what is called matter, or ignorance of God or Wisdom." Yet matter and the body were very real for Quimby, in ways that perhaps contributed to the disavowals made by his one-time patient Eddy (then Mary Patterson) about the degree of his influence upon her. In point of fact, Quimby's writings are highly ambiguous on these themes, and it is fair to conclude that his own views of the causative workings of mind and matter were not fixed with the precision of a mathematical theorem. Enough of mesmerism remained integral to Quimby's position, long after he had officially discarded it, to prevent him from denying the weight of material substance altogether. Mind was not simply the opposite of matter for Quimby, nor matter itself a delusion in the manner that Eddy would later claim. Letters written to his patients reveal his characterization of mind as "the name of the fluids of which your body is composed, with 'thoughts' representing changes in these fluids." More consistently, Quimby represented mind as "spiritual matter," an expression interpreted (and perhaps distorted) by his posthumous editor, Horatio Dresser, as meaning "subconscious mind." Quimby appears to have intended it as a mediating term between more static notions of mind and matter that he believed most people to hold.[4]

A wonderfully vivid illustration of how Quimby believed spiritual matter to work emerges in an 1861 letter to a patient afflicted by a cough. To help the patient see both the cause and the cure of his affliction, Quimby offered as an example the effects of being told about someone else's death from bronchitis, which he described in evocatively material terms. Error, borne of another's words, entered the porous body through the ears and then passed into the stomach, where the antagonistic forces of heat and coldness materialized into mucus: a condensed form of thought and the unmistakable sign of sickness. But the process was not one of direct mental cause and physical effect; rather, it was one of multiple shifts and exchanges between "so-called matter and mind."

You listen or eat this belief or wisdom as you would eat your meals.
It sets rather hard upon your stomach; this disturbs the error of your
body, and a cloud appears in the sky. You cannot see the storm but you
can see it looks dark. In this cloud or belief you prophesy rain or a
storm. So in your belief you foresee evils. The elements of the body
of your belief are shaken, the earth is lit up by the fire of your error,
the heat rises, the heaven or mind grows dark; the heat moves like the
roaring of thunder, the lightning of hot flashes shoot to all parts of the
solar system of your belief. At last the winds or chills strike the earth
or surface of the body, a cold clammy sensation passes over you. This
changes the heat into a sort of watery substance, which works its way
to the channels, and pours to the head and stomach.

Ultimately, Quimby concluded, the substance of sickness would be dissolved
by Wisdom so that it would pass through the pores and also exit the body
by means of coughing, which he called "one of Truth's servants."[5]

Mind as "spiritual matter" was a process, signaling the ever changing and
interpenetrating movement between one state of being and another. And
the site of these exchanges, interestingly, was the stomach. In another letter
written the same year, Quimby told a patient, "Every word I said to you is
like yeast. This went into your system like food and came in contact with
the food of your old bread or belief. Mine was like a purgative, and acted like
an emetic on your mind." Ingestion was no mere metaphor. Quimby told
Miss S. of New Hampshire, like his other patients at a distance, to drink
water while reading his letter, sipping and swallowing and opening herself
up for Quimby to work on her body every night at nine o'clock.[6] Together,
doctor and patient employed multiple techniques enabling them to shift
from the mental to the physical and again from the physical to the mental,
in a seemingly inexhaustible series of spirit-matter manipulations.

Consonant with his view of mind and matter as successive gradations of a
singular reality, Quimby retained an emphasis on bodily routines as vital to
the healing process. Besides regularly advising distant patients such as Miss
S. to drink tumblers of water as they read his letters, in practice Quimby often
applied water treatments to parts of the body such as the face, neck, and
head.[7] Indeed, his letters frequently demonstrated a preference for combining
physical procedures, practiced by the patient, with mental healing systems
that he himself directed, often in absentia. "Remember how I explained to
you about standing straight," he wrote one patient from afar in 1861. "Just
put your hands on your hips, then bend forward and back. This relaxes the
muscles around the waist at the pit of the stomach. This takes away the pressure from the nerves of the stomach and allays the irritation. Now follow this

and sit down and I will work upon your stomach two or three times in three or four days. It will affect your bowels and help your color." Thus Quimby's work on the stomach was accomplished at a distance, but the patient himself had a vital, somatically active role to play in the process.[8]

In contrast to Quimby, Mary Baker Eddy promoted the view that matter was erroneous, plain and simple, because God or Spirit was all in all:

> The realm of the real is Spirit. The unlikeness of Spirit is matter, and
> the opposite of the real is not divine,—it is a human concept. Matter
> is an error of statement. This error in the premise leads to errors in the
> conclusion in every statement into which it enters. Nothing we can say
> or believe regarding matter is immortal, for matter is temporal and is
> therefore a mortal phenomenon, a human concept, sometimes beautiful,
> always erroneous.[9]

Like matter more broadly, the human body itself was a "sometimes beautiful, always erroneous" delusion. In her formulation, "The true relation of Soul to body is that of God to man; in other words, of Principle to its idea; these are forever inseparable; and when the true idea, which is the immortal body, is perceptible, we shall have become acquainted with its Principle."[10]

Though she taught the unreality of the human body, however, Eddy did not eschew but, in fact, relished the possibility of physical immortality. A tempting prospect detailed in the first edition of *Science and Health* (1875) was the future achievement of perpetual youth and corporeal immortality. "To understand Intelligence nor Life are in the body, is to conquer age and hold being forever fresh and immortal," she wrote. She illustrated her statement with a story of a young woman whose heart was broken by a lover and who lived her entire life in that moment of loss and hope: because she never considered herself to age, according to Eddy, her physical body complied, such that at the age of seventy-four she appeared no older than twenty years old. Elsewhere in the same first edition of her text, she wrote, "Life is Spirit, not matter, and if you understand the law of Spirit you understand how to make the body immortal." Death itself, she insisted, "can be cured."[11]

By no means were bodily perfection and immortality prompted by such material tools as food, drink, exercise, fresh air, or related methods—only through perfect obedience to mind. Eddy especially belittled the dietary reforms of the day, from the systems of Sylvester Graham to all manners of therapeutic fasting, as she regarded such practices as misguided at best and as seriously detrimental to their disciples. The frequency with which she discussed food in her writings is intriguing, however; eating and food had a substantial but ambiguous, if not ambivalent, place in Eddy's original *Science and Health*. On the one hand, she upheld the principle that food had absolutely no effect upon human life—it was able neither to help nor to hurt men and women but was utterly neutral. "We learn in science," she wrote, "food neither helps nor harms man." On the other hand, Eddy was not so rash as to suggest that followers of these principles should—or could—simply stop eating altogether and live on Spirit. No one could change overnight: "To stop utterly eating and drinking until your belief changes in regard to these things, were error," she emphasized. "Get rid of your beliefs as fast as possible, and admit the Principle, for it is the platform of health, joy, and immortality. To reach this proof by degrees, and only as we are capable of doing so with increasing health, harmony and happiness, is the only proper method."[12]

The suitable attitude to take toward food, Eddy variously reiterated, was simply to give it no thought whatsoever. The cure for such sicknesses as dyspepsia (indigestion) was to be found in "eat[ing] what was set before us, asking no questions for conscience' sake," according to Eddy: "yea, to consult matter less, and God more." In the ancient world, she noted, no one had the luxury to be dyspeptic: "People had little time then to be selfish, or to think of their bodies, and for sickly after-dinner talk." Likewise, she wrote, "The primitive privilege was to take no thought about the bowels, or gastric juices, letting these act in obedience to Truth, instead of error. A ghastly array of diseases was not constantly kept before the mind by works on physiology, hygiene and materia medica; hence the greater longevity and more harmony of man."[13]

Besides its aptness for the teachings of Christian Science, Eddy's disregard for food may have been influenced by her own negative childhood associations with fasting. The first edition of *Science and Health* contained this grim description from her own experience, worth quoting in full:

> When quite a child we adopted the Graham system for dyspepsia, ate only bread and vegetables, and drank water, following this diet for years; we became more dyspeptic, however, and, of course, thought we must diet more rigidly; so we partook of but one meal in twenty-four hours, and this consisted of a thin slice of bread, about three inches square, without water; our physician not allowing us with this ample meal, to wet our parched lips for many hours thereafter; whenever we drank, it produced violent retchings. Thus we passed most of our early years, as many can attest, in hunger, pain, weakness, and starvation. At length we learned that while fasting increased the desire for food, it spared none of

the sufferings occasioned by partaking of it, and what to do next, having already exhausted the medicine men, was a question. After years of suffering, when we made up our mind to die, our doctors kindly assuring us that this was our only alternative, our eyes were suddenly opened, and we learned suffering is self-imposed, a belief, and not Truth. . . .
As a natural result, we took less thought about "What we should eat or what drink," and, fasting or feasting, consulted less our stomach and our food, arguing against their claims continually, and in this manner despoiled them of their power over us to give pleasure or pain, and recovered strength and flesh rapidly, enjoying health and harmony that we never before had done.

Again and again, Eddy insisted that just as food did not have the power to harm, it did not have the power to help the body or even to provide enjoyment. Truly, she wrote, "we never afterwards enjoyed food as we expected to, if ever we were a freed slave, to eat without a master."[14]

Servants and companions close to Eddy in her old age noted, however, that she was actually fastidious about the quality of her food. Eddy's recent biographer, Gillian Gill, remarks that Eddy's cook at her Pleasant View estate in Concord, New Hampshire, "liked to have an extra dinner on hand in case Mrs. Eddy found the soup too salty, the baked potatoes too hard, or the sponge cake too heavy." She was, in fact, "very particular about the quality of what she ate." The woman who had disparaged the enjoyment of food was an especial lover of bacon and kept pigs on the farm for that purpose. She "took a cup of soup at dinner and supper, loving cream of tomato particularly, and she liked milk custards and above all ice cream." In her letters as well, she frequently complained of the poor fare her servants prepared and asked students for help: "Will you get me a cook that will try to get something palatable for me to eat?" she asked one in 1900. "You will have no peace if you love me to see how I am starved in my own house. . . . Now dear this is your duty. Come to me at once and bring your COOK WITH YOU and then see that she cooks what I can eat."[15] Food was, then, of rather greater interest and pleasure to her personally than she recommended in her writings.

This gap between Eddy's tutoring in culinary dispassion and her own more refined eating habits points toward a larger variance between her ideals and daily experience of embodiment. Derogatory sketches of Eddy, such as Mark Twain's vitriolic treatise *Christian Science* (1907), poked derisively at this apparent incongruity: why surround oneself with servants and cooks if matter is an erroneous notion? Why insist on living in beautiful surroundings, choose a home with views of great natural beauty, and redecorate it to live amid stylish interior furnishings? If Eddy considered her own body a delusion, Twain sardonically implied, it was one she surely cherished and enjoyed.[16]

Eddy's private correspondence elaborated her close attention to matters of savory food, fine clothes, and physical appearance. During her final years Eddy wrote scores of letters to loyal students in New York, Boston, and London, urging their assistance in procuring such items as wigs, fur cloaks, and silk gowns for her, along with commissioning portraits painted from her photographs. In a typical example, Eddy wrote more than three years of cajoling letters to Caroline Frame, chronicling her receipt and impatient return of numerous wigs to be altered by the hairdresser. "I return all but one coiffure," she remonstrated in 1901. "They are a shame a disgrace to our cause and [to] your promise to send one that is right in return as you said for the class in which you received the degrees of C.S. . . . Return the coiffure you now have at once, as soon as possible. I shall not be seen in YELLOW hair." After eventually relieving Frame from this strenuous task, Eddy briefly took up with the wigmaker Carrie E. Smith, to whom she was soon writing more angry letters:

> I cannot wear either of the two last coiffures you have sent to me. One of them, the old one, is far from the color of my switch and I have thrown it away. The last one you made, and the new one, the long hair is SO THIN on the SIDES of the HEAD it shows my white hair under it, and shows the roll that I coil it over. O how can you give me so much trouble over hair in the midst of all my persecution for righteousness, for what I have done for your salvation and for all who CAUSE ME TO SUFFER?

Wearing hair and clothes befitting her station was vitally important to Eddy, and her voluminous correspondence on such matters regularly despaired at the inability of her underlings to suit her needs.[17]

Eddy devoted steady attention as well to her own portraiture, and at least occasional thought to statuary. Discussing with her onetime student Augusta Stetson her projected embodiment in marble, Eddy averred, "When I was 20 years of age my waist measured 18 inches. . . . My form was not thin but perfectly full yet slender as the Venus de Medici's." To artists attempting to paint her portrait from photographs, she composed explicit and lengthy instructions to correct apparent flaws captured by the lens. "Please in your work avoid the hump on the nose of the photo in gray hair," she wrote to James T. White in 1897. "It is not true to my face. It was the mistake of light ill-directed." To Sarah Winslow in London, another student, she requested a very particular kind of portrait in 1899.

Now darling I want ONE GOOD LIKENESS of myself. You spoke to me of several artists. This is the favor I ask. Will you employ for me the best you can find, give them my photos and tell them they are poor resemblances but if they will give to them the expression of a life LIKE MINE then they will succeed and success is millions of money. It must be done in EUROPE and not in the U.S. Please tell them of the love UNSELFED, the inspiration, the FAITH, patience, courage of the author of S. & H.

Fifteen months later, after frequent letters urging on Winslow with further details, Eddy received the highly anticipated painting in January 1901. She responded with heated fury at what she considered a poor likeness and sought not to remunerate the $2,000 Winslow had paid from her own pocket, now claiming the idea and desire for Eddy's picture had been Winslow's own. "People who see it hide their eyes," she bitterly protested. "It has NO resemblance to me. It is a sinister face and dressed in the most unbecoming style of over a hundred years ago. It is masterly in its ugliness of face and form."

Within days, as Winslow showed she had kept Eddy's serial letters of instruction and began complaining publicly about Eddy's behavior, the livid leader sent payment "for caricaturing me in a portrait"; accused the student of being under the influence of malicious animal magnetism; and sought to have her surreptitiously banned from Christian Science circles (two years later, the correspondence shows, Winslow refunded the $2,000 and sent Eddy numerous gifts, in an apparent effort to return to the leader's good graces). Within five months of the Winslow debacle, however, Eddy was writing to the artist D. E. Fultz, "O that you would paint an oil painting of me as true to my life and labor as you have that of our great Master to his wonderful life." Once again she stipulated that though her hair was then white, it should not be so in the portrait, but dark auburn as it once was: "I want your soul work for my picture that leaves no look of decay on the canvas." Whatever happened with Fultz, Eddy was soon arguing over portrait details with more artists, including Willis Kimball ("The hair is even more painfully stiff in this last portrait than in the original") and Emilie Hergenroeder, to whom she returned her portrait and complained, "The poise of the picture is too INARTISTIC, too stiff, unnatural or rather unlifelike. More consecration, devotion, abstraction, spiritual expression is needed in the eyes." Such examples, multiplied many times over in her letters, show Eddy's enduring concern for her form to be idealized and rendered physically beautiful, in order to reflect the radiant inner life within.[18]

Nonetheless, unlike numerous later New Thought teachers, including many of Eddy's own apostate students, Eddy in her public writings maintained an unambiguously clear position on embodiment. The body, like all matter, was simply a false belief, and the path to spiritual truth required a thoroughgoing denial of its claims: "The indestructible faculties of Spirit exist without the conditions of matter and also without the false beliefs of a so-called material existence," she taught. If the necessity of eradicating such false beliefs remained in doubt, Eddy made an urgent case throughout her writings that, as she worded it in one passage, "Denial of the claims of matter is a great step towards the joys of Spirit, towards human freedom and the final triumph over the body." Excessive attention to bodily matters, even in private, prevented the spiritual progress of the entire human race. Conversely, "If half the attention given to hygiene were given to the study of Christian Science and the spiritualization of thought, this alone would usher in the millennium."[19]

Spiritual progress was not all that was at stake, of course; as had Quimby, Eddy preached the possibility, indeed the godly necessity, of perfect health. The healthy body had about it the beauty of holiness (ever distinguished from physical beauty, which was to be despised) and was purified by Mind. Purification, indeed, was a topic of much consequence for Eddy, and cleanliness a clear marker of distinction between "the refined" and "the gross." "A hint," she wrote, "may be taken from the emigrant [sic], whose filth does not affect his happiness, because mind and body rest on the same basis. To the mind equally gross, dirt gives no uneasiness. It is the native element of such a mind, which is symbolized, and not chafed, by its surroundings." Such a condition was hardly acceptable for the spiritually enlightened, however, for "impurity and uncleanliness, which do not trouble the gross, could not be borne by the refined." The lesson? "This shows that the mind must be clean to keep the body in proper condition."[20]

While a clean body might simply mean one that was regularly bathed and free of disease, it could also convey a body that was sexually pure. "It is," she wrote, "chastity and purity, in contrast with the downward tendencies and earthward gravitations of sensualism and impurity, which really attest the divine origin and operation of Christian Science." Elsewhere she wrote, "Chastity is the cement of civilization and progress. Without it there is no stability in society, and without it one cannot attain the Science of Life." In a third passage, where she commanded readers to "conquer lust with chastity," the consequences of sexual sin were clarified with the rendering of an army delivering the sinner to justice and "the sentence of mortal law . . . executed upon mortal mind and body. Both will be manacled until the last farthing is paid,—until you have balanced your account with God."[21] The body might be an error, but its cleanliness, as a symbol and mirror of spiritual purity, was absolutely vital.

In all, Eddy developed a system that turned her teacher Quimby's theoretical system of mind and matter into a denial of the human body's reality. In formulating this doctrine, Eddy diverged not only from Quimby but also from many of her contemporaneous rivals in the metaphysical movements of the day, as well as the New Thought thinkers who were to come. As the New Thought historian and philosopher Alan Anderson has noted, Eddy went beyond the form of idealism purveyed by the majority of New Thought thinkers by denying matter in two senses: "matter as real in itself," and "matter as phenomenon or experience or idea." Eddy's system is one that Anderson terms "idealistic dualism," in which God vies against the errors of "matter," "mortal mind," and "malicious animal magnetism."[22] Yet her conception of embodiment could not escape the flesh entirely, both because she relied so heavily on the notion of purity and because she relished—or at least relied upon—her own material existence. The paradox lay not only between Eddy's life and her teachings, then, but also within those teachings.

For believers in Christian Science, relegating the flesh to "mortal error" may well have posed other kinds of difficulties. The detailed journal entries of one Midwestern homemaker and avid twentieth-century follower of Christian Science, Margaret Fowler Dunaway, affectingly depict her battle to conquer the false evidence presented by her senses in her quest to deny bodily experience and soar in the Spirit. In February 1929, amid financial difficulties, lingering sickness, and dissatisfaction with her husband, Maurice, she urged herself upward:

> Write a Journal of the Soul—the journey, triumphs and travail of the Spirit on its way—thru childhood, young womanhood, marriage, wife and motherhood—wrestling and battling to keep the laws of Life from being choked out by the flesh, appetites, and struggles with lack and want.—The glory of daily inbreeding of character into the children— always the lifting of the eyes to the perfect model of Life—the constant claiming and confidently walking toward Achievement, Prosperity, Oneness, Sureness—Health always known and ever demonstrated thru divine consciousness of possession————Why can I not write these things—these Realities—into my Journal?

Despite frequent admonitions to herself to stick to the highest truths revealed by Christian Science, Dunaway wrote long, fretful accounts of her husband's lengthy unemployment, his apparent infidelity, and her guilt at exposing him before the children, as well as her ambivalence at postponing her own creative ambitions for the sake of her family. Willing herself to cheerfulness, she typically then denied all such unpleasantries. "The prick of

Poverty! We will not feel it nor acknowledge, nor bind to it. 'Tis only another temptation to deny His sufficient care for me and mine." The one death account in her early journals typified this painstakingly bright tone: "Betty Fowler, dear friend, passed away. Buried her winsome little body yesterday. Exquisitely beautiful she looked in her pale pink robe of softest crepe or chiffon. To we [sic] it seems as if she has only gone to another city. Nothing there seems to me of Death in it all. When will the race quit play-acting and perpetuating this farce of Death?"[23]

Chronicles of Christian Science childhoods also explicitly recount the complexities of adhering to a body-denying faith, some wrenchingly so. The former Christian Scientist Barbara Wilson sought to replicate a child's confusion in her anguished memoir, *Blue Windows.*

> And what did it mean that my body too was matter and thus had no reality? What did it mean to be inside a body that did not exist, a body that was not made up of brain, blood, and bones? . . . I knew that Mind was real and matter was unreal, but it seemed that some aspects of matter were more unreal than others, more objectionable and thus more to be struggled with, and those aspects always had to do with the body. . . . [I]n my metaphysical childhood, to have a body was also to have a kind of enemy scout between your mind and Divine Mind, a secret agent whose dispatches from the physical world had to be ignored at all costs.

For Wilson, sexually abused by her uncle as a child, the consequences of a body-denying faith were particularly horrifying, for "there was something specific in Christian Science that made it impossible to incorporate acts of sexual aggression into the metaphysical view of the world that was being drummed into me":

> Being touched down there, being forced to lie there while it happened, was so far out of my experience and the experience of a totally good universe, that I couldn't assimilate it. All my young life I'd heard that evil was a lie, was a bad dream, and that all we had to do was say it didn't exist for it not to exist.[24]

In *The Unseen Shore,* his own memoir of a Christian Science childhood, Thomas Simmons recalled the child's paradoxical experience of physical pain within a religion that defined freedom as denial of mortal mind and disease.

> And so, lying in bed all those nights with ear infections, I was free. I was free through all of my innumerable colds and fevers, and I was free when at the age of three I walked in front of a moving metal swing that tore a jagged gash in my forehead. I was free when, in third grade, I had

bronchitis for three weeks. . . . Because I was free (I was reminded regularly in Sunday school), I was not to question the extent of my suffering; the suffering was simply unreal. . . . And yet, after an illness, the memory of the cruelty and the suffering did not simply go away. It lingered, an evil competing reality, raising an insistent complaint: was the pain really unreal? Was it necessary to endure so much?

Underlying the ceaseless assurances of freedom, Simmons writes, was simply fear. "We were afraid of everything—afraid of sickness, afraid of deviating from God's word, afraid of mortal mind, afraid of the body, afraid of sex, afraid of people, of difference, of strangers, even of love." As she was dying of cancer, his devout grandmother—once a Christian Science practitioner—reverted to the Southern Baptist faith of her childhood, bitterly telling a family member, "Christian Science offers no comfort for the dying." And when Simmons's own mother lay dying of the same disease, she could only feel that she had failed yet again to trust sufficiently in the power of divine Love to heal all ills. "When no healings came," writes Simmons, "the language of the religion broke down." Since death itself was considered unreal, neither funeral nor grieving for his mother was permitted.[25]

Such angry retrospectives hardly convey the full measure of Christian Science's impact on the bodies in its fold: positive narratives of successful healings saturate Christian Science literature, after all, and it would be perverse to reduce these to lies and fancies. What the dissenting voices do forcefully illustrate, however, is the sheer complexity of living—and dying—in a flesh-denying, death-renouncing religious context. Simmons recalls a gruesome incident from his late adolescence, in which his parents and five other church couples flew in two private planes to a fly-in picnic in California's Central Valley. When his parents returned home that evening, a bit later than they'd planned, they reported that the day had been "OK" albeit "tiring." When Simmons opened the next morning's newspaper, however, the lead story informed him that the other plane had crashed, killing the Christian Science Sunday school superintendent, Mildred Valentine, and her husband. Simmons instantly felt revulsion toward his parents' reticence and the "falsehoods" surrounding the retelling of this incident.

> My parents could not tell me about it because they were afraid it would shake my religious faith; I had to find out from the newspaper, like any stranger. Later, as I reflected on what had occurred, I realized that they could not tell me because it was simply too horrible. They could not even really admit it to themselves, because they had only the language of "the real and eternal." Their own silent suffering must have been enormous. Like them, my Sunday school teacher could not admit the

reality of these deaths; he too was afraid it would shake our faith, and thus seemed to blame the Valentines for their fate.

But the plane had crashed, the Valentines were dead, and the accident "hovered . . . like a pliant lie, cooperative but inescapable."[26] For Simmons, at least, materiality turned out to be an elemental fact.

If in this, the most antimaterialist of religions, the body proved a powerful and ultimately inescapable referent, still more in the systems developed by Eddy's followers. Eddy was notoriously irascible with those of her students who began to show some ambition of their own, and the history of early New Thought is to a degree a history of those whom she rejected as apostates. Very few, it turns out, sustained her unyielding posture of denying matter altogether. These later metaphysical thinkers mined both Quimby's language of spiritual matter and Eddy's language of a clean mind and purified body, seeking to refine the perceived rough edges or contradictions of previous systems.

CORRESPONDING BODIES

Though today less well known than Eddy, their mentor-turned-rival, celebrated women such as Emma Curtis Hopkins and Ursula N. Gestefeld were widely read and influential as New Thought teachers and writers. Hopkins, especially, trained various influential New Thought teachers, including H. Emilie Cady, Malinda Cramer, Myrtle and Charles Fillmore, Annie Rix Militz, and Helen Van-Anderson. Even before some of Hopkins's pupils began to deviate overtly from Eddy's exacting antimaterialist stance, Gestefeld and her contemporaries were putting forth a theory of compound bodies, earthly and spiritual, that invested physicality with both significant innate power and meaningful symbolic resonance. Over time New Thought proponents would develop multiple systems of body-oriented practices and provide an alternative philosophy that was unequivocally opposed to Eddy's strict tenets. Gestefeld's, one of the least occupied with actual techniques, nonetheless disclosed some important sources of New Thought's appeal to forward-looking audiences.

Gestefeld (1845–1921) was first healed of illness by reading *Science and Health* in the early 1880s and later enrolled in classes taught by Eddy herself.[27] She developed what she termed the "Science of Being" in the 1890s, and she spread the word by traveling the lecture circuit, writing at least fourteen tracts and two novels, and preaching regularly to her midsize Chicago congregation. Like Eddy and like many other teachers under the

New Thought rubric, Gestefeld distinguished between the visible or physical body and the "thought" body. Yet the relationship between these two bodies was complex: "You, the living soul, are more than you were. You are more conscious of your true being and its possibilities, and this 'more' is embodied in your physical body as a finer body which is not visible to the outer sense of sight. It is what has been built into the nature-body." It was, in fact, changes in the thought body, "its higher quality" that would actually make one appear different to friends and family, "even though they still see flesh and blood." She described the thought body as "a finer body which is not visible to the outer sense of sight," yet for Gestefeld this body would literally "pervade" the physical body and work toward the latter's transformation.[28]

Compared to later innovations in New Thought, nothing seems especially radical about this doctrine of correspondences, certainly not within the context of New Thought. Quimby himself had written about the "real man" and the "natural man" as parts of the selfsame being, while the doctrine of a "perfect unity between the soul and the shape" can be read back into Emanuel Swedenborg (and forward into some faith healers interpreting disease as a fleshly sign of sin). Gestefeld, in fact, echoed Eddy by arguing, "The visible physical body is not the seat of disease but only the plane of its visibility. By the relation of subjective and objective, the objective body is the means by which is made visible what is held in the subjective soul. If there be the power to cast out of the soul what has been held within it, it follows that there must be, eventually, corresponding disappearance from the objective body." Likewise, even as the soul evolved upward, "from the minimum toward the maximum of self-consciousness," so would the body rise. The thought-body was incarnated in the natural or basic body so that the latter could ascend "to the plane of Likeness to God."[29]

But if the natural body was not able to transcend the material world, neither was the thought-body wholly invulnerable to material afflictions. In a remarkable passage about the transmission of sickness from one human being to another, from a chapter acknowledging the existence of germs (even while noting they could be rendered innocuous), Gestefeld discussed the potential for the "germs or emanations" of people in a room to poison the air within its walls. The individual, unless he opened a window or left the room for more open air, breathed in this poisoned air, so that "the poisonous element enters his lungs and, therefore, penetrates his physical body and leaves its deposits." The very thoughts of "sickness, suffering, and death" emitted from others' bodies overwhelmed the individual who did not seek clean air. So long as the soul was passive rather than aggressively resistant to the thought emanations of others, "the human race is bound to be disease-ridden, for the causes of disease are constantly at work and effects must follow."[30]

Illness and contagion were live problems facing Gestefeld and her readers. While the promise of purification aimed to soothe, however, her graphic acknowledgment of poisons and their power to sicken and even kill—a stark contrast to Eddy's denial of both matter and evil—stoked further unease. In Gestefeld's writings as in many other New Thought texts, an apprehensive undertone sounded softly (and sometimes not so softly). Not surprisingly, fear of disease linked up with a host of other matters, for which the terminology of poison and purification worked equally well. In *Each Mind a Kingdom,* her interpretation of New Thought as a women's movement, the historian Beryl Satter describes Gestefeld's dread of sexuality and the tension she posed between love and freedom in her 1892 novel, *The Woman Who Dares.* Here, Satter argues, lies evidence that the driving force of Gestefeld's doctrine was her anger at a male-dominated world that suppressed women's independence and sexual freedom. In Satter's reading of Gestefeld and other female New Thought leaders, the whole appeal of this metaphysical movement lay in its attempts to wrestle freely (if cryptically) with the problem of desire as it faced late Victorian middle-class women: whether "masculine" ambition or, its opposite, "feminine" self-abnegation was to be the model for the future.[31] Gestefeld fits this model fairly well (though few of the other figures discussed in this chapter similarly do). But however slippery female selfhood appeared in *The Woman Who Dares*— Murva, the novel's heroine, came into her own only by means of sexual exploitation and then merely shifted her self-sacrifice into new arenas—by the time Gestefeld published *How We Master Our Fate* five years later, she had shifted to a decisive position advocating determined self-mastery. Handwringing over proper female behavior toward husbands and domestic life occupied her no longer (her own husband had died some years earlier): instead, Gestefeld attended to her readers' public responsibilities, in particular the power of women and men alike to reform the gritty metropolis fast changing around them.

With the evils of civilization as an underlying subtext, disquietude continued to dog these later writings. Crime, drunkenness, and prostitution hovered as spectral presences in the background, problems of male vice and female victimization to which Gestefeld offered a characteristically spiritualized solution. She sought, that is, to ease the discomfort of her audience by persuading them that city youth, however "weak, wicked, dissipated," possess "the germ of divinity" that "will develop as sure as God is God."

Though the outer personal shape is rolling in the gutter covered with
the filth which is found there, through this covering may be seen, by
those who have enlarged their soul-capacity, that which is not native
to the gutter. And these know that sometime in the great Forever he
will come to himself, arise from the gutter and go to the Father's house;
and this even if the physical shape were to be found there, dead.[32]

Incongruity between outer and inner selves was an old, deeply familiar
source of anxiety, and Gestefeld sought to replace unease with determined
optimism, even as she reminded readers, over and over again, of the "burden of suffering" under which "the whole human race is groaning and will
continue to groan."[33]

Elsewhere returning to this theme of "the murderer or the thief or the
rascal," she wrote similarly: "However this visible person may appear to
you, however wicked and altogether vile this man may be, that soul must
ascend. Ascension is compelled by the nature of its being, and the almighty
resistless primal energy which is the creative power of God pushes it along
the upward path." When she finally assured readers that any "effort we
make for ourselves is equally an effort for the whole race," that "our
thought, redeemed and purified, is a saviour of men as well as of our own
souls," Gestefeld spoke vividly of overcoming the blights of modern existence. Corruption was provisional, not absolute, so that even the most vice-
ridden society could be redeemed. "No more murders, robberies and crimes
if we get and hold the true self-idea," she coolly assured. "All is good. There
is no evil."[34] Having addressed the endlessly vexing question of differenti-
ating inner truths from the deceptive outer shell that housed and disguised
them, she commanded readers to ignore the evidence of the latter so as to
live in a perfect, sinless world.

Fear and forced optimism had just as surely motivated Gestefeld's predecessors (not least Eddy herself), accruing to mind power much of its dynamic
appeal. But other New Thought writers developed strategies for championing bodily practices as vital means to higher spiritual ends. Prentice
Mulford (1834–91), less well known today but a major New Thought writer
in his own time and for some years after his death, likewise theorized a palpable distinction between the spirit body and the natural body. Atkinson
credited the popular works of Mulford, an erstwhile journalist, failed miner,
and general drifter, with bringing New Thought to wider prominence and
"open[ing] a new world of thought to many." The biography (one might say
hagiography) of Mulford by the British theosophist Eva Martin, written two
decades after his death, likewise noted that he had "yet made himself known
and remembered in two continents entirely by the fruits of his mind."

Mulford, she wrote, "was an early pioneer in these now well-trodden paths" of New Thought.[35] For a time before his mysterious death (he was found dead in his own canoe), Mulford had lived, Thoreau-style, in a small cabin in the New Jersey woods, breaking the spell on one occasion for a journey to Boston in which he immersed himself in New Thought teachings. From his semi-isolation, between 1886 and 1891, he produced a series of pamphlets (thirty-seven essays in all) that were published in the White Cross Library and later (posthumously) compiled in a six-volume work entitled *Your Forces and How to Use Them.* Here, titles such as "The Law of Success" and "How to Push Your Business" mingled with "Immortality in the Flesh," "The Process of Re-Embodiment," and "The Uses of Sickness." Mulford sounded like a conventional New Thought writer as he distinguished between material and spiritual selves and promised that the latter would vanquish the former: "There belong to every human being a higher self and a lower self—a self or mind of the spirit, which has been growing for ages, and a self of the body, which is but a thing of yesterday."[36]

When his own bodily self expired, numerous manuscript pages were discovered beside the corpse, recording Mulford's lengthy channeled correspondence with an unnamed spiritual being. Described in a genial if somewhat mystified obituary on the front page of the *New York Times*, the letters were "filled with assurance that the 'spirit' was close beside him, watching over him and guarding him from harm, and that brighter days were in store for him." This account was influenced by Mulford's U.S. publisher, F. J. Needham, and rendered the dead man's life as one of "constant changes and many disappointments," evoking a rugged individualist who conquered all obstacles—even once wandering alone through the Sierra, lost and severely frostbitten—until his untimely death.[37] Bleaker, less understated reports on Mulford over the years indicted him for drunkenness, indigence, an ignominious marriage (he was derided as a pitiable cuckold), and eccentric abandonment of all friends. At least one renowned American intellectual, the poet John Greenleaf Whittier, reportedly praised Mulford as "a sage and seer."[38] Whatever curiosity surrounded his demise, he retained a strong reputation as a well-traveled essayist who had once worked with such luminaries as Bret Harte, Mark Twain, and John Muir and had talked up American frontier life on trips abroad. Like Gestefeld and other New Thought popularizers, Mulford wrote of the world as he dreamed it could be, a world utterly distinct from his own life's pain and modest, only intermittent achievements. His metaphysical writings sold widely after his death.

Despite the spirit-body pecking order that supposedly reigned, Mulford made explicit claims about the body's importance, including prolonged attention to the development of healthy appetites and to the joys of physical life. Contemplating the prospect of fleshly immortality, for instance, Mulford highlighted his conviction "that a physical body can be retained so long as the spirit desires its use, and that this body, instead of decreasing in strength and vigour as the years go on, will increase and its youth will be perpetual." The role of the spirit in this meditation, of course, raised perplexing questions. Why would spirit-minded persons desire immortal life in the flesh? In Mulford's view, the human desire for longevity and physical perfectibility signaled mental maturity, as people learned to "appreciate more than ever the value of living in the physical." As the demand grew for eternal life in the flesh, supply would eventually follow: that is, the spirit would act upon the body in order to create a newly spiritualized form of matter, "an ever-changing and refining body." The stronger the craving for physicality, in other words, the greater one's chances would be of receiving an eternal body. Indeed, the last obstacle to everlasting life was finally surpassed when spirit and body were conjoined: "It is very desirable for the spirit to be able to keep a physical body which shall refine as the spirit refines, because in such equality of refinement between the spirit and its instrument, our increase in happiness is greatly advanced, and the relatively perfected rounding out of our powers cannot be realised until this union between spirit and body is effected."[39]

Mulford continued to talk about "spirit" and "body" as separate entities, even in the ideal state of integration. But matter was wily and not easily vanquished: food, for instance, could enter even the refined body and do it evil. Why did some victuals nauseate, and why were others cast out of the body through its orifices? Mulford taught that the spirit undertook such action "through a knowledge of its own that the cast-out substance is unfit for it."[40] Eventually, he assured, the spirit could grow so advanced and sensitive to such evils that it would not allow them to be ingested, warning the body in advance of those things that it should refuse to receive. (One might wonder what Mulford's own spirit had to say about the pint of St. Croix rum found with him when he died; or perhaps, since the bottle was reportedly unopened, death was simply his creative avoidance strategy.) Yet Mulford's view of matter clearly depicted it as both powerful and potentially hazardous, hardly the willing slave of the more refined spirit.

Matter could, however, also be benevolent and was absolutely essential to the life of the spirit. Mulford took care to note: "As faith increases many material aids will be called in by the spirit which will greatly help the renewing processes. These aids will come in selection of foods, in choosing proper associations, and other changes of habit and custom."[41] The spirit itself demanded "varying dishes and flavours," and indifference to sensory enjoyment "proves there is a deadening or blunting of the spirit." By contrast, "The higher the spiritualisation of any person the more vigorous and appreciative becomes the palate." The pleasures of eating, like other physical pleasures, directed themselves to spiritual rather than animal ends. Tasting and savoring food with such refinement was the opposite of gluttony. "The glutton does not eat," Mulford observed. "He swallows. Proper eating dwells on every morsel with relish, and the longer it can be so dwelt upon, the longer it serves as the physical medium for the conveyance of life to the spirit."[42]

Should the conscience-ridden eater fret at so much time being devoted to the delights of the palate, Mulford reassuringly promised that this was an expansive, even socially responsible good. Indeed, he wrote, "Your spiritual force when you eat with the proper mind is working on others, possibly far from your body, as much and even more than at some other times." Any pleasure, he concluded, if rightly used was a source of strength both for the individual and for the wider world. In fact, enjoyment itself should be the result of "every effort, mental or physical," that was undertaken, and gratification taken in eating (and any other effort) was "the proof that life is rightly lived." It was this pleasure principle that impelled Mulford to recommend that his readers "Eat what most pleases your taste." Eating for health, when the food was not pleasurable and its consumption a mere duty, was of no benefit.[43]

At this point Mulford strained his blend of seemingly incongruous principles by unselfconsciously chasing advice to eat only personally toothsome foods with a lengthy exposition on the proper and most spiritual diet. Topping the list were fresh meats, vegetables, and fruits, said to "contain the most force." Salted and pickled products possessed reduced might, as preservative processes drained the life present in food newly "plucked or dug." Meat itself had ambiguous value: on the one hand, Mulford taught those who craved it to eat it without guilt: "You can while eating meat desire the best and purest for body and spirit as easily as when eating fruit. If you do this you are making meat a conveyance to your spirit of such higher thought."[44] On the other hand, meat was admittedly "a food grosser and coarser than some others," and, as Mulford noted elsewhere, "The regenerative process will involve the eating of less and less animal food, until we shall eat none whatever."[45] He cautioned readers to realize that they were not ready to give up meat until the desire for it had gone; yet he associated reduced intake of food in general, and meat in particular, with higher spiritual attainment.

Mulford explicated the high value of "natural" (as opposed to "cultivated") foods as an analogy of humanity. "All grains, fruits, and vegetables cultivated by man are natural types captured and enslaved by him. They are bred to forced conditions. They are dependent on man's care. Remove that care and they cannot sustain themselves. . . . In consuming these artificial growths, man absorbs also their spirit of dependence, of slavery and unnatural condition. All this tends to cripple and retard the growth of his spiritual powers." Human beings today had the same choice Adam and Eve had, to consume only foodstuffs in the wild, "so that they should absorb only the natural and more powerful spirit of such growth." Yet most, like the sinners in the Garden, failed to trust in this spiritual power that "would make all and any food desired out of the elements at will" and so were forced to cultivate the soil and to rely upon "forced and artificial growths of animal [and] vegetable." Thus they acted unnaturally, "killing and slaying, and renewing . . . the human body's life by the unnatural life or spirit from another body." In this way, the terror implanted in both animals and plants (by awareness of their impending slaughter) was, through ingestion, transferred to the human eater. "We absorb the helplessness of the plant or animal which is entirely dependent on man's care."[46]

Helplessness was Mulford's life companion, from his failed expeditions to the California gold and silver mines through his disappointing marriage and into his final authorial (perhaps alcoholic) seclusion, where it took a spirit being to assure him of better times to come. It is not difficult to read more deeply into the disquiet that nourished his urgent appeal to retreat from artificiality and civilization so as to return to the ordering of nature. He soon wrenched other implications into full view as well: Adam and Eve were not, as it turned out, the parents of all humanity; rather, they were "the ancestors of our present white race . . . possessed [of] an intelligence superior to the dark races then on the earth." The link between Mulford's dietary teachings and his racial ordering was intriguingly tortuous (and by no means limited to his writing; Progressive Era literature on eugenics, for instance, often made very similar associations). He associated the "dark races" with the animals of the earth, closer to nature and instinct than their white counterparts, whose history of slave-owning he more or less condemned. Yet Mulford blamed what he also called "lower races" for imparting to Adam and Eve the knowledge of capturing wild animals and plants and transforming them into artificial products, hence beginning the whole process of civilization and decay! At that point this fairly ordinary, if quirky, defense of a spiritualized diet unexpectedly exposed an overarching racialized worldview, one that, Satter's work makes clear, was hardly uncommon in many New Thought circles.

New Thought systems such as those put forward by Gestefeld and Mulford did not merely argue that the importance of bodily health was primarily as an indicator of spiritual maturity. Even where they described physical perfection as an ultimate end of existence, the flip side of spiritual perfection, they often depicted its primary route as through the mind. And yet a close reading of these and many other New Thought authors reveals the surprising degree to which bodily techniques themselves served as aids in the pursuit of spiritual matters—the body not simply an "illusion" but important in its own right as a key to the spiritual life. Appropriating aspects of bodily discourse from the medical realm, proponents could divorce the spiritual or real from the so-called natural or material but still talk of natural (good) and artificial (bad) in matters such as food. Smiling serenely through its ambiguities allowed writers to tether New Thought's contradictory impulses into a quasi-coherent, authoritative logic that contained the body's hazards while elevating somatic pursuits and pleasures to a higher plane. Some emphasized spiritual prowess as the key to mastering the universe, others would focus on sexual ecstasy, and still others became ever more vehement about the role of bodily disciplines in sustaining the life of the soul.[47]

FEMALE SEXUAL PLEASURE AND MYSTICAL COMMUNION: REPRODUCING A CIVILIZED RACE

Diet and exercise were not the only, nor perhaps the most alluring, of New Thought preoccupations with human appetite. Though religious discussion in mainstream literature typically suppressed the subject of sex, New Thought and likeminded writers (particularly occultists, who overlapped with New Thought teachers in crucial and largely overlooked ways) considered the subject vitally important to the life of the mind and spirit.[48] Regulation of sexual function, of course, had long drawn its Christian advocates, who shored up their moral views with medicalized theories of seminal power and enervation. The nineteenth-century crusades against masturbation and prostitution found a natural ally in the campaign for marriage-based continence, variously promoted by such disparate figures as Sylvester Graham, John Humphrey Noyes, Mary Gove Nichols, and Henry Hanchett.[49] New Thought writers developed their own version of continence theory, drawing more on Asian and specifically Hindu models than on Christian notions of depravity but reflecting modern society's growing attention to female sexuality (and victimization).

The most famous and widely read New Thought writer to promote sexual control within marriage was Alice Bunker Stockham (1833–1912), one of the first female physicians in the United States and a specialist in the health of women and children.[50] After the pronounced success of her 1883 volume *Tokology: A Book for Every Woman,* which would become a widely recognized textbook on pregnancy and childbirth and would earn her international fame, Stockham became involved in the mind cure movement in Chicago under the tutelage of Emma Curtis Hopkins. Later revised editions of *Tokology,* in fact, included a section titled "Mind Cure a Reality," urging readers, "Cheerfully, hopefully bring the soul into harmony with the good in the universe. Where there is light there can be no darkness, where health reigns, disease disappears."[51] And in her 1896 book *Karezza: Ethics of Marriage,* she expounded in fullest terms her influential theory of sex and continence.

Like other New Thought writers, Stockham argued that sex was a spiritual as much as a physical deed. "Copulation is more than a propagative act; it is a blending of body, soul and spirit, ennobling or degrading according to the attitude of the participants." As she had in *Tokology,* Stockham argued in *Karezza* against the common view, propounded by figures such as Havelock Ellis, that men and women had fundamentally different experiences of sex, with men focused on the carnal and women on the spiritual. Rather, both husband and wife participated in the physical as well as spiritual dimensions of sexual intercourse; the key was to balance them properly. She decried prudish antipathy toward the genital organs, writing, "No part of the body should be under condemnation." At the same time, Stockham sought to purify intercourse itself, calling her audience to a new method for "the control, mastery and consecration of sex energy" that she termed "Karezza" (Italian for "caress," in sound if not spelling). The term suggested a mode of sexual intercourse in which both partners would intentionally forego orgasm, thereby ensuring "a conscious conservation of creative energy." This practice, a "complete but quiet union of the sexual organs" that included only carefully controlled motion and would ideally last for an extended period of time, was to be the exclusive mode for marital sex except when the couple desired procreation. "With abundant time and mutual reciprocity," she assured readers, "the interchange becomes satisfactory and complete without emission or crisis. In the course of an hour the physical tension subsides, the spiritual exaltation increases, and not uncommonly visions of a transcendent life are seen and consciousness of new powers experienced."[52]

At its most transparent, Stockham's concern for self-control evoked the possibility of rechanneling sexual desire into a spiritual exercise that would elevate both parties. She even suggested that before or during the sexual act itself, "there may be some devotional exercises, or there may be a formula of consecration of an uplifting character in which both unite." Such spiritual applications would "aid in concentration and in removing the thoughts from merely physical sensations." Stockham cited Noyes as calling it male continence but noted that it was just as much about female continence, since "the husband and wife equally conserve their forces under a wise control." The goal was to focus on a process of "spiritual unfoldment," a form of creative expression and not merely "asceticism or repression." Thus Karezza would help one to be "put in possession of new powers and possibilities."[53]

This language of power grew increasingly bold, as Stockham noted how "Western people" had only recently come to this knowledge of conscious control. With this knowledge, "man is no more the machine to be buffeted by circumstances and environment; he is rather the machinist having control of both the mechanism and the power of the bodily instrument." The machinist had "unlimited resources" and no real limitations. "He enthrones his divine nature which gives dominion and mastery," she reported euphorically, "and at no time does this dominion serve him with more satisfaction than in the marital relation and in making possible the attainment of Karezza." Women under this liberating system would be "freed from the usual dread of excessive and undesired child-bearing," while men would properly "conserve the virile principle" so as to possess more power in the world. Comparing semen to tears, in that regular secretion of neither was essential to physical health, Stockham compared the "unmanly" shedding of trivial tears to the likewise degrading habit of ejaculating "without rational and proper cause."[54]

The social consequences of Stockham's progressive program were monumental, since newly discovered "control of the fecundating power" would stop the inflow of unwanted children into the world, including those who, "if poor," were currently forced to "seek their own diversion" so that "all their activities thus lack wise direction." Generations of the future would thus be offered "a rightful inheritance" now lacking among the burdened lower classes. "Every child has a right to a parentage of thoughtful preparation, to the best that can be given him," she sermonized. "In Karezza this right of the unborn child is fulfilled." In this way a child's character could be wholly protected and shaped to be wise, loving, and cultured. With the eradication of selfish desire and indulgence, "wise control" rather than "the ordinary chance procreation" would be the norm. "As future generations understand the law of spiritual growth and mastery, their children will be superior in power and achievement to any heretofore known." At last, the eugenic implications of Stockham's project came to light:

Shall not the world cease to be peopled by unloved and undesired children? Let love be the fulfillment of law, and let us have a race of men
and women that will bless the wisdom and deliberation of their progeni-
tors. Breathe the spirit of progress into the institution of marriage and
let all strive for descendants that shall glorify the centuries to come. . . .
Let us multiply the Emersons, the Savonarolas, the Catherines of Siena,
for they in turn will bless the earth.

Ideal conditions for procreation, in short, would lead to a whole race of "ideal
children." And virtues of self-control would generate virtuous middle-class
citizens.[55]

Also addressing these matters around the same time as Stockham was the
Philadelphia-born Ida Craddock (1857–1902), a noted expert on stenogra-
phy and systems of phonetic shorthand who was also a practicing sex counselor in Chicago during the 1890s before relocating to New York. A Quaker
by birth, Craddock was drawn to occult and theosophical teachings during
her thirties, and she read widely in Eastern philosophy and diverse mytho-
logical traditions. She once held the position of secretary to the National
Liberal League and was more generally associated with the Free Thought
movement, lecturing widely on topics such as "Survivals of Sex Worship in
Christianity and in Paganism" and "What Christianity Has Done for the
Marital Relation." Pursued and prosecuted by anti-vice crusader Anthony
Comstock for her "obscene" writings, Craddock committed suicide on the
morning she was to be sentenced to prison. Her blunt and sometimes hilar-
ious proclamations on sexuality—evoking the later beloved sexpert Dr.
Ruth Westheimer—sought to deal candidly with everything, including the
clitoris (which "should be simply saluted, at most, in passing") no less than
the penis (the "one lawful finger of love with which to approach [the bride's]
genitals" but which the innocent young woman might first view as "something of a monstrosity"). Craddock's relative obscurity among later historians, almost none of whom noticed much less wrote about her, stems in part
from her occult views, including insistence that she was married to a "heavenly bridegroom" and had nightly passionate sexual relations. Her 1894
work that made this revelation, *Heavenly Bridegrooms*, attempted to allay
the suspicions and questions put to her about her status as an unmarried
woman writing so graphically about sex.[56]

Like Stockham, whose works she knew, Craddock strongly emphasized
the propriety of sexual relations within marriage and their impropriety outside those bounds. Yet she was a stronger advocate of erotic pleasure than
Stockham and emphasized more than the spiritual blessings to be derived
from intercourse. An early published writing on this subject was her *Danse*

du ventre, which defended the undulating dance of the same name performed by Fahreda Mahzar ("Little Egypt") at the 1893 World's Columbian
Exposition in Chicago. When Comstock sought to have the dance shut
down, Craddock defended it as "a religious memorial inculcat[ing] purity
and self-control."[57] And when Craddock's essay was published in the
Chicago Clinic, a journal dedicated to alternative medicine and "pantherapeutic" endeavors, Comstock declared the issue unmailable.[58] Despite the
fact that Craddock advocated limited sexual relations within marriage and,
like Comstock, decried prostitution, masturbation, contraception, and other
practices deemed deviant, her emphasis upon the importance of sex for both
men and women as a practice that "never debilitates" but rather "freshens
and renews" earned her Comstock's wrath again and again.[59] Her blending
of eroticism, female pleasure, and self-control earned her other enthusiasts,
however: occultists such as Aleister Crowley (who praised her in 1919), on
the one side, and investigators of the links between sex worship and the history of religion, on the other.

Craddock's final booklet, *The Wedding Night,* appeared the same year as
her death, 1902. Here, the no-nonsense Craddock deplored the "impenetra-
ble veil of secrecy" that so often shrouded this "night of mystery and passion" as she sought to give sexual advice to both bride and groom. Besides
urging the man to be "gentlemanly and considerate" and to avoid seeking
genital contact before the bride indicated her own desire for it ("My dear sir,
you must be indeed lacking in manhood to be unable to arouse sex desire in
a bride who loves you with even a half-way sort of affection"), she urged
couples to remember that the true purpose of union was "the exchange of
sexual magnetism which will strengthen and refresh," a process she preferred to call yoga after Hindu notions of oneness with the divine. Orgasms
were vital to women's health, but men should expend semen only when
both parties wanted to beget children. Sexual self-control, Craddock has-
tened to add, "does not mean less pleasure, but more pleasure than by the
ordinary method of sex union." Men who learned to control themselves also
knew better than to think of intercourse as unclean or of women as interchangeable receptacles for male excretions. "When the higher law is known
and kept—that of genital union in self-control and aspiration to the
Divine—the sex relation at once becomes refined and spiritualized, and the
morbid ideas about its being impure cease." Each should seek to please the
other, with God also "included in this pleasure-giving partnership."[60]

Besides Stockham, Craddock had also read Albert Chavannes, the
Tennessee-based author of a number of New Thought books, including
Magnetation, and Its Relation to Health and Character. The term "mag-

netation" carried similar suggestions as Stockham's *Karezza*, in that it meant "the blending of sexual magnetism, not for procreation, as is the case among undeveloped men and women, but for the purpose of benefiting the persons themselves." That force of magnetism itself, wrote Chavannes, was "a substance, not evanescent like air, but more in the nature of a fluid like water," and sexual magnetism was stored in the reproductive organs. Civilization's advance, and the concomitant diminution of humanity's enemies (wild animals, disease, and aggressive passions) meant that "the procreative powers of mankind are far in excess of the normal demand, and are either largely wasted, or the cause of much misery and crime, and that if a profitable use can be found for them, it will prove a great blessing to humanity." Shifting sexual magnetism away from reproduction to the spiritual communion of souls, avoiding orgasm, would not only help those particular sexual partners but would also improve the character of the race and even "do away with the crimes and miseries due to an excess of procreative power." Only an evolved individual, "the fully developed man or woman," had sufficient brain power " to control and direct all the desires due to the influence of sexual and emotional magnetism." Self-controlled, powerfully minded persons would advance the civilized race, by sharing one another's magnetism without overly exciting themselves and risking conception. "In procreation the excitement is so great that the overflow of sexual magnetism caused by it has no time to diffuse itself, and the blending takes place where it can be followed by conception, while in magnetation, the excitement being kept under reasonable bounds, the flow of sexual magnetism is more moderate and better controlled and has time to diffuse itself."[61]

In 1899, Chavannes sent Craddock a letter thanking her for sending him her pamphlet *Right Marital Living*, though he noted that her citation of his work misidentified magnetation as "magnetism." The two authors discussed the possibility of writing a novel together, and they also described their somewhat different theories of sexuality and marriage. Chavannes's thesis was that monogamy as currently practiced was a disaster for any number of reasons and that sexual relations should evolve to encompass greater variety, along the lines of complex marriage. Exclusive monogamy bred jealousy, stress, and boredom. "As to variety, I might say that it is the logical result of my belief as to the best sexual relations, but I defend it on other grounds. Progress comes from the blending of human efforts in all directions. Now that we have reached a little higher stage of development, we recognize that it is those nations and individuals who exchange the most intellectual knowledge who stand the best chances of success." More than pleasure, he wrote, sexual variety was "one of the most beneficent practices of social life" improving both the health and character of those who engaged in it. With breeding controlled, sexual expression should be given free reign: "It is true that many good reasons can be advanced to discourage sexual freedom from the procreative standpoint, but none can be advanced from the magnetative standpoint, except such as are based upon authoritative morality, a thing I have entirely discarded."[62]

Sexual power, then, could be turned toward greater ends than animalistic gratification, these New Thought teachers argued, and self-control of this kind both signaled and advanced a new stage in human civilization. Sexual discipline tallied perfectly with other teachings concerning mental power, since the mystical powers of sex likewise had tangible force in the material world. Craddock cited the "Oriental occultists" for teaching that a prayer breathed during rapturously controlled sexual communion would unfailingly be granted: "All power is ours," she concluded, "when we rise in thought to oneness inwardly with the Divine Central Force." Without orgasm—what Chavannes called "reaction"—sexual energy would be "thoroughly diffused all through the organism," so that it acted as a source of healing, "like oil upon the troubled waters," while "the tempest running riot in the excited nerves" due to overwork and the turmoil of modern life would be "quieted down as if by enchantment." Sexual control and proper diffusion of energies would create health and strong character, beauty, and longevity, all signs of "the development of the human race." The appropriate channeling of human appetite, once again, paved the way for the reproduction of only the most virtuous citizens, centering bodily discipline as both the portent and instrument of the future race.[63]

Most New Thought writers, of course, avoided sex as a topic for investigation. But many spoke no less forcefully about the vital significance of human appetites and the ways in which modes of restraint distinguished the virtuous from the wicked. Plentiful numbers of adherents vigorously extended the time-honored search for physical signs of spiritual regeneration, some finding hope in systematized food and exercise regimens more or less consistent with those promoted throughout the broad reaches of popular culture. Even those who paid little attention to such systems (or at least neglected to write about them) began to sound a harmonious note of approval for slimness, most notably a slender body type that would become ever more allied with particular configurations of class and race. As thinness, already a token of thrift and capitalist success, enhanced the New Thought project of self-regeneration, fat evinced clogged mental thinking, obstructed spiritual pathways, and death.

REGIMENS SHAPING BODIES TO COME

The most widely read of New Thought writers at the turn of the century was Ralph Waldo Trine (1866–1958). His 1897 book *In Tune with the Infinite* was a multimillion best seller in its own time and had broad appeal in a culture ripe for the word that individuals could be in charge of their earthly lives, if not their final destinies. The book has remained in print (most recently reissued by the New Age publisher Thorsons in 1995 and by Oaklea Press in 2002) and is one of the best selling New Thought books of all time. The enduring popularity of this classic New Thought inspirational text make its references to the body particularly meaningful, revealing some evocative assumptions about the body and leanness.

The version of New Thought represented by *In Tune with the Infinite* charted another seemingly direct course for subjugating matters of the flesh. Here again, however, things were rather less simple than Trine wished to acknowledge. Writing of the "Spirit of Infinite Life" as the deep background to human existence, Trine taught, "The great central fact in human life, in your life and in mine, is the coming into a conscious, vital realization of our oneness with this Infinite Life, and the opening of ourselves fully to this divine inflow."

> Mankind has not yet realized that the real self is one with the life of God. Through its ignorance it has never yet opened itself to the divine inflow, and so has never made itself a channel through which the infinite powers and forces can manifest. When we know ourselves merely as men, we live accordingly, and have merely the powers of men. When we come into the realization of the fact that we are God-men, then again we live accordingly, and have the powers of God-men. *In the degree that we open ourselves to this divine inflow are we changed from mere men into God-men.*

As Mulford had, Trine turned his attention to bodily matters not simply as methods of bodily healing but as signposts of spiritual progress.[64]

"Our bodies," wrote Trine, "are given us to serve far higher purposes than we ordinarily use them for." Lamenting the "numerous cases where the body is master of its owner" rather than vice versa, Trine repeated the common refrain of harmony between body and spirit yet, with a censure of fat, transposed them into a new key.

> In the degree that we come into the realization of the higher powers of the mind and spirit, in that degree does the body, through their influence upon it, become less gross and heavy, finer in its texture and form. And then, because the mind finds a kingdom of enjoyment in itself,

and in all the higher things it becomes related to, *excesses* in eating and drinking, as well as all others, naturally and of their own accord fall away. There also falls away the desire for the heavier, grosser, less valuable kinds of food and drink, such as the flesh of animals, alcoholic drinks, and all things of the class that stimulate the body and the passions rather than build the body and the brain into a strong, clean, well-nourished, enduring, and fibrous condition.

The "finer," leaner body would be an efficient machine, able to utilize a smaller amount of nourishment more ably than a large body could; moreover, in the "less gross and heavy" body, there would be "less waste" all around, keeping it in "a more regular and even condition." Such ideas were growing into Progressive Era staples of alternative health lore, while the dread of food's excessive temptation and stimulation of the passions harked back to the Graham and Alcott systems of yore, long past their prime but soon to benefit from a New Thought revival.[65]

The slimming body was not merely a sign of spiritual progress, in Trine's telling. Far more, it provided assistance to the spirit, acting as the center from which progress was attained. "As the body in this way grows finer, . . . it in turn helps the mind and the soul in the realization of ever higher perceptions, and thus body helps mind the same as mind builds body."

Later in the same book, Trine made the workings of the body's assistance somewhat more explicit, noting:

As the body becomes less gross and heavy, finer in its texture and form, all the senses become finer, so that powers we do not now realize as belonging to us gradually develop. Thus we come, in a perfectly natural and normal way, into the super-conscious realms whereby we make it possible for the higher laws and truths to be revealed to us. . . . As we thus make it possible for these higher laws and truths to be revealed to us, we will in turn become enlightened ones, channels through which they may be revealed to others.

Though Trine did not say so directly, the implication was clear: the science of nutrition, which included all the practices of feeding the body, was vital not merely to the preservation of the biological body but to the much grander life of the soul.[66]

Two other widely influential New Thought teachers who were persuaded of the body's crucial import, particularly that of nutritive practices, were Charles (1854–1948) and Myrtle (1845–1931) Fillmore, co-founders of the Unity School of Christianity in 1889. Both became vegetarians around 1895, with Myrtle Fillmore explaining that she had "outgr[own] the demand for murdered things." She encouraged hundreds of correspondents and followers to eat what she called "spiritual foods which wash out the accumulations in the tissues, clear up the brain structure, and soothe and quiet." In her view, "the spirit will more readily handle the flesh when the body is denied the foods which make it heavy and dense and which irritate the stomach and cause it to crave more food." Her preference was for fresh fruits and vegetables as the basic building blocks for strong, healthy bodies. Other foodstuffs, by contrast, merely became "a burden to the organs."[67]

Meanwhile her husband, the more prolific author, had other things to say about food and bodily health. His commitment to vegetarianism was the subject of numerous reflections in Unity's early years. In one article published in *Unity* magazine in 1903, for instance, Charles Fillmore accentuated the "life ideas" hidden within the "material forms" of food as a way of teaching that what one eats should "be full of life in its purity and vigor," rather than depleted or dead. He lamented the violence inflicted upon animals in "shipping pens . . . and packing houses," arguing, "These very sufferings are through the law of sympathetic mental vibrations transferred to the flesh of those who eat the bodies of these animals. The undefined fears, the terrors of the nightmare, and the many disturbances in stomach and bowels that man endures may be in a measure traced to these unsuspected sources."[68] Under the magazine's later title, *Weekly Unity*, a Vegetarian Department ran weekly from the October 25, 1911, issue through October 1930, edited for some years by the Fillmores' son, Royal. Like Eddy, however, Charles Fillmore was uninterested in literal fasting, noting instead fasting's more figurative meanings: "In fasting, we as metaphysicians abstain from error thinking and meditate on spiritual Truth until we incorporate it into the consciousness of oneness with the Father."[69]

Despite their concern for proper dietary habits, the Fillmores' hope, like that of so many of their New Thought contemporaries, was that eventually human beings could forego food altogether and live entirely on air. For Myrtle Fillmore, this idea, like the regimens she practiced so assiduously, seems to have been strengthened by her frequent correspondence with Dr. Bengamin Gayelord Hauser, a popular nutritionist and physical culturist who wrote numerous best-selling books and counted many celebrities among his clients. In one letter to Hauser, she wrote:

> There will come a time when we can draw forth the universal mind stuff, just the elements we need in the right proportion and relation, to maintain the proper balance in our organisms. We shall be able to draw chemical substances from the fourth dimensional realm, down into our physical body. But in the meantime, we need to make practical

all the knowledge we have concerning bodily renewal, through using intelligence and discrimination in the selection of our food.[70]

Yet hope for the ideal world to come, in which eating would no longer be necessary, did not prevent her from paying close attention to the body in the here and now. Elsewhere she noted: "We must know the chemistry of the body. We must feed the whole man. We have to have this outer man and have to make the mortar that builds him up. Sometimes the soul gets so anxious about what it wishes to do that it tends to neglect the body. This is not fair to the body or to those who must take care of the body when it is neglected." Indeed, she noted, "Your first duty, then, is to bless your body." One was to praise and nurture the flesh, understanding and supplying all its needs, while ever hoping for the day when subsistence would come through air alone. As she once wrote to a friend, in response to curiosity about the Fillmores' kitchenless home, "Mr. Fillmore and I have not come to the place where we do not eat, although we find more and more the substance in the bread of heaven."[71]

Myrtle Fillmore's desire to live on air, which endures in the latter-day breatharian movement, was shared by many of her New Thought contemporaries, including the animated publisher and author Elizabeth Towne (1865–1960).[72] The journal she founded and published, the *Nautilus*, endured for some time as the most prominent New Thought journal in America, regularly publishing authors such as Ella Wheeler Wilcox, William Walker Atkinson, Edwin Markham, Sinclair Lewis, and Florence Morse Kingsley.[73] Throughout her writings she often advocated fasting, including in the introduction for Wallace D. Wattles's *Health through New Thought and Fasting*, which she also published. Towne's writings are also notable, however, for their concern with physical development. Like Fillmore and the other New Thought writers who looked to a fully spiritual future yet sought to deal concretely with the material realities of the present, Towne worked hard to display for her readers the beautiful harmony between body and mind as a means of giving positive value to daily physical care.

In *Practical Methods for Self-Development: Spiritual—Mental—Physical* (1904), Towne wrestled with the role of food and exercise in a world governed by spirit. "Our food," she noted, "has something to do with the incarnating of ideas," though what that "something" was she could not say with complete confidence: "Just what becomes of assimilated food nobody yet knows. . . . I suspect we really take the soul, the highest of its 'vibrations,' the least dense part of itself, the 'energy,' from what we eat;

much as fire takes the soul or energy from wood. And as the fire leaves an ash, which must be got rid of if we would keep digestion in good order. Neither a choked digestion nor a choked stove will run well." Though careful always to note that food, like all material substance, was comprised simply of thought, Towne held that one's daily fare remained nonetheless an enemy to the higher life of the spirit. "What makes your body hard and dull and burdened? It is clogged with dead or half-dead matter; *which is dead or half-dead thought.*" Yes, food was made of thought, but it was in the form of "condensed mind." "*And condensed mind is mind on the way to death,*" she warned ominously. Though some condensed mind was necessary for sustenance, "our bodies grow *too* substantial, too condensed."[74] Restraint in daily eating, combined with frequent fasts, was the key to physical health and so also the basis of spiritual power, joy, and wisdom.

Towne also considered mental power to be an important motivating force for bodily reduction of this kind. "To reduce flesh the only successful method I know of is that of applying new thought to the reduction of the food supply to fit the real and scientific *needs* of the body," she wrote. What this meant in practice was simple: stop eating, or at least eat less. To the flabby, she advised: "Use your 'new thought' to command your food supply and your 'natural tendencies.' Keep choking off the fat producing foods and using your energies in active physical exercise until you get your body into a healthy, beautiful shape. . . . Fruit, water and air are the great eliminators; and the first thing you need is to have all those stagnant fat cells dissolved and eliminated." Was fat, then, really the product of ill thoughts? Though she had sounded that note before, her chapter on Jack Spratt's wife gave a different answer: "Too much flesh means too much eating, and it *never* means anything else."[75]

Vigorous physical exercise was also important to the work of somatic "combustion" so necessary for health, since it increased oxygen to the body like a damper opened over a fire. Towne turned to the example of children, whom she considered naturally physically active. "A baby," for instance, "is never still. All its running and playing *shakes down the ashes.* This keeps its body clean." But since adults exercised less, breathed less, and ate more than children, they were generally far less healthy—and their systems far more obstructed: "There are ash deposits, lime deposits, uric acid deposits literally at every turn—all for the want of a good shaking down and opening of dampers. We call it 'constipation' or 'indigestion' or 'rheumatism,' or some other long name." What all of these diseases really represented was an overabundance of negative thoughts, which were then incarnated throughout the cells of the body and given no release in exercise and deep breathing.

Without exercise, at any age, the body's ashes would inevitably "clog the fires of life."[76]

Body cells, of course, reflected the situation of the spirit, according to Towne, and yet her musings pointed more substantively to the myriad ways in which corporeal activity created a particular state of mind or spirit. All might well be spirit, as she taught, but not all spirit was created equal. The distinction she drew between free-flowing mind and condensed mind was a fairly tidy one, imagining the two elements less as permeable states along a spectrum than as categories with discernible boundaries and identifying characteristics. Moreover, her method of glossing this distinction—noting the impact of food and exercise upon the individual spirit, for instance— threatened to upend her whole system, unmasking her as a covert materialist. For amid assertions of the primacy of mind—"A dull, heavy, unwieldy body is made up of a preponderance of heavy, dull, unwieldy thought"— Towne relied on physiology as the gateway to spiritual progress. Outlining the process by which exercise drew extra blood to whatever body parts were in motion, she noted, "To breathe enough and exercise enough and eat enough (but not too much) to keep up a positive circulation of blood, is the key to control of thought and feelings as well as body." Which element, body or spirit, was ultimately in charge? Her answer: "Healthy, positive thought cannot be generated in a body whose circulation is persistently uneven or sluggish; and you may depend upon it that the easiest way, and perhaps the only way, to acquire thought control is to establish a positive circulation of blood."[77] Indeed, the longest chapter of Towne's book was that devoted exclusively to physical culture, giving advice on breathing, stretching, bathing, softening and whitening the skin, and pulling the hair to make it grow long and thick. Matter mattered after all.

Towne's manual was followed by Alice M. Long's *My Lady Beautiful: The Harmony of Mind and Body Finds Its Expression in Beauty* (1908), which copiously illustrated many of Towne's most cherished precepts. Long, a New Thought teacher of some repute, described her system as "menti-physical culture" and wrote to women struggling against "weariness, despondency, and ill health" to "grop[e] and reach upward toward the light." Topping its list of regimens for transforming dull lethargy into feminine grandeur was exercise. Long taught readers how to perform a series of "Sara [sic] Bernhardt exercises," utilizing a bamboo wand so as to tone the upper arms, expand the bust ("every well sexed woman desires a beautiful, well rounded bust"), flatten the stomach, improve posture, and "get rid of superfluous flesh." While these exercises would create "the form superb," other tips relating to dress, voice training, proper bathing, and toiletry together helped produce the sum total, a model described by Long as the "winsome woman." New Thought precepts were properly enhanced by these regimens, especially for women, wrote Long: "While the purpose of presenting this book is to guide you in the care of the physical organism, to teach you that only with internal health and cleanliness can there be beauty and wholesomeness, to direct your thoughts to things of a bright and uplifting character, yet I would not have you overlook the little, harmless external aids to further enhance your charms." In other words, as Towne intoned to her listeners, "Faith *and works* will accomplish anything."[78]

Another forward-thinking writer in this regard was Sydney Flower, the Chicago-based publisher of *New Thought* magazine and an explorer of topics such as hypnotism and clairvoyance. In 1921 Flower produced his *New Thought System of Physical Culture and Beauty Culture*, a title that by this time was utterly conventional. In his introduction, Flower noted that the four tools for establishing health were "RIGHT THOUGHT, RIGHT MEDICINE, RIGHT EXERCISE, and RIGHT DIET." In a book dedicated to exercise, Flower proclaimed the conditions of middle age and old age to be "wrong and false": "The only right and proper and natural condition of the physical body and brain is the condition of youth, no matter what your age may be when numbered in years." Flower did not advocate weight lifting for muscular development—he disparaged both Jack Johnson and James Jeffries and called this pursuit a "false god"—but rather promoted what he called "QUICKNESS" as a condensed symbol for "the alert body and the alert brain."[79]

The "ideal human body" would not only be quick but also free from pain, muscular stiffness and soreness, and disease. Furthermore, he argued, "there must be also a comeliness of face, feature, and form" as well as "a feeling of pleasure in mere living, which is the natural heritage of the human body." Humankind had moved far away from that heritage, according to Flower, as witnessed by both men—"fat, bald, short of breath . . . minds gloomy, despairing . . . or hard, bitter"—and women—"too fat for beauty or too thin, . . . cantankerous and unloving, . . . a dreary lot." Speaking like a practiced evangelist, Flower called to his readers: "Let us go back and follow the right road. It is never too late. . . . The way is open, and it is very necessary that we make ourselves over, physically and mentally. It is the thing for us to do that is most worth our while."[80] The journey began with morning breathing and stretching exercises that, Flower insisted, nature intended to be performed—not just anywhere, any time, but "IN BED."

No exercise in the book went much beyond clenching and "hardening" the various muscles of the body in turn. Such actions of contraction and release, accompanied throughout by deep breathing and supplemented by

4. "Bernhardt Exercise A2" (left) and "Horizontal Chinning" (above) from Alice Long, *My Lady Beautiful,* 121, 187.

facial massage, were all that was needed to create the kind of catlike physique that was sought: sleek and soft in repose, rippling with smooth yet steely muscle under the skin, lightning swift in action. Flower's goal was to teach readers to attain "the biggest results with the least effort and in the shortest time." Older venerations of the sheer difficulty of bodily disciplines evaporated with nary a trace, as Flower urged his audience to pursue the quick, simple, and easy. Forget "hard training," weight lifting, running, hard walking, or jumping, he soothed: "Nothing whatever is required of you but the practice of this alternate contraction and relaxation of your muscles by a simple effort of the will." This process would stimulate muscles to "get rid of their waste," tone their fibers, and stir the cells to take in more oxygen, all of which would "convert weak muscle into muscle of quality."[81]

As for other forms of stimulation, Flower took rather a dimmer view, setting narrow limitations around sexual practice that harked back to Ida Craddock and Alice Bunker Stockham. The book's most vehemently written chapter, "The Sex-Instinct; Its Use and Abuse," roared with righteous indignation: "It should be taught in schools, it should be read in books, it should be thundered from pulpits, that a woman pregnant is a woman sealed from a profane touch. Are we lower than our four-footed kindred in the scale of right and wrong that we do not know this, or do not heed it?" Citing Craddock and Stockham, Flower noted the twofold purpose of intercourse as the production of children and the increase of love between spouses. In the latter case, however, the sexual act should never be completed, "neither by the man nor by the woman," so that conjugal love and affection would be increased by means of "perpetual desire of each for each." This was Flower's "inspired truth": "The practice of self-denial in marriage, to the extent of avoiding the completion of the sexual act is, to the student of Physical Culture, desirous of training mind and body to the highest state of excellence, a necessary means of preserving that sexual energy which is the potential of all the sum of his energies, muscular, nervous, mental and spiritual." Once again, the body had the power to disrupt, enervate, and ultimately destroy the purer realm of the spirit.[82]

But that power to destroy was also the power to heal, strengthen, and release from bondage. Flower's chapter on the right diet, essentially a condensed version of his contemporaneous book published as the *New Thought System of Dietetics*, gave food a central role in the nourishment of the body that was also nourishment of the soul. His mediating position on meat eating versus vegetarianism recommended less meat and more vegetables while not excluding the animal kingdom altogether. He separated himself from the more extreme vegetarian diets promoted elsewhere, noting, "If a choice had to be made between beefsteak, on the one hand, or beans, on the other hand, or some pressed compound of walnuts or peanuts . . . we should without hesitation prefer the beefsteak as being more alluring in flavor, more digestible, and more easy of assimilation, conferring greater benefit upon the body." Moderate use of coffee and tea was recommended, and Flower took a soft stance on tobacco, noting optimistically that one could "use tobacco for half a century without any perceptible ill effects."[83]

Most of all, Flower praised the New Thought system of diet as a method by which women and men could liberate themselves from all the "conditions of physical disorder" that beset them, mostly old age and fat. "Our system of exercise and massage holds out to the aging man and woman and to the fat man and woman the means of getting back to normal, and this means, especially for the fat woman, is supplemented by valuable information on the effect of right diet upon the fat-storing properties of the cells."[84] Flower's view on fat, however, was moderated by his awareness of the importance of fat beneath the skin in the creation of beauty. Fat per se was not evil in Flower's view, except when a body carried an overly abundant amount of it. When excessive, however, fat reaped from Flower a disgust that was widespread in America, with many rather more vocal in their denunciations than Flower himself.

What distinguished Flower's plan as an authentic part of the New Thought tradition was clarified in *The New Thought System of Dietetics*. Here Flower praised the well-known and beloved health reformer Horace Fletcher's teachings on thorough mastication and loosely paraphrased the latter as saying, "Fatheads, it matters little WHAT you eat; the important thing is HOW you eat." Flower then highlighted the trajectory of Luigi Cornaro, the obese Italian whose dietary conversion, weight loss, and impressive longevity had made him a model for later health reformers; and yet his commentary on Cornaro was revealing:

> The writer does not hold up before you the example of Luigi Cornaro as a pattern for your guidance. His regimen was too exacting for the multitude. It compelled certain austerities of self-denial which most of us have not the inclination to perform. We argue, and sanely, that there are not so many joys in living that we should voluntarily restrict ourselves to a few crumbs of bread and a thimbleful of wine three times a day as a steady diet, and thereby deny ourselves the satisfaction of eating and drinking good food with enjoyment.

Fletcher was the better example, as one who taught the masses to eat all they wanted so long as their appetite did not advise them to stop. Fletcher's advice was "very comforting," Flower wrote. "No asceticism here. Nothing of the pale martyr about it. Only a protracting of the enjoyment." Eating properly had the reward not simply of health or strength but of enabling one to luxuriate in the delectable quality of food.[85]

Another New Thought writer, David Van Bush, described a rather more stringent diet in his contemporaneous *What to Eat*. The back cover noted Bush as the author of such texts as *Grit and Gumption, The Universality of the Master Mind,* and *Will Power and Success* when he turned to diet; and he perceived no contradiction between his advocacy of a vegetarian raw foods diet—he referred to meat as "corpse"—and his teaching that "Unhappiness, sickness, mental disturbances, bad habits, lack of success and practically all unsatisfactory conditions in life are the result of wrong mental activity and negative thinking."[86] In promoting somatic methods as foundational for the higher things in life, namely spiritual advancement, Bush was merely a man of his time. In 1923 Bush published his fully illustrated encyclopedic manual *Character Analysis: How to Read People at Sight,* whose meticulous readings of body parts—the alimentive double chin, the osseous cheek bones, the muscular neck, the spendthrift thumb—perfectly exemplified the continued coupling of New Thought and phrenology, along with more general theories of correspondence between body and soul. Reserving his fullest contempt for the alimentive "type"—"The fat man is the baby of the race"—Bush indicated the convergence of teachings within the New Thought tradition that worked to demonize fat and worship thin. The peculiar spiritual underpinnings of this devotional matrix hardly hampered its appeal for ordinary Americans; far more, as later chapters clarify, the religious links invested the classificatory scheme of body types with righteous certainty and power. As typological procedures simultaneously gained ground in other realms, the degree to which character was readable upon the body seemed virtually inescapable.

While New Thought writers often seemed to be saying that personal power was accessed by means of mind energy alone, for many the *body* was the real source of might, site of potential transformation, and basis for revealing the inner truth about the human self. Though New Thought disciples remained apprehensive about materiality and doggedly insisted upon the ultimate power of spirit, they and their positive-thinking therapeutic progeny would intensify the already strenuous attention devoted to the flesh. Marginal as an organized movement by midcentury, New Thought filtered its suppositions about thought power shaping physical reality through elite sectors of American society then and later, including religious groups (evangelicals, among others) who had little else in common with such reputedly crackpot ideologies but who turned out to be, on similar albeit not identical grounds, stalwart defenders of beautiful bodies. Such concerns, we well know, were by no means limited to some sphere narrowly defined as the religious: America's manic pursuit of health that New Thought served and intensified until the activity became its own supposed type of religion still echoes the old theme of body as dangerous yet revelatory of purity and perfection, or else filth and decay. Elusively, but by no means insubstantially, New Thought played a key role in helping assemble the framework within which the bodily preoccupations of later Americans would take shape.

The New Thought movement did not materialize only out of spiritualized air, of course. Indeed, horror at particular types of bodies—Gestefeld's gutter drunks and Mulford's dark races, among others—played a crucial role in the formation of New Thought, a system that did not spiritualize all matter in the way of Christian Science so much as aim to distinguish between pure matter and pollution and to separate good bodies from bad. Again, this fixation within New Thought carried weight in other parts of the culture generally, aided by discourses in medicine (eugenics, dietetics, and eventually bariatrics, or the science of obesity) that enabled its doctrine of the perfectible body to prevail. The notion that New Thought opposed the body is correct only in the sense that many New Thought thinkers, especially those who came out of Christian Science, endeavored to deny the body a primary role and placed mind above materiality in the hierarchy of power. All the same, they played out their passions upon living bodies, closely scrutinized for signs of self-control or dissolution and attuned to promises of beauty, longevity, corresponding suppression and fulfillment of desire. New Thought advocates posited no end of dietary regimens, exercise routines, and recommendations for personal toiletry, recurrently betraying a presumption that the body was ultimately the true source of might—that the mind could not really do it all alone.

In sum, New Thought advocates persuaded of the body's crucial import to the life of the self in its fullest capacity sharply countered the conviction of Eddy and others that mind or consciousness was the only reality worth considering. Quarrels in New Thought literature over mind, matter, and spirit were also, as Satter has rightly contended, deeply resonant of broader issues and problems within American culture at the time. But where Satter sees these debates as a gendered power struggle between white middle-class men and women, a more powerful undercurrent may have been one in which status-conscious women and men joined forces to urge their fellow citizens to rise and grasp hold of the felt destiny of their civilization, realizing the potential inherent in self-mastery to promote the new and perfect race. This is not to say that gender was not an issue; after all, many female New Thought writers spent their careers writing books only for women, and not a few were suffragists who contributed to Elizabeth Cady Stanton's massive *Woman's Bible.* Rather, other issues of identity and power loomed large in the quarters populated by advantaged spiritual proponents, enabling white middle-class women and men to join together in furthering their shared interests.

New Thought writers aimed to raise their readership to a higher awareness of the power of self-mastery and control, qualities allegedly made visible on the flesh. As anxious warnings about obesity, dissipation, and infantilism repeatedly made plain, sloth, greed, and vice were just as transparently perceptible in the body. The pure civilization could not make headway so long as its citizenry stank of filthy habits and capitulated to poisonous appetites. New Thought leaders alternately upbraided and flattered their followers in hopes of making good citizens who would transcend the maddening limits of physicality and soar high with spirits and angels. Here, in this airy religion of the mind, bodies were formed anew.

3 Minding the Body

*Divergent Paths of
New Thought Perfectionism*

The spread of New Thought's cultural influence is not easy to map, especially since so many of its distinctive themes overlapped and merged with other motifs in American Christianity and culture. A hodgepodge of psychological and physiological techniques for attaining health, wealth, and happiness took many forms in Pentecostal circles, for instance, as preachers and healers such as Aimee Semple McPherson, William Branham, and Oral Roberts insisted that such blessings were part of God's plan for all obedient believers. The early twentieth century also witnessed a rising interest in particular physical routines that proponents taught would have a profound effect upon the strength and longevity of the nation's populace. By this time, in fact, Anglo-American diet reformers were achieving favorable success in their quest to demonize flab and preach brawn as necessary to economic and spiritual salvation. Progressive advocates inspired by New Thought culled fresh meaning out of texts ranging from ancient scriptures to contemporary eugenic and hygienic literature, inspired to do so by their own disgust and dismay at the degradations of modern urban life that ostensibly turned men into milksops and healthy bodies into mere repositories of disease and sludge. In this crusade for purification and power, appetite restraint played a key role. Disciplined flesh formed the compliant receptacle for the satisfaction of inward desires—the source of true fulfillment. Purged, regulated, and self-contained, those who purposefully abstained from excess would reap extraordinary fortune.

Various spiritually motivated channels to power and happiness developed followings, both within Anglo-American circles and also outside them. Even those that diverged widely in ideology, however, shared a central emphasis on physical practice and appearance as revelatory of much deeper, otherwise invisible truths. As New Thought aged over the first half of the twentieth century, its varied teachers continued to preach bodily perfection—assuring audiences that internal and external selves had far more to do with one another than previous generations may have imagined—but did so in dramatically disparate ways. This chapter looks at some of the salient consequences of New Thought perfectionism in three distinct venues: the health craze of fasting in the early twentieth century; William Sheldon's religious psychology and somatotyping procedures; and racialized theologies of divine materialization in Father Divine's Peace Mission movement and Elijah Muhammad's black nationalist Islam. While none of these projects became so enduring, widespread, or revolutionary as their formulators believed they were destined to be, all illuminate much broader corporeal themes in American culture that were influenced by metaphysical hopes.

LIVING ON AIR: GOSPELS OF FASTING, CONQUEST, AND PURGATION

"Starve and Be a Samson!" This invitation opened an illustrated article in the *New York World* in 1907, describing the well-known bodybuilder and athlete Gilman Low, who trained for his popular weight-lifting feats by living abstemiously on one light meal per day. Later that same year, experimenting with ever smaller amounts of food, Low endured a series of seven- to fifteen-day fasts, after which he performed further weight-lifting exhibitions in venues such as Madison Square Garden. Elaborating on the increased power he received while abstaining entirely from food during one such occasion, Low issued a forceful challenge to medical skeptics in a letter: "At the end of my fifteen-day fast . . . I could have thrashed my weight in wildcats. If the doctors . . . think a man will be so weak in a week's time he cannot walk, I will fast fifteen days and if any two of them can handle me (in any way suitable to them) I will give them each $100." The reliability of these swaggering assertions was corroborated by the letter's recipient, the osteopathic physician Irving James Eales, who chronicled his own thirty-one-day fast in *Healthology*, his 1907 book written in muscular prose with photographs to match.[1]

Low's burly sales pitch for fasting, no less than Eales's own, was by no means original, either in content or tone. Both were directly inspired by male-authored texts going back several years, Progressive Era volumes that stressed the religious roots of fasting (looking to Jesus as the prototype of strength in abstinence, for instance) while yet accentuating fasting's worldly benefits. When Low bragged of his increased virility or Eales wrote of the manly figures whose health had been restored by fasting, they fit into an

5. Gilman Low, from Irving James Eales, *Healthology*, across from 86. Low performed a number of weight-lifting exhibitions after extended fasts.

established pattern of Protestant male fitness writers convinced that food abstinence was the secret to virility and a key to the regeneration of the Anglo-American race as a whole. "Jesus was no ascetic," warned the evangelist Billy Sunday, but a "robust, red-blooded man"; while the businessman Bruce Barton later enthused about the "physically powerful and handsome" Jesus who was "the founder of modern business." Unlike the evangelicals, however, this innovative crop of New Thought fitness writers made food abstinence the key to strength and masculine subjectivity. As Upton Sinclair (1878–1968) wrote in the first of two books devoted to health and fasting, the present day witnessed "a movement of moral regeneration," exemplified in each individual's "conscious effort . . . to eliminate his own unfitness" and supported harmoniously by Christian Science, New Thought, and contemporary health reform.[2]

Nearly all advocates of fasting between 1890 and 1930—Edward Hooker Dewey, Charles Haskell, Bernarr Macfadden, J. Austin Shaw, Irving James Eales, Hereward Carrington, Robert Baille Pearson, Edward Earle Purinton, Upton Sinclair, Wallace D. Wattles, and Frank McCoy, for example—were male.[3] In one way or another, they explicitly connected their own experience

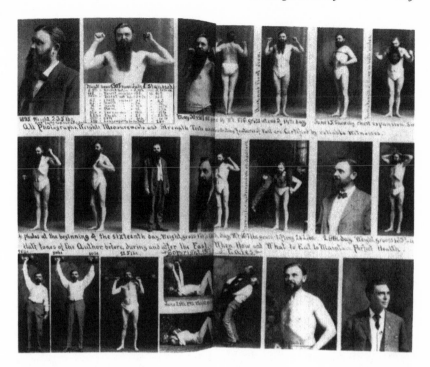

6. Images of strength during a thirty-one-day fast, from Irving James Eales, *Healthology,* front matter.

of fasting to virility and defended the practice as intrepid and heroic—a clear sign of (or path to) financial and social success that would invigorate the race. Eager to record their experiences in print, these vigorous fasters displayed a near-consuming fixation on the body's interior and exterior functions and, more precisely, on purification, disciplined self-control, and the pleasurable pain of food refusal. These preoccupations, incidentally, were already clinically associated with anorexia nervosa, a condition first identified by British, French, and American doctors during the 1870s and linked for half a century with that most thoroughly feminized of illnesses, hysteria.[4] But since male advocates of the fast generally ate plentifully when not fasting, refused food only at set intervals and for bounded durations, and carefully marked their behavior as masculine, they were able to elude pathologization as anorexic.

Dewey's 1895 book, *The True Science of Living,* subtitled "The New Gospel of Health," was a masterpiece of drama, a sermonic tour de force that nearly all subsequent fasting masters cited as their inspiration. It blended the persuasive intimacy of the revivalist, the zeal of the social reformer, and the scientific precision of the medical professional to articulate a dietary plan for health and moral uplift that the physician and onetime Civil War field surgeon claimed as his own "original discovery." Dewey's text had been reprinted at least four times in the United States and Britain by 1908 and was followed by an even more successful sequel, *The No-Breakfast Plan and the Fasting Cure* (1900), which was translated into French and German and entered a third American edition in 1921, seventeen years after its author's death. The central tenet of Dewey's gospel was fairly simple: abstain completely from breakfast, thereby consuming only two meals per day, and eat these only when "natural hunger" calls for food. Virtually all physiological evils began with excessive eating, gorging oneself on immoderate quantities of food out of habit or "morbid hunger" (as opposed to the "natural," calmer kind). Diseases of all sorts took hold in overfed bodies, whose cells fairly groaned under the weight of this extravagance and whose exhausted defenses were laid too low to prevent the entrance of foreign adversaries.

Even crime was a product of intemperate habits that began in the nursery, a site that Dewey held responsible "for more human misery, more of lunacy, of homicide, of suicide, of disease, of pestilence, of premature ending of lives, infinitely more than can be charged to the saloon, because infinitely more universal." Mothers carried heavy blame in this gendered discourse, and Christian women especially had to accept their accessory role: echoing William Andrus Alcott, Dewey called church suppers "life-depressing . . . sin-enticing repasts" that should be obliterated altogether. He further called male pastors to account for "go[ing] into your pulpits with loaded stomachs to teach the word of life," when instead they ought to undergo a solemn Sunday fast and uphold their duty to "be our highest types of physical as well as of spiritual life." Dewey was so certain of the magnitude of ills caused by overeating that he called for "a new W.C.T.U. [Woman's Christian Temperance Union] association" to wage a "war on irregular feedings," instructing all citizens to avoid excess and to fast when sick or out of sorts.[5] In practically every imaginable instance, the key to exchanging illness for health, vice for virtue, and social chaos for order was a sincere, thorough, and extended fast.

Abstinence was the key to individual and social regeneration because it inculcated both virtue and fortitude. Restraint in eating, like other forms of self-control, was a sacrifice that elevated practitioners to a higher humanity and an improved fulfillment of their social and domestic roles. Dewey counseled his readers, "If you are Christians, you will become a great deal better Christians; if husbands, a great deal better husbands; if wives, a great deal better wives; if parents, you will be a great deal more kindly, considerate, reasonable in all your relations to your children. There will be such moral strength added that in all your relations to the family, to the church and society you will become *better, stronger men and women."* Habits of work would also be fortified by means of the fast, with workers more punctual, economical, and dynamic than before. By focusing on heightened productivity, Dewey persistently appealed to fasting as a manly practice, one with Franklinesque overtones of restraint and self-discipline. This view was ever linked with Dewey's insistence that fasting was a cure for debility-inducing illnesses such as neurasthenia, which sapped their victims' pep and drained energy from the workplace. Extreme food reduction appropriately suited the period's capitalist ethic of increased, efficient production.[6]

Dewey was well aware of fasting's ancient devotional meanings, though he refrained from stressing them directly; his health plan was, in any case, far too dependent on "cheer of mind" to traffic in repentance or mortification.[7] Yet as an active Protestant writing to a largely Protestant audience, he sought throughout to affirm the harmony between his own gospel of health and the Christian gospel. The introduction to Dewey's *True Science of Living*, written by the famed evangelist George Frederick Pentecost (1842–1920), gave the entire endeavor a distinctly Christian spin and traced out key scriptural passages to buttress the orthodoxy of Dewey's plan. To overeat, Pentecost argued, was to "defile the body" and was thus "an offence against our salvation and the honor of God." More concretely, "to deliberately undermine the health and strength of the body by persisting in an injurious . . . way of living, is a sin of great enormity." Like drunkenness, gluttony was an "offence against both body and soul which no self-respecting person, not to say Christian, ought for a moment to allow."[8] Pentecost's language echoed the older reformist tradition of Alcott and Graham, not to mention George Cheyne and John Wesley, but it was Dewey whom the Reverend Pentecost, like so many who came later, esteemed as the originating sage of such wisdom.

Drawn to Dewey's confidently prophetic voice, his modern "discovery" and repackaging of an old religious practice, or perhaps merely his simple promise to restore health to all who followed him, a vast and motley parade of apostles soon entered the scene, expanding and popularizing Dewey's gospel of fasting to a degree he could scarcely have imagined. One of the most important of these was Charles Haskell, Dewey's friend and publisher who grandly titled his own 1901 disquisition *Perfect Health: How to Get It and How to Keep It, by One Who Has It.* Like virtually all health reformers before and since, Haskell laid claim to a long history of disease and despair prior to his discovery of fasting as the path to "perfect health." In the midst of one financial crisis, feeling defeated and decidedly unmanly, exhausted in body and mind, Haskell took comfort in modeling himself after a rather more famous sufferer:

> For a time life and death seemed to balance evenly in the scales. I was in the distress and darkness of Gethsemane and before me was the cross. It did not seem possible that my mind could stand the awful strain that was upon it, but through "The New Gospel of Health" and two good angels who stood faithfully by me, I was enabled to . . . come out into *peace, life* and *safety,* and to have Perfect Health of body and Perfect Health of mind, which is "The Kingdom of God within you."

Like any good convert, Haskell was motivated to share his "good news" with others, writing that Dewey's plan "had indeed proved 'A Gospel'" to him and his wife, and that they "desired above all things to give it to other sufferers." Haskell's histrionic writing was drenched in biblical language and reached out to its audience with an urgency that bordered on pathos. He took pride in printing effusive, weepy testimonies from multiple "disciples" of this gospel so as to circulate the "glad tidings" it was destined to bring to all humankind. Haskell's text was to serve as the authoritative commentary on Dewey's scriptures, and he gave joyful praise that "Thou has made known to me the ways of life."[9]

Haskell himself did not add anything new to Dewey's dietary regimen, only undergirding it more thoroughly with a spiritual foundation deeply indebted to the New Thought currents of his day. Like his mentor, he was particularly enamored of the virtue of self-control that fasting cultivated, noting that this was the Apostle Paul's true meaning in the scriptural verse, "I keep my body *under* and bring it into subjection." But if Haskell was a latter-day Paul, polishing another man's gospel while paying homage to the man himself, reformers with loftier ambitions also emerged, vying to be crowned a new messiah. The first of these was Bernarr Macfadden (1868–1955), owner of the Physical Culture Publishing Company and destined for later notoriety as the editor of such popular magazines as *True Romances* and *True Detective Stories*. The pompous Macfadden was a laughingstock to many for flamboyantly displaying his own developed musculature (and a bane to Anthony Comstock for featuring scantily clad male and female bodies in his theatric exhibitions), and he remained a controversial figure throughout his adult life. Despite his indecorous behavior (or perhaps because of it), his magazine *Physical Culture,* launched in 1899, as well as his many published books drew a wide audience of readers concerned to improve their physiques and enrich their lives. Ever committed to the project of reinvigorating urban and suburban mollycoddles, of remasculinizing the once robust race of white American men whose muscles had turned to mush, Macfadden published his first book on fasting in 1900, claiming his own inspiration and originality in discovering this remarkable antidote to softness. Macfadden treated fasting in many writings during the several decades after *Fasting-Hydropathy-Exercise*, briefly in *Superb Virility of Manhood* (1904) and more expansively in *Macfadden's Encyclopedia of Physical Culture* (originally published in 1911–12 and periodically revised into the early 1940s) and *Fasting for Health* (1923, 1934), among others.[10]

Where Dewey and Haskell had expected fasting to cultivate virtue, Macfadden took for granted that the real appeal, the attraction that would make men hunger for greater and greater bouts of abstinence, was the experience of absolute power evoked by a fast. Through fasting, Macfadden promised, a person could exercise unqualified control over virtually all types of disease while revealing a degree of strength and stamina such as would put others to shame. In short, fasting was a stunning weapon of mastery, an instrument with which to prove one's superiority over menacing perils ranging from microbes to men. Nor did Macfadden hesitate to puff his program's redemptive implications; the first chapter opened with the reverberating evangelical question, "What shall we do to be saved?" and implicitly assured readers that salvation was to be found not along the sawdust trail but in the regimens propounded in his book. "Civilized man" needed to throw off the artificial tastes and cultivated habits accrued over time, in favor of the practices observable in animals and "primitive" people (one of Macfadden's favorite subjects). This shift would restore the lost strength and vitality that every man supposedly coveted, enabling him to conquer all that was debilitating and feminizing about modern civilization.[11]

Macfadden's philosophy was basic enough: in all things, trust nature, and employ only "natural" remedies to heal disease and maintain health. The body was a "self-regulating apparatus," a "house that cleanses its own chambers" of intrusive substances when properly cared for. What made this system malfunction were the "baneful . . . superstitions" that caused people to mistake "poison for food" and to pour toxic substances into the body until the physical self developed cravings for excessive aliment (especially meat), drugs, and alcohol, which the unwitting spiritual self would dutifully supply. Eventually this overabundance of toxins would so thoroughly deplete a person's vigor that constant sickness and premature death would result. The cure was not mere avoidance of overeating (which hardly proved one's hardiness) but protracted, cleansing fasts. Fasting during times of illness was instinctive (and hence "natural"), freeing the body's vital energies that were normally monopolized by digestion to be utilized in the war against disease. No virus or microbe stood "a living chance against that method of expurgation." Whenever the warning signs of impending illness appear, Macfadden urged, cease all food intake and let the body concentrate its energies on ridding the house of unwanted intruders, sweeping out germs like so much "rubbish." Example piled upon example certified that in virtually every case—influenza, asthma, catarrh, even cancer—this remedy would reap success. Most important of all, fasting could restore that "superb virility of manhood" so easily enfeebled by decadence, laziness, sedentary lifestyles, and ill health.[12]

How long to fast? In general, Macfadden recommended a seven-day recess from food. Even a fast of two days' duration, however, would do some good, especially for those inclined toward gluttony. The dilemma, for Macfadden as for other devotees of abstinence, was how to persuade a food-loving audience of fasting's benefits. Macfadden, himself an open lover of pleasure and an advocate of frequent, vigorous sexual intercourse, did not exactly sing the joys of austere living; instead, he marketed his plan by arguing that brief periods of fasting were pleasurable in and of themselves and, even more, in their results. Forget humiliation and repentance: "No need of aggravating the sickness of dyspeptics by mentioning the 'duty of self-denial,' and evok[ing] visions of spiritual advisers helping themselves to the assets of world-renouncing idiots," he wrote acidly. Rather than glamorize ascetics and mystics, Macfadden defended fasting "from the epicuric point of view": food would be relished more thoroughly, rest would be sweeter than before. In short, fasting opened the way to a richer savoring of bodily experience.[13]

Macfadden took perhaps his own greatest pleasure in exhibiting his expertly chiseled body, finely carved not simply through exercise but also, and just as important, by means of fasting. His entire oeuvre was filled with naked photographs of his sinewy frame, as he performed feats of strength or simply posed in likeness of classical sculpture. A number of these images were "before and after" shots of a fast, the "after" pictures depicting a leaner, meaner Macfadden whose veins and muscles strained almost to bursting out of the tight skin that overlay them. Through these powerful visual representations (which other fasting masters would also utilize), he presented himself as the perfect model of robust strength and beauty to which his readers, and most especially his male readers, could aspire: the exquisitely fit, hale, and hearty body, as immune to disease as it was scornful of weakness. For Macfadden, the body was no mere receptacle of some elusive higher self but a "machine that thinks," as he often put it, the final evolution of which was to be the "superman" of physical supremacy.[14] Fasting, the body's literal

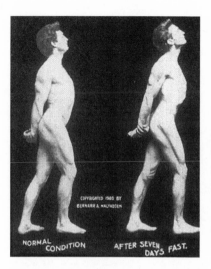 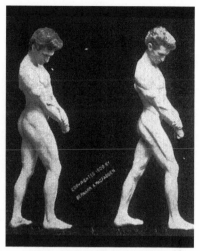

7. "Normal Condition" and "After Seven-Day Fast," two views from Bernarr Macfadden, *Fasting-Hydropathy-Exercise*, 74, 80. Macfadden enjoyed displaying his muscular body, made tauter by fasting.

victory over its own craven desires and dependencies, was a crucial tool in this progression, the key to winning life's perennial battle against fragility.

A comparative glance back at Alice Long's contemporaneous manual of physical culture for women, *My Lady Beautiful*, suggests just how much this language of food abstinence was explicitly gendered male. Besides the exercise regimens noted before, Long advised female readers, both obese and thin, to sip water throughout the day, using auto-suggestion to declare: "Every time I sip I shall say to myself, this will give me a good, healthy appetite and I shall be hungry, hungry, hungry for each meal and every mouthful of food I eat will taste good and digest thoroughly. . . . I shall feel hungry, hungry, hungry every morning; for the body must be supplied with nourishment, as the engine is supplied with coal, that the machinery may be kept in working order." Long addressed herself as much to readers seeking to gain weight as those wishing to reduce, and far greater priority was given to the mastery of facial expression and emotions, along with the need for sunshine and fresh air for clearing the complexion and promoting health, than to dietary laws or the precise shape of the body. While the foundation of mental, moral, and spiritual life was taught to be a "strong and healthy body"—"for it is that through which the real I must function"—such a body was attained through satiation, rather than restraint. The life essentials—air, sunshine, food and water—were to be taken "in proportion to the needs of the body." Readers pledged, "Every day I shall exercise in the fresh air and sunshine; I shall eat nourishing food and drink an abundance (at least two quarts) of good, pure water."[15] Such habits produced the smooth complexion, sparkling eyes, rosy cheeks, and spry step that were the markers of womanly perfection. Outside anorexia, fasting played no tangible role in the fashioning of female subjectivity, though the body-as-factory undertones link Long's approach to the dreams loitering amid abstinence, hinting again at a shared motif in contemporary physical culture manuals of sacralizing the market economy.

Only two women wrote well-known treatises on fasting similar to those produced by male writers: Linda Burfield Hazzard, a physician, and Julia Seton, an author of many New Thought and occultist books. We have already seen how Elizabeth Towne also advocated fasting in some of her writings, such as *Practical Methods for Self-Development,* but she did not focus on the practice as intently as Hazzard and Seton; moreover, her own commentary on fasting focused on the masculinist example of the muscular showman Gilman Low. While Hazzard's book was often cited as authoritative by her male counterparts, especially Macfadden, her career was blotted by the 1912 death of a fasting patient at her Seattle sanatorium and Hazzard's subsequent two-year prison sentence. With her reputation thus sullied, Hazzard's appeal diminished. It is worth noting, however, that Hazzard's book was more explicit than those of her male counterparts in claiming that the fast would diminish sexual desire to its proper proportions, reducing its excesses to a "normal" condition and leaving the passions "controlled and in all senses subservient to will." Menstrual difficulties entirely disappeared, as menses ceased during the fast only to return "odorless and healthy in appearance." The copious monthly flow from human females resulted, after all, from thousands of years of "perversion" in which the sexual organs were used "for other than legitimate purposes": pleasure over procreation.[16] Similar to Alice Stockham's *Karezza,* Hazzard's text urged men and women alike to achieve better health through a disciplined sexuality. Male authors couched that theme rather differently, as when Macfadden insisted upon his own sexual prowess or when Irving James Eales, the osteopathic doctor who recounted Gilman Low's experiences as well as his own in *Healthology,* exulted that even his "sex powers" were invigorated by the fast.[17] As a preponderantly masculine genre, fasting literature typically focused on sexual discipline only to support eugenic reproductive programs.

Therapeutic fasters of the era also sought to harmonize materiality with transcendence, cresting the heights of spiritual enlightenment while basking in earthly and bodily gratification. Fasting healed, according to many writ-

8. "Winsome Woman," from Alice Long, *My Lady Beautiful*, 37.

ers, because it enabled the spirit to soar above and beyond the body, free from the animalistic, even grotesque indignity of eating. Edward Earle Purinton (1878–1945), the widely read author of such success manuals as *The Triumph of the Man Who Acts* and *Efficient Living* as well as *Personal Efficiency in Business*, voiced this dualism in his *Philosophy of Fasting* (1906): "There is no enduring power save transcendence of soul. Money tarnishes, fame withers, friendship wanes, beauty fades, success palls and worlds end in dust. But to the soul that can leave the mortal when it chooses, sustaining itself on air, water, light, faith and love—there are no limitations, no disappointments, no doubts, no fears, no disabilities, no misunderstandings, no tremors whatsoever."[18]

For the soul to endure on ethereal things, the body would have to do the same, and writers like Purinton urged fasting not predominantly for physical health or beauty (at least not as ends in themselves) but for spiritual well-being, empowerment, and virtue. This insistence on abstinence as the key to attaining all one's desires signaled a powerful aversion, not so much to the body qua material substance as to the vulgar limitations of corporeality, its pathetic vulnerability and untrustworthiness, its conflated needs and desires. In that sense, the visionary dream of these fasters was to discover the means by which they could go without eating altogether, living only, as Purinton had it, on "air, water, light, faith and love."

Haskell himself manifested that hope when, in one of his published letters to J. Austin Shaw during the latter's forty-five-day fast, he expressed his intention to visit Mollie Fancher, the young Brooklyn woman renowned for her extended fasting (which turned out to be fraudulent). "She is certainly a very remarkable person, and she shows how little food one can subsist upon," wrote Haskell wistfully. "If she could be in the open air where she could breathe in more of the tonic of life from the atmosphere, I think she would live all right without even the fruit juice." After Shaw had finally broken his fast, Haskell urged him to remain vigilant against falling again into excess. "See how little you need to eat in order to keep yourself in equilibrium and at your normal weight. If it is but one ounce a day, then let it be that, and if it takes two ounces or more, let it be whatever you need. Every ounce of earth matter that you accumulate in your body detracts from your strength." Fasting was indeed a sacred activity, because it purified the "Divine Temple" and established the spirit's ascendancy over the insubordinate body.[19]

New Thought advocates, patently disenchanted with what they perceived to be an overly routinized this-worldly Protestantism, craved the magic and mysticism of an older faith. Obsessed with transcending the dreariness of the body, they longed to live on air. The publisher's introduction to Wattles's *Health through New Thought and Fasting* invoked as a model for readers the heroic figure of Atlas, "standing on air, living on air and lifting the earth." The writer looked forward to the day when the body would store enough material not only for a fast of forty, fifty, or sixty days but for "eternal famine," a blessed state of perennial abstinence. Wallace D. Wattles (1860–1911) argued that human powers of strength were not drawn from food at all; instead, "food is to the human body what the soil is to a plant—merely raw material; tissue elements, to be built into the organism, but not in any sense a source of life." Vital power, the life force that sustained a person's energy, was received into the body during sleep through the brain; it had literally nothing to do with what one ate. The belief that life had any material basis was a well-worn fallacy, sighed Wattles: "We are spiritual beings; we get our life in the Great Silence, out of which we came. We shall live after we cease to eat, for we do not live by eating now; our physical bodies are kept up by a mysterious power which comes to us while we are unconscious. God is Spirit; and He giveth life to all." Since vital power did not come from food, fasting—and living daily on as little nutriment as possible—could open the

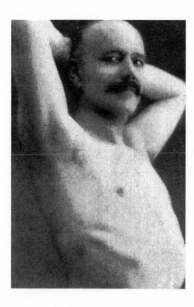

9. J. Austin Shaw, on day forty of a forty-five-day fast, from Hereward Carrington, *Vitality, Fasting, and Nutrition,* across from 206.

door to the possibility not only of spiritual immortality but also of eternal physical immortality, the theme of Wattles's penultimate chapter.[20]

This decorporealized philosophy of fasting seems a pointed repudiation of the versions espoused by some other fasting masters, whose goals for abstinence were frankly carnal—muscular strength and even sensual experience for the likes of Macfadden. Indeed, this conflict over "spirit" or mind versus "matter" or body was one in which Americans more generally were deeply embroiled around the turn of the century, a debate in which clear definitions of manliness and womanliness were supremely at stake. As Beryl Satter has persuasively argued, this broad cultural debate, engaged by New Thought authors no less than social theorists, feminists, reformers, and physicians, centered on the contested meaning of desire. The question at hand was whether "desire" itself—for wealth, pleasure, materiality, power, or simply individual autonomy—should be denied, as befitted the austere norms of late Victorian propriety, or celebrated, suiting the dynamic ideal appropriate for a progressive, consumer-oriented civilization.[21] For New Thought writers like Haskell and Wattles who wrestled with this dilemma, fasting could be utilized as a check against excess, a hopeful summons to the realization that matter was utterly insignificant and desire, therefore, patently senseless. The path to heaven was paved not with corrupt desire but with virtuous renunciation.

At the same time, however, the discourse of fasting was lithe enough to adapt itself for antithetical ends. Seton, one of the occasional female fasting writers, posited a literal distinction between the "misfit food body" (the site of old age) and the "life body" that was "young, fresh, unwrinkled, not fat or flabby nor skinny, but just whole." To one dismayed by the burden of his or her own flesh, Seton's vision, revealed in *The Short Cut—Regeneration through Fasting* (1929), was appealing indeed. Extended abstinence, according to Seton, erased the tell-tale signs that mental and physical stress had imprinted upon the body's features. It also proved that the body's willful, petulant greed, manifested as much in double chins and wrinkles as in hunger pangs and stomach growls, could be disciplined and the spirit freed for higher work. Together with conscious breathing and exercise, fasting enabled the life cells to create a "new flesh suit" of whatever type one chose, changing face or form as easily as clothes. Desire, then, was ambivalent: to want food was a source of shame, while to want a whole new body was perfectly appropriate and deserving of fulfillment. Even more, the fat-free, flab-free "whole" body was the body truly fit for spiritual ends—"misfit" bodies merely languished on the sidelines. In Seton's view, the flesh should be an index of what lived beneath it, the authentic self within.[22]

For those occupying more obstreperous bodies, whose beastlike voracity seemed to know no bounds, authors offered another kind of comfort. The more rebellious the carnal substance, after all, the more the spiritual self could revel in its mastery over this chastened savage, a mastery that extended far beyond the disciplined self. More important, this phraseology of forceful dominance seized the desireless state from late Victorian femininity, realigning it with the cause of sovereign, masculine power. Purinton, for instance, labeled his special mode of fasting the "Conquest Fast," describing it as "a combination of the early Church Fast with the modern Therapeutic Fast." The benefits of this Conquest Fast were multiple: it would sever one's "thralldom" to useless things and people, reveal the "insignificance of the brain," refine one's faculties of reason, and "perpetuate the joy of living." Above all, however, Purinton noted that the Conquest Fast had revealed to him his "oneness with Omnipotence."

Even as Purinton continued to rhapsodize about both regular fasting and spiritual pursuits in later published writings, his practical side soon emerged forcefully into view, as the author entered business and redirected his time to the furtherance of the "efficiency" dogma that so captivated American engineers, businessmen, workers, scientists, and housewives during the 1910s.[23] Wattles followed a similar career path, writing a variety of success manuals with titles like *The Science of Getting Rich* (1910) and *The Science of Being Great* (1911), editions of which have been translated into French and Spanish and reissued into the 1990s. Both Purinton and Wattles blended themes of sacrificial austerity, business efficiency, and the pleasures of consumer-oriented success, effecting their rapprochement not simply in bodily metaphors but, more important, by means of physical practices that promised omnipotent control over need as well as desire. The careers of Purinton and Wattles, among other fasters writing in the same vein, display how the practice of fasting resonated with the self-help literature that relied on and fortified market capitalism, even among seekers unlikely to reap its grandest fruits. Indeed, because fasting could incorporate the themes of excess and renunciation so exhaustively, the ideology of fasting could perform crucially important work in service to that market system. The New Thought currents of the day cloaked fasting in the sacred garb of mystical transcendence without undermining its profoundly materialist ends. Fasting's ultimate enticement, eternal life, may have remained unrealized, but its intermediate pleasures, from weight loss and purification to the felt experiences of strength, control, and transcendence, would live on for many hopeful seekers of regeneration, men and women alike.

Before Dewey and Macfadden popularized food avoidance, few if any people conceived of the fast in terms of ordinary therapeutic practice, valor, or vitality. Above all, these expert fasters shared a keen curiosity about ingestion and expurgation, a fascination with all that entered and exited the body's orifices. While this was a familiar topic of interest and concern, articulated by both medical physicians and natural healers concerned about America's dietary excesses, fasting advocates were especially fervent about both somatic interiority and the mysterious outer limits of abstinence and consequently wrote in a different vein altogether. It was this symbolic repertoire used by fasting advocates to convert their American audiences— a repertoire easily tuned to play on timely anxieties about race, gender, and national identity while prompting and relentlessly exploiting a severe dread of personal filth and death—that gave fasting renewed power.[24]

The sensuous, even autoerotic dimensions of fasting emerge from the lavish descriptions writers gave of all aspects of the process: the carefully selected last meal eaten before a fast; the roaring pain of hunger during the fast's early days; the cool liquids sipped and savored in place of food; the bloated stomach and fetid gas expelled from the body; the minutely measured size, substance, and smell of one's excrement during a fast—a prize obtained through compulsively repetitive enemas; the color and viscosity of the urine; the foul breath and coated tongue, assurances that so much poison was being swept from the body; the hot and icy cold baths; the daily weighing and measuring of one's chest and waist dimensions; the ritualistic planning of the foods with which one would break the fast, down to the smallest ounce; the willingness to cook and serve rich, fragrant meals to family and friends without touching a single morsel oneself; the climactic photographs of the fasting body, defiantly posed to convey strength, beauty, and vitality; the strenuous daily exercise carried on throughout. Fasters reveled in their bodies with lush self-absorption, entranced by the effluvia that passed out of them as much as by their seeming attainment of utter emptiness. As these enthusiasts weighed and documented every substance ingested, each visible and tactile change in the body, and most of all every smell and particle that exited its orifices, materiality was at one and the same time wondrously revered and violently extirpated.

Nothing better illustrates this dynamic of bodily sanctification and revilement than the obstinate longing for odorless excrement, a concern in keeping with (but more frequently mentioned than) Hazzard's odorless menstrual blood. The turn-of-the-century reformer Horace Fletcher, whose teachings on mastication had so pervasively reached the middle and upper classes, had already planted the notion that healthy intestines produced only infrequent and perfectly scent-free stools, which he preferred to call "ash." The offensive smell of most bowel movements, Fletcher asserted, was simply a sign of poor eating habits and meant that poisons had been trapped in the body. Odoriferous feces were, quite literally, toxic waste. Fasting advocates, similarly committed to ridding the world of this putrid stuff, effused about the marvelously innocuous excrement that passed from their bodies toward the end of a fast, proclamations often preceded by almost unbearably vivid descriptions of what had come before. The scatologically obsessed Robert Baille Pearson (b. 1880), a construction engineer who daily collected and probed his own evacuations and who advised readers to take enemas of up to thirty quarts per day during a fast, published an exceedingly graphic account of his own experience, describing how "large quantities of catarrhal mucus came out with the foulest excrement," until eventually "the excreta became perfectly odorless." Pearson also noted that though he had read Horace Fletcher's book *The A.B.–Z. of Our Own Nutrition* years earlier, he had "utterly failed to attain odorless excrement" until his technical experiments in fasting.[25]

Like other fasters, Pearson was indignant that the mainstream medical profession dismissed routine stool-and-odor examinations as offensive and of little diagnostic use. He used his own vocational experience as proof of doctors' idiocy in this area, writing that one in his trade "would never think of judging the efficiency of a boiler plant without at least a rough estimate of the unburned coal in the ashes and partly burned gases going up the stack." It seemed patently clear to Pearson, by contrast, that Fletcher had been right: each individual should learn to examine and interpret his own excretions, knowing that healthy human stools were "no more offensive than moist clay [with] no more odour than a hot biscuit." Even the Bible, long an ambiguous source on the proprieties of fasting, acted for Pearson as a proof text of the practice's tremendous benefits. Quoting—or rather, misquoting—the Bible as saying, "Fast ye not and ye cannot enter the kingdom of heaven," he queried, "Could not this mean that eternal life (on this earth) is obtainable, but only through fasting, and in no other manner?" Fragrance-free feces were redolent of paradise.[26]

This obsession with filth and stench might appear to be little more than a peculiar effect of the massive urban sewer projects taking place at this time. Devastating epidemics of yellow fever, cholera, typhoid, and other diseases had long spurred efforts toward sanitation measures, and no undertaking was more important to the reform movement for public health than the construction of massive underground pipe systems and wastewater treatment facilities to contain, do away with, or purify human waste. Though Boston's underground sewer had kept the city streets dry and clean from the early 1700s on, other urban areas—notably New York—were lined with squalid alleyways and dotted with overflowing cesspools until well after the Civil War. The crowded slum areas were especially reputed to reek of fecal muck. One nineteenth-century inspection officer in New York reported families "living in basements with privy vaults located at higher levels than the apartments and oozing their contents into them, amidst offensive odors," while another noted the "insalubrity of privies in which masses of human excrement were found on the seats and floors." Poor or rich, residents lived amid such smells: cities literally stank throughout, a fact that undoubtedly lent appeal to Pearson's fantasy of "ash."[27]

Yet anxiety over defecatory products and odors does not merely reflect the desire for more hygienic streets and living quarters, especially since this uneasiness emerged with greatest intensity well after sewage systems had made successful inroads at sanitation. More pointedly, a fanciful vision of replacing foul bodies with clean, healthy ones overlay the trepidation, drawing on a lavish symbolic repertoire of racialized representations to evoke its urgency. The vocabulary of bodily contamination fit contemporaneous anxieties about "dung" in the public square, played out in the steady tides of racial enmity, the rising currents of nativism, and the zeal for eugenic research (including forced sterilization for the "feeble-minded") that swept both England and the United States during those years. Odor, of course, has perennially lent itself to use as a conspicuous indicator of difference, within literal catalogs of smells compiled to distinguish the "stink" of particular races or classes of people from the "sweet" smells of one's own kind.[28] Anglo-Americans during the late nineteenth and early twentieth centuries (among other times) displayed intense disgust toward the supposed fetor of foreign bodies, not to mention that of dark-skinned bodies in their own midst. The pure body would be thoroughly deodorized, one's skin emanating only the most pleasing, subtle, and respectable fragrance (at least to olfactory organs like one's own). In crusading for odorless excrement, Progressive Era fasting advocates took this obsession to its farthest extreme, but their enthusiastic labors remained firmly ensconced within the American dialectic of fascination with and repulsion from filth, contagion, and all things alien or inassimilable. As one longtime fasting advocate put it, "The real nature of disease . . . is the encumbrance of the system with effete, mal-assimilated, foreign material . . . 'the presence of foreign substances in the body.' "[29]

An oft-used clinical term for this kind of situation was "auto-intoxication," a condition of being poisoned by pernicious elements within one's own flesh, often signaled by body odor in general and more specifically by that of feces. Auto-intoxication was a particular obsession of Hereward Carrington (1880–1959), the author of *Vitality, Fasting, and Nutrition* (1908) as well as numerous later books on medical, psychic, and occult topics. Not only germs but excrement itself invaded the body's tissues by absorption, so that the human organism was "constantly saturated with poisonous germs and filth, re-excreted, re-absorbed and re-secreted—no one knows how many times—by the various organs of the body."[30] Sickened by this ghastly procedure of self-poisoning, Carrington bemoaned the porosity of human bowels, deploring the fact that bodies were themselves composed of putrefaction: "That beautiful form; that God-like intellect; the very soul itself, is on any theory, dependent upon the material body for its manifestation, in this life; and *these* materials (and foul air), are the materials from which our bodies are built!"

Rather than the "bloated faces, blotchy skins, and foul breath . . . encountered on every hand," Carrington longed for "the clean, sweet, healthy body that results from perfect nutrition, and a strict observance of hygienic laws." Fortunately, there was no need to continue living with the indignity of putrid fecal matter: if one ate only just enough to meet the body's requirements, Carrington prophesied, then evacuations themselves could be rendered virtually unnecessary! All that would occasionally pass from the rectum would be less noxious waste products deposited by the blood—a hygienist's dream come true at last. Through enemas, one could annihilate those filthy poisons that otherwise putrefied in the body to the point of death, creating an enticing alternative to the drone of mortal fate. Only when the civilized human family began to practice this and other hygienic laws would one begin to see "the clean, healthful, pink complexions that should encounter us on every hand."[31]

That one of the main issues implicitly at stake for Carrington and others was the health of "pink" complexions—and bodies—cannot be underestimated. Indeed, the larger framework of meaning in which fasting played a key role relied on notions of hierarchy—the strong versus the weak—that were themselves often racially charged. Bernarr Macfadden's written corpus was especially suffused with an ideology of racial hierarchy, which he glossed as the scientific "study of physical measurements and of their relationship to the prehistoric and modern racial development of mankind." Echoing associations long elevated in phrenology and other popular science arenas, he contrasted black and Asian women and men with their white counterparts in order to illustrate the superiority of Caucasian facial characteristics and physical prowess. "The broad high forehead," he wrote in the *Encyclopedia of Health and Physical Culture*, "is a sign of intelligence which distinguishes the white man from the Australian Bushman"—and, as the photographic images made clear, from black Americans as well. Clearly, "the more advanced races have over their eyes more brain capacity than the lower races."[32]

Such declarations did not directly have to do with fasting, but his other writings made clear that the will and strength needed to conquer one's own bodily appetites were in fact only accessible to beings of advanced mental power, those with the good sense to recognize their physical dominance over craven appetite. In Macfadden's evolutionary schema early men who survived imposed starvation—having been compelled by the "rigors of existence" into "enforced fasting periods"—developed the "capacity to sustain life and gain renewed vitality from periods of temporary abstinence from food" and thus helped propel the progress of the race. But none were so advanced as to have given up food voluntarily, as he exhorted modern civilized (white) men to do. By focusing so intently on the arduousness of manly self-denial, the discourse of fasting bolstered a larger thematic agenda of distinguishing hearty, Anglo-Saxon stock from "degenerate" races of men and women, those who remained bound to the animalistic gratification of eating and were much too weak to fast.[33]

Fasting and whiteness, then, conveniently merged into a larger logic of bodily domination and superiority, for some fasting masters more explicitly than others. While Macfadden's language concerning the advancement of the white "superman" was somewhat more strident than that of other fasting writers, the general fixation on dirt displayed by his counterparts, not to mention the insistence that starving was the best way to cure the body, resonated deeply with other anxieties and strategies regarding the so-called polluted influences of racialized others in American society. Moreover, the vocabulary of health that these writers employed was used to racialized ends by more virulent ideologues of racial hierarchy and eugenic science, such as the physician William S. Sadler (1875–1969).

Sadler's *Race Decadence* (1922) developed an alarming portrait of the declining health of American citizens and recommended a "health revival" for the nation's hearty that emphasized the rational breeding of children (the "feeble-minded" would undergo involuntary sterilization) no less than the stamping out of that most awful bane to health, auto-intoxication. Sadler was so concerned about the latter as the most common cause of high blood pressure, kidney trouble, and various degenerative diseases that he included a special appendix entitled "Special Diet List for Auto-Intoxication." A rational eating plan was a crucial part of the overhaul of America's best racial stock, which according to Sadler was becoming "more unstable, less self-collected and less self-controlled . . . more and more panicky and hysterical." Though Sadler never went so far as to encourage periods of complete food abstinence, his menu of dietary regimens otherwise echoed the prescriptions of those who did (two daily meals instead of three, less meat, thorough mastication, raw and natural foods, etc.). Male fasters were thus invoking a broader lexicon of health, purity, and pollution used to shore up the boundaries of the physical as well as the social body, monitoring the orifices of the one no less rigorously than those who policed the more expansive borders of American democratic society.[34]

The compulsion to control the appetite so thoroughly as to obliterate the smell of one's excrement thus fit into late Victorian constructions of manly self-restraint. At the same time, the precision that guided these fasters' exploration of their own feces—the meticulous processes of weighing, measuring, poking, and purging to which they were so committed—suggests a deep attraction to a Progressive paradigm of scientific mastery that they sought to rescue from the tightly bounded world of gentlemen physicians, those who operated in the mainstream of American medicine. Yet the exemplary self to which the fasters aspired was equally overlaid with cherished ideals of masculine potency and physical conquest, ideals that in the past had conflicted with Victorian manliness more than harmonizing with that model.[35] Part of fasting's allure, then, was surely its expansive capacity to combine more traditional, refined sorts of training the manly will with the era's newer masculine interest in raw strength and power—the businessman and the bodybuilder fused into one omnipotent, invincible white body.

The habits that surrounded the practice of fasting celebrated sensuality as much as self-denial, paving the way for a model of virility in which even the most extreme forms of narcissism could be revamped as self-sacrifice.

WILLIAM SHELDON'S METAPHYSICAL SOMATOTYPES

The pictorial culture of bodily display promoted by New Thought physical culturists and fasting masters took various forms after spiritualized starvation, caricatured and recurrently scarified in the media, faded into relative obscurity. Historians of advertising, fashion, and mass media have illustrated the radical shifts in physical ideals that took place after the twentieth century's early decades. Less well analyzed are the midcentury attempts to typologize human bodies, a goal that followed upon the efforts of clinical physicians and psychologists to develop models of mind-body interaction that would enable a more holistic medical practice. For many such holists and practitioners of constitutional medicine, it is a powerful historical irony that the most popular and widely influential of these efforts, Sheldon's somatotypy, drew on deeply racialized notions of biological determinism and hopes for eugenic breeding. Once again the body, fit or unfit, was destiny.[36]

William Herbert Sheldon (1898–1977), a Rhode Island native, attended Brown University before taking a PhD in psychology and an MD from the University of Chicago in 1925 and 1933, respectively. Apparently reflecting the influence of William James, his alleged godfather, Sheldon had a lifelong interest in religion and believed that psychology ought to rescue religion from the crises facing it in an age of consumer hedonism and scientistic skepticism. Sheldon's first book, *Psychology and the Promethean Will* (1936), was funded by a grant from the National Council on Religion in Higher Education and argued that psychology's first and perhaps best task in this resurrection process was to develop better systematic models for describing differences among human beings. Four years later Sheldon published *The Varieties of Human Physique*, where his opening words returned to this hope of classification: "From such a point of view the first task of psychology seems to be that of standardizing a method for describing quantitatively the varying physical endowments of individuals. In order to systematize the science of human behavior, we must start with some kind of descriptive classification of the behaving structure: the physical constitution. The present volume provides a three-dimensional system for the description of human physique."[37] Read together, these and later books reveal the religious underpinning of his classificatory desires: a worldview steeped in metaphysical assumptions about the revelatory power of human bodies.

With his onetime popularity buried under a cloud of scholarly embarrassment, Sheldon's name is no longer renowned, despite the fact that over the course of his career he taught or had affiliations at the universities of Texas, Wisconsin, Harvard, Columbia, and California as well as Chicago and its Theological Seminary, the University of Oregon Medical School, and the U.S. Army Medical School. Legal actions taken by several major academic institutions during the 1990s have meant that Sheldon's papers, housed in the Smithsonian Institution's National Anthropological Archives, were eventually closed to the public, including scholarly researchers. Why such secrecy? Sheldon elaborated a taxonomy of bodies whose truncated version survives in familiar parlance as *endomorphy* (a state associated with being short and round), *mesomorphy* (square and muscular), and *ectomorphy* (tall and thin). He first published these ideas while doing research and teaching in the anthropology and psychology departments at Harvard University, where he was enthusiastically promoted by figures such as the physical anthropologist Earnest Hooton. By examining thousands of naked human bodies, which he photographed from three different angles (standing front, back, and side), Sheldon derived a measure of a person's constitutional physique and assigned it a three-digit numerical combination that revealed the degree of each of these variables. This number comprised the somatotype, based on a seven-point scale that matched one number to each morphological indicator. The survival of an enormous cache of photographs, capturing America's privileged youths and future leaders in their birthday suits, is the source of the Smithsonian's unusual restrictions on Sheldon's collection.

But Sheldon's point was not merely to typologize human physicality, for he further correlated these somatotypes with particular psychological qualities and motivational drives termed *viscerotonia* (characterized by being happy and relaxed), *somatotonia* (energetic and aggressive), and *cerebrotonia* (nervous and intelligent). He made these correlations the primary subject of his second constitutional study, *The Varieties of Temperament* (1942), which was highly influential among American physicians and vigorously promoted in the popular press by such well-known figures as Aldous Huxley and Christopher Isherwood. From Harvard he went to work for the U.S. Army Air Corps to devise somatotypes for potential pilots, and in 1946 he moved to Columbia University to succeed George Draper as head of the Constitution Clinic (he changed its name to laboratory, presumably to make it sound more authoritative) at Columbia's College of Physicians and Surgeons. While at Columbia, Sheldon published two more constitutional studies, *Varieties of Delinquent Youth* (1949) and *Atlas of*

Men (1954), before Columbia closed the Constitution Laboratory in 1959. He then returned to Cambridge, Massachusetts, to continue his research supported with the private funding of the Texas businessman Eugene McDermott. In 1975 he published his final work, an updated and little-circulated version of *Psychology and the Promethean Will*, and titled it *Prometheus Revisited: A Second Look at the Religious Function in Human Affairs, and a Proposal to Merge Religion with a Biologically Grounded Social Psychiatry*, making plain yet again his life's interest in constructing a "*biologically grounded* religion" for the future.[38]

Sheldon, along with those who supported his work during the 1930s and 1940s, believed that his morphological findings comprised a breakthrough discovery of great relevance to fields such as medicine, nutrition, and physical education, not to mention eugenics and criminology. His interests in the latter two areas overlapped with his Harvard patron's, the anthropologist Hooton, who examined criminals by categories of race and whose eugenicist books such as *Crime and the Man* and *The American Criminal* (both published by Harvard University Press in 1939) argued that "the elimination of crime can be effected only by the extirpation of the physically, mentally, and morally unfit, or by their complete segregation in a socially aseptic environment." Like Hooton, Sheldon described his aim in *Varieties of Delinquent Youth* as making "a direct attack on our most deadly enemy—careless reproduction." Stephen H. Gatlin, in his doctoral dissertation on Sheldon, has described the ways in which eugenics and constitutionalism served together in this period as channels for articulating reactionary discontent to the problems of modernity, issues that were engaged rather differently by modernist artists and literary figures. Comparing American eugenics to Nazi propaganda art, Gatlin traces how "the human body . . . became not just the site of the spiritual but the soul itself," quoting one of Sheldon's undated letters to that effect: "The profession of physical education has always seemed to me to be the most religious profession. [Its advocates'] faith is secure, and their worship serene, for they have found the immortal Soul. The soul is the body. . . . Physical educators derive an ecstasy from seeing the soul stand straight up." Sheldon's romanticism built upon Emerson and William James no less than Blake and Nietzsche, writes Gatlin, as he sought "to fashion a humanist religion out of the Promethean possibilities for splendor, vitality, and social order invested within the human physique. . . . To obey 'God' was to obey eugenics. To violate 'God' was to ignore biological, eugenic reality." Sheldon's somatotyping project extended older ambitions for self-realization, and "eugenic breeding became an essential ingredient of these humanist and essentially 'religious' designs."[39]

Though typing so-called feeble-minded defectives and offenders had been a recurring interest in eugenic criminology and phrenology, Sheldon borrowed widely from other traditions as well, which was particularly evident in his work on the affluent, privileged youth who offered loftier prototypes than their delinquent counterparts. His chief subjects for such photographic studies were college students at elite institutions including Yale, Harvard, Radcliffe, Wellesley, Vassar, Mt. Holyoke, and others. Many colleges, along with elementary and secondary schools, already had their own traditions of photographing nude students in order to measure bad posture and correct the improper habits that supposedly accompanied it. Indeed, as early as 1913 Jessie Bancroft, founder of the American Posture League, carried out posture tests at public elementary schools in Brooklyn and used a stereopticon to make shadow pictures of each student, to be projected onto a screen in front of the whole class for purposes of assessment and correction. By the 1920s, incoming freshman at the most exclusive northeastern colleges, including the Ivy League and Seven Sister institutions, were photographed in the nude from various angles; and some schools even claimed the right to deny final admission to students whose posture or overall physical condition was exposed as unfit when these photos were taken.[40]

Sheldon's research outwardly shifted what had professed to be a concern about posture—marking discipline, control, and good breeding but still treatable—to a subject more unequivocally focused on constitution and heredity: the science of reading internal truths in external signs. He, at least, knew this was an older occupation, as he cited the intellectual lineage of the phrenologists Gall, Spurzheim, and Samuel Wells: if these pioneers "leaned heavily upon subjective judgment," they were nonetheless "able to size up a human being with shrewdness, possibly with rare insight." Whether or not college officers of the time perceived such a shift from posture reading to a new phrenology, later administrators energetically distanced themselves from the project as an embarrassment to their respective institutions' venerable reputations. For instance, after a *New York Times* journalist wrote in 1995 of unearthing a treasure trove of nude photographs in the Sheldon papers at the National Anthropological Archives at the Smithsonian Institution, Yale University lawyers intervened to demand that the museum shred all photographs and negatives of its outraged alumni.[41]

Certainly, in his own time and beyond, numerous scientists and scholars denounced Sheldon as a shoddy researcher and fringe character whose distaste for non-Anglo-Saxon peoples—evident as early as his 1922 master's thesis at the University of Colorado, "A Comparison of the Intelligence of Mexican and White Children"—signaled a severe personality disorder. It would seem hard not to conclude this when reading repeated descriptions of delinquents' familial origins, mostly immigrant, alcoholic, and urban, as in these wholly typical examples:

> Third of six, urban family, both parents immigrant Poles. Father of average physique, described as "hard drinking, cunning, and sly with social agencies." He has several court appearances for drunkenness. Mother short and heavy, called "emotional, greedy, exploitative." . . . First of three, urban Negro family. Father a tall, active man of about the same physique as this [19-year-old] boy. He has been a semi-alcoholic singer and entertainer, is regarded as unreliable and exploitative. . . . Only child, urban family. Both parents Portugese [sic] immigrants. Father described as a vigorous, healthy, improvident alcoholic . . . Mother large and excessively muscular, described as a "hypomanic [sic] go-getter who can fight like a man. Her second husband committed suicide. The third is now a chronic alcoholic."

Here, in *Varieties of Delinquent Youth*, he decried Jews and Italians as "vermin" and relentlessly lamented "mongrel," "socially chaotic" American culture.[42] Barbara Honeyman Heath, Sheldon's onetime devoted assistant and apparent lover during the 1950s, later sharply distanced herself from his views while developing new methods of somatotyping; her final evisceration of Sheldon's reputation appeared in a lengthy personal and professional arraignment of him published in her coauthored book *Somatotyping— Development and Applications*, published by Cambridge University Press in 1990. But as Gatlin has rightly argued, Sheldon's extreme views, while criticized by many educators and professionals especially after the fall of Adolph Hitler's Third Reich, were still widely tolerated, supported for instance by grants from the Rockefeller Foundation well into the 1950s.[43]

In fact, Sheldon remained comfortably situated in the Ivy League world, taking naked photographs of the nation's elite young men and women, precisely because his work fit so well into previous models of character examination by bodily measurement. As David Yosifon and Peter N. Stearns suggest in their historical analysis of American posture norms, American scientists and educators believed that posture was a key indicator of character until the 1960s, even as popular standards were drifting downward and most young people themselves were choosing to adopt more relaxed, less stringent models for appropriate standing and sitting positions. Sheldon's somatotypy adopted distinct criteria for measuring psychological health and may even have appeared more democratic than posture standards in showing the many varieties of body and temperament that could succeed at getting into an exclusive East Coast college, while yet upholding elite presumptions about class and race that were part and parcel of the posture movement. Sheldon's form of body typing appeared so seamlessly mainstream, in fact, that between 1940 and 1952 it received acclaim in household magazines ranging from *Popular Science* and *Scientific Monthly* to *Harper's Monthly*, *Time, Cosmopolitan, Ladies Home Journal, Women's Home Companion,* and *Life.*[44] How much the readers of these articles knew about Sheldon's withering assessments of the low mental capacity of African Americans, Mexicans, Eastern Europeans, Irish, and others is hard to say, but his system seemed to sit well with newsstand audiences for a lengthy time.

Sheldon's love of the aristocracy, his racist views, and his strong eugenic aspirations make Sheldon's Ivy League connections an awkward subject for university archivists and overseers who wish to excise him from their history. It is hard to believe that *Varieties of Delinquent Youth* was republished in 1970, with Sheldon's disparaging comments about New York as "this rather Negrophilic city" still intact.[45] Whatever else, the endurance of the naked photograph experiment into the 1960s—the practice continued at Yale until 1968—exposes the resilience of cultural faith in the unclothed body's expressive meanings, the belief that there were secrets embedded in the flesh that provided essential classificatory information for American educators. Being forced to walk into a glaringly bright room and stand nude before a stranger holding a camera lens must surely have felt, to many, like an invasion of their most private, inmost self. The journalist Ron Rosenbaum, the last to examine many negatives of these photographs before they were destroyed in the mid-1990s, described the mostly "diffident, oblivious" faces of the men, already accustomed to naked self-display during draft physicals and sport weight-ins, but he also made note of the "deeply unhappy" faces of many women, grimacing as if in pain, or else furious.[46] Most of these women had presumably been examined by physicians along the way, and some had undoubtedly also been photographed as early as elementary school, but having a camera trained on one's adult body may well have felt new and intimidating. Feelings of shame or humiliation at this practice were not, however, grounds for exemption or even, it appears, sympathy.

Enacting these procedures, after all, ostensibly served higher ends. Like earlier systems of phrenology and physiognomy that Sheldon cited directly as part of the ancestry of his own work, his somatotypy spoke the revered language of science (and carried the authority derived from his University of Chicago medical degree) and for a time gained respect in both academic and popular circles. But religious interests were paramount for Sheldon, who thereby made morphological classifications meaningful as systems for identifying those persons who exemplified humanity's divine potential. Religion, wrote Sheldon in *Psychology and the Promethean Will*, was simply "in a practical sense the application of techniques for the development of character." Religion and psychology went together, particularly since psychological research had ostensibly surpassed religious thought in terms of articulating insights into human desire. Yet Sheldon held religion to be the more elementary and essential of the two fields: "Through the years I have come to feel that professional work in psychology and psychotherapy can be only a rather superficial palliation of the more fundamental orientational problem of religion until religionists at large shall become equipped to make use of the best available intellectual and technical resources for dealing with conflict; more particularly and more immediately with the conflict in their own minds."[47] If religious leaders themselves refused to recognize the means at their disposal to resolve such conflicts and reunite intellect with feeling, power with discipline, then psychologists would step in as the new ministerial class. It was a situation, Sheldon repeatedly argued, too urgent to leave to the future.

The year after Sheldon published *Psychology and the Promethean Will* in 1936, Aldous Huxley raved about this "very remarkable man" to his biologist brother, Julian. Sheldon had "evolved a genuinely scientific conception of human types," Huxley wrote: a "genuine algebra" through which to quantify scientifically "the typological factors present in varying amounts in different individuals." Already famous for *Brave New World* (1932), Huxley was Sheldon's friend and steadfast promoter for years afterward, championing him in a *Harper's* article in 1944; and he continued to praise Sheldon for clarifying and confirming "the old insights and intuitions about the different kinds of human beings." As Gatlin illustrates in depth, Huxley shared Sheldon's views not only on eugenics but on psychology and mystical spirituality: "Sheldon's tendency to mystify, spiritualize, the body (his empiricist rhetoric notwithstanding) appealed to Huxley's quest for a naturalized religion." Biological determinacy and somatic aristocracy were no less foreign to Huxley than to Sheldon, however differently their reputations have fared over time. But in his day, Sheldon's works sold extremely well: published by Harper in New York, for instance, *Varieties of Human Physique* (1940) went through later editions in 1963 and 1970, while *Varieties of Temperament* (1942) was reissued in 1944, 1945, 1962, and 1970.[48]

The world was going to hell. Hell's road was paved with all the marks of overbreeding by poor stock, so-called counterselection, and various kinds of Anglo-Saxon desecration, and Sheldon's hoped-for solution was a spiritualized nationalism at once comfortably concrete and highly metaphysical that would—in Sheldon's golden-age view—again allow order and hierarchy to suffuse American society with perfect precision. Through the new religious psychology of the body, restraint, simplicity, and humility would arise to correct the "escape" religions of the day: systems that "a mind embraces at some level below that of its own best development" and that promise only amusement and overstimulation. The churches, Sheldon noted, were "filled with thousands of individuals who have bought a cheap religion," so that for many intellectuals, the wisest course seemed abandonment of the institutions and contempt for the people still in them. For Sheldon, the problem was a poignant one, since "unintellectual souls" who accepted these cheap religions evinced "the heavy stupidity and the dreary piety of a Protestant horse and buggy Sunday in New England" yet also showed affection and kindness. They were "the salt of the earth." True religion properly found a compromise to "embody the simplicity and humility of the old religion of faith" while yet supporting the wider intellectual developments available ("unfortunately," noted Sheldon) in cities. Qualities of discipline would not drown the Promethean man in a sea of inaction—Sheldon was far too influenced by Nietzsche to think that—but rather propel him ahead to new heights of vital creativity and true joy. The greatest temptation on this road to heaven was to fall into the "urban influence . . . near the environs of massed population" and thereby develop habits of what Sheldon called "waster" personalities: the unchastened, opportunistic sensualists who scoffed at the traditional order in favor of personal authenticity and experience.[49]

Sheldon's descriptions of these wasters, who represented a grave threat to western civilization, ever revealed potent race and class undertones:

> The real enemies of character are not to be found among atheists or critics of religion or non-conformists, but they are the lusty, noise-loving expressivists, who believe in living for the present, in having their fling. . . . Wasters perforce seek overstimulation, love city life, and have a profound horror of the inferiority complex. Their god is Expression, and their spiritual counselors are sometimes the psychoanalysts. Flushed with sudden release from Christian inhibitions, they are resolved to smash away all that was ever associated with the spiritual, or religious, or reminiscent, or chastened mental outlook, and their exultant ecstasy finds its channels of expression in the material processes of manipulating things, of social domination, and of sexual conquest.

Jews and Italians always offered vivid examples for Sheldon's historical narrative, cast in the role of the seductive tempter tricking innocent Anglo-Saxon youths into abandoning the religious moorings of their ancestors in

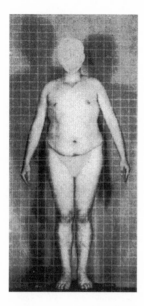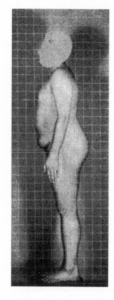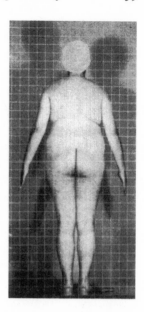

10. Somatotype 712 (endomorph), from William Sheldon, *Varieties of Human Physique,* between 162–63.

favor of chaos and commerce. "Al Capone did not become a great commercial and political power in Chicago through the intentional support of his own kind," Sheldon noted ominously, "but through the herding and flocking and drinking of callow, hip-flask souls who, having been shorn by education of their morality, stood naked and characterless before the wind."[50]

Perhaps Sheldon's photographic project was an attempt to depict this young nakedness in a new light, so that the nation's raw youth could rise to the call of their characters and live up to the destiny determined by their somatotype. For if it was the case that biology was destiny, it was also true that Sheldon found positive points to make about most of the different kinds of bodies that he examined, with the exception of the fat, "excessively endomorphic" types such as the 712. The person of this somatotype seemed to swim in his (or more often her) own fat, punctuated by features that were "soft and sodden, as if no muscles were present."

> The 712 . . . is a rare somatotopye, but it is so conspicuous that nearly everybody knows one or two. The body is literally swamped with first component, and the extremely weak second is barely able to carry it around. Locomotion is difficult, and everything "shimmies" or wiggles up and down, when the 712 walks. This somatotype is much more com-

mon in the female than in the male, and it is not uncommon for the female 712 in middle life to give up locomotion altogether and to become chair-ridden, if the family or government can afford it.

Fat indicated a person for whom "eating is one of the principal pleasures of life, if not indeed the greatest pleasure," he wrote in *Varieties of Temperament*. When not eating, such a one would need to be sucking or chewing ("Viscerotonic people are indefatigable kissers"), and while an educated person of this sort might become a culinary expert, "at lower levels he tends merely to become a glutton." (Sheldon also typically noted the obesity of delinquents' mothers, another sign of their unfitness.) Sheldon hardly invented these associations, but his authoritative tone and wide renown lent them a kind of popular scientific credence.[51]

Earnest contemplation of one's own body type, of whatever kind, showed a person to be a serious pupil, and this gusto for self-improvement proved ultimately better than the inattentiveness of a waster mentality, however powerful its body. As with other subjective sciences that sought to classify and predict character by relatively malleable somatic characteristics, participants could read almost anything they wanted into their own somatotype. The brilliance of Sheldon's system was that it promised to reveal destiny but left room for the individual's sense of his or her own distinctive qualities. The habits it encouraged for reading other bodies, however, made for a much more virulent than happy science, one that drew on prior stereotypes about the poor character of people who lived in cities or had dark skin or were fat while it wrapped these beliefs ever more tightly in the seemingly smart dress of constitutional medicine. As it turned out, however, persons inhabiting those bodies had their own ways of describing them, even when they shared the faith of Sheldon—and the fasting masters before him—in harmony between body and spirit.

GOD IN A BODY: GASTRONOMY AND BLACK POWER

New Day, a newspaper published by the Peace Mission movement beginning in the 1930s, frequently featured boldface headlines like "That Which You Vividly Visualize You Will Materialize," or "The Invisible Is the Reality of the Visible," mixed with titles such as "Your Bodies Are the Temples of God" and "The Physical Bodies Are the Realizers." Then there were headings like "The Material Food We Eat . . . Is the Actual Tangibilization of the Personification of God's Word, God's Love and God's Presence" and "God Is God in a Body Just Like a Doctor Is a Doctor in a Body—God Has a Body

Just Like a Doctor Has."[52] The instructor behind these vivid headlines was Father Divine, one of the most intriguing figures of twentieth-century American religious life, who was himself considered by his followers to be "God in a body."[53]

Perhaps because rumors and controversies surrounded him through most of his adult life, not to mention unconventional claims of divinity, Father Divine (born George Baker, 1879–1965) has received little scholarly attention, though he was one of the most prominent religious leaders of the time. During the heyday of his movement in the 1930s, he drew thousands of devout African-American followers, who frequently traveled to his Sayville, New York, mansion to be near him, and later to his headquarters in Harlem and scattered other missions elsewhere. He attracted nearly equal numbers of dedicated white supporters across the country and in Britain, including some extremely wealthy and socially prominent members. During that decade, he claimed a global audience in the millions, many of whom were reached through the circulation of newspapers such as *Spoken Word* and *New Day*. Though finding this number inflated, historians have estimated Divine's following in the 1930s as being at least thirty thousand and probably closer to fifty thousand people—no mean number by any standard.[54] Countless enthusiasts and onlookers, the curious as well as the devoted, came to visit his headquarters in person, many waiting days and even weeks for the chance to consult him privately. Even forty years after his 1965 death, a small but devoted following endures, communing together at his latter-day headquarters in Gladwyne, Pennsylvania.[55]

Those who wholeheartedly accepted Divine's teachings he called his "angels," and he had them take on new spiritual names as a sign of having been born again into the kingdom of God. Many lived in communalist enclaves, sharing property and contributing their labor to the good of the whole. While this collectivist mode of living secured the derision of the movement's critics, who viewed Divine as a schemer living off the wealth produced by his minions, communal labor also guaranteed meals, clothing, and long-term housing to many destitute people who were otherwise at chronic risk of poverty and homelessness. But at least until very recently, critics have used the narrow and often racialized category of "cult leader" to lump him with Bishop Charles M. "Sweet Daddy" Grace and other "black gods of the metropolis."[56] This blurring of disparate figures has deemphasized or entirely neglected their substantive teachings. In the case of Father Divine, the doctrinal content of his instruction is especially important to explore, as it opens up a window on African American practitioners of New Thought and on black leaders in New Thought's continuing popularity and dissemination. His teachings also set out in bold relief a presumption of the body's infinite perfectibility that was already working its way into the mainstream culture and would only intensify in the coming decades, so that it is not too much to describe Divine as a prototype and augur of broader salvationist fixations on the flesh.[57]

It was primarily at his Holy Communion banquets, the central public event of his ministry, that Father Divine expounded his intricate theology of matter and spirit. His sermons on these elaborate occasions were painstakingly transcribed by the two dozen secretaries in his employ and were reprinted in each week's issue of *New Day*. Divine's sermons and related writings give evidence of a view that was at once deeply influenced by various New Thought theological streams and at the same time strikingly original, rejecting conventional dogmas where he considered them inadequate for his own following. Providing a critique of both traditional Christianity and the seemingly radical New Thought currents of his time, each of which appeared (in his view) overly hostile to the bodily substance of life, Divine tendered in their place a renewed veneration for embodiment: a symbolic feast with offerings as sumptuous and plentiful as the dishes served daily at his banquets.[58] His ideas as well as his practices touched a broad spectrum of women and men, black and white, rich and poor, and were influential beyond the strict bounds of his Peace Mission communes.

Divine's early interest in the work of Mary Baker Eddy gave way to rejection of her thoroughgoing antimaterialism but praise for the teachings of Charles Fillmore (Divine noted that he had once distributed Unity literature). Jill Watts has persuasively argued that Divine's "later vocabulary, ideas, and the organization of his ministry" resemble those of the Unity School more than any other New Thought group or thinker and that, in fact, Fillmore had "the strongest influence over the young preacher."[59] Fillmore's emphasis on living things extended well beyond vegetarianism, even to what he frequently referred to as the living body of God: "The real body of God is a living body. Above all, it is a beautiful body, a temple. And God Himself is in that temple, and it is not necessary to have any light but His light, the light of life and health." Body and mind were crucially integrated in Fillmore's worldview, just as crucially as were humanity and divinity. "The body of man must rest upon a divine body idea in Divine Mind, and it logically follows that the inner life substance and intelligence of all flesh is perfect." In other words, wrote Fillmore, "We have a perfect body in mind, and this perfect mind-body expresses itself through our I AM, or the Christ in us; it brings itself into manifestation just as fast as we let it, just as fast as we perceive God in the flesh." Divine's words closely replicated Fillmore's on this and other key issues, even as he developed a philosophy of bodily holiness and pleasure well beyond what Fillmore would have found acceptable.[60]

Father Divine's ministry, whatever other functions it performed, had as its cornerstone the practice of feeding hungry bodies, bodies who were trained to see this sustenance as distributed to them by God himself. At these communion banquets, Father Divine instructed his followers in the esoteric mysteries of "tangibilization"—the spirit of God made manifest in material form. His typical greeting began with the words, "Peace everyone! Good Health, Good Will and a Good Appetite." He taught hearers to recognize that the feast set before them, and available every day of the week, was a fulfillment of scripture, a materialization of what they had traditionally been taught was the mere spiritual promise of feasting at the Welcome Table in the afterlife. Food was depicted as the concrete symbol of heavenly love, a love poured out upon all who were willing to partake of it; and the purpose of dining at this holy table was to tangibly unite body and soul. "I came to supply the Abundance of the Fulness [sic] of the Consciousness of Good of every necessary food for the sustenance of your bodies and for the benefit of your souls, to keep your soul and your body together so that your soul will be your body and your body will be your soul!"[61] Keeping body and soul together was no mere metaphor but had practical ends, bringing about the hoped-for kingdom of God on earth rather than postponing it to some ethereal fantasy of the future. God in a living, breathing body! If even the source of all things was willing to become manifest in human form—if perfection itself could be, in Divine's parlance, visibilized and tangibilated—then those already in earthly bodies must regard their bodies in a new way.

It was this theology of materialization that earned the Peace Mission movement its most bilious denigrations. Journalists heaped contempt upon the man whom they termed "the squat little Negro messiah with the shiny bald head" wearing an "absurd mustache," no less than "the angels throwing themselves into a frenzy wilder than the wildest camp meetings," and such descriptions were not only the stuff of Anglo-American newspapers but also regularly turned up in venues such as the *Negro Digest*.[62] Yet this same doctrine of the divine presence purged the contempt in which the body had been held by more traditional New Thought and Christian Science thinkers. We have already seen how Eddy, who outright denied the reality of material substance, left her own followers equally wary of pleasure and sickness and forcefully minimized attention to bodily functions. Though many of Eddy's rivals who crossed over to New Thought opposed this rigid separation between mind (or spirit) and matter, they seemed just as committed to curtailing, even disguising, the life-sustaining activities of the physical self, particularly the alimentary and digestive kind. Father Divine, raised in poverty and moved by the suffering of hungry people, had no interest in making light of the body's daily functions. What could possibly be grotesque about eating, especially a communal meal modeled after the disciples' supper with Jesus? Surely starvation, whether forced or enacted as a supercilious rejection of God's bounty, was the real sin to combat.

Just as God had earlier become manifest in the human body of Jesus, so now God was materialized in the body of Divine himself—a body that was rotund, required little sleep, and radiated health to those around him. What it took to persuade those initially skeptical of Divine's divinity is largely beyond the scope of this examination, but it is clear that a major source of his followers' trust in him was the abundance of provisions which he provided them, as if effortlessly. Charles Samuel Braden, who made an early and very thoughtful study of Divine during the 1940s, asked believers how they knew Divine was God; most answered him by pointing to the elaborate feasts and respectable accommodations that he bestowed upon them, gratis. "Nobody but God could do that," they repeatedly averred. One of Divine's secretaries reminded Braden of Jesus' feeding the five thousand with only five loaves and two fishes, while a German farmer in New Jersey noted of Father Divine's kitchen, "If they prepare ten pounds of meat, they then can serve ten thousand people, so is God's blessing. When they take a piece of meat out of the pot there is another piece in the place." Others recounted Divine pouring endless cups of coffee out of his coffee pot without needing to replenish it.[63] The serving of the food along with its apparently inexplicable abundance acted as proof that Divine was God in their very midst. The reality—stuff and substance—of God was vital to Divine's teaching, and he never ceased reminding his followers to "acknowledge GOD in matter, in this food, in our own bodies, in the Body of One Whom you call FATHER DIVINE. Acknowledge Him in matter—that is an important thing to get."[64] Like the God conceptualized by New Thought adherents, Divine's God would make real whatever was imagined or desired, but because this God resided in a living body rather than some mystical plane of consciousness, He both recognized and honored the bodies of his followers.

The personal body of Father Divine was a source of immense joy for those who believed him to be God. His followers loved his body; a typical song sung by the Rosebuds went, *"You brought us Happiness when YOU brought YOUR Body, Real Happiness lies in YOUR Holy Body!*[65] The secretaries who transcribed his communion messages for reprinting in the *New Day* often prefaced the messages with adoring descriptions of the ecstatic atmosphere that preceded his arrival, as followers began calling and singing for "the PERSONAL BODY OF GOD" to arrive: "Song sung by the audience: The BODY! The BODY! The BODY! I love YOU [etc.], The BODY of FATHER DIVINE."[66] Divine regularly kept his adherents waiting until midnight or later, which led to scenes of intense longing such as this one:

> Father found the BODY lovers waiting patiently for their Lover to come in the PERSONAL BODY. The dining room and auditorium were both filled to capacity as usual, and the walls echoed with praises to GOD ALMIGHTY, which was evidence to show how happy the children were, that the BODY was with them, although they are always happy with the Presence of His Spirit, but the BODY is what caused them to have BODY SALVATION.[67]

That the short, round, balding body of a black man was the chosen vehicle for God's reincarnation seemed a wonderful thing to Divine's black and white supporters alike, and they did all that they could to keep their own bodies near that holy form at all times.

Even his most avid followers, of course, were not initially accustomed to thinking of God as presently embodied, and Divine took care to explain to them how a concept that conflicted with their prior teaching and experience could possibly be true. Why did God need a body, anyway, especially one that was evidently not that of Jesus? If this question was not answered to his critics' satisfaction, his response made perfect sense to the angels: "GOD gave you a body before He gave Himself one. . . . Just because you had a body before I did, it does not mean to say that I should not have a BODY, I have one!" Because God was originally spirit, taught Divine, human beings continued to expect that God would never have a body. Even those who believed in the first incarnation of Jesus and in his eventual second coming were deceived in the present day, not expecting God to return so soon and especially not in the body of an ordinary-looking black man. But now that such a miraculous event had taken place, true believers had no recourse but to bow down to the truth of God's latest revelation.[68]

Indeed, it was dangerous not to recognize Father Divine's body as the body of God. According to Divine's teachings, God in turn would refuse to recognize those who had rejected his body on earth, leading to horrific torments that he described in detail: "With the disrecognition of the BODY of GOD, when GOD disrecognizes your body and redeems that which is called 'your Soul,' or 'your Spirit,' . . . your body will stay in misery and be tortured until it is consumed from the face of the earth."[69] These dreadful portents seemed to come true in the tragedies that reportedly befell those who opposed Father Divine's ministry, including the judge who sentenced him to prison and died a week later of a heart attack. There was, as well, the famous case of Faithful Mary, a once loyal angel who toppled from wealth to scrabbling poverty after publicly betraying Divine with scandalous stories of sexual and financial impropriety. The frequent retelling of these and many other calamities served to warn the curious that the Peace Mission leader possessed the inviolable power of God and would smite those who challenged his divinity.

Along the way, some supporters tried to have it both ways, confessing their adherence to many of Divine's teachings while remaining silent on the question of Divine's place in the holy pantheon. In the view of the most devout, however, professions of religious commitment were empty without visible attachment to the body of God, as one was compelled to leave all other ties—spouses, parents, children—and cleave to Father Divine as the true beloved. Eager adherence to such an extreme obligation fueled the vituperative assaults on Divine's Peace Mission movement as merely a cult of poor, deluded blacks desperate for an authoritarian protector. Critics lambasted Divine by pointing to abandoned children, husbands, and (though much less frequently) wives, permanently discarded by those who wanted to live in full-time communion with Divine and his closest associates. Divine's well-known requirement of celibacy for all his angels, including the promise of restoring the once married or soiled to virginity, led his opponents to hypothesize repressed sexual energy as the source of the followers' panting admiration—either that or the possibility that Divine himself was satisfying the angels' lust via raucous, orgiastic encounters.[70] (Divine claimed personal celibacy throughout his two mortal marriages, both representing God's deep love for and fusion with humanity, the uniting of heaven and earth.) Such reductive explanations aside, the testimonies of male and female adherents alike suggest that the leader was thought of in the highest terms as a lover as much as a father.

For his part, Father Divine was intensely interested in the bodies of his angels, not only their presence in his midst but also their shape and state of health. Susan Hadley, the Harlem resident who secretly infiltrated Divine's Sayville estate on behalf of the Suffolk County district attorney's office, focused significant attention upon his meticulous physical care of the angels in residence. Many were in various stages of recuperation from illness, while others told stories of having been healed by his touch. She quoted Divine as telling her, "I have come on earth to save people from dying if only they will listen to me. People who live out to the world are living in Hell." Size, interestingly, was a chief component of his health plan (his own wife was estimated to weigh 250 pounds). Hadley reported, "He weighs everybody twice a week to see if they gain any. He always weighs on Sundays and Thursdays.

If any one loses he tells them to eat more so they can gain, for he wants them all to be very large." Of course, it would have been difficult to lose weight on the menu served nightly at Sayville: the first magnificent spread witnessed by Hadley featured "hot tea, milk and postum, rice, macaroni, white potatoes, green peas, baked beans, mashed turnips, corn, baked tomatoes, turkey, ham chops, corn meal bread, biscuits, graham bread, cake, pie, peaches and a salad."[71]

Divine's emphasis on fat is especially intriguing in light of his own family history. His mother, Nancy, reportedly weighed 480 pounds at the time of her death in 1897—an enormous size for any human figure and particularly for a woman who stood five feet tall. As Watts reports, she was so large that a special coffin had to be made for her and the door cut out of her home to remove the body.[72] But whereas Watts surmises that Nancy Baker's obesity must have embarrassed her family, including the eighteen-year-old son who would become Father Divine, the record suggests almost the contrary: that Divine saw lasting value in fat and urged it upon his followers. Nancy had been a slave for the first twenty years of her life, but by the time her son was seven years old the family was able to purchase a small lot and live in their own home. While the circumstances surrounding her physical condition are unclear, her extraordinary weight gain would have been unlikely under slavery, where watchful eyes and grueling work would have set limits on her body (and the evidence indicates a much later date for her obesity). At the very least, young George, later Father Divine, likely viewed her weight as something other than sheer catastrophe.[73]

That both Divine and his first wife, Peninniah, were heavy (particularly the latter), and that the diet served to Peace Mission believers was hardly one aimed at weight loss, bespeaks a worldview in which corpulence could symbolize victory over poverty—black poverty born of slavery—and its shame. Fat bodies had presence: they could not be ignored, as white masters once hoped to ignore the "fitter" bodies of obedient slaves. Many other black religious leaders of the time carried such weight; one was Elder Lucy Smith, the founder of Chicago's All Nations Pentecostal Church, who weighed over 300 pounds.[74] Those of Father Divine's followers who were large (and certainly not all were) carried their weight not because they were forced to eat the diet of cornmeal and pork fat that sustained Divine as a child but because of the sheer wealth and multiplicity of nutriment available to them every day. Others outside that community might interpret obesity differently, whether as a sign of poor health, laziness, or (ironically, in this case) poverty, but to those within its walls fat was a blessing, not a sin.[75]

Alongside heft as a key indicator of health, Divine applied the same tactics as more traditional New Thought practitioners, going so far as to argue that no true follower of his could ever fall prey to sickness or death. "Sickness may be in the very atmosphere in which we are living, but unless you are susceptive to such germs of sickness and disease, you cannot make that which is invisible, visible; therefore, you will not materialize it, for you shall have refused to visualize it and to recognize that which was invisible and was not recognizable; for it was not observable." The rigidity of this tenet undoubtedly had the power to terrorize those who, though faithful followers, inexplicably became sick. For these, Divine had no tolerance, noting, "If perchance you have brought affliction upon yourself from any angle of expression, it is because of deviation and failing to follow Me perfectly or whole-heartedly." Even the minutest ache or pain in the body was a sign of not living completely according to God's will, of some secret disobedience or rebellion. The burden of staying well in this sacred community was severe.[76]

More often, however, Divine did not convey the message in this way but rather turned it into a promise of perfect health. To his followers, he vowed, "I will make the way possible where you will not suffer in or out of the body." Death itself, in fact, was perfectly avoidable, since all that was required was refusal to give up the "Ghost of Life." "If you are at the bottom of the sea six weeks," Divine assured those listening, "you could not die unless you give up the Ghost. Your conscious mind must be stronger than death, backed by love combined with CHRIST Himself." Thus even life eternal was seemingly made possible through adherence to Divine's teachings and to his holy body.[77]

What made Divine unique in the arena of New Thought was not that he held out an eschatological promise to the world; most other New Thought writers had focused on spiritual immortality and some also lauded the doctrine of physical resurrection, the body purified from the dross of earthly existence. Distinctive to Divine's theology, however, and deeply tied to the culture of poverty and racism in which the man himself was formed, was the linking of that promise to a high view of bodily experience *in this life*, assurance that just as God had once again become incarnated in flesh the bodies of those who believed in him were immediately redeemed. If such redemption necessitated a lifetime of celibacy, it did not require mortification of other pleasures such as eating. The angels needed only to look at the example of their leader as he presided over their feasts to be persuaded that enjoyment of epicurean pleasures was a sacred undertaking. Here was a foretaste of heaven, holding all of the pleasures and none of the suffering of the streets beyond the banquet hall.

Abundant food was surely an aid to good health, especially for those for whom poverty had been a way of life before joining the Peace Mission movement. Yet the provisions served at Divine's communion banquets offered no ordinary sustenance; in fact, they contained immense transformative power. A communion message in 1941 made this point explicit, when Divine noted that the people "eat this food as blessed food. They cannot think as they have been thinking. They cannot have those antagonistic and malicious thoughts when they partake of the food that I have blessed." Distinguishing between the symbolic, custom-bound ritual of communion practiced by ordinary ministers, and the more practical, sustenance-oriented sacrament that he performed at every banquet table, Divine noted that the simple thought of God's literally handling their food helped believers develop purer, more wholesome bodies and souls. "This is the way I bless you all—by giving you blessed food to eat, to drink and the blessed comfort and convenience such as we have for the nourishment and for the comfort of your bodies, and for the unification of your body and your soul, that they might be severed no more."[78]

While the tangible, nutritional quality of food was vital to Divine's communion banquets, the victuals were also richly suggestive of the greater gifts promised to those who would choose to give up their former lives and follow him completely. The feasts, though supplemented by a network of affordable restaurants and grocery stores run by Peace Mission supporters across the country, were distinct in supplying vast quantities of food at little or no cost to anyone who wished to enter the premises, whether rich or poor, black or white. Outsiders who made their way there might wonder at the luxuriant meals, but the angels knew better. As Divine taught, "The material food is only a sketch and a reflection of a percent of a percent of a fraction of a grain of a percent of a fraction of a grain of the mystery of GOD's Presence and of GOD feeding His Children!" The cuisine, however scrumptious and wholesome in itself, was a mere shadow of true reality, pointing to the far more considerable sustenance that Father Divine could and would provide. "You marvel at the Banquets we serve daily," he teased his unconverted guests. "It is a matter of course with us. It is a daily occurrence! Why marvel at the material side?" Wonderment ought to be reserved for that which was genuinely miraculous, namely the all-benevolent, embodied manifestation of God in their humble midst. Food was not mere food: "This material food we are eating is the actual tangibilization of GOD's Word, of GOD's Love and of GOD's Presence; they have been made bread and meat for you to personally eat."[79]

Marveling aside, the promises of bodily comfort were important to both Divine and his followers. Never did anyone in the Peace Mission movement seriously suggest that the body could or should be done away with alto-gether. Even if spirit was ultimately higher than body in Divine's New Thought calculus, bodily satisfactions remained vitally important. Though food remained a mere shadow, he promised, "As long as you walk in the light, you will have the shadow." The two were inextricably linked for Divine, in a concrete way—with food the element that bonded them together—that no New Thought promoter before him had so confidently articulated. "Abide in My Spirit and walk in the light of My LOVE," vowed Divine, "and your spirit, your body and your soul will be bountifully sup-plied, and your bodies of all of their desires as well as your souls, and your minds will be perfectly satisfied. Aren't you glad!"[80]

Divine's angels seemed very glad indeed, basking in both the material and mystical aspects of these holy banquets. And, on the surface at least, their convictions did not go unrewarded, as the daily communion meals worked miraculous effects on those who were faithful to Father Divine. Testimonies of healing abounded in printed accounts of these sumptuous banquets. Preston Dudley, visiting the Harlem Peace Mission from Washington, DC, told of being healed from consumption and gaining weight because of his faith in Father Divine. He also recounted the healing of another man, whose disease was so far advanced that doctors had given him up and burial plans had been made. One look at Divine was all it took to heal the man, according to Dudley's account. He concluded with an appropriately food-centered anal-ogy: most people were like hogs who root around acorn trees looking for nuts instead of picking up that which was right in front of them. "I have been here and seen the FATHER and talked with the Son," he finished, thanking Divine for charging his batteries and keeping them charged.[81]

If Divine's own claim of godly authority limited his appeal in many quar-ters, it expanded his influence among many whose own flesh had been bro-ken by the world, his assurances richly alluring to those who wished to recommence their lives in entirely new flesh. Indeed, the appetite, the senses, and all disparate parts of the body would be fully renovated upon conversion, for "when you become to be a different one characteristically, dispositionally, naturely and actually as well as mentally and spiritually, you become to be new creatures physically and your bodies will take on new cell tissues in the remodelling and the renovating of your body in which you are now living." The new birth that Jesus memorably commanded his disciples to undergo was here translated into the reality of a new body. "The very blood in your veins will not be the same. You will have a different heart-beat, hence you will have a different beating-pulse; for you are being renovated as you are regenerated, as you are born again." Even a trained bloodhound, with its highly advanced instinct of smell, would no longer be able to recognize its own newly born-again owner, for the complete transformation meant that "YOU HAVE A DIFFERENT ODOR." Ultimately, one's entire physical body, from its physiognomic expression to its shape to its internal system, would become the "personification" of all that one had previously emphasized in thought.[82]

Such a lesson could not have always been joyously received, especially among those who knew their former thought patterns to be harmful and whose mirrors reflected faces lined with dread and bodies frail or ill. But no body, however old, was ever finished changing in Divine's kingdom. It was never too late for one to make a new beginning, to open oneself up to new mental and spiritual conceptions of peace and love and watch one's very physical self undergo transformation. "Your physical bodies and your actions and expressions, your emotions and vibrations in your physical bodies, are but your mental and Spiritual conception of yesterday." But today! Today was a new day, "and your physical bodies are expressing it," shedding the skins of former selves and becoming "new creatures in reality," the decisive sign of which for any individual was a visibly refurbished body.[83]

If such a body remained identifiable to the people in one's old life—jilted mates, parents, and children, after all, continued to pursue their loved ones well after the latter had joined the angelic circle around Father Divine—it was not susceptible to any of its older infirmities, afflictions, or iniquities. Ties to whatever cursed genealogical lineage one came from were forever severed, so that even "the wickedness of your ancestors" no longer had power. Those outside the fold, that is, those not born again, were tormented by all the transgressions of their forebears, according to Divine, as well as their sicknesses and diseases. This was why it was so crucial for the angels to break completely with their families of birth and marriage, to shun terms such as "my mother" (and heatedly correct any outsider who dared to use the phrase) in favor of "she who was called my mother" and to treat even their own biological children with the aloofness of a total stranger. Those who remained tied to their old bodies represented sickness, unhappiness, and the miseries of death, spreading contagion throughout the land.[84]

What it meant for God to spiritualize one's body was not always completely clear to outsiders, especially in the context of the sumptuous daily meals to which the body was privy. But Divine called upon his followers to practice strict self-denial in manifold ways, almost as if to prove that in reality they existed on a plane high above that in which their bodies partook of raw gustatory pleasures. They could simultaneously have their pleasure and etherealize it too. The title of one of Divine's communion sermons summarized this notion perfectly: "When You Deny Yourself after the Manner of the Flesh You Will Unify Yourself with the Infinite Spirit and the Universal Mind Substance."[85] Denial had more than one meaning in Divine's kingdom, but its clearest referent was sexual intercourse. In his childhood, Divine had become familiar with the celibacy practiced by Catholic nuns and priests and later expressed admiration for this form of devotion.[86] The angels who lived in his Peace Mission communes, even married couples, were housed among their own sex, with occasional warnings not to become overly attached to their roommates in those close quarters. Virginity, as practically all previous observers of Divine's movement have noted, was crucially important in the movement, with Divine promising to restore to virgin status all those who had been "soiled" by sexual relations in their unredeemed lives. Here again God's own body, the body of Father Divine, was the power source by which all human beings could be purified, if they denied the lusts of the flesh.

Interest in celibacy, we noted, was not outside the bounds of classic New Thought. Indeed, in a worldview that glorified spirit and held a rather low view of matter, the wonder may be that more New Thought leaders did not disdain copulation as sharply as Divine. Stockham's *Karezza* (1896), the best-selling New Thought text on the subject, had taught strict mastery of sexual desire while yet encouraging regulated intercourse as a spiritual act that ennobled both husband and wife. For Father Divine to demand complete sexual abstinence (and separation of spouses to guard against cheating) even as he sanctioned gluttonous abandonment to food created an apparent paradox that outsiders, then and later, found difficult to comprehend. Yet functionally these practices were not at odds: the discipline of sexual abstinence would have worked to center the affection of Divine's angels almost solely on him, and of course this was essentially the same effect that the banquets had—especially so, perhaps, for those unused to such luxurious spreads or unable to afford them elsewhere.

Excessive feeding could in this way become its own form of regulation, whether serving to sap the energy of the banqueters (research has shown that both heavy eating and obesity are correlated with reduced energy and the latter also with sleep apnea) or drawing them into a closer circle of gratitude toward the fulfiller of their needs. Divine was most definitely in charge of his followers, though his form of control hardly seemed malicious: most reports of the time, including Hadley's and Braden's, suggest a fatherly regard toward those who joined his community. Nonetheless, these practices surrounding sex and food both acted as means to channel human affection away from its former objects and concentrate it wholly upon this god in a body. The point of abstinence was not to deny the physical but to focus the full self and all of its desires entirely on Divine.

The rejuvenation that Divine offered to his followers was one lived out in bodily experience, not in a ghostly spiritual realm beyond flesh. As he noted more than once, "I did not come to save the SOUL . . . but I came to save the BODIES of the children of men." Emphatically targeted on health, nonplussed by illness, Divine refused even to speak of those who died in his midst—asserting only in the abstract that those who allowed themselves to expire had not believed fully in him. The death, sometime in 1943, of his wife, Peninniah, was not immediately acknowledged, then was later explained away when Divine remarried a much younger woman and said that Peninniah had desired to leave her former body and be reborn in a "more youthful body."[87] Yet at Divine's death in 1965, his followers interpreted it in Christological terms, that is, as an act of supreme sacrifice for the world; then, with no perceptible sense of contradiction, they reshaped his theology to account for his continuing spiritual presence in their midst in ways still observed by the small, aged remnant of his movement (led by his second wife, Mother Divine). The inconsistencies in Divine's own musings on death, nonetheless, reveal how forcibly he tried to eradicate it from his world, and how fervently he believed that such was possible.

If Divine's ultimate promise of victory over death resonated with that of other New Thought and Christian Perfectionist thinkers, his intermediate path was highly inventive. He led his followers, black and white alike, to celebrate their bodies, however feeble, ugly, contaminated, or worthless they had once believed their flesh to be. Likewise, Divine called his supporters to venerate the body of a black man, and that in an age when most Americans found it difficult, ludicrous, or simply downright impossible to imagine such flesh as holy. He taught everyone who visited him, from the angels to the skeptics, to take delight in the corporeal pleasures of food, to see in the act of eating multiple possibilities for wholesale regeneration of the self. And he instructed them never to discount the importance of the physical body—its sensory capacities, cell structure, and organic unity viewed as a profoundly miraculous system that reflected the state of the spirit. Indeed, more than simply reflecting the spirit, the body provided the material out of which spiritual maturity and health were literally forged: the foundation without which nothing else was possible.

Critics who have rued Divine's attempt to erase racial categories altogether—his refusal of the terms "black" and "white"—have failed to recognize the radical direction of his thought and practice concerning bodies and of the alternative categories he imagined transforming the world.

"Race" was of diminished importance, and "sexuality" altogether erased, because these seemed trivial in light of the holy immanence that Divine professed to represent. Distinctions among bodies vanished as these bodies communed together in celebratory feasting and enthusiastic acceptance of a celibate life. With bodily perfection attainable right here on earth, visible markers of that state shifted dramatically, so that what one sought as evidence of goodness was not skin color or markings of gender but signs of good appetite, health, and peaceful well-being.

Yet it was arguably the very culture of poverty and racism into which Divine was born that prompted such an inversion of standard New Thought precepts. Raised in a world in which obesity could signify *presence* no less than an end to slavery-bred poverty, a sign that neither blacks nor whites could pretend to ignore, Divine enabled his followers to give up forever the "poor food" they once knew and grow fat on a more luxurious diet (though one still linked to southern soul food). Father Divine's version of New Thought was different from that of his white precedents and contemporaries because of where he came from and what he had seen in the poor black community of Rockville, Maryland. Raised by a mother who had once been enslaved, and bred in a world still thick with hunger and racial inequity, Father Divine could ill afford to conclude that the world of matter was an illusion. Where many of his New Thought forebears had looked ahead to a bodiless future, fasting vigorously in search of a way to sustain life without food, Divine's paradise was precisely the opposite: a world in which nothing was more real than steaming hot, sumptuous meals, available virtually around the clock. Though he cloaked his background in secrecy as a strategy for universalizing and purifying his message to the world, Father Divine never split himself from George Baker or forgot the hunger endured by that child and millions more.

Finally, the story of Divine and the Peace Mission movement cautions contemporary observers to recall that sexuality is not the only criterion for viewing the human body. The celibacy requirement that so many scholars and critics have taken as proof of Divine's rigid dualism does not tell us nearly as much about his attitudes toward fleshly existence as do his pronouncements and practices regarding food, physical perfectibility, and the sacredness of human embodiment. More exactly, neither celibacy nor epicureanism presents the full picture of Divine's instruction on the design of the human self. He sometimes joined the sexually ascetic way of life that he required of his angels with potent inducements to bodily pleasure, even ecstasy. Thus mundane bodily habits of discipline and release fused seemingly disparate impulses and heightened attention to transcendent experience. Together, Divine's angels sang of a day beyond racism, when, "Away down in Texas, and in the farthest parts of the south, we shall eat and drink together, racism shall be wiped out. There will be no more race riots and lynchings, there will be no more division or strife, when they recognize *God's Body,* they will value each other's life. Father will make them love each other so much . . . Racialism shall be wiped out!"[88] The tangibilization of God in a vigorous, food-loving man meant not merely that common flesh could be sanctified; far more, it signified the annulment of ordinary categories of distinction between body and spirit, black and white: the materialization of a once unimaginable, mystical world.

Father Divine's materialist theology ultimately lost favor among all but a small remnant of followers, even as other African American religious leaders propounded very different kinds of body regimens. During the 1950s and accelerating into the 1960s, movements for black power and liberation spurred forceful discussions about the need for bodily care, nutrition, and general health. Food, in fact, was at the center of black political debates during the civil rights movement and beyond, as a range of religious voices sought to transform the lives of African Americans by overhauling their food practices. It may be useful to look briefly at one of these, as a way of comparing some of the later innovations in black nationalist treatments of religion and the body. The devotion to dietary regimen by groups such as the Nation of Islam (NOI), the African American liberation movement headed by Elijah Muhammad between 1934–75 and made famous by Malcolm X during the 1960s, relied upon common American cultural themes. In two books titled *How to Eat to Live* (1967 and 1972), Muhammad began his text with the promise, "Eat to live to bring about a return to perfection and long life."

Good food and good thoughts went hand in hand, taught Muhammad, so that one had to be careful not to eat the "wrong mental food" when on an otherwise healthy diet. Proper food comprised the heart of the liberation message that Muhammad sought to bring to black men and women:

> Master Fard Muhammad, to Whom Praises are due forever, comes to prolong our lives, not to shorten them, by correcting our eating habits to one meal a day instead of three, and by teaching us to eat the proper foods that will not destroy us or shorten our lives to less than 100 years. His (Allah's) teaching us to eat better food and to cut our eating from three and four times a day to once a day will certainly prolong our lives and increase our beautiful appearance.

In this view, the "Christian race," and specifically the "white man," had created a state of affairs in which the "Black nation" had been poisoned by overeating and by habituation to the slave diet of meat, greasy foods, starch, sugar, alcohol, and tobacco. And not only these foods: "Every meal that we put in our bodies has some poison in it," he noted. "If we do not wait until our previous meal has been digested [and] we add a new meal to the previous meal we have new poison, in its full strength, to aid the dying poison of the previous meal or to help it revive in strength; and we will continue to be sick."[89]

Fasting was central to the Nation of Islam's dietary teachings, and Elijah Muhammad's many reflections on this practice included one chapter entitled "Fasting, Eating Right Foods, Keys to Long Life." Here and elsewhere, his teachings on food abstinence went well beyond Koranic justifications for religious fasting—indeed, Elijah Muhammad often wrote directly against Orthodox Muslim methods, including fasting during Ramadan—as he spoke in harmony with the New Thought apostles of abstinence some decades hence:

> Fasting is a greater cure of our ills—both mentally and physically—than all of the drugs of the earth combined into one bottle or into a billion bottles. . . . ALLAH TAUGHT ME that one meal a day would keep us here for a long time; we would live over 100 years. And eating one meal every two days would lengthen our lives just that much longer. He told me you would never be sick, eating one meal every three days. The fact that fasting is the cure to 90 per cent of our ills is known by the medical scientists. But, they do not teach you that.[90]

Longer life, increased wealth, better health, sharper thinking, and reduction of evil or filthy desires would all accrue to the abstinent eater, he stated. Nation of Islam adherents were advised to fast monthly for three, nine, or twenty-seven days, in order to eliminate the poisons in the bloods accumulated from nondigested foods. Though Elijah Muhammad did not explicitly mention thinness, adherence to this dietary regimen would produce a beautiful appearance and result in a happier, freer, and elongated life. Twenty years later, in "Exercise to Stay Alive!" the later Nation of Islam leader Louis Farrakhan noted God's abhorrence of obesity and asked a question any Christian dieter would have understood: "What would you think of Jesus if you saw him in his holy robes, overweight, with a stomach that made him look eight months pregnant, fat jowls and a fat neck?" Imploring his readers to do away with the grease and garbage infesting their bodies, he urged, "Anytime you see an ounce of fat that shouldn't be there, I want you to see that excess fat as an opposer, an adversary, a devil . . . Satan robbing you of life."[91]

Purity and filth, then, have been key tropes in the Nation of Islam's discourse of diet. Leaders such as Muhammad and Farrakhan upended white appraisals of dirty blackness so as to link filth with the "devil" white race, European lineage, and western Christianity. Pork, the filthiest of all food-stuffs in this worldview, was beloved by the white race, which had then imposed it upon others; to refuse such disgusting fare was to reject both white values and historical associations with slavery. Abstinence—again, Elijah Muhammad urged his followers to eat only one daily meal and to fast frequently—lifted the individual above the consumerist hedonism of ordinary citizens who were drugged out on food and other sensual attachments. Private bodily practices carried powerful meanings about black strength and racial supremacy, and Nation of Islam leaders urged their followers to be models of disciplined restraint (a quality that was also embodied in the pristine adornments NOI men and women wore to reveal their adherence to this abstemious life). Whereas Father Divine had vocally underplayed the existence of racial categories (despite their centrality to his religious and political program), the Nation of Islam put race front and center in order vigorously to oppose the evil white racism that suffused American society. And whereas Divine focused on the body's pleasures, Elijah Muhammad's writings damned pleasure by connecting it both implicitly and explicitly with death.

The pleasures of the appetite were tools of deception that would shorten a black man's life. "In the past, our appetites were as the appetites of swine," wrote Muhammad, but "the swine's life is very short, because it comes here eating itself to death, and death soon takes it away."[92] This was a powerful message to a community for whom pork had long been a dietary staple and had particular salience after the civil rights movement amid the new espousals of "soul food." "Black is beautiful" was a mantra that extended to such practices as cooking, and soul food cookbooks grew in popularity among the black middle classes. Many of these texts, incidentally, were published as "church" cookbooks, and the mainstream black Christian denominations settled themselves squarely on the side of soul food, an expression of black pride that nonetheless avoided the revolutionary implications of Elijah Muhammad's abstemious program.

Despite NOI's small adherence in comparison to black church membership, however, its influence went well beyond its numbers. Figures such as the black comedian Dick Gregory crusaded for natural foods and fasting among black people, a direct result of Elijah Muhammad's influence. Traditions of African American feasting battled it out with fasting as starkly different symbolizations of black pride, practices with competing messages to send about bodily expression and constraint. In these two divergent communities, though, hopeful believers could imagine a connection to "God in a body"—whether Divine himself as God incarnate or Elijah Muhammad's teacher, Wallace Fard Muhammad. Notably, Muhammad's ideas about discipline and pleasure were much closer to those reigning in white middle-class circles than Divine's were, even as Muhammad was the one lodging more serious claims against the wickedness of white people and their religion. While both leaders attracted the majority of their followers from the urban lower class, they appealed to different needs; for while Divine's program of abundance surely reflected the way that many Americans *wanted* to be able to eat—copiously but without negative consequences—Muhammad tempted his listeners to believe that they could construct a superior self by rejecting most of what the world had to offer.

The literary critic Doris Witt has cogently argued that the Nation of Islam's use of dietary prohibitions, particularly Elijah Muhammad's and Farrakhan's, signals a particular project of constructing black manhood and erasing—or at least radically constraining—women's roles in that religious world. She describes how the foods that Muhammad associated with the slave diet were linked to black women *as mothers*. Eating, she contends, "calls into question the origins of self in the mother and grandmother, who are here rescripted by Muhammad as takers rather than givers of life. Muhammad was facing a problem common to all patriarchal religions: how to elide the role of women in procreation so as to locate the origins of life in a male god."[93]

Witt's argument serves as a useful lens for viewing ways in which sex, food, and death intersected on the site of the female body. In a chapter titled "The Death Way," Muhammad clarified these connections between the "poisonous foods, milk, and water" that fed blacks from the beginning and led to "such a great percentage of delinquency among minors." Mothers were self-centered: "The child is not fed from his mother's breast—she is too proud of her form. Therefore, she lets the cow and other animals nurse her new-born baby." Hence the baby "loves the bottle that its food is in— food that his mother robbed from the cow's baby to feed her own baby."[94] By insisting that NOI women rededicate themselves to their roles as mothers, Muhammad once again departed from the program of Father Divine. Peace Mission movement women were celibate and freed of all child-rearing responsibilities, though Divine seemed to see them as bodies of life rather than death.

Both Divine and Muhammad worked to free black people from the injustice and ongoing indignities inflicted upon them by white American society, and they built their programs around new practices of embodiment.

Exacting leaders both, each demanded that their followers ingest new ideological doctrines just as thoroughly as they shifted the religious and social meaning of food and body. Later black Christian diet writers such as T. D. Jakes and Jawanza Kunjufu combined aspects of both programs, urging African Americans to rethink their gluttonous potluck dinners but also celebrating other kinds of abundance, such as—particularly in the case of Jakes—consumer spending. Kunjufu didn't mince words about the dangers of gluttony; in his 2000 book *Satan, I'm Taking Back My Health*, he wrote, "God wants us to have life and to have life more abundantly. God is not pleased with his children dying of cancer, heart disease, strokes, and diabetes, nor suffering from obesity, arthritis, and rheumatism." Proverbs 23:3 came in handy as a reminder that disciplined believers should *"Put a knife to your throat if you are a man given to appetite. . . .* We have a much greater chance of dying at the dinner table than from a gun, an automobile, or a nuclear weapon."[95]

Jakes and Kunjufu were not only influenced by black liberationist food regimens, however, for by the time they began publishing their work in the 1980s, a substantial corpus of Christian dietary advice had been generated by white Protestant authors and fitness leaders. For while Father Divine's sumptuous theology of body and soul and Elijah Muhammad's intensive dietary regulations were largely confined to their respective followers, other gospels of bodily perfection were flooding twentieth-century American senses. Most of these gospels, traversing decades of repetition and reinvention, were indebted no less than the onetime fasting masters and William Sheldon to the positive thinking habits bestowed by New Thought, and nearly all would center on disciplined thinness. What happened when white American Christians entered more vigorously into this tradition, creating an ever livelier amalgam of abstinence and consumerism, repression and exuberance, is the story to which we now turn.

4 Pray the Weight Away

Shaping Devotional Fitness Culture

Disparate twentieth-century programs of masculinized fasting, Sheldonian somatotypy, and epicurean empowerment inspired many in their day, but they give less than a full picture of metaphysical preoccupations with the flesh. Devotion to thinness, at least among white middle-class Americans, took lasting hold on the culture between 1890 and 1910, as we have seen. But if the decades surrounding the turn of the twentieth century marked the development and ripening of American diet culture, the postwar years provided vital nourishment for that culture's intensification, a process built upon ever mounting certitude about the inward truths supposedly revealed by the condition of the external body. Even as black urban leaders were urging followers to eat for their spiritual and physical lives, white Protestants put forth their own survival regimen, its latent stringency matched by its formulators' down-home affability and cloaked by its reassuring familiarity within the wider milieu of American diet culture. Here Christian piety and health reform reunited, in a coupling seemingly impervious to the poverty and prejudice that had inspired Divine and Muhammad to accentuate the religious politics of gastronomy. Yet the ultimate aim proved in some ways analogous to black nationalism, in that faithful Christian dieters believed their disciplined lives would serve higher ends than private pleasure or individual health: at stake, ultimately, was the creation of a holy people beloved by an approachable, stern yet merciful God.

As white middle-class body fixations extended and secured their cultural hold in the United States during the postwar years, religious diet culture took its own concentrated course, though critics have tended to condemn its theology rather than explain its appeal.[1] What accounts for the assiduous cultivation of thinness as an American ideal? Historians and other observers, whether applying Weberian or psychoanalytic models, have regularly invoked accelerating American anxieties with affluence and consumerism to explain the persistence of this ascetic-looking ideal: body disciplines, they claim, have provided compensation for the loss of other forms of restraint and meaning. From this perspective, commentators have further envisaged the pursuit of thinness as a new kind of secularizing "religion" to replace older forms of faith. As earlier chapters in this book demonstrate, however, Protestant and New Thought influences helped shape the dominant American diet culture, as the upward currency of disciplined, meditative thought imbued authors and expectant dieters alike with hope in the power of mental therapeutic methods to boost weight loss. Moreover, as sociologists and historians of religion have repeatedly documented, religion hardly faltered but rather flourished in the latter decades of the twentieth century, and its greatest proliferation occurred among those groups happily allied with consumerist, body-conscious ideals: chiefly conservative evangelicals. The case for a widespread secularizing impulse, entwined with guilt and nostalgia for moribund norms of Puritan fortitude, appears to rely more on conjecture than visible evidence.

Psychological explanations of shame and self-punishment, coupled with dubious secularization theories, in fact display much less agility in accounting for America's love affair with thin bodies than theories of religion, particularly those that highlight religion's cultural role in legitimizing and fortifying divine-human relationships. Persons believing in the real presence of holy beings who are amenable to human contact and interaction approach such deities through a variety of ritual methods, providing data for comparative religious studies. In western Christianity, linked by customs of asceticism and communicative prayer, such devotional exchanges between humans and their gods often entail notions of intimacy and obedience, as well as punishment and exclusion; and these relational dynamics are in turn essential for structuring power relations within and across religious communities. This concern for a very tangible form of connectedness with sacred power carries vast cultural import in postwar American culture, and nowhere does that concern appear more acutely than in Christian diet culture. As this and the next chapter of *Born Again Bodies* seek to show, purveyors and consumers of religious fitness culture raise such relationships to foremost levels of concern: ideal bodies serve not merely private or even political ends—though the power interests of individuals and social factions have been more than incidental—but, still further, perform indispensable work as effective agents of devotional intimacy.[2]

SHEDD-ING POUNDS: SCRIPTURE AND DEVOTIONAL
PRACTICE IN SERVICE TO WEIGHT LOSS

"I was the fattest girl on the campus—or at least I felt that way," wrote twenty-two-year-old Deborah Pierce in 1960. As a 208-pound college student at the University of Tennessee, she had never had a date, and she wept while other girls cruelly scorned her as "Fatty." One night, according to Pierce's narrative retelling, "I comforted myself with a midnight snack consisting of a pint of ice cream and a box of cookies. 'I'll show them,' I thought, 'I'll go on a diet and I'll get so slim that I'll be able to call *them* fatty.'" Having failed on numerous commercial diets, Pierce turned to God, began praying daily for the grace to avoid food until her one daily afternoon meal, and dropped 82 pounds in ten months until at 5'9" she weighed a lean 126 pounds. She went on to become a high-fashion model and beauty contestant, becoming a finalist in the Miss District of Columbia pageant (a step in the competition for Miss Universe), and then a beaming bride.[3]

To readers of her *American Weekly* article and subsequent book, *I Prayed Myself Slim*, Pierce—a southern Episcopalian—outlined a strict regimen, including an abstemious thirty-day diet that rarely went above 1,000 calories. Alongside each day's menu was a prayer, set to liturgical cadences and meant to be repeated throughout the day for humility, recollection of gluttony as sinful, and strength to overcome it. Her text rang with appeals for divine assistance "never to return to my old reprehensible food habits" but rather "to be truly grateful for each morsel of the small amount that I can eat with impunity and with beneficial results."[4] Enfolding this type of self-denial within the long history of Christian asceticism reaped wondrously modern-day results, as Pierce embraced the body and beauty standards of American white middle-class culture as God's will for all, marking deviance from that model as sin.

Just three years before Deborah Pierce's book, the Presbyterian minister Charlie Shedd had published *Pray Your Weight Away* (1957), which denounced fat in no uncertain terms. "We fatties are the only people on earth who can weigh our sin," he wrote straightforwardly: "Stand on the scale. How much more do you weigh than you should weigh? There it is: one hundred pounds of sin, or fifty, or eleven." Shedd's aptly titled book, published when the author was in his early forties, sported a jacket topped with the propitious headliner, "How one man found the help he needed for the greatest act of self-discipline of his life." Here Shedd, who professed having lost 100 pounds himself, announced a "new truth" that was "glorious news for the obese." Far from promoting a wrathful God of anger, Shedd

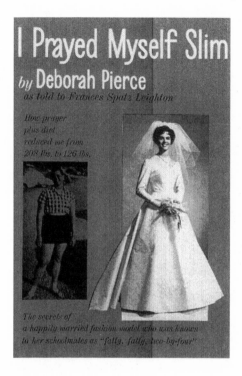

11. Front cover of Deborah Pierce, *I Prayed Myself Slim.*

affirmed a God of love, the sure proof of which for God's "chubby children" was the visibility and measurability of sin as body fat: if they could see it, they could do something about it. Writing to an audience as yet not jaded by diet books—or by the combination of spirituality and weight loss—as later readers would be, Shedd promoted a gospel of slimness that condemned portly bodies in the explicit language of sin and guilt, while guaranteeing weight loss by means of sustained prayer, devotion to the Bible, and unshakeable faith in thinness as a sign of sanctity.[5]

Being by now mostly adjusted to this softened version of New Thought wisdom in their theology, few of Shedd's Protestant readers found it heretical or scandalous. For some, the response came closer to resigned acceptance, as if understanding that Shedd augured the future of practical, therapeutic Christianity. Among the commentaries on his book, for instance, was a droll review by the Christian literary scholar William R. Mueller, who made light fun of "the originality of Dr. Shedd's religious perspective" while confessing to the resonance of Shedd's spiritual diet in his own life. (Mueller's fat-hating Presbyterian mother had hung coupled portraits of John Calvin and Bernarr Macfadden above her dressing table and subjected her young son to

12. "Before" and "After," from back cover of Charlie Shedd, *Pray Your Weight Away*.

carrot juice and a "grueling order of calisthenics" each morning before school.) Writing for the liberal Protestant magazine *Christian Century*, Mueller noted the relentless perkiness of this "new theology," with its "streamlined soldiers of righteousness" who would divest their mountains of flesh and march lithely into heaven.[6] A similarly amused evaluation of *Pray Your Weight Away* appeared in the *New Republic* from the pen of the drama critic Gerald Weales. In the era of Norman Vincent Peale and Gaylord Hauser, Weales observed, Shedd's joining of theology and diet was a farsighted and savvy promotional move, especially when seasoned with the doctrine that fat was sin (a belief that, as Mueller pointed out, many Christians had long held about gluttony, though perhaps rarely stated so forthrightly). Weales predicted great success for the book—"unless some canny health-food expert is about to turn out a competitive volume, called *Salvation through Diet*."[7] This whimsical title may have been too clunky for the times—*I Prayed Myself Slim* won the day instead—but his forecast for the success of this genre proved prescient.

For Shedd and Pierce to claim that "reducing," in the parlance of the day, was a spiritual problem rather than merely a medical one echoed older themes rehearsed by the fasting masters of the Progressive Era but played them in a new key. Modulated in these books, for instance, was the obsessive concern with bodily purification and toxicity endlessly detailed in texts by

Bernarr Macfadden and his cohort. As James Whorton has documented, the fixation upon feces as being capable of poisoning the body—and the accompanying language of "autointoxication"—had virtually disappeared from mainstream medicine and general parlance by midcentury.[8] Yet the ultimate aim of eradicating disease, and the belief that such was not only possible but divinely ordained, was nothing if not stronger by the 1950s than it had been even among the New Thought prophets some decades earlier.

At the time that Shedd and Pierce wrote, however, there had been very little public attention paid to fat as something that itself required healing from divine hands. Though the postwar era was a time of increased consciousness about weight and an upsurge in dieting for beauty and health, the religious literature remained mostly silent on the issue, with an occasional exception such as the National Council of Churches executive J. Carter Swaim. In 1957, Swaim argued that obesity prevented persons, perhaps especially men, from being their most effective selves and advised the mainline Protestant audience of *Religion and Health* to "avoid the addition of excess poundage" by pushing their chairs away from their dinner tables. "Temperance is a good thing but the Bible enjoins upon us a better," Swaim insisted. Looking wistfully to the model of military discipline ("The army can court-martial a man who will not reduce"), Swaim urged Christians to revisit the scriptures and by their teachings attain perfect self-control.[9]

Shedd's perspective was both gentler and sterner than Swaim's: gentler because it relied on a soft-hearted God and eschewed talk of military discipline, sterner because it spoke louder and more ominously about fat as sin. "Sin," Shedd noted, was so commonplace in scriptural readings that modern readers could not fail to avoid it, yet its very frequency dulled the mind and the senses to its import. Christians encountered the word so often, in fact, that sin merely "skittered lightly" across the surface of their reflections. To take sin more seriously, for Shedd, was to allow it to "fall heavy on our bulging contours," to recognize the gravity of failing to meet the standard that God had set for all people. "Now step on the scale!" he commanded. "You know approximately what you should weigh. How much does the needle 'miss the mark'? The spread between your proper weight and your current weight looms large before you." The glory of this simple measuring of sin was that fat people could "see with their eyes the exact extent of their evil," by looking bluntly at the numbers on the scale and the figure reflected in the mirror. Fat was the embodied mark of disobedience and distance from God, while weight reduction signified the restoration of holiness.[10]

As for Pierce, her text reiterated and extended some of Shedd's key themes while adding to his chirpy meditations the sonorous rhythms of the *Book of Common Prayer* and the historical religious resonances of "gluttony" (a concept that Shedd, for whom overeating signaled psychological needs rather than simple greed, avoided altogether). While her book detailed a plan for combating the sin of gluttony that had inflated her figure to a size 20, Pierce also described herself as a compulsive eater who continued to think of food as her enemy. She conveyed little of Shedd's routine humor and proffered a much more severe course of discipline than her Presbyterian forerunner, a rigor closely akin to other female-authored diet books of the period and in that sense a nascent sign of the powerful gender dynamics already at play in this genre. There could be no respite for the offenders of God's diet plan, whom Pierce seemingly held in lower regard as miscreant sinners than had Shedd. Later sections of her book gave "additional prayers to help you keep that new slim figure," with the reader called to beseech God for help remembering "how long and painful was the struggle I underwent to conquer gluttony and attain this slimness." Gratitude mixed with guilt and desperation, "that I may never fall victim again to ugly and self-destroying obesity," nor ever "sin against Thee again, now that I have realized the error of my ways and the enormity of the sin which I committed against Thee."[11]

Tenets of sin and love were thus closely interwoven in both Pierce and Shedd's slimness creeds: the joys of earthly existence that were forsaken by the heavy were abundantly supplied to the physically fit. For the obese, "out of tune" with God, the Holy Spirit's knocking on their hearts could not be heard through the layers of fat. Once those layers were peeled away and the Spirit could enter into the body, the results were confidence, direction, energy, and love, all of which created a new dynamism, radiance, and true health. Modern scientific research that attributed multiple infirmities to obesity aided this worldview, which set such diseases (diabetes, arthritis, heart problems, and the like) in opposition to God's design for a healthier humanity. Moreover, because fat preceded and in some sense seemed actually to cause these and other maladies, fat in any amount could not logically be part of God's plan. "When God first dreamed you into creation," Shedd chided his heavy readers, "there weren't one hundred pounds of excess avoirdupois hanging around your belt. No, nor sixty, nor sixteen."[12] In this way, Shedd and Pierce shifted the discussion surrounding religion and health by insisting that fat itself, and not simply the medical illnesses it helped create, could be—and should be—subject to God's healing, slimming power.

That some could riotously indulge their appetite yet remain thin was a common source of envy for the corpulent, Pierce realized, and so she provided prayers to guard against jealousy of those who could devour rich foods without visible consequence. Such people did not appear, in her mapping of transgression and redemption, to partake in "gluttony," which even as a sin was indexed by body size and nothing more. Moreover, the idea that the indignity of their "abnormal" bodies disgraced fat people was perfectly reasonable to Pierce, who recommended prayers not for tolerance of the heavy but for the strength to stay slim: "Dear Lord, now that I have a normal-sized body and can hold my head high and not be ashamed among people who once regarded me with scorn, help me to look upon food . . . not with the eyes of a glutton, but with those of a normal human being."[13] As Shedd did, she uncritically embraced the body and beauty standards of the wider white middle-class culture as God's will for all, with deviance from that model indelibly marked as sin.

Shedd was an especially ideal figure to inaugurate the modern Christian diet movement, in part because he was one of the twentieth century's various popularizers of New Thought ideals within a Reformed evangelical context. In words that echoed Norman Vincent Peale's wildly popular *Power of Positive Thinking* (1952), Shedd enthused about the power of prayer to effect change and produce the thing desired. Prayer was "healing power" that removed the obstacles standing "between things as they are and things as they ought to be." Prayer would open channels to " permit the free flow of God's plan in you." Whether conscious or "subconscious" and dreamlike, prayer could generate a healthy body, transforming the ideal into the real by turning that which was visualized and desired into a material reality. Thought power was the key. In another passage recalling the New Thought writers to whom his language was so indebted, Shedd wrote, "Here is the great value of the prayer approach. You've not only lost your pounds, you've lost the thought patterns which were producing those pounds. You've opened your mind, removed the blockages and let in the light of God on previous shaded thinking."[14] Pierce echoed these New Thought ideas in somewhat softer terms, her confident optimism perfectly matching Shedd's.

Several factors made these ideas palatable to a wide swath of white American Christians, including many traditionalists who were deeply suspicious of New Thought. Shedd had solid Presbyterian credentials, a respectable pastorate at a fast-growing church in Houston, Texas, and the comforting "Reverend" label before his name on the book jacket. Pierce's popular appeal lay in her beauty pageant semi-celebrity, but she also underscored her familiar Episcopal faith. These Protestant pedigrees may have drawn many devout apt to be skeptical of the looser spiritual moorings of another major positive thinking physical culturist of the time, Jack LaLanne (the "Norman Vincent Peale with muscles," who said of the evangelist Billy Graham, "He puts people in shape for the hereafter, and I get them fit for the here and now").[15] In theological terms, Shedd and Pierce insisted upon a loving, personal God, one who wanted the best for Christians and was happy to bestow upon them all that they sincerely requested, from affluence to health and happiness. The God of whom Shedd and Pierce wrote was a patient deity who forgave sin and tenderly assisted his obese children to lose their excess weight, never closing the door of possibility but always keeping it open with hope for fat persons to commit to the celestial weight-loss plan. "He wants," Shedd wrote, "to share every moment of my living, every cell of my brain, every pound of my body."[16] Finally, these Christian slimming programs were attractive because of their practical aspects, which linked each book to the popular diet literature of the day and so lent it an air of sensibility without subtracting from its devotional message. Both authors urged heavy readers to learn as much as they could about nutrition, and to read widely in the medical literature for information about protein and carbohydrates, vitamins and minerals. And each doled out generous portions of pragmatic advice for choosing food at restaurants, dealing with emotional triggers for overeating, and planning a suitable exercise regimen. Prayer was the key to a thin body, but more commonplace activities played a no less essential role.

Even these functional routines were as indebted to New Thought as to the Protestant heritage that had produced such earlier diet reformers as Sylvester Graham. Where Graham, more than a century before, had advocated a severely ascetic program of behavior and linked dietary restriction with a desired reduction in the sex drive, however, Shedd and Pierce both focused on the fun that one should have while getting and staying fit as well as on the happiness that was its reward. The 1950s tone alternated between homespun humor, pastoral sympathy for those beset with excess flesh, and sharp reminders of the perils of disobedience. Along with repeated injunctions to self-discipline, Shedd's treatments for successful slimming included vocal mealtime affirmations straight out of the New Thought mode, such as: "Today my body belongs to God. Today I live for Him. Today I eat with Him." With a heavy dose of positive thinking to balance his rebuke of excess poundage, Shedd assured readers that beneath their bulk, "there is a beautiful figure waiting to come forth. Peel off the layers, watch it emerge, and know the thrill which comes when you meet the real you."[17]

When I found Charlie Shedd, more than forty years after the publication of *Pray Your Weight Away*, he was eighty-five years old and had, over the previous two years, lost 50 pounds after struggling with a serious heart ailment. He genially related his lifelong struggle with weight and continued to stress overeating as a psychological problem of loneliness: "People who are not happy are eating to give themselves calm and peace and a feeling that somebody loves them," he remarked. His own ups and downs "were pretty much based on whether or not I was spiritually tuned in to the body that God wanted me to be using and that he had given me." Along with these mental therapeutics, Shedd insisted that a motivating factor for the overweight to reduce should be occupational achievement and social connectedness. "[If] you want to be getting somewhere in the world, you want to move up the ladder, you ain't gonna do it if you're carrying 20 pounds too much. . . . I think most people do not cotton to the big person, the obviously overweight person. That is not a popular thing. Once in a while you find some fatty who is a big success, but he's generally a buffoon. There's just a lot to be said for keeping the body in good shape because it is respectable to a large share of the populace." Pleasing others by fulfilling their aesthetic ideals reaped relational rewards, which would in turn reduce the lonesome feelings that triggered overeating. After I asked whether another theological approach might stress God's equivalent love for persons whether fat or thin, Shedd responded, "Sure, he's going to love you, no matter what you do. But he's going to look at you with pride if you have kept yourself in good condition." As he spoke, a picture emerged of how that God looked upon his fat children: with the sad eyes of a parent hoping carefully to shame a child into obedience, promising more abundant approval for toeing the line. Discerning and then following the Lord's fitness ideals would, noted Shedd, bring about deepened, more fulfilling relationships with God and others.[18]

A decade after Shedd and seven years post-Pierce, a second Episcopalian entered the devotional diet arena, as Pastor H. Victor Kane published *Devotions for Dieters* (1967; reprinted in 1973 and again in 1976). Renewing and resolving the tension between the "sin" and "disease" paradigms for overeating that had structured the books of Shedd and Pierce, Kane confessed himself to be the victim of a "compulsive eating pattern which rendered me impotent in controlling my own appetite." He spoke easily about his affliction—and that of others who ate to excess—as the evil of "dietary idolatry," pure and simple. Though few people might now bow down to molten cows as in Moses' time, still "plenty of people put a pork chop or a piece of pie on a pedestal—as if these were their greatest good, their 'god.'" Such obeisance bred obesity, Kane taught, and must be counteracted with a fresh commitment to self-discipline.

The effortlessness with which these two models of wrong eating—victimization and transgression—blended spoke to the reconciliation of sin and sickness, their fusion into a set of behaviors that grieved (rather than angered) a loving, compassionate God. Whether sin or sickness, gluttonous behavior was to be defeated by a merger of God power with human will power, since the impotency spawned by overeating was a source of human disenfranchisement amounting to slavery. "You were not born to be flabby and fat," exclaimed Kane indignantly. "Your physical birthright is to be healthy and firm, even as your citizenship guarantees you the right to think and vote as you wish. Heredity and habit may seem to dictate otherwise, but they are frauds and cheats. You have the right and the power to be trimmer than you are." Kane intended his readers to wake up to the gravity of their condition and realize the consequences of sacrificing their God-given inheritance. With strengthened grit and fortitude on the part of Christian disciples, God's corporeal blueprint for humankind could be fulfilled.[19]

Like the wider diet culture of which these books were part, authors like Shedd, Pierce, and Kane aimed their messages at individuals who sought to be healthy, happy, and attractive in order to be well liked; and both readers and writers presumed that a necessary (if not sufficient) condition of such an achievement was a slender and properly disciplined body. "Don't kid yourself about everybody's loving a fat man," cautioned Kane, warning readers of the inevitable deception undergirding exchanges between fat and thin persons. "Even though they may not say it, your friends probably feel sorry for the sight of you under layers of fat; and those who really care about you are secretly worried."[20] What identified this message as a distinctively Christian one was its rhetoric equating fat with sin, though these writers identified the source of that sin differently: for Shedd, it was ill health and distance from God; for Pierce, gluttony and ugliness; and for Kane, self-indulgence and dietary idolatry. In virtually every other way, these devotional dieters were in full unison with the American diet culture surrounding them. Overeating, as diet writers throughout the century had increasingly lectured, was related to loneliness, isolation, and emotional deprivation. Its cure—self-control leading to thinness—supposedly bred more satisfactory social and familial relationships, thereby satisfying deep needs for intimacy and community that were previously unmet.

Yet despite this attention to the dynamics of individual and community, theirs was a message dramatically lacking any larger social vision of food, or an awareness of what "hunger" really meant for the world's nonaffluent. Shedd and Pierce mentioned the problems of famine and global hunger not at all, whereas Kane devoted a mere page and a half of his sixty-four-page book to the "thoughtless indulgence" that rendered the world's privileged "incapable of caring about the other person." Kane's lament, surrounded by blithe appeals to individual vanity and personal happiness, rang a bit hollow, as he noted, "Dieting will not make you a philanthropist overnight but it does give you the self-respect of feeling that you are not a physical embodiment of one of the great social tragedies of our time. Probably you will not give away the money you save by curtailing that ravenous urge for food. But you might! And it could be fun." This "fun" was as far as Kane went. Yet even his feeble attempt at turning a personal concern with weight loss to broader social ends was virtually unique in the religious diet literature of the time. Writers more often lamented the Depression-era taboo against throwing out food before asserting, in one woman's words, "it was far more of a sin to put weight on" than to let food go to waste. Lest readers grow overly "myopic" about "world starvation," another cautioned readers to remember that such a concern was "only part moral, forgetting that God is concerned with *our* diets too!" Astonishingly, Christian diet culture seemed better suited to create negligence than sympathy for the poor, those who lacked the means and perhaps also the intentional discipline of dieters.[21]

In that sense, this embryonic genre promoting slim bodies for the sake of God's kingdom was highly individualistic, in much the same way that New Thought, positive thinking, and the burgeoning therapeutic culture represented a multifaceted venture aimed at personal perfection. Older theories of the body as being loaded with toxic matter yet ultimately perfectible were replenished (with toxicity now defined in the language of calories) and joined anew with condemnations of fat and flabbiness, in a discourse that distinguished the righteous from their sinful brethren with the implacable seriousness of the era, characterized by fear of global conflict and dismal apprehension for the future. The shift "from salvation to self-realization," so persistently documented by social scientists, theologians, and psychologists for much of the century, culminated for many Christians with a newly severe dogma of fleshly perfection, embodied in personal fitness. Here, the Christian body was not a feeder of other bodies but a model of self-restrained eating and unblemished physical splendor for others to follow. In a curious logic, bodies that neither fed nor shared food to excess—bodies, that is, that relinquished or at least reduced the social value of cooking and eating communal meals—gained through that sacrificial renunciation a closer relational intimacy with God. That there could be a contradiction in this system for religious persons who would not or could not stomach the passionate attention, vast expenditures of time, and sizeable cost involved in achieving a slim body at others' expense seemed unthinkable within the wide reaches of this literature.

THE BURGEONING CHRISTIAN DIET CULTURE

Soon after the 1967 publication of Kane's *Devotions for Dieters,* Christian diet literature expanded from a trickle to a torrent of books printed by religious presses and eagerly consumed by hungry disciples throughout the country. Again leading the way in the devotional diet book parade was Charlie Shedd, whose sentimental best sellers *Letters to Karen* and *Letters to Philip* made him a well known Christian writer during the 1960s. His book *The Fat Is in Your Head* (1972) remained on the National Religious Bestsellers list for two years and sold more than 120,000 copies in its first three years.[22] One year after *The Fat Is in Your Head* was published a retired Air Force chaplain, the independent fundamentalist C. S. Lovett, wrote *Jesus Wants You Well!* to outline God's laws for perfect health, including food and weight, and argued that the body provided "concrete evidence that God means for us to be well." Four years later Lovett would focus more intently on diet in *Help Lord—The Devil Wants Me Fat!,* which spent several months on the National Religious Bestsellers list and sold close to 100,000 copies between the fall of 1977 and 1978, despite being published by a tiny independent press. In 1975 the evangelist Frances Hunter produced *God's Answer to Fat: Loøse It!,* a top religious best seller that far exceeded even Shedd's numbers, with 1977 sales figures nearly matching Charles Colson's prison memoir, *Born Again,* and the inspirational autobiography *Joni.* Also in 1975, Ann Thomas published *God's Answer to Overeating* in the Bible Study Series of Women's Aglow Fellowship, which at the time described itself as the largest evangelical women's organization in the world.[23]

The summer 1976 issue of the *Bookstore Journal,* the official publication of the Christian Booksellers Association, noted the mushrooming trade in health books and contained an extensive list of books on "physical fitness" from Christian publishers (though with notably nonspecific titles). Several other popular Christian diet and fitness books appeared during the last half of the 1970s, many of them striking successes, including Joan Cavanaugh, *More of Jesus, Less of Me* (1976); Shirley Cook, *Diary of a FAT Housewife* (1977), which sold 100,000 copies in its first year; Patricia B. Kreml, *Slim for Him* (1978); and Marie Chapian and Neva Coyle, *Free to Be Thin* (1979), which in its original edition sold 1.4 million copies worldwide and spawned a virtual industry of diet products marketed by the Pentecostal Coyle,

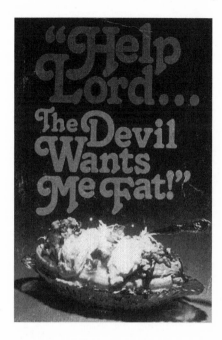

13. Front cover of C. S. Lovett, *Help Lord—The Devil Wants Me Fat!*

including an exercise video and a low-calorie inspirational cookbook.[24] By now, it was standard fare to contend that God expected Christian disciples to display fit, slender bodies. Far more than in earlier years, moreover, devotional diet literature was dominated by conservative evangelical authors and publishers (as opposed to those from mainline denominations). While the claim that Christian devotion entailed thinness was first issued in print from the pen of Shedd, a pulpit minister, laymen and (especially) laywomen had by the middle years of the 1970s procured the argument for themselves, recasting it in apocalyptic tones and reading ever more dire messages into the problem that fat Christians exemplified for the spread of the gospel and the quest for perfection.

In concert with this escalating literature arose biblically based diet groups, which had emerged in scattered fashion during the 1950s and 1960s as prayer-diet clubs (Deborah Pierce advocated these in *I Prayed Myself Slim*), only to bloom into full-blown organizations during the 1970s and 1980s.[25] These groups materialized as women who had failed to lose weight on their own took a cue from "secular" weight-loss groups like TOPS (for Taking Off Pounds Sensibly, founded in 1949), Overeaters Anonymous (which, though generically spiritual, was not specifically Christian; its founding date was 1960), and Weight Watchers (incorporated in 1963).

14. Front and back covers of Joan Cavanaugh, *More of Jesus, Less of Me.*

Christian women began seeking help from other struggling dieters, adding a scriptural and devotional dimension to these groups, and to the ideal body size they hoped to achieve, that was unavailable elsewhere. The first of these was developed by the homemaker Carol Showalter, the wife of a Presbyterian pastor in Rochester, New York. Dejected and overweight again after years of yo-yo dieting, Showalter gave up the strict regimen of Weight Watchers in 1973 to form a local group called 3D, a designation that stood for Diet, Discipline, and Discipleship. She advertised the group as "a Christian counterpart to national weight-watcher programs," and after starting with ten women meeting in the church lounge the group expanded to more than 5,000 churches and 100,000 participants by 1981. As 3D was hitting the national scene, 248-pound Neva Coyle from Minnesota, having failed at every commercial diet program she tried, turned to the Bible, lost 113 pounds, and founded Overeaters Victorious in 1977, which launched her successful career as a best-selling author and inspirational speaker. Though both programs eventually, and for different reasons, fell on hard times—3D was hurt in 1982 by a negative *Christianity Today* article that accused the leadership of authoritarianism, while Overeaters Victorious folded after Coyle regained her weight and subdued her message—they created a winning formula that others would emulate with mounting success.[26]

15. Front cover of Patricia B. Kreml, *Slim for Him*.

This trend expanded into the 1980s and swelled still more in the 1990s, as growing numbers of Christian diet groups emerged locally and went national. Some, such as Step Forward! and Jesus Is the Weigh, enjoyed modest success: for instance, the nurse and former compulsive overeater Julie Morris started Step Forward! in her Birmingham, Alabama, church in 1992, and while the program allegedly took place in churches "all over the country" (including African American congregations) as well as New Zealand and England, Abingdon Press took the curriculum out of print in 2002. The PRISM weight-loss program was created in 1990 and eventually developed an enthusiastic online community, as well as clustered local groups.[27]

More explicitly denominational programs also emerged, such as the United Methodist Church's curriculum *Body and Soul* (later *Health Yourself! 10 Weeks to a Healthier Lifestyle*), whose author specified it as "not a weight loss program" but rather "a healthy lifestyle adventure" and "a plan to become more healthy through better personal habits." When I later interviewed that author, the registered nurse Margie Hesson, she noted that she had wanted the program to be a more positive health program than other religious and secular programs on the market, "not a diet program that creates shame or seeks to measure people by how much they weigh."[28] However, Abingdon Press chose to stress the weight-loss component and marketed Health Yourself with the more explicitly diet-oriented Step Forward! books before retiring both to out-of-print status in 2002. Increasingly emphasizing health more than weight loss, Christian programs nonetheless consistently upheld the fitness ideals of the wider culture in much the same way as their earlier counterparts.

Over time, the two most successful organizations (numerically and financially, at least, if not demonstrably in terms of weight loss) have been the Texas-based First Place (1981), affiliated with the Southern Baptist Convention, the nation's largest Protestant denomination; and the Weigh Down Workshop (1986), headed by Gwen Shamblin from her corporate headquarters in Nashville. First Place was founded by twelve members of Houston's First Baptist Church who wished to form their own Christian weight-loss program. By the 1990s groups had reportedly met in approximately 12,000 churches in the country, including each of the fifty states, and abroad. Like the early participants in Showalter and Coyle's programs, most early First Place members had experience with national programs like Weight Watchers or Nutri/System but had never been able to keep off the pounds they lost in these groups. Many felt, they testified, depressed, ugly, and out of control because of their size, whether they were seriously obese (as were some) or merely a stubborn 10–20 pounds over their "ideal" weight (as were most). First Place leaders, devout evangelicals all, believed the key to losing weight successfully was to combine rigidly controlled food intake, which they termed a "live-it" rather than a "diet," with regimented Bible study and prayer. Their chosen readings focused on those scripture passages commanding discipline, obedience, and submission to God. Participants learned, as one later wrote, that they would be "better representatives of the Lord with a healthy body"—the primary index of health, significantly, being slenderness. (To illustrate the point, the woman who led the group, though she weighed only a slim 110 pounds, went on the same 1,200-calorie per day diet as the other participants and cheerfully lost weight right along with them—to the point that her clothes ceased to fit her diminishing body.) To signify that they were consciously displacing their love of eating with a renewed commitment to God, they chose the name "First Place," meaning that God—not food—would now take first place in their lives.[29]

The largest devotional diet program, by far, has been the Weigh Down Workshop, a twelve-week Bible-study program founded by the nutritionist and fundamentalist Gwen Shamblin in 1986 and, by 2000, offered in as many as thirty thousand churches, seventy countries, and sixty different denominations. Originally founded as a secular program in Memphis,

Weigh Down became explicitly Christian in 1990 when, Shamblin recounted, she asked God for guidance and took Weigh Down to the churches. The program remained largely local into the early 1990s, with most locations offered in Memphis and surrounding areas, but by 1994 Weigh Down was offered in as many as thirty-three states as well as the United Kingdom. (First Place, by then thirteen years old, was at the time offered in forty states.) The program gained national attention with the publication of Shamblin's first book, *The Weigh Down Diet* (1997), which was published by Doubleday and distributed at chain bookstores across the country. As the book quickly reached sales in the millions, Shamblin's program received national press coverage on television programs (as noted earlier, CNN's *Larry King Live* and ABC's *20/20*) as well as in print venues such as *Good Housekeeping* and even the *New Yorker* magazine.[30]

Shamblin quickly became well known for her insistence that there are no "bad" foods and that dieters can eat anything so long as they do so in strictly limited quantities. For those in doubt about how much to eat, Shamblin counseled prayer, advising her audience that God will answer them in no uncertain terms. Advertising herself as a "size 4–6" even as a middle-aged mother of adult children, Shamblin remained an advocate of marked thinness and denounced excessive fat as a sign of unholy disobedience to God's spiritual laws. In one 1994 article, Shamblin was quoted as saying she had gone from weighing 125 to 107 pounds on the program; at 125 pounds, she said, "I looked like a potato with toothpick legs. I had three tires around my waist. I looked very dumpy." Putting her program in more positive terms, Shamblin echoed other popular diet writers of the period in her descriptions of overeating as the misguided attempt to fill what was instead a spiritual hunger for God. New Thought perfectionists of yore had long made the same point in different ways; in Linda Hazzard's 1908 formulation, "Appetite is Craving; Hunger is Desire. Craving is never satisfied; but Desire is relieved when Want is Supplied. Eating without Hunger, or pandering to Appetite at the expense of Digestion, makes Disease inevitable."[31]

Programs based on more countercultural diets have included the vegetarian raw food plan advocated by the North Carolina minister George Malkmus, who called his plan the Hallelujah diet. In one of his books, *God's Way to Ultimate Health*, Malkmus wrote that the "key to preventing heart attacks, cancer, diabetes, arthritis and a host of other physical problems is in our own hands." In his view, people "can literally control whether we are going to be sick or not and how long we are going to live by simply choosing how we live our lives . . . the world's way or God's way! God's way leads to a long, happy, pain-free, sickness-free life! While the world's way usually leads to a short, unhappy, sickness-filled life with lots of pain and suffering, to say nothing of the financial costs." Other similar organic and "natural" Bible-based diet plans have appeared, and Don Colbert's 2002 book, *What Would Jesus Eat? The Ultimate Program for Eating Well, Feeling Great, and Living Longer,* garnered extraordinary popular attention in American newspapers, most of it positive.[32]

Alongside this slew of books devoted to natural foods plans, the old standard diet regimens remained strong sellers. Well into the 1980s and 1990s, seasoned devotional diet authors such as Charlie Shedd, Neva Coyle, and Roger F. Campbell continued to publish weight-loss guides, most of them reiterating the standard view that true Christianity is embodied in thinness (Coyle eventually recanted this view, but only after publishing widely in the field). In the same year that Shamblin's *Weigh Down Diet* appeared (1997), the African American evangelist T. D. Jakes published *Lay Aside the Weight,* replete with before and after photographs of himself (from 338 to 228 pounds) and his wife, Serita (from 210 to 169 pounds). Another popular evangelist, Joyce Meyer, published *Eat and Stay Thin: Simple, Spiritual, Satisfying Weight Control* (1999), while Shamblin's own program provided the impetus for the first-time author Jan Christiansen to publish *More of Him, Less of Me* (1998) and *Desert Morsels: A Journal with Encouraging Tidbits from My Journey on the Weigh Down Diet* (2000). While all of these authors except Jakes were white, more African American authors soon entered the market: the nutritionist and chiropractor Deidre Little wrote *Fit for Eternity: Balanced Living through Better Nutrition and Spiritual Health* in 2002, followed in 2003 by the ordained charismatic minister and fitness trainer La Vita Weaver's *Fit for God: The 8–Week Plan that Kicks the Devil OUT and Invites Health and Healing IN.*

Christian exercise programs also took the country by storm, beginning in 1981 with Body and Soul Ministries (founded by Jeanne and Roy Blocher) and expanding into programs such as Believercise, Word-a-Cise, Cross Training, Jehobics, Praise Aerobics, and more. Catalogs from the Texas-based Christian Aerobic Resource have been successful at selling a vast array of Christian music tapes, workout clothes replete with religious slogans, and training manuals for "Faithfully Fit" aerobics instructors. In 1996 Sheri Chambers' *Praise Aerobics* video immediately went gold, quickly selling over 50,000 copies to compete numerically with then current offerings from pop music stars like Bon Jovi and Janet Jackson. Not many years later, the faithfullyfit.com Web site advertised a two-part video series titled "Bodies for Christ," with subtitles "Breakthrough Fat Burner" and "Firm and Tight." The ad stated, "Breakthrough Fat Burner is a simple cardio fat burning work-

16. "Fun to Be Fit," from *Today's Christian Woman,*
May–June 1985 (photo by Stephen Harvey).

out that will truly create a 'new creature' in spirit, soul and body. This work-out program will help you melt away fat so you can be slim, mobile, and heart healthy so you are prepared to be God's hands and feet on the earth."[33] But for the constant mantra in this literature that an aerobics program can be a "ministry," it would be difficult to say how Christian aerobics differ from other programs at any local gymnasium: Chambers and other instructors have worn the same spandex to display the same sculpted hamstring, quadri-ceps, calf, and arm muscles, glistening with sweat, as one sees in any Nike ad commanding women to "Just do it." Testimonies have followed scripts simi-lar to the First Place narratives, with self-transformation (from, say, lethar-gic couch potato to perfectly chiseled athlete) the goal.

How successful have these programs been at helping their members lose weight and maintain a slimmer physique? No one knows. Not surprisingly, Christian leaders have regularly contended that their plans assist dieters in achieving their goals to a far greater extent than non-Christian programs, but no studies exist to support or refute this claim. Promotional materials from First Place have long put a positive spin on these sparse data by pre-senting the program's leaders as exemplars of the victory others can expect from following their regimen. While noting, "No weight-loss program has conclusive statistics on their members," they affirm, "First Place can claim five leaders in Houston who have lost a cumulative 100+ pounds and kept it off for over five years." Gwen Shamblin has avoided talk of statistics by placing the burden of failure directly on the hopeful dieter. To the question, "What is the average weight loss for people attending The Weigh Down Workshop?" Shamblin has responded: "God has made each of us wonderfully unique. Some people take the program only to lose five or ten pounds, while others need to lose 100 pounds or more. It doesn't matter how much weight you have to lose; being obedient to the way God created the body to maintain itself will allow everyone to achieve their weight loss goals."[34] Those who do not lose or maintain their losses, in other words, are simply disobedient to God's will.

If purveyors of these and many other American Christian fitness and diet enterprises have not spoken in a wholly unified voice, it is partly because they have competed for the same market and so have invariably sought to characterize their own message as unique truth. What they have enthusiastically shared, however, is the conviction that thinness is (or should be) the visible marker of godliness. In the words of Dan R. Dick, author of one of the various books sporting the title *Devotions for Dieters* (1989), "To care for our appearance and health is pleasing to God, and he will bless us richly in our endeavors." Writers have not been in the business of distinguishing between God's demands and the pressures imposed by the wider American culture of slimness; in fact, their reflections on this point have rarely gone deeper than affirming that because the body is God's temple, being slender is part of living the true Christian life. After all, one author mused, "I can't imagine Paul or Peter—or any of the apostles—with stomachs hanging over their girdles!" Emphasizing the same point, another writer insisted, God "want[s] us aware that sloppy fat, hanging all over the place (or even well girdled) is not a good Christian witness." Occasionally this message has been delivered in more severe terms, as when Frances Hunter wrote of hearing God chastise her, declaring, "Fat Christians are the biggest liars of them all—and you're a FAT Christian."[35]

Frequently authors have rebuked the American church for no longer preaching against gluttony and, indeed, for being a place where overeating is encouraged if not downright celebrated. In *God Even Likes My Pantry*, Mab Graff Hoover made a cutting reference to "food orgies" at church, while others agreed that the church has been a den of iniquity when it came to consumption. "How many Sunday school picnics have you gone on," asked Chapian and Coyle in *Free to Be Thin*, "where you heaped your paper plate so high with food, you could hardly get it back to your seat without losing some of it along the way?"[36] Even worse, Christians, in the view of some writers, have been the most heated critics of physical fitness. Pastor

Haydn Gilmore, in his 1974 book *Jog for Your Life,* caustically labeled his detractors as "supine in their fat and lethargy" and asked why those so urgent in "verbalizing the body as the temple of the Holy Spirit" were "so slow in caring for the function of that temple?"[37] Just as pastors preach against other forms of self-indulgence, noted these writers, so too should they talk openly about gluttony. As Jakes put it, eternal consequences await Christians who shorten their lives by overeating: "When I get to heaven and all the disciples are sharing their testimonies, telling how they laid their lives down on chopping blocks and were beheaded for preaching the Gospel, I don't want to be ashamed. I refuse to be the only set of lard-wrapped hips sitting on a cloud saying, 'I was slain by a slab of barbecue ribs!'"[38]

Authors have, nonetheless, been forced to deal with the fact that large numbers of Christians, female and male, are overweight, even obese. What the sociologist Kenneth Ferraro has documented about the correlations between religious adherence and obesity—that "many 'firm believers' do not have 'firm bodies'"[39]—American Christians since at least the 1960s have noted as well. Sadly, these purveyors have argued, fat Christians are a poor reflection of the God they profess to serve and actually sabotage efforts at evangelization. In her 1977 book *Diary of a FAT Housewife,* Shirley Cook recalled looking at "that fat lady" in the mirror: "I thought of the scripture that says, 'Beholding as in a glass, the glory of the Lord.' I didn't see His glory reflected in my glass. I saw my own lack of discipline and moderation. Is this what others see too? Is my overweight a hindrance in reaching my friends for Christ?"[40] Her answer, widely echoed in American Christian culture, was yes.

FROM EMPATHY TO AUTHORITY: SHIFTING MODELS OF EXPERTISE

Even as Christian diet writers have professed intent to amend the hollowness of losing weight solely for the sake of public image, their horror of fat and celebration of thin have continued to ring strong into the twenty-first century. New Thought fasters and body salvationists from the first half of the century laid important groundwork for this kind of somatic devotion, but Christians from the 1950s into the twenty-first century have added a crucial twist by invoking the fear of divine disapproval for those who continue to love food and fail to lose weight. The equation of fat with sin has been parsed many ways, from the gentle picture of God submitted by Charlie Shedd—God is disappointed by his children's dietary excess—to the much more severe theology of discipline and obedience supplied by

Gwen Shamblin—God is rightly offended or even angered by overeating, as indicative of a betrayal equivalent to adultery. The exceptional sales of Shamblin's books and the numbers who have flocked to her program suggest a steady appetite for her exceptionally rigorous doctrine of the body, one requiring believers not simply to adhere to her dietary regimen but to comply with a totalistic and uncompromising worldview.

As Shamblin has put it, to love both food and God is a doomed attempt to serve two masters. "You are either losing weight or not losing weight. This lets you know whom you obey. The one you obey is your master. You are serving *the* God or the food god." Shamblin's exacting system came under fire and scrutiny beginning in 2000–2001, when it became clear that she was a critic of trinitarian theology—discarding the traditional doctrine of three persons in one God in favor of a hierarchy with God at the top, and the Son and Holy Spirit below—and thus heretical to most of the evangelicals who had joined her program. After the early furor diminished, it appeared that while many churches had ousted her program and a group of her former devotees had shifted gears toward the online Thin Within program, the numbers of those choosing to retain Weigh Down or start it anew were high enough for her program to retain its title as the largest Christian diet plan on the market. Shamblin has been resolute in her view of God and her stringent emphasis on sin and punishment (some have, not without justification, accused her of preaching damnation for the obese) that make her, in one sense at least, less an exemplar of Christian diet culture as a whole than an agent of one particularly austere strand within it. Like other fundamentalist leaders such as Jerry Falwell and Pat Robertson, she interpreted the 2001 al Qaeda attacks on the World Trade Center and Pentagon as the result of American's disobedience to God's laws, of which—for Shamblin, anyway—food indulgence is an especially visible sign.[41] Yet her program's ongoing success is noteworthy in comparison to others, including those still in existence and competition with her own (such as First Place). Her forceful managerial style includes an unapologetic concentration on both dieters' and Weigh Down employees' submitting in all matters to their boss as well as a propensity when addressing her audience to wear commanding business-style suits rather than softer, more feminine attire.

Notwithstanding her distinctive theological stance on the trinity, Shamblin's program illustrates both continuities and changes in the Christian diet literature of the 1970s through the 1990s, and beyond. One link has been the sheer urgency characterizing many texts, from Patricia Kreml's *Slim for Him* to Shamblin's *Rise Above*. Kreml urged her readers to remember Sodom and Gomorrah as "two cities in which sin ran rampant" (from adultery to gluttony) such that "the Lord had to destroy them." Like the gluttons of old, wrote Kreml, modern "gluttons and compulsive eaters continue in their sin: they love what they are doing and they don't believe destruction is just around the corner." In fact, "God sees greed and gluttony as sin worthy of death," Kreml noted, and the Bible was full of examples of those whom God smote or let die because of such sins. Here and elsewhere, the millennial fervor of the mid-1970s, and the powerful images of Satan that permeated evangelical culture, accompanied a zeal for thinness as a sign of victory. "Lord," Kreml prayed, "it's so easy to think food is the problem in itself, but I recognize now that food is only an instrument used by the devil to try to keep me in bondage. Thank you for making clear the battle plan and equipping me with the necessary weapons for a sure victory."[42] While earlier authors such as Shedd, Pierce, and Kane had long characterized fat and overeating as sin, evangelical authors began in the mid-1970s to speak in a much stronger tone of condemnation and exigency, as if salvation itself hinged on body size.

What Hillel Schwartz has called the "tight conjunction between the act of dieting and the fear of an End" in that era was reinforced by the expectation of perfect (thin) bodies in the world to come.[43] Hal Lindsey's *Late Great Planet Earth*—the single best-selling nonfiction book of the 1970s in the United States, selling nearly 7,500,000 copies in that decade alone—sustained this hope in his depiction of the eternal afterlife. "If you're not too satisfied with the face or body you now have, you will have a glorious new body. . . . We won't have to eat to be sustained, but the Scripture says we can eat if we want to—and enjoy it. For those who have a weight problem, that sounds rather heavenly in itself. Our eternal bodies will not be subject to aging, or pain, or decay. . . . How . . . excited we should be about acquiring a new body!"[44] The latter wave of publications on such topics as "spiritual discipline for weight control," "Biblical principles that will improve your health," and achieving "greater health God's way" retained the chatty pitch to which their targeted readership would presumably respond; yet their injunctions to thinness were repeatedly reinforced with a sense of peril. By the time Shamblin emerged on the national scene, blending a fiery rebuke of Christian apathy with excoriations of fat, the course of history itself could well have seemed, to some anyway, inexorably conjoined with fluctuations in body mass. Equating thinness with obedience, godly submission, and the thoroughgoing self-abnegation required for salvation, later authors like Shamblin reinforced the sunny picture of paradisiacal slimness along with its grim obverse: damnation by fat.

Amid the increasing pressure to be thin for the sake of redemption, fewer authors presented themselves, as they once had, as homespun folk, most of them women, whose weight had ballooned after marriage and childbearing. Those who did—Jan Christiansen is one, a onetime proponent of Shamblin's Weigh Down diet who later distanced herself from it— worked with small, independent Christian publishers and wrote intimately to small audiences of their struggles. Meanwhile, managerial types like Shamblin, experts rather than fellow strugglers, forged ahead with massive conglomerate-affiliated publishers like Doubleday and Thomas Nelson, who stocked books in chain bookstores across the country. As in the wider culture of weight watching, younger, skinnier writers rose to the fore in the publishing world, striking athletic, self-assured poses and generally dispensing with the personal "before and after" photos that were the bread and butter of most earlier writers. The chummy, experiential tone endured— even Shamblin never tired of telling her audience, "I just love y'all!"—yet there arose a stronger emphasis on expertise in the diet and fitness world, vying with the more traditional criteria of a personal "fat healing" narrative combined with fluency in scripture.

An early sign of this growing professionalism was increased systematization in Christian fitness literature: the utilization of meticulous tables, diagrams, charts, and graphs depicting proper weight; workbooks for recording dietary intake and the emotions that surrounded each meal, snack, or binge; and general pretensions to numerical precision, therapeutic certainty, and scientific authority. Dee Brestin and Peggy Johnston's *Joy of Eating Right* (1993), for instance, contained a characteristic plethora of fill-in Weight Graphs, Habit Charts, Calorie Worksheets, Menu Planners, and Food Journals, a combination that went far beyond the older reliance on insurance company weight tables. Like national diet programs such as Weight Watchers and Nutri/System, Christian diets relied far more on participatory systematization than they once had, even as authors drew ever more stringent analogies of their programs with the "discipline of Jesus." The body was likewise increasingly disciplined by this renewed attention to number-oriented charts, where emotions around eating were condensed into structured types even while being labeled illusory. ("What is your perspective when you choose to eat food you don't need? Write down your thoughts so that you'll better be able to recognize their deceptiveness next time.")[45] Readers were invited to record their individual specifications and experiences straight into the text, then were instructed precisely how to make these data match the author's own normative standards.

The professional style of Christian fitness leaders also increasingly relied upon an image of scientific training and assurance. Well into the early

1980s, few Christian diet writers aspired diligently to medical understand-ings of nutrition, trying instead to shed light on the distinctive appetites motivating human desire. Soon enough, however, authors seemed to catch on to the idea that readers accustomed to secular diet books distributed by physicians would be more likely to buy a devotional fitness manual if it laid claim to medical science, giving rise to methodical assertions of an author's dietary credentials and the scientific legitimacy of her weight-loss tech-niques. Pamela Snyder's *Life Styled by God* (1985) justified her program's emphasis on behavioral-change techniques by mentioning their use by psy-chiatrists and physicians at Stanford University Medical School and the University of Pennsylvania Medical School. She filled her book with anec-dotes of women struggling with their weight and asked readers to fill the lined pages with their own experiences, feelings, sufferings, and successes. Snyder herself, a registered dietitian and vice-president of "a health promo-tion corporation serving business and industry," personified the mixture of medical, corporate, and therapeutic expertise sought by an emerging cohort of Christian diet writers.[46]

This corporate-therapeutic model was widely adopted by Christian fit-ness writers, women and men alike. Laying claim to proficiency in the com-petitive business world required extensive citation of personal credentials, and back-cover bios were substantially larger by the early 1990s than they had been in previous years, as writers typically swelled their qualifications to distinguish themselves from other experts and support their pioneer sta-tus in the field. In her book *Food for Life* (1994, 1997), for instance, the evangelical nutritionist Pamela M. Smith was described as the founder of "one of the original private practices of dietetics in America," "the nutri-tionist for the Orlando Magic NBA team and for individual players and other professional athletes nationwide," and a "consultant to industry giants such as Walt Disney World and Hyatt Hotels and Resorts," as well as the "director of culinary development for General Mills Restaurants, New Business Division." Listing her educational degrees as RD and LDN, Smith was said to be "in demand for corporate, top-management programs, semi-nars, conventions, and corporate wellness programs." In line with the cor-porate ethos she represented, with its emphasis on inspirational motivation, Smith sprinkled her prose with rousing slogans like "Born to Be Free," "Take a Risk," "Getting the Vision," and "Just Say No!"[47]

The upsurge in this style of fitness managerialism also included male writers, their book covers emblazoned with authorial credentials—once again, both as nutritional experts and as corporate motivators—and with promises of longer life and happiness. One, *Eating by the Book* (1999), listed the degrees of its author David L. Meinz as MS, RD, FADA, CSP: Master of Science in Nutrition, Registered Dietitian, Fellow in the American Dietetic Association, and Certified Speaking Professional in the National Speakers Association (his author bio boasted that Meinz was "the only individual to hold both designations" of FADA and CSP). The dust jacket, featuring two runners silhouetted before an orange sunrise, pledged to teach readers "how to lose weight, lower cholesterol, prevent cancer, eat more, get fit, and feel great!" Making the usual claim to originality, Meinz's bio also informed readers that he "believes that physical health and *prevention* of illness have, for the most part, been overlooked by the Church." Beginning with "Jehovah's Top Ten List" (traditionally known as the Ten Commandments) and including paeans to the harmony of science and scripture ("The foods God originally gave us were carbohydrates"), Meinz concluded his main text with the contemporary corporate/spiritual mantra par excellence: "Just do it."[48]

The message conveyed by this growing assemblage of corporate fitness specialists was one of both optimism and certainty, based less on personal experience than professional expertise: yes, God wants you to be thin and yes, you can change your lifestyle to lose weight! Gone were earlier notions (however scarcely achieved) of a Christian culture separate and apart from the secular world: now, identical norms for health and beauty were simply assumed to apply to Christians and heathens alike, and acceptance in the secular world evidently bolstered the credentials of Christian dietitians. Smith's back-page bio focused almost exclusively on non-Christian credentials, with her appearances on *The 700 Club* and *Focus on the Family* the only signs of religious affiliation. All the rest—her training from Florida State University and continuing education from Harvard Medical School, her recognition with awards in the State of Florida and appearances on *The Today Show*, America's Health Network, and the TV Food Network, her work as consultant to various corporations—gave only the impression of a top-rank nutritionist helping companies achieve maximum productivity from their slimmed-down workers. There was no conversion narrative here, as there were in earlier books; believers simply needed to learn how to harness "God's power" in their lives for, as Smith noted, "[God's] desire is for us to 'prosper in all things and be in health' (3 John 2 NKJV)." New Thought leaders a century before could not have put it better than she did in concluding her final chapter: "You have been designed to accomplish, engineered to succeed and empowered to achieve greatness. Don't let any life trap hinder you another second. . . . [K]eep your eyes lifted up to the vision of living life well. You deserve the best!"[49]

This trend toward professionalization was part and parcel of larger trends occurring during the final third of the twentieth century within the American Protestant and particularly evangelical culture, whose spokespersons had increasingly achieved not merely a public platform but the aura of professional expertise and corporate acceptance. The immense networks presided over by figures such as James Dobson supplied models for a new era in American evangelicalism, in which professional specialists in fields such as medicine, psychology, and politics rose to exceptionally high religious prominence without necessarily holding ministerial credentials or working primarily in a pastoral role. Dobson's Focus on the Family empire, replete with daily national radio broadcasts and a publishing house of extraordinary range and influence, became a chief source of Christian thought and practice for millions of American believers, and Dobson himself—a physician and psychologist by training—expanded his range of purported expertise from child rearing to the full spectrum of social, political, and cultural crises, from welfare reform to U.S. foreign policy. Part of his success in this field was due to his ability to embody the paternal ideal emphasized in his child-rearing books: stern yet potentially affectionate, offering approval and affection to those who disciplined themselves and obeyed the father's will. Dobson's course for achieving broad authoritative power echoed ever more thunderously in American evangelicalism into the early twenty-first century, with the trajectory in Christian fitness writing only one of other relevant sites.

Within that devotional diet world as elsewhere, authoritative voices and stricter messages, coupled with the promise of relational intimacy through obedience, found a willing audience. Women like Rebecca (twenty-five years old when I interviewed her), who lost 20 pounds in a Weigh Down class held on her Pentecostal college campus, have focused on weight as an issue of "integrity and consistency and being truthful about every area of my life" rather than appearance alone. "I recognized that this [eating] was an area that I did not know how to say no in, that I did not have control. Well, I just think anything in excess is wrong. Even good things can be bad if they're done too much." As Rebecca saw it, being a Christian meant that every aspect of her life should be surrendered to Christ, eating included. "The real problem was I was out of control, and I needed to deal with that in the heart of me, which is where I deal with myself in relationship with God." It was this last point, the relationship, that Rebecca ultimately wished to emphasize to me:

> You can't say, "Oh, it's a spiritual journey," and then try and do all the
> rules and not have the relationship part. . . . It wasn't that I felt like I
> didn't have a relationship with God before, but I felt like that sense of,

I am being honest; I am being complete here; I'm not hiding behind an issue or not letting him see an issue of my life. There was just a greater sense of fulfillment in that relationship. I guess you could say it's like in a love relationship the more you share intimately the closer you feel. The more that I shared of myself with the Lord about this [food] issue the closer I felt to him. I don't want to say that trivially because that sounds kind of sing-songy, "oh, it wasn't the weight." But honestly it was awesome. I was so grateful to lose that weight, and I felt like it was a tremendous blessing. But it wasn't the only blessing.

Rebecca was not interested in a program, Christian or otherwise, that would simply focus on calories and healthy eating—she had done those before—but much preferred Weigh Down for focusing, as she said, on the deeper issues of obedience to and subsequent intimacy with her highest authority, her divine father, the Lord.[50]

Eighteen-year-old Anna, a former anorexic who turned compulsive overeater and became overweight, also agreed wholeheartedly with Shamblin's message of discipline and hard-won love. As for her struggle with food, "I realize it's not about me and it's not about how my body looks; it's all about being obedient to God. I'm just trying to practice that more, because I would put my body and food as an idol before God for all those years that I've done that." Her description of the benefits of the Weigh Down class in which she was participating invoked the motivating power of fear:

It's a wakeup call to remind me how important it is to be obedient to God. How you will perish if you don't. The main thing that helped me is that the world does not see overeating as a sin. Many people in my church don't see overeating or obesity as a sin. I like the fact that this [program] is saying how wrong overeating is and the more how wrong it is, the more I don't want to do it.

Rather than remain in fear, Anna took comfort in the message of sin and obedience because it gave her a compass to repent and thereby find true intimacy with God. Her own drug-addicted parents had died when she was seven years old, and she had had many emotional problems since then: "I was bounced from counselor to counselor to counselor. Now I realize that the Lord is the best counselor."

While Anna expressed some uncertainty with Weigh Down teachings during our interview, she repeatedly reminded herself that Shamblin spoke the truth, as in this exchange between us:

MG: I think some of the questions you're raising are really good ones. It could be good to have the group [Weigh Down class] discuss, too, like let's think together about what is sin, where's the line between what's sin or what's not sin. People may have different ideas about that.

ANNA: It's like something that you can't argue with, because you just don't know. It's just so weird to me.

MG: What's weird?

ANNA: Overeating is disobedience, but so many very obedient people are overweight. Gwen says the only problem [that causes] overweight is overeating. She says it's not a metabolism problem. You just overeat. I guess a lot of things she says are right and God ordained.

Anna, like other Weigh Down participants I interviewed, was very attracted to the power of this message because of the passionate conviction that emanated from Shamblin herself, as she taught listeners to think of God's love as something they had to earn through hard work, rather than accept as a cheap and easy (and so easily dismissed) gift. Anna wanted and needed to believe in Shamblin as a prophetic leader speaking God's truth, even when that truth seemed to conflict with Anna's own experience—as she said, "so many very obedient people are overweight." In her case, the kindness directed to her by the local Weigh Down group participants and by Darlene, the coordinator, were also potent; but what Anna seemed particularly to crave was a method of strict discipline that would allow her to emerge at the end thin, upright, and at last wholly deserving of God's love.[51]

Shamblin's theological teachings are important in this context, for she has emerged as a thoroughgoing perfectionist, severe even for the fundamentalist pole of American evangelicalism. The goal of the Christian life, in her view, is to "lay down sin" completely, so that for an alleged believer to assert that she continues to struggle with sin is itself to commit a sinful act. Food is a major aspect of this teaching but not the whole of it; and Shamblin has also addressed topics of sexual immorality, excessive shopping, and other vices termed strongholds that prevent people from focusing on the will of God. Shamblin has called her audiences to a grand if arduously obtained version of the Christian life, one in which there should be no lazy "resting in sin" and wallowing in what she regularly terms "false grace." "To obey is better than sacrifice," she quotes from scripture, and the point is to follow Jesus' example when dying he said, "Not my will but Thine be done." The highest standard of behavior is one in which a person foregoes the self and relinquishes all private hopes, desires, ambitions, and expectations in favor of hearing the voice of God and surrendering to his will. If that will is only faintly discernible through prayer or private scripture reading, through her own voice Shamblin—like other authoritarian Christian leaders of the day—turns up the volume. The impact this teaching has on the bodies of her followers is, of course, extraordinarily powerful.

Rita, a middle-aged former Weigh Down participant, spoke of Shamblin with common admiration: "I love her teaching, I really do. She's just a very classy, beautiful woman of God. . . . I just love every technique she has to teach, and even her voice is very soothing. . . . I can say that for the whole group. We all enjoyed it very much." Throughout my interviews with Weigh Down participants, only a few people expressed disagreement with Shamblin, and most of these focused more on style than substance. Joe, a middle-aged Catholic businessman and the only male in his Catholic Weigh Down class, described his admiration for the principles of the program but noted, "The problem with Weigh Down Workshop, Gwen, puts herself up on quite a pedestal. . . . Nobody in our group liked Gwen at all. We're Catholics. We get uncomfortable around that evangelical way. . . . But Catholics, we're old. We're used to hearing so many voices. . . . The Pope is a very cool guy, but he's not *the* guy. We're used to a number of people pointing us to God." Participants in faith-based diet groups other than Weigh Down occasionally noted a similar discomfort with Shamblin's evangelistic style or with her message of hard-fought salvation ("works over grace," is how critics have typically described it). Many combine what they like best from Weigh Down with teachings from other programs, as when fifty-three-year-old Angela, a Pentecostal of Italian Catholic heritage, told me in our interview, "I'm like a Heinz 57 person. I've extracted things from different programs. From O[vereaters] V[ictorious] I've learned that you have a personal responsibility to take care of yourself and to eat because your body is a temple of the holy spirit and to take care of it. Through Weight Watchers I learned how to eat healthy. I don't have to obey the list, but here are some choices you can make. Through Weigh Down, the good part that I learned was that any behavior that I have is because of a choice that I'm making and that Satan has basically wallpapered my mind with lies and that I have believed those lies by choice. I can turn to God and trust God. . . . It was through [Weigh Down] that, again, my relationship with the Lord, it seemed like it got stronger." More relevant than any visceral response to Shamblin herself is the widespread belief among the faithful that disciplined eating accrues relational benefits, a point of her teaching that echoed among participants in other programs as well.[52]

Twenty-three-year-old Tish, also a Catholic-born convert to Pentecostalism, lost 60 pounds on Weigh Down before making the transition to another program, Thin Within. In her narrative, the Holy Spirit was already teaching her about hunger and fullness before she discovered any of these programs, and the appeal of following them was clarity and deeper closeness to God in prayer.

> I've noticed when I am overeating when I go to pray, I'm not as clear. Now I'm not a big theologian or anything, but I think that's one of the principles why God had fasting in the Bible is it just lets you have focus and bring clarity to your mind. Because you know when you overeat it's like you kind of feel you want to take a nap and you don't really feel like doing anything. It kind of makes me more lazy when I overeat. When I'm eating within the boundaries that God wants me to eat, I just feel more energy and so it allows me then to be able to pray more focused and enjoy my time or prayer rather than thinking about food I'm going to eat or thinking about how stuffed I am.

While Tish was not able, despite having led two Weigh Down Workshop classes in the past, to think of any biblical verses to reinforce her case for disciplined eating, she could express the spiritual clarity she felt and the sense of feeling "more on track" when she ate sparingly. She had gained 20 pounds since getting married and was hoping at the time of our interview to reduce in size down to the "healthy six or eight" that was her personal ideal.

As she continued speaking, Tish expressed her preference for Thin Within over Weigh Down because the group stresses that even for those who remain overweight, "of course God doesn't necessarily look down on us or he's upset with us or he doesn't love us." Tish articulated this intricate balance as she understood it:

> Thin Within is real good with explaining this. They talk about how it doesn't break our relationship with [God], like he's still in a relationship with us. He still loves us, and still he's there for us and answers our prayers. But that fellowship with him is going to be hindered. I from experience agree with that. I know some people don't like to agree with that because then they have to take food away. . . . I think people make up excuses, even women sometimes, that "God loves me and this is how I am. I'm getting older, and my metabolism's slowing down." They make excuses, and it really comes down to they don't want to deny themselves the extra food that they want. I think it comes down to that.

At the same time, Tish assured me that she knew "people with wonderful hearts" who had not managed to lose weight on Christian weight-loss plans. "I don't necessarily think God is so mad at them, and spiritually they're not at a place they should be because they're still in a process. Until we go to heaven we're going to live in this fallen world. . . . His love doesn't change for them but his desire is for them to move out of this because it is like a bondage." Weight loss, an embodiment of sacrificial obedience, would enhance a person's relationship with God and raise it to a higher level, and while those who did not exemplify such discipline were not left out completely, they did not receive the same degree of approval. "I know this is kind of harsh," Tish remarked about Weigh Down, "but I honestly believe that the principles work if they're followed honestly. . . . If [people] were really eating the way they should, they would lose weight."[53]

First Place participants, while adhering to a less severe message than that of Weigh Down or Thin Within participants, have focused just as intently on issues of relational intimacy through disciplined eating. Their foundation has not been the perfectionist notion of "laying down sin," as with Shamblin's Weigh Down Workshop. Indeed, in one of the groups I attended, the talk centered on the women's own daily struggles to "be good" and not sin, and the struggle itself seemed both expected and even noble: women such as Jenna identified with the apostle Paul in his struggles with sin: "We're always struggling to overcome in our own willpower." The group discussed their persistent temptations to skip First Place meetings and avoid the group scrutiny of their bodies and their behavior, with Gloria even noting that she dropped out of the group and her husband put her back into it. The women blamed Satan for weakening their resolve to eat less and lose weight: "The Enemy is right there saying, 'You'll never do it. You can't do it,'" commented Kim. Carla, the heaviest in the group, noted that she had given over every area of her life to God except food, and Gloria echoed that she had faith for every one of God's gifts except for faith that she could lose weight and reach her goal size. Susan, whose husband was also overweight but refused to worry about it, remarked upon the frequency of her passing thought that, "if my husband likes me this way, why do I care?" But her immediate response, accompanied by heads nodding around the room, was "But that's wrong!" The point, they acknowledged to me, was to cultivate self-control and obedience in order to defeat Satan and please God in a way that would deepen their relationship with him. Here, as elsewhere in Christian diet culture, authority seemed to trump empathy every time.[54]

RELIGIOUS DEVOTION TO THINNESS OUTSIDE MAINSTREAM PROTESTANTISM

Mainline and evangelical Protestants have not cornered the market for religious concern with diet and thinness. The Seventh-day Adventist (SDA) Church, for example, has long stressed the importance of health regimens, encouraged its members to eat sparingly and only of wholesome foods, and founded numerous health-care institutions such as hospitals and medical schools. Its nineteenth-century prophetess Ellen White promoted health reform, as did the erstwhile member John Harvey Kellogg, and later generations have continued to lay stress on dietary restraint. Those who follow SDA guidelines generally avoid alcohol, caffeinated beverages, tobacco, and red meat; and many are vegetarians. Various denominational writers have appealed as well to health enthusiasts outside the church, drawing a more religiously diverse readership interested in vegetarianism, natural foods, and alternative healing. Virtually all of this literature, at least until recently, has aimed its attention at health and longevity, rather than slenderness: typical titles would include Aileen Ludington's *Feeling Fit: True Stories of People Who Turned Their Health Around* (1997) and William D. Scott's *In The Beginning, God Said: Eat Raw Food* (2000), both based on personal narratives of newfound health generated by an SDA diet. As Andrea, a thirty-ish physician raised in the SDA church, told me, "Most Adventists are healthy and exercise focused, into dietary healthfulness etc.," and yet theirs is *"not* a culture of 'Slim for Him.' "[55]

Nevertheless, other recent book titles may augur subtle but substantial shifts, as a few SDA authors turn their message more explicitly toward weight loss and slimness ideals. In 1991, for instance, Random House published *The Seventh-Day Diet: How "the Healthiest People in America" Live Better, Longer, Slimmer—And How You Can Too,* a book that one of the authors revised and republished in 2002 as *Seventh-Day Diet: A Practical Plan to Apply the Adventist Lifestyle to Live Longer, Healthier, and Slimmer in the 21st Century.* Even if these books have not radically departed from the longstanding emphasis on healthy living, the invocation of "slimness" and the pragmatic, positive thinking subtitles signal an altered way of packaging health for a mass audience. By trying to reach diet-conscious readers beyond the Adventist fold, such books have tacitly proposed unraveling Ellen White's health precepts from the other facets of the tradition, presumably including its strict sabbatarianism, bans on gold jewelry, and ordinances against idolatrous materialism, which such texts generally neglect. Adventists have long been well known for proscribing flashiness and worldly adornment of all kinds, but outsiders wishing to follow their dietary precepts for the sake of getting "slimmer" have operated under no such injunctions. To my knowledge no explicitly SDA weight-loss groups have emerged, certainly none with the national recognition of Weigh Down or First Place or the explicit emphasis on slender femininity; nonetheless, the popularized Adventist message on health may easily converge with that of its mainstream evangelical counterparts.[56]

Alongside programs promoted by evangelicals, fundamentalists, charismatics, mainliners, and Pentecostals there are also a few Latter-day Saint (LDS, or Mormon) diet books, and the trajectory of this literature follows a course similar to that of the Adventist publications. A foundational text for later books such as *Joseph Smith and Natural Foods* (1976, 2001) was a 1937 book by the LDS authors John A. Widtsoe and Leah D. Widtsoe, *The Word of Wisdom: A Modern Interpretation*. The book emphasized both the positive and the negative commands in the Mormon code of health revealed to Joseph Smith in 1833, a code best known for prohibiting alcohol, tobacco, and hot stimulating drinks such as coffee or tea. The Widtsoes blended searing analysis of the contemporary health conditions facing the U.S. population—including the food contamination, fraudulent claims, and fad diets generated by American food corporations—with arguments seeking to prove that the precepts found in Mormon revelation could reverse climbing mortality figures associated with cancer, diabetes, and heart disease. The authors were particularly disturbed by the high death rates of Latter-day Saints from these and other preventable diseases and noted, "It is evident that the people of the Church are not observing fully all the factors of health as given in the Word of Wisdom, else they would have an even greater immunity from all diseases." Eating more nutritiously meant avoiding meat, adulterated stimulants, and nonnutritive substances in favor of more fruits, vegetables, and grains; and those who followed this plan would be rewarded with increased "strength and vigor of body," "protection against disease," and "the possession of knowledge and wisdom," and "temporal salvation," including economic welfare.[57]

Fifty years later, the businessman and LDS adherent Earl F. Updike authored *The Mormon Diet a Word of Wisdom: 14 Days to New Vigor and Health* (1991), citing the Widtsoes' inspiration and quoting copiously from their book. His plan also echoed the vocabulary of George Malkmus's Hallelujah diet, as he denounced the "standard American diet" and urged LDS members to live up to their heritage of health and happiness. Mormon tradition obliged its members to do all that they could to eat well and improve their bodies. Updike approvingly reprinted "ideal weight" charts for women and men, originally composed by Dr. Walter Kempner in 1972. At 5'3", a fully dressed woman should weigh 104 pounds; if she were 5'4", 108 pounds, or at 5'6", 117 pounds was the ideal. As Updike noted, "Compared to average weights in the Western world, these numbers seem low. But if you live by the Lord's law of health, you will find they are a real possibility." At the lower end of the height range especially, Updike's standards for female health were extremely lean: his ideal 5'4" woman was far thinner than the *Seventh-Day Diet* author Chris Rucker's, whose suggested weight range for women that height was 114 to 146. In his follow-up cookbook, Updike listed the everyday rewards of healthful eating: "You'll lose excess weight. You'll enjoy boundless energy. You'll be free of degenerative diseases. You'll look young well into old age. Simply stated, you'll enjoy the best possible health!" Without liposuction, plastic surgery, cosmetics, or diet supplements, Mormons could enjoy this program "sent to us by the Lord through the prophets, a program that can make you look and feel your physical best." Dire consequences would, moreover, result from evading this mandate's full import: "Disease, fevers, and unexpected deaths are some of the consequences directly related to disobedience." Perhaps to appeal to a more expansive audience of non-LDS readers, the word "Mormon" dropped out of the title and off the cover when Updike's books were reprinted in 1995 and 1996 as *The Miracle Diet* and *The Miracle Diet Cookbook*.[58]

A different kind of LDS text, and one more focused on issues of weight loss, is the book by the LDS author Colleen C. Harrison, *He Did Deliver Me from Bondage*. Written in 1990 (originally under the name Colleen Bernhard) and into its sixth edition by 2002, the book offered a personal and prescriptive account of combining the *Book of Mormon* with twelve-step principles in order to overcome addictive behavior, particularly compulsive overeating. Like evangelical writers such as Joan Cavanaugh and Neva Coyle, Harrison's own narrative detailed weight loss following severe obesity. In 1981 her weight peaked at an extremely unfit 315 pounds. At that point, "I stepped off the scale and dropped to my knees. . . . I literally crawled to my bedside, and crumpled there, the tears finally came. Tears of complete surrender to God. . . . Today, I know those tears were, at least in spirit, mingled with blood—Jesus Christ's own atoning blood; for from that hour my deliverance began." By 1994 the author reported a loss of 140 pounds, and by 2002 she was within 10 pounds of her maintenance weight. The author and some LDS friends eventually formed Heart t' Heart, a 12-step international network of LDS women and men chiefly focused on issues of eating disorders, sexual addiction, and codependency.[59]

While nothing in these materials stressed a particular fitness ideal, ongoing online forum discussions suggest that achieving certain standards may preoccupy LDS women no less than others. "Robin," an LDS woman who had lost 100 pounds by avoiding carbohydrates and sugar, wrote to the group in April 2002 about her ongoing depression. While "most people around me looking from the outside think that I have it all . . . thin, beautiful, excellent career . . . inside I feel like I'm ugly, undesireable [sic], emotionally unstable, and quite insecure." She chided herself for her failure to accept God's plan: "I know that it is what He thinks of me that is important and our true self esteem comes from Him. [But] I am having difficulty trusting that He will bring me a mate in my life . . . so I go about dating and relationships second guessing myself and Him. The emotional turmoil is enough to keep me from God's light."[60] However officially irrelevant to LDS theology, thinness and beauty continue to resonate as though, despite all odds to the contrary, they could possibly open new doors to love and total happiness. When they do not, as Robin's narrative indicates, women struggle to remember that the only relationship that really matters and can provide ultimate joy is that with God. But is that really all they want?

Mormon views on these matters seem, in fact, paradoxical and double-sided in ways that correspond in interesting ways with popular Adventist and evangelical norms. Lynn, an LDS woman in her twenties, told me, "there is a big part of the general [Mormon] culture that stresses thinness, health, and beauty as a way of showing that Mormons are a chosen people, as a missionary tactic, and as an emphasis on a beautiful couple getting married—which are all tied into the Mormon plan of salvation." As a teenager attending her church's Sunday young women's hour, Lynn studied *The Inside-Out Beauty Book,* a popular Christian grooming guide first published in 1978 that urged women to beautify themselves for God's sake: "We talked at length about being appealing on the outside (to attract men as well as nonmembers) and so had weekly lessons in make-up application, hair styling, and food preparation (which instructed us both in how to make pies and pastries, and how to avoid eating them . . . or eating very little of them yourself)."[61] Jill, another young LDS woman who described herself as "morally pretty conservative" but politically very liberal acknowledged that the importance of dating and marriage in LDS theology does make health and thinness important for Mormon women, since they want to be appealing to decent, marriageable LDS men.

Jill's own narrative is worth citing at some length, revealing both one devout LDS woman's depiction of a seamlessly affirmative body-spirit theology and the fissures beneath its surface. In our interview, this articulate, vegetarian student expressed a strong interest in healthy eating habits as an expression of temperate living and described her consciousness about eating moderately as "a general setting up my life in a way that I feel like I have control over my physical desires and my physical attractions." The spirit should master the temporal body, she said, even though "we [Mormons] don't believe in a big divide between spirit and body." In her next comments, however, Jill shifted focus: "I would also like to be thin, like honestly to lose fifteen pounds if I could." Since she appeared athletic, attractive, and well within both the cultural and medical range of approved thinness, I was surprised and asked if she wanted to be slender for the sake of her outward appearance. She demurred, noting instead: "I know I'll feel better spiritually and physically." When I next asked whether she cared at all about her appearance, she smiled wryly at either the query's obviousness or her own mixed motives: "I definitely do care how I look. Absolutely! And I do think about how I'll look in a bathing suit this summer. I mean, I definitely do, I mean I've got to be totally honest." Jill's repeated insistence that her interest in thinness had nothing to do with her spirituality was sincere, and her words compellingly echoed the careful way that LDS leaders aim to prescribe healthy living without falling prey to the body obsessions reinforced in American culture. Still, as she talked she herself grew pensive about Mormon descriptions of the appearance of true believers: in the idealizing rhetoric, she mused, "you have this light about you" and "that's how you show people that the church is a good thing . . . that there's something different about you, and that's this idea of being a daughter of God." This impression of "something different," conceptually elusive to outsiders even if precise to LDS participants, may surely—however unintentionally—generate anxieties of the kind that appear more blatantly in Protestant evangelical culture.[62]

Notwithstanding the undercurrents of anxiety over beauty and thinness in these circles, the vast majority of energetic work in the arena of religious weight watching has been Protestant. In fact, not a single book of this type seems to have yet surfaced from the pen of an American Catholic writer.[63] A 1967 account by a male convert to the evangelical Mennonite Church noted that he had grown up "in a nominal Roman Catholic home where we ate large amounts of food," until as an adult he became a "384-pound blob"; then and only in a Protestant context he came to realize that overeating was sinful so that he eventually "claimed the victory" of weight loss; this narrative, we have seen, persists among former Catholics who now participate in Protestant fitness programs.[64] It seems fair to say that Catholic bodily obsessions have typically focused on matters other than food: in the words of twenty-eight-year-old Alicia, a "cradle Catholic" still active in the church, talk of bodies in her Catholic upbringing did not emphasize "body image so much as leading chaste sexual lives." Indeed, she said she wished greater attention would be given to dietary discipline in Catholic life: after we discussed Protestant weight-loss programs, Alicia pondered the Protestant-Catholic comparison and commented on "all those overweight priests" who encouraged Catholics to eat and drink together. "What about control?" she asked rhetorically. "I almost was like, well, maybe some of those [Protestant] programs should come to my church!" Alicia noted that she never heard "abstinence" or self-control discussed in terms of food and drink in her parish, nor was gluttony a major theme outside Lent. Protestants, she affirmed, seemed far more obsessed with food and Catholics with sex.[65]

This point is not, of course, an assertion that American Catholics have cared nothing about thinness or beauty; to make such a claim would be absurd. No evidence that I have seen suggests that Catholics in the United States have been less affected by American body-image anxieties, including eating disorders, than their non-Catholic counterparts. Alicia also described her encounter with the Catholic lay order Regnum Christi (affiliated with the Legion of Christ), whose well-dressed members apparently work to recruit model-type beautiful women from elite college campuses to their conservative order. When some young, slender, and expensively attired women approached Alicia at the Vatican, they turned out to be nuns who defended relinquishing the temptations of earthly romance in order to be married to Christ; but, in Alicia's paraphrase of their worldview, "that doesn't mean we need to put on a habit and be ugly." To me she explained, "they really want young, good-looking women who are outgoing, because these are the people who are going to revitalize the vocational crisis in the church. 'Because you're beautiful and you're outgoing, you're the chosen; you're who Christ would want to marry.'" According to Alicia, the nuns described themselves as "the women men would want, but no, we're going to choose Christ" instead.[66]

Despite this richly illustrative example of a conservative group finding use for a culturally desired body image as a model for young people, most Catholics who have participated in the wider American diet culture appear to have done so for other than religious reasons.[67] Still, tantalizing signs may indicate a growing interest among some Catholics to link religion, diet, and body weight. In 1997 the Catholic homemaker Suzanne Fowler of Leawood, Kansas, developed a Catholic weight-loss program, the Light Weigh, after the birth of her sixth child. In Fowler's words, "My excess weight was just a sign that I did not understand temptation and how to overcome it; but the great, grand and Godly news is that Jesus did understand temptation and defeated it. The Saints of the Catholic Church (faithful followers and students of God the Son) actually developed methods to overcome temptation. The Catholic Church has everything we need by the power of Jesus Christ to help us triumph over temptation!" Her twelve-week program—with its motto "Learn to eat the food you like, for the Lord you love"—cost $117 per person in 2002, by which time one thousand groups had run in the United States (with groups in every state), Canada, Ireland, and Australia.

While many of Fowler's lessons resembled Shamblin's Weigh Down diet—for instance, overeating indicates a spiritual hunger, dieters should eat only when a growling stomach indicates true hunger, there are no bad foods but only sinfully sized portions—participants looked beyond the Bible to the writings of Saints Ignatius of Loyola and Thérèse of Lisieux. Ads in church bulletins straightforwardly promoted the plan as a "Catholic spiritual growth weight loss program" that was "designed to help deepen your relationship with Jesus while learning to eat the food you enjoy in moderation," and coordinators (seemingly all women) ranged from parishioners to parish nurses to nuns. Like Shamblin, Fowler also set a daunting standard for body size: after a lifelong weight battle, wrote Fowler, "Now this mother of seven wears size 6 jeans everyday."[68] Perhaps for American Catholics, at last, maternity may comfortably coexist with vanity.

But Light Weigh turns out to be quite different from Weigh Down on several points, as Fowler noted to me when I reached her for an interview. As did her Protestant counterparts, Fowler assured me that the program was in no way about beauty or thinness per se but was really about overcoming temptation. One distinguishing point of her program was the Catholic way of interpreting sin, she noted: "The Protestant perspective of sin is different from the Catholic perspective. That radically changes things." The difference between mortal and venial sins is not replicated in Protestant theology:

> Protestants view sin as sin, and so overeating is a sin, a terrible sin.
> Well, Catholics would view it differently. It's not a terrible sin, it is
> a temptation, it is a struggle, and you're going to have to build virtues
> in yourself to overcome that; but it's not going to send you to hell if
> you overeat. So the Protestant programs, ironically, end up fostering
> more guilt in people, because it's this, "you're a sinner, you're sinning
> against God if you overeat," and I mean some people who founded those
> programs do say you're going to go to hell. And that isn't the case!

The other Catholic feature to distinguish the Light Weigh from its Protestant counterparts, noted Fowler, is the notion that suffering has meaning. "In the Light Weigh, your obedience to God, really, when you want to eat something and you're not eating it, it's a form of suffering." Suffering has meaning because it is united with the suffering of Christ on the cross, giving people the "spiritual weapons they need to overcome temptation." Suffering can also be "offered up for a specific intention, and God in his goodness allows us to do this" for the sake of another.

Fowler strongly resisted the idea that her program was about external appearance or body image; rather, she stressed, it is about helping people find "peace with food" and enter into a loving relationship with God. "God loves you no matter what you weigh," she emphasized, but those who gluttonously abuse their bodies "are not pleasing [to him]—that's a big difference." Some of these same themes do appear in Protestant programs, of course—the notion that God loves his children no matter what they weigh, even if he disapproves of or is disappointed by their lack of disciplined eating, is a truism in most evangelical diet groups as well—and Fowler similarly echoes the point that these programs are not really about weight loss but rather "a spiritual journey" in which the goal is closeness to God. Likewise, however, the implication that slimmer bodies have better relationships suffuses her program no less than its Protestant counterparts.[69]

Outside American Christian and Christian-derived traditions, religious motivations for seeking a slim figure have been far less commonly invoked, though examples occasionally surface. Jews have only rarely participated in religious diet culture, for instance, however much they may have participated in its secular versions. But at least one prescriptive text explicitly aimed at weight loss has come from the pen of a rabbi, Moshe Goldberger of the Staten Island Yeshiva: *Watching Your Weight . . . The Torah Way* (1989). Goldberger referred to halachic sources and the *Mishna Avos* 2:8 to remind Jews, *Marbeh basar, marbeh rima!*: the more a person increases in flesh and fat by overeating, "the more he will be increasing worms [which will devour his flesh in the grave]." Hence, along with increasing the study of Torah and *Tehillim* as "a substitute form of indulgence" to resist overeating, Goldberger urged readers to "Repeat the phrase 'More food means more worms!' 40 times in the morning and 40 times in the afternoon or at bedtime." If particular foods were especially tempting, one should "imagine that tempting dish crawling with worms." Goldberger interspersed his text with (boldface) motivational statements such as "The Torah's Program has helped millions of people!" and "The Torah's Program is guaranteed by Hashem Who designed and created us all!"[70]

Jews could also purchase the thirty-minute video *Shvitz! My Yiddisheh Workout*, produced entirely in Yiddish with English subtitles and set to klezmer music and Yiddish tunes; the socialist Workmen's Circle on Manhattan's lower east side sponsored and sold this self-consciously humorous program, "the one and only exercise workout tape in Yiddish." (The video box sported a young man in fedora, performing a bicep curl with a Star of David dumbbell under the caption, *oy vey iz mir!*) For others, there was *Rise Like a Lion*, a fifteen-minute video depicting stretching and flexibility exercises, performed by a Hasidic man with uncut beard and *payess* (side curls; he'd look dumpy next to Shamblin and Macfadden would mock him unmercifully). Still, rather than adopt an exceedingly marginal genre, adherents of mainstream American Judaism—like Catholics—have thus far tended to pick broader, nonreligious weight-loss groups such as TOPS, Weight Watchers (founded by the Jewish homemaker Jean Nidetch), or Overeaters Anonymous rather than set up explicitly Jewish ones.[71]

Concerns about body image nevertheless affect Jewish women, and not purely for so-called secular reasons. Twenty-three-year-old Debra, who as a preteen in New York converted from her family's loose Reform Judaism to Orthodoxy, recalled to me the intense emphasis placed on thinness and beauty in her parents' household and the interesting links between that focus and what she discovered in more strictly observant communities. Her mother was bulimic during Debra's childhood and attended closely to the minutiae of femininity; while Debra's grandmother used to say, "Women are never ugly, they're just lazy," a saying she apparently read on a plastic surgeon's wall plaque. When Debra became Orthodox and transferred to a religious high school, the religious notion of female modesty seemed worlds apart from her upbringing, and she developed what in her words was a "split personality" of trying to combine sexiness and modesty. Nor was she the only one of her peers to blend these ideals: there was "a huge anorexia problem" at Debra's Manhattan yeshiva, alongside other obsessions with attaining what she called a WASP standard of female beauty through procedures such as nose jobs and expensive hair removal. Being sexy and modest at the same time, girls typically wore "black tight skirts, black high platform boots, and tight bodysuits tucked in," which—though suggestive by many strict religious standards—were allowed in the religious school unless one's knees were showing. After leaving Orthodoxy, Debra came to think of both models—her family's and her yeshiva's—as fostering rigorous bodily control, albeit plainly different kinds, and she eloquently described the "body-mind problem" that she faced as a Jewish woman. Whereas in her home, female bodies had to be disciplined for the sake of beauty, Orthodoxy taught that women's sexuality "had to be constantly under ropes, and . . . not an intimate part of my personality," at least not until marriage.[72]

At still another point on the spectrum of non-Protestant religions, the widespread appeal of Asian traditions for American baby boomers and their children has resulted in their appropriation for pragmatic ends. As growing numbers of American diet writers have discovered the practical usefulness of meditation, vegetarianism, and mindful exercise, they have found weight-loss resources in Buddhist texts and traditions: witness, for instance, Ronna Kabatznick's *Zen of Eating: Ancient Answers to Modern Weight Problems* (1998). Other popular texts have addressed the spiritual dimensions of food, such as Donald Altman's *Art of the Inner Meal: Eating as a Spiritual Path* (1999). Various American fitness instructors and health enthusiasts have also increasingly appropriated Hindu systems of yoga as an aid to the goal of thinness. Typical titles range from *Beauty through Yoga: Slim and Trim in 14 Days* (1989) to *The Yoga Mini Book for Weight Loss and Fitness*. The last promises to help expectant seekers "burn calories and lose weight; strengthen and sculpt your abs; boost metabolism and banish cellulite; tone your body from head to toe; [and] improve cardiovascular fitness and flexibility," all through "traditional hatha poses" and "powerful asanas" that are "specially designed to melt off extra pounds and boost muscle tone." Inner spiritual tranquility would harmonize, produce, and in turn be sustained by the perfect American body.[73]

Communal groups founded on Eastern teachings have frequently focused on dietary and related bodily regimens as pathways to spiritual evolution or enlightenment. Divine Madness, a community influenced by the teachings of the Russian mystic G. I. Gurdjieff (1877?–1949) and located in Boulder, Colorado, has attracted media coverage for the athletic success of its elite members in running ultramarathons, ranging from fifty to one hundred miles. Journalists have noted the dietary stringency of the group, founded in 1977, and its leader, Marc Tizer: members eat only two strictly controlled daily meals and train themselves to sleep as little as four hours a night (Tizer himself has claimed to sleep only twenty hours per week and to eat as little as three figs per day). Julie, who lived in the community during the 1980s when it was called "The Work," spoke with me about the community's practice of discerning individual bodies' proper portions of food and sleep. Highly restricted food intake was crucial for all community members "not because of weight, per se," noted Julie, but rather as part of the path to spiritual evolution: the more spiritually evolved one became, the less one would need to eat or sleep. Eating and sleeping the absolute minimum amount required, members, said Julie, were "very, very thin." Eating more than one's portion was to indulge selfishly in the animalistic appetites, and it was an infraction that would reap harsh condemnation from the leader and community members alike. Sex likewise served as "a spiritual discipline" though in a very different way: sexual activity was encouraged while monogamy was eschewed, the point being to learn to get over attachments and jealousies. Discipline, obedience, and structure ruled all. Julie concluded our interview by speculating on why such a high proportion of the group members—including herself and Tizer but also many others—were Jewish, perhaps because they were drawn to the emphasis on intentional regulation found also in Jewish tradition.[74]

Beliefs and practices commingle in many ways, however, and as persons living in the United States reshape both long established and recently transported religious practices, it becomes impossible to establish a determinative source of particular prejudices toward body size. Gauri, the twenty-five-year-old daughter of a marriage between a fourth-generation "old-school" New England Unitarian and an "atheist Hindu" who migrated to the United States, told me of imbibing messages about disciplined regimen from both sides of her family. Her Unitarian relatives denounced gluttony, frivolity, and waste: from them she learned to clean her plate, compost the surplus, speak matter-of-factly, be ever punctual, and shun the vanity of makeup. The Hindu side of her family, by contrast, stressed the importance of both excess and regimen: women were to cook copious amounts of food to share with others, for instance, even as everyone stressed female slenderness and beauty for the sake of attracting a good husband. Predictably enough, these competing ideals of frugality and hospitality created internal familial conflicts, especially at holidays, as each set of relatives sought to avoid affronting the other. Gauri and her younger sister responded in different ways to the mixed and even contradictory messages given by their parents and extended kin, her sister becoming extremely thin and anxious about her body—"vaguely anorexic," in Gauri's words—and Gauri developing a rounder figure that was a few pounds (not many) past slender. Relatives from both the Hindu and Unitarian sides periodically "berated" the girls about weight, albeit for different reasons.

But Gauri's unease with her body hardly ended with her protective if well-meaning family. When she eventually sought ministerial ordination in the Unitarian-Universalist Association, she made a required visit to an interdenominational career assessment counselor who among other things rated her on attention to personal grooming. Despite her meticulous preparation for this encounter, Gauri's score on a scale of 1–5 was a mediocre 3. When she later asked for detailed information about what she could have done differently and what she should do in future to improve, the counselor refused to be more specific, instead recommending that Gauri visit a personal appearance consultant ("like those women who used to do your colors," Gauri drolly informed me), and also "maybe join a gym and get a personal trainer." One can only speculate that Gauri's weight—150 pounds on her 5'2" frame—prevented her from attaining a ringing endorsement of her ministerial candidacy. Bright yet emotionally bruised from all sides of her heritage, Gauri was trapped by disciplinary ideals that she either could not or would not attain.[75]

Not surprisingly, other spirit-oriented groups, many of New Thought derivation, also offer reasons and resources for thinking concretely about "ideal body weight" in relation to prayer. One local Church of Religious Science had an ongoing program of this kind for many years, while New Age-inspired public figures such as Oprah Winfrey and Norris Chumley enduringly preached the necessity of harnessing spiritual forces for the purposes of weight loss. The Unity School book catalog advertised Debbie Johnson's 1996 book *Think Yourself Thin: The Visualization Technique That Will Make You Lose Weight Without Diet or Exercise,* while Unity health authors Richard and Mary-Alice Jafolla assured readers, "Your body is right now seeking the slenderness and the perfection that are really you." New titles such as *Daily Word for Weight Loss: Spiritual Guidance to Give You Courage on Your Journey* (2002) continue to appear from the editors of the Unity School's monthly magazine.[76] Even Christian Scientists, still denying the materiality of the body and declaring the true nature of human beings to be nonmaterial spirit, addressed the problem of excess weight and diet control in a special 1997 issue of the *Christian Science Sentinel,* where readers were encouraged to pray about what foods to eat.[77]

While those outside the mainstream Protestant world typically speak in different tones about the spiritual dimensions of diet, they agree with countless other American Protestant fitness entrepreneurs that God commands human beings to glorify their bodies as God's own temple, and they diet vigorously to keep healthy. Still, Protestants unquestionably lead the way in creating a broadly appealing diet culture that speaks to specific issues of ethics, divine will, and salvation; and the didacticism of that culture only intensifies with the passing of time. Christians of many stripes have long been preoccupied, certainly, with food and with the suffering that accompanies bodily existence and have sought in diverse and sundry ways to transcend, ameliorate, or simply survive the everyday dilemmas of the flesh. The idea that the appetite is treacherous and that the faithful should be thin has a lengthy history, as we've seen, making the modern devotional diet culture seem not so new or unusual after all. Much of what marks the contemporary message as distinctive, in fact, is not its concern with food and fitness per se, but the apparent willingness of authors to accept and even celebrate the most extreme cultural body standards, converting them from social constructs into divine decree. "Think of your 'promised land' as a thin body," bubbled Chapian and Coyle in 1979, a depiction echoed twenty years later when another writer affirmed her certainty that she would soon "enter the Promised Land of thinness!"[78] Whether all others would express it so forthrightly, the formulation articulates a guarantee of righteous success that has ever more aggressively permeated religious and secular diet cultures alike.

As with Shedd, later diet purveyors rarely distinguished between those whose obesity could seriously affect their health by medical standards and those who were merely a few pounds over the extremely lean ideal celebrated in the American advertising and entertainment industries. None could afford to relax completely, for there would always be room in the arena of Christian discipline for improvement. Fitness writers persistently cite the Bible as the final authority for their views on fat and thinness, celebrating the apparent congruence between medical opinions about body weight and the much older scriptural writings. Weight reduction is still about beauty, but with stakes much higher than earthly attention and praise. Far more important is the certainty of a familiar, influential relationship with God, the closeness of which may be taken as divine approval for other agendas, personal and political. As we turn to the final chapter, we see that other, more chilling, themes have been exceptionally long-lived in Christian fitness culture, fueling the industry throughout its development and into what appears to be its nonstop escalation into the twenty-first century.

5 "Don't Eat That"

*Denial, Indulgence, and Exclusion
in Christian Diet Culture*

The practice of shaping the body in service to particular religious ideals subsists on the rhythms of desire and restraint, excess and exclusion. Like other acts born of longing piled on necessity, eating can be an act of passion and anticipated satiation, while also carrying live possibilities for regret and shame. Some appetites are not easily slaked. For American Protestant people—who have restricted or eschewed sex, alcohol, smoking, dancing, leisure activities, and other bodily pleasures for the sake of obedience and virtue—eating has long carried dense and contradictory meanings. Early modern Protestants, we recall, made creative and sometimes paradoxical use of fasting as a religious observance; while later Protestant-derived traditions, including New Thought and its various offshoots, stressed the centrality of both ingestion and abstinence to religious devotion. Overlapping and intertwined with these impulses was the project of "visibilizing the soul" by dissecting somatic indicators of inward spiritual renewal—a project sustained by a range of diet reformers, physiognomists, and phrenologists, among others, and one that transmogrified into such programs as the somatotyping work of the mystically oriented William Sheldon.

But nowhere has the mandate to personify purity appeared more richly expressive than in modern-day Christian diet culture, where food is at once the object of desperate longing and embittered loathing. Markers of gender, race, and class also figure deeply into attitudes formed toward physical appetites, in ways that may cloak the trauma sometimes motivating dietary disciplines—the afflictive experience of an eating disorder, for example, triggered by silent suffering—even while generating other forms of pain and distress. This chapter traces the effects of the religious ambivalence about sin and pleasure upon bodies that eat, feed others, and aim toward godly distinction within a putatively corrupt and anguished world.

POISONED BODIES, BLEMISHED SOULS:
FOOD AS TAINT AND TRANSGRESSION

As in earlier historical periods, latter-day religious diet reformers have promoted a variety of messages, some advocating fasting as a useful means of
weight control and others urging against it, several advocating vegetarianism while opponents uphold the benefits of meat, more and more recommending special vitamin supplements to fight toxins while the conservative
proffer basic dietary variety mixed with exercise. And as in the wider diet
culture of which Bible-based writers have been part, there is no general
consensus as to the most proper and righteous way to eat (indeed, authors
sometimes seem to thrive on denouncing each other's programs), but few
authors if any question the belief that following God means taking a deeply
suspicious stance toward food. If you listen to the Lord, urged Marie
Chapian and Neva Coyle in *Free to Be Thin*, you will often hear his voice
telling you, "Don't eat that."[1]

Food, in fact, has consistently remained an evil temptation in the literature of the past half-century. Most authors have echoed the idea suggested
by Deborah Pierce in *I Prayed Myself Slim*, that while they were once
taught to say grace for their food, they now pray for the grace to stay away
from food. For decades, Christian diet writers have likened love for food to
idolatry. "Did you know," wrote Chapian and Coyle in *Free to Be Thin*,
"that you stifle God's working in your life when you habitually overeat?"
God will always be there to advise believers about the proper amount to eat;
in fact, these divine instructions are far more important than any humanly
constructed diet plan: "He loves you more than anybody in the whole world
and is more concerned with your weight than anyone else you know. Let
Him speak to you and direct *every morsel you eat*." Discerning God's voice
from other, earthly voices is sometimes difficult, Chapian and Coyle
acknowledge, and a good test is generally to check with a doctor. "If you
think the Lord is telling you to go on a fad diet of, say, only grapefruit and
eggs for a certain time (or some equally unhealthy scheme), please pray
again. God's ways aren't faddy—they're eternal and everlasting."[2]

For Chapian and Coyle, as for most other writers, particular kinds of
foods have been evil and others virtuous. In *Free to Be Thin*, victuals ranked
as "World Food vs. Kingdom Food." Foods from the world defile our bodies,
the authors argued, and are ones "that have appealed to our flesh, not our
spirit." Tootsie rolls, pizza, candy, and cookies, as well as the low-calorie substitutes and artificial sweeteners marketed as diet products, all come under
fire as being "fattening" and hence "worldly" foods. Foods from the king-

dom of God, by contrast, consist of lean meats (steamed, water-packed, skin-less), dairy products ("lo-cal," not processed), fruits and vegetables (raw or steamed, without butter), and whole-grain breads and cereals. The authors recommended the daily food guide published by the U.S. Department of Agriculture, which they advised adapting to individual daily calorie limits. And they urged readers to pray: "Dear Lord, help me to develop an interest in nutrition and what my body needs to function beautifully for your glory. . . . I renounce the lusts for those foods that are harmful to my body. I refuse to be a friend of the world's system and foods. I choose to eat Kingdom food to the glory of God. In Jesus' name, Amen!"[3]

The anticonsumerism evident in such refrains against "worldly food" was rarely taken very far by diet writers—certainly not the most popular ones, who were in any case benefiting handsomely from the consumer culture rising within American evangelicalism and witnessed powerfully in the publishing industry. Yet a persistent lament against processed foodstuffs rang strong, with evil heaped in correlative increments upon the more "commercialized" types. Good foods were plainer in their packaging and preparation, unembellished by sauces, dressings, or immoderate spices. The biblical figure of Daniel provided the ideal model for this system of austerity and renunciation, inasmuch as he rejected the rich food and wine of King Nebuchadnezzar in favor of simple vegetables and water. Quoting Daniel, Chapian and Coyle noted that his spare diet was a choice against "defiling himself," according to the scripture. They concluded on a dismal note: "Think of the last time you binged on some rich or fattening food. By eating that food, you were actually making your body filthy, unclean, unfit, desecrated." The authors also tried to appeal to their readers' personal revulsions, observing, "You wouldn't want to eat a hair, a roach, or a rat, but that éclair or those greasy french fries may be just as defiling."[4] Authors such as these worked hard to upend readers' own food hierarchies and unhealthy tastes, here and elsewhere utilizing disgust in an attempt to turn tempting treats into aversions.

Mab Graff Hoover's 1983 book of "meditations for munchers," inspired by Chapian and Coyle's bestselling volume, cited Paul's letter to the Colossians as proof of the need to annihilate lust for food, a procedure she attempted by recalling her dead mother's corpse: "When mother died, the body looked like my mother, but it wasn't she. Mother liked to eat, but that body never grew hungry. Even though her body had no appetite, I knew mother was still alive—hidden from me, but alive in Christ. The apostle Paul says that *my* life also is hidden with Christ; because I have died to self, I am commanded to kill my earthly nature!"[5] And like the lifeless body that no longer hungers, so should living Christians adopt indifference toward food, slaughtering their appetites if necessary, so as to diminish its power over them. Those who care too much about food, Hoover notes, make a "god" of the stomach (another reference to Paul) and are hypocrites as she herself sometimes was: "I see myself sitting in church, hands folded over the Bible, innocent eyes on the pastor, but with my mind on waffles, sweet rolls, pancakes."[6] Heavy, sweet foods were tempting as a fantasy no less than as items actually partaken, for they drew her mind away from God's word to the evil things of this world.

Hoover mocks her own struggle to choose righteous foods over wicked ones, writing, "Can I imagine myself picking up a grease-filled, chocolate-covered donut, and saying, 'I eat this in the name of the Lord Jesus?'" Indeed, she laments, "When I look at chocolates or a beautiful birthday cake or Danish pastries, it's hard for me to believe they are being offered through the Evil One. But I know from Scripture that Satan continually tries to ruin the temple of God, the church, (my body!)." Instead of giving in to her temptation to eat such foods, she resolves to emulate Paul and Jesus, eating sparingly as she presumes they did. "Today, I will eat one piece of chicken (without the skin), a lot of salad (chewing it well), some vegetables, fruit, and one small slice of bread! I will imitate the Lord." Yet the struggle continues, admits Hoover, and perpetually she must "come to the place where I am totally convinced that sugar, chocolate, and fat are also [with alcohol and nicotine, her former vices] dreaded enemies."[7] As Pamela Snyder taught in *A Life Styled by God*, "We have a choice to make: living within the *bounds* of Christ or living in *bondage* to Boston cream pie."[8] The front cover of C. S. Lovett's *Help Lord . . . The Devil Wants Me Fat!* made the same point, picturing a devilishly tempting banana split (see figure 13).

That liberal Protestants were as subject to this mode of thought as their conservative counterparts was made clear in a 1981 article in the *Christian Century* by the Unitarian Universalist minister Bruce Marshall. Noting that "in this age salvation by diet seems easier to conceive of than salvation by grace," Marshall gently lampooned what he called "the Protestant approach to eating" as "purification through sacrifice": "Virtue is won through deprivation. The faithful are warned against the lure of pleasure. If you enjoy what you are eating, chances are that it's bad for you. Your menu has been formulated by the devil to tempt you to ruin. . . . If I don't drink wine, I'll be a more virtuous person. If I don't eat sugar, if I don't eat meat, if I avoid cream sauces and rich desserts, God will shower his blessings upon me. Salvation is earned by not eating things." Arguing that this theology, like other contemporary theologies of eating he outlined, was "sacrilegious," Marshall sought to promote a more joyous, less constricted notion of divine feasting. Yet he spoke for many in noting that his own occasional indulgences in such "illicit" foods as doughnuts sparked an inner voice warning of the torment soon to follow this pleasure.[9]

An example of the occasional Christian diet book that aimed to promote a more positive view of food was Edward Dumke's book *The Serpent Beguiled Me and I Ate: A Heavenly Diet for Saints and Sinners* (1986). An Episcopal priest and licensed counselor in the state of California, Dumke described "seven lessons" about food as taught in the Bible (and, he argued, religions more generally) that included "food as a symbol for the sacred," "food as a symbol for love," and "food as a symbol for community." Dumke titled another section "Enjoy Your Food," recommending the benefits of eating slowly for enjoyment as well as moderation; and he urged readers at one point to "Eat the foods you really like. Many people associate dieting success with deprivation. It doesn't have to be this way. Remember, if you enjoy what you eat, you will not need to eat as much and you won't get bored with your diet." Yet the very title of Dumke's book, evoking the biblical theme of temptation and the transgressive dangers of eating, conveyed a primary equation of food with sin—or, in the book's more nuanced passages, a line demarcating foods into opposing categories of virtue and indulgence. Intermittently in the text, as in his "Ten Commandments of Good Nutrition," Dumke instructed readers in religio-scientific terms: "Thou shalt consume sufficient protein but thou shalt limit the amount of animal protein. . . . Thou shalt create a diet in complex carbohydrates. . . . Thou shalt create a diet low in saturated fat. . . . Thou shalt limit the amount of chocolate thou eatest." His test at the end of this section was to have readers distinguish between the "good" and "not-good" foods in a list of pairs that included such combinations as chocolate cake and grapefruit, fried chicken and boiled chicken, steak and filet of sole, pastrami and tofu. "Remember," he concluded, "you are what you eat."[10]

Well into the 1980s, most writers readily admitted their own failures concerning food and weight. The knowledge that certain foods and ways of eating are sinful may be simple to grasp, but the life change that is supposed to follow such awareness is more difficult. At one point Hoover confessed that while "most mornings" she was "thrilled with the Scriptures" and knew she loved God, "this flesh of mine is like a hungry tiger, always ready to break out of the cage of discipline and gobble everything in sight. And *I* am the one who opens the door." But because the Bible's teachings against self-indulgence were irrevocable, she advised herself sternly to resist: "Participating in food orgies (even at church!), helping to plan unhealthy dinners, or offering junk foods to my loved ones is sin. As long as I overeat or poison my body with chemical additives, I shall not become the righteousness of God."[11]

The poisoned body: the image thrusts us back among health reformers of earlier eras, who similarly equated gluttonous eating with contamination and filth. Naturalists and alternative health advocates have long deplored the toxins and impurities allegedly infecting the body ignorant or blasé about its intake, and, as we saw, they have counseled abstinence as an indispensable therapy for this gloomy situation. Even mainstream Christian diet books that oppose the alternative health culture have absorbed many of these ideas about bodily poisons, as evidenced in Hoover's concern about chemical additives or this passage in the Jewish convert Zola Levitt's *How to Win at Losing*: "God has, in a sense, already committed himself on the matter of eating. The foods found easily and naturally on the earth are the ones that do you no harm. The weird combinations made by men—the processing and drying of grains, the 'enhancing' of foods with sugar—are the ones that got you where you are today."[12] Chapian and Coyle repeat the belief that fasting "giv[es] the overworked internal organs and tissues of the body a good rest and time for rehabilitation. Fasting (over six days) flushes out toxic matter and poisons from the body system. Fasting improves circulation and promotes endurance and stamina. Fasting renovates, revives and purifies the cells of the body."[13] Twentieth-century technological innovations in food production and pest control have emphatically given new force to old fears, making for a much expanded list of sinful foods than those that are simply "fattening."

George Malkmus's Hallelujah diet consists mainly of raw fruits and vegetables and is grounded in Genesis 1:29: "I give you every seed-bearing plant on the face of the whole earth and every tree that has fruit with seed in it." On that early diet, Malkmus argues in *Why Christians Get Sick* (1989), people lived over nine hundred years, but once meat and cooked food were added to the human diet sickness came into being and radically reduced the life span. Whereas raw fruits and vegetables are "good" foods, junk foods are bad and to eat them is morally wrong, a point Malkmus proves by citing Paul in the New Testament: "If any man defile the temple of God, him shall God destroy." Modern bodies, heaving with meat and other animal products, saturated fat, insecticides, artificial preservatives, chlorinated water, bleached-white bread, caffeine, sugar, and packaged convenience foods, are "so full of poisons that the cells are literally being drowned in these pollutants." Though some bodies may appear strong enough to withstand such abuse, warns Malkmus, "You can count on all abusers having a payday some day, because of an irreversible law which says: 'Be not deceived; God is not mocked: for whatsoever a man soweth (in ignorance or with knowledge), that shall he also reap' (Galatians 6:7)."[14]

Malkmus's view toward the evils of what he called the Standard American Diet (SAD) is unambiguous. In God's Way to Ultimate Health (1995), he described typical eating habits in terms used by his own Christian mentor in natural foods, the evangelist Lester Roloff (1918–82): modern foods were impoverished, ghostly, doped, adulterated, embalmed, decomposed, rancid, fumigated, corrupt, desiccated, lifeless, "injured by decomposition, toxins, age, vermin, rodents, metallic contamination, and by other agents of decay and corruption."[15] Raw fruits and vegetables, by contrast, were alive, fresh, pure, life-saving, sweet, vital, clarifying, economical, energizing, healing, and of course natural. The consequences of improper choices were presented in dire terms: cancer, arthritis, gout, and diseases of the colon were only a few of the stark signs that the body had been poorly treated. Making only a handful of doctor-recommended dietary changes— less red meat, more produce, reduced salt, and so forth—was too half hearted an effort to matter, leaving the dieter as reliant as ever on artificial, cooked and therefore "dead" foods. One either adopted the Hallelujah diet in all its entirety or not; as with the particular branch of fundamentalist Christianity Malkmus preached, one was either "in" or "out." The partition of the world into such stark classifications of good and evil provisions is similar in its urgency—while being profoundly different in its details— to the systems proffered by more mainstream dieters like Coyle and Hoover, or Shamblin. The tensions among these programs over which foods to demarcate as "good" or "evil" represent, in a sense, larger disagreements over which parts of so-called secular culture to appropriate and which to reject.

Gwen Shamblin's writings frequently imply that food is something to transcend or even to avoid altogether: it is a devilish lover, tempting human beings to betray their covenant with God and enter a lascivious relationship with food. In her words,

> We fell in love with the food by giving it our heart, soul, mind, and strength. . . . We obeyed it. It called us from the bed in the morning, and we used our strength to prepare it. We also used our strength to force more of it down into the body than the body called for. We gave it our mind all day long by looking through recipe books and discussing the latest diets with our friends, asking, "What do you get to eat on your diet?" We lusted after the foods that were on the menu, and we gave our hearts to the 10 o'clock binge.[16]

Shamblin explicitly links food with sex, with the corollary that to overeat is a sin closely aligned with adultery. Though she notes that food can be enjoyed if it is not desired too much, her teachings throughout suggest a deeply embattled relationship with food and a strict regimen of asking God for guidance at each and every bite. Shamblin's image of food as a seductive lover who entices the overeater away from her true husband, God, is unusually graphic for this literature; yet her theme of sinful surrender to temptation is widely shared.

Human beings must eat to live, however, and since conservative Christian theology assumes God to be the author of all things, food cannot be unredeemably evil. In fact, authors often linger at great length on the deliciousness of approved foods, which they claim to enjoy more now that they are liberated from eating obsessions. Shamblin writes about food with erotic abandon, in sensual language that makes her experience of it sound as lush as that of Father Divine.

> As soon as I get to the movie theater, I can smell the popcorn and the hot dogs. I like to make sure I am hungry when I arrive, so most of the time I won't eat supper before going to the movies. . . . I find the best kernels of popcorn with just the right amount of butter and salt on them. I like to eat one kernel at a time so I can savor the combined flavors of the popcorn, salt, and butter. . . . Keep in mind that I still have my box of candy, so I do not want to fill up entirely on the popcorn. . . . If the candy comes in a variety of colors or flavors, I will eat my favorite colors and flavors first. I take a bite, savor it, and take a sip from my diet drink.

Sometimes Shamblin's descriptions of her food habits seem as obsessive as any overeater's, as she recounts skipping lunch prior to special dinners "to make sure that I am really, *really* hungry!" Her writing lingers teasingly over finding the "best morsels" of the steak's "juiciest pieces," loading "plenty of real butter and sour cream" on her baked potato, and topping off her meal with "the ultimate brownie topped with hot caramel, chocolate fudge, whipped cream, nuts." She encourages her readers to search their plates for "the perfect bite" that "will just melt in your mouth." It is easy to forget, when reading such mouth-watering descriptions, that they come from a text that denounces fat Christians for loving food to the point of idolatry.[17]

But for Shamblin, unlike so many of her predecessors, food itself is not sin (recall that there are no sinful foods in Shamblin's world, only sinful worshipers of it); *fat* is sin, and so long as one can eat joyfully without gaining weight, none of God's rules have been broken. The ideal attitude toward food is a kind of thoroughgoing indifference precariously combined with a

sensual basking in its pleasures. Achieving this delicate balance is not difficult, in Shamblin's view: God wants people to enjoy food, after all, and as
soon as one fully surrenders one's will, he will restore the joy of eating that
remains unavailable to the person obsessed with food. Set free from enslave-
ment to food, the truly Christian eater may revel in all good things and
inhabit a kind of earthly paradise. Those who greedily indulge their desires
will never be satisfied, but the obedient will gain the infinite bliss of a thin
body *and* bodily pleasure—the appetite lusciously emancipated through
abstinence!

Shamblin's followers echo her equation, describing the taut balance
between discipline and delight. A Weigh Down participant named Tracy, for
instance, told me that she has learned that food could become an addiction
that displeased God, who created food for pleasure instead. "I like a nice
tawny port, but I don't get drunk," she remarks in explanation. "I like a few
puffs off my husband's fine cigars, but I don't smoke cigarettes. I love
movies, but I don't spend all my time in theaters. I found out that, like Paul
said in, what, 1 Corinthians 6, I think, that all things are allowable but we
must not be brought under the control of any one thing." Even those who
have not managed to keep weight off may praise these teachings about
appetite while continuing to strive to meet the ideal. Nina, a woman influenced by Neva Coyle's teachings on food, described to me her relentless
food cravings and sinful capitulation to them: "I can honestly say that the
Holy Spirit convicts me constantly about the terrible eating habits I have
and I believe that if I kept my mind focused on the Christ-like eating habits
I should have I would not be an overweight person. It is just a matter of fact.
As Peter took his eyes off Jesus he began to sink . . . so shall we!!! I truly
believe our body is the temple of Christ and we should keep it in tip-top
shape. I am a food addict with a weakness I have not completely turned over
to the Lord."[18] The degree of responsibility Nina bears for her addiction is
unclear, although this is a crucial point of difference among programs such
as Weigh Down, 3D, and First Place.

As media attention increasingly focuses upon the growing incidence of
obesity in the United States, gluttony has become popular fodder for pulpit
pronouncements even in churches that do not sponsor Bible-based diet
groups. A 2003 Lenten sermon series on the seven deadly sins, delivered at
Boston's evangelical Park Street Church, began with gluttony. "Growing up
I remember church pot luck supper tables overladen with fried chicken and
potato salad with which we were encouraged to gorge ourselves in the name
of Christian fellowship," remarked the associate minister Daniel Harrell.
Piling up other ecclesial examples, Harrell erased any Norman Rockwellian

innocence from this picture. "At its rotten core, gluttony is fixated self-love that impedes love of God and of neighbor. Gluttony obscures your vision toward the needs of others by distorting your perception of your own needs." Eating too much becomes an unfortunate means of trying to alleviate boredom or escape life's everyday sorrows. "We indulge in order that we might inoculate ourselves against potential suffering," Harrell preached, but the true Christian way was to "reorient your hunger heavenward."

Harrell's inspiration for this subject was an online Christian forum thread on Greg Critser's book, *Fat Land,* since Critser argued that a factor in the fattening of U.S. citizens was the declining emphasis on gluttony as sin. Harrell's oration echoed many forum discussants who agreed that modern-day Christians should retrieve older denunciations of overeating, though he stayed far away from the subject of fat itself. Perhaps with good reason: the *Re:Generation* discussion participants were less restrained, as one subscriber generated several heated replies from fellow Christians when he called obese people "lazy sacks of shit" and refused to recant his point (though he adjusted his lingo and deleted "sacks of shit" from the original post). Forum members approached the topic from various perspectives (some clearly shaped by their own body size, lean or large); shared advice about food choices, diet soda, and the power of prayer; and struggled together to carve out a religious stance that could denounce gluttony as sinful without damning fat people themselves. As with so many other "hate the sin, love the sinner" matters, however, this latter task proved exceedingly difficult and divisive until the thread finally tailed off into silence.[19]

Christians clearly differ on the finer points of righteous eating, but their chorus of voices has left little doubt for many churchgoers as to the appropriateness of eyeing food behavior through a religious lens. Most of these, moreover, train that lens on transgression, viewing it from a wide variety of angles and in seemingly innocuous settings. By focusing on scriptural precedents for eating well—from Adam and Eve to the exiled Israelites (who ate only manna and meat), Daniel (who fasted on vegetables and water), John the Baptist, and Jesus—Christian authors try to deflect criticism that their instruction conforms too closely to the body standards of the wider American culture. At the same time, they proffer biblical justification for their readers' desire to be lean and appealing; for though this literature repeatedly decries the material rewards of slenderness offered by the secular world as superficial, Christian writers appeal to them constantly. And while they urge all Christians to be fit for God and to serve as models of perfection to those around them, their tone is especially severe when addressing women, constrained to subsist upon the spare diet of pious femininity.

LOVED ON A SMALLER SCALE: WOMEN, WEIGHT,
AND THE DIVINE LOVER ABOVE

Few writers may have followed Deborah Pierce's trajectory—from self-professed "object of campus ridicule" to fashion model, beauty pageant winner, and beaming bride—but most focused close attention on the prize attainments of beauty and femininity at the end of the arduous diet road. Patricia Kreml's 1978 book *Slim for Him* (whose cover sported an extremely thin woman standing triumphantly atop a mountain of whipped cream and strawberries; see figure 15) modeled the common pattern of urging readers against vanity even while assuring them that beauty would result from prudent regimen. "We don't diet, lose weight, and firm our bodies just so we can look nice and get compliments. This will be a result of our efforts but not the main reason for them," Kreml earnestly maintained. "Our first reason has to be keeping our bodies under subjection that we might live the temperate, Christ–like life we are called to live."[20] Likewise, in *Diary of a FAT Housewife* Shirley Cook told her readers that the motive to be thin "can't be that I want to be pretty . . . Or that I want better health . . . Or even to make my husband proud of me." The motive had to be "pure," solely focused on loving and pleasing God. "And He will not abuse my love, but will gently and lovingly lead me in His way."[21] The body is God's temple, authors reminded their readers, and while the real aim of keeping it "under subjection" was professedly obedience to God, weight watching had the additional benefit of making Christians more beautiful, more appealing, more envied by those who failed where disciplined believers thrived. Deliberately provoking such envy was itself a guilt-free pleasure, since it could serve as an evangelizing tool for bringing nonbelievers to Christ.

This message was reinforced in the beauty books written by and for Christian women during this same period, a genre that overlapped the diet books. One, *The Inside-Out Beauty Book* (1978), repeatedly assured women that their desire to look beautiful was not self-centered but truly godly. "If there is one thing you must be sure of in your heart," the authors wrote in urging readers to join Christian diet groups, it is the goal of *"becoming the slimmest, healthiest, most vital and alert self you can, because you are made in the image of God! (This is not selfish vanity!)"*[22] Another, *Disciplines of the Beautiful Woman* (1977), likewise noted, "That's the reason to look good! God's children, when compared with the children of darkness, should declare without a word that God is good." The author's solution was to give just over an hour a day to her appearance, and she challenged her readers to moisturize their skin, style their hair prettily, tone their muscles, "stay supple," and "stand tall; to be a good advertisement of God's wonderful care of his children." Weight was "a key factor in being a beautiful woman for God," in her view, and God could "help you get to and keep the weight that is right for you."[23]

Diet writers recognized that men as well as women struggled with gluttony and so frequently strove to address persons of both sexes. Certainly the number of books by men struggling with their own weight problems demonstrates food as a pitfall for all persons. Yet in the genre as a whole, as in many other areas of Christian publishing, female authors both dominated and aimed their work explicitly at women. As the *Bookstore Journal* noted in 1975, 90 percent of the authors of all clothbound religious best sellers were women, compared to 15 to 20 percent of the general best sellers' lists compiled by *Publishers Weekly*; and, by the estimate of the Christian News Service, which published the National Religious Bestsellers lists, fully 70 percent of the religious book buyers were women.[24] Such a predominantly female slate of authors and readers made particular sense in the devotional diet arena, since women were likewise the main purveyors and consumers of diet literature outside religious circles. They not only contributed to but, in effect, regulated and presided over the themes guiding the Christian diet industry.

Equally important in the formation of the gendered dimension of this message was a well-honed scriptural and theological interpretation of gluttony as the special province of women, both as victims and as devilish tempters for other individuals. Women not only fell into bad eating habits with greater ease and rapidity than men but also often caused family members—husbands as well as children—to commit the same sin. Behind every gluttonous man, so it was often presumed in this literature, lay a food-bearing woman.

Scripture provided a wondrously useful standard for this notion in the Old Testament account of Adam and Eve in the Garden of Eden, in which Satan tempts Eve to eat the forbidden fruit and she tempts Adam to do the same. As Joan Cavanaugh noted in *More of Jesus, Less of Me*, "Most of our men would agree with the original Adam and say, 'That woman you gave me, she did eat.'" While Eve was actually tempted by the food, according to Cavanaugh, Adam's temptation was not food but the woman, the "beautiful Eve." This scenario continued into the present, wrote Cavanaugh: women's lives were consumed by food, while men were obsessed with women and sex. "Adam could have said, 'You big dummy; now isn't that just like a woman? Let her out of your sight and there she is, stuffing her mouth.' But he loved her, so he went into the land of death to bring her out, and he couldn't get back."[25] Charlie Shedd, in *The Fat Is in Your Head*, took the Genesis passage as evidence that women often ruin other people's diets: "In any crowd we can count on it: There will be somebody near to ruin our resolves! Aunt Helen, maybe. She majors in strawberry pie and looks so wounded if we turn her down. Mrs. B., the nervous flibbertigibbet at the church dinners who can't take no."[26] Shedd concluded that to yield to such temptresses was wrong, yet the presumption remained that, as in the Genesis story, women are gluttons and may lure men into the same trap.

Fully six chapters of Shedd's book (and much of his earlier *Pray Your Weight Away*) were devoted to the impact of mothers on their children's food habits, habits that carried into adulthood and could well result in obesity. Basing his analysis on popular psychological theories of the period, Shedd emphasized the point that *"Heavy eating as a love search is futile,"* and asserted, "There are parents who cannot love properly no matter how hard they try. With some mothers, all available energies are drained off in their own neurotic trends." Elsewhere, he mused, "Uncanny how many obese people I have known came from a pushy, pushy mom. . . . Every fatty knows we eat for hidden reasons. . . . And fearless research on our mother's domination may be of special value." Mothers, as the first feeders, were responsible for the "oral syndrome" that might beset their children well into adulthood, and while Shedd urged readers to realize that most mothers did the best they could, he also recognized that "my compulsive obsessive drives are often mother oriented."[27] Whether because they gave their children too much love or not enough, whether they taught their offspring to clean their plates or were overly restrictive of their intake, whether they used food as a means of love and comfort or an instrument of seduction and control, mothers were the source of countless—indeed, probably most—adults' food problems.

Even when authors placed the burden of guilt squarely upon the overeater rather than those around him or her, then, women were presumed to be the mistresses of temptation. "Just because mother sets a homemade lemon meringue pie in front of you doesn't mean you have to eat it," wrote Kreml. "Mother may have been the tempter, but we are the ones who give in to the temptation." With somewhat less neutrality, Victor Kane had earlier written of the biblical figure Samson (remembered mostly for his seduction by Delilah) and concluded, "Poor Samson and his women! Come to think of it, many a man has been cheated out of some new clothing in a smaller size by a wife who unwittingly conspired against him with a cookbook in one hand and a frying pan in the other."[28] Virtually every Christian diet book of the period had at least one story to tell about an older female figure who pushed food on those around her and measured others' love for her by the amount they would eat. In *Diary of a FAT Housewife*, Shirley Cook recounted how her friend Bertha ended their friendship after Cook refused to go with her to their usual all-you-can-eat restaurants and ice cream parlors; and while Donna, another friend, provided a counterexample to such behavior, supporting Cook in her endeavor to reduce to her "formerly fine figure," even Donna's initial response had come closer to that of Eve coaxing Adam to eat.[29] The weight of scripture, history, and personal experience was patently clear: women, fat or thin, were agents of sin.[30]

Beyond the role of seductress, women were consistently portrayed as weaker than men when it came to their diets, a characterization that was equally present in literature written by men and by women. Frances Hunter, in *God's Answer to Fat*, wrote in typical fashion of being a "foodaholic" with a husband who "has never had a problem with weight because he has never had a tremendous desire for food." In the early years of her marriage, Hunter wrote, she cooked huge meals and pretended they were for her husband, Charles; but whereas he only gained a little bit of weight, Hunter herself gained 50 pounds in the first five years of marriage, and more than that as time passed. Like Hunter, Cavanaugh made a promise to her thin husband to restrict her eating; her motivation was the memory of her husband telling her, when she outweighed him by 65 pounds (she weighed 230), that he did not love her anymore. Some weeks after making a written contract claiming God's power to "win the war over gluttony," Cavanaugh craved chocolate cake; but her husband forbade her to eat any, though he himself had eaten some in her presence. The narratives of Hunter and Cavanaugh were typical in describing women as out-of-control food addicts, and in perceiving men as far less susceptible. That men could and should act as a source of support as well as admonishment for gluttonous wives was both necessary and seemingly natural.[31]

Archetypes of women as irrepressible gluttons and vamps were didactic counterparts to the paradigm of sacred femininity to which Christian women ought to align themselves. Models of ideal Christian womanhood are, of course, longstanding, but the prototype that emerged in the postwar period has been notably rigorous in its steady focus on extreme slenderness. That image blends an inherited religious emphasis on abstinence with a seemingly contradictory stress on luxury, abundance, and even indulgence. Its disciplines for diet are not penitence or the desire for mortification (two main impulses for premodern fasting) but rather the belief that diet provides the basis for a grand transformation of the self in which the outcome is beauty, wealth, and thinness. Particularly since the 1970s and most relentlessly since the 1990s, its twin ideals of beauty and femininity have been forged by white evangelical women such as those representing the public face of First Place and analogous diet programs, women who have been influenced by and have, in turn, reproduced an exemplar for "true Christian womanhood" that is ever more narrow and exclusive.

Between the 1980s and 1990s, more books emerged that were explicitly directed to women, such as Pamela Snyder's *Life Styled by God* (1985) and Dee Brestin and Peggy Johnston's *Joy of Eating Right* (1993), marketed as "A Bible Study for Women." Such books aimed their message less at individuals than at diet support groups, where Christian women could receive "accountability, encouragement, and prayer." Heavy reliance on charts, graphs, and structured responses grew, as the authors stressed weekly "weigh in" procedures, inspection of physical measurements such as waist size, numerical calculations such as body fat percentages, and systematic memorization of scripture.[32] By this point in time, Christian womanhood had long stiffened its back against American feminism, which was deemed a movement of self-centered, power-hungry women—a movement antithetical to true piety. The arguments against feminism, in fact, were organized quite similarly to those against overeating: both feminists and fat people represented greed, selfishness, and the purloining of goods to which they held no right. Both the feminist and the fat woman could be contrasted to the sweetly self-sacrificing female Christian. Body weight, more and more, indicated whether one was in the category of the saved or teetered into the realm of the damned.

When books eventually emerged to challenge this dominant model of thinness, they did so only weakly and in such a way that undermined that very challenge by blaming the slim ideal on American culture and failing to see the crucial role played by Christians in its formation. Lisa Bevere's *You Are NOT What You Weigh* (1998), for instance, documented the author's struggle with eating disorders and overweight and worked to free readers from overreliance on the bathroom scales. In her view, the image that American women wanted to conform to is "an image molded and forged by the spirit of this world." After turning to God and fasting, she writes that God delivered her from obsession with weight. "No longer was I interested in pleasing everyone else; I wanted to please God."

Yet Bevere's message is ultimately one of assuring readers that if they simply overcome their fears about weight and surrender these to God, He will in fact help them maintain a gorgeous figure. Her own experience is apparently illustrative: "I have four children, and though they periodically tax my strength and back, I have found God faithful for my figure. I relaxed, nursed, and enjoyed them without worrying about exercising back down to my prepregnancy size. With each one, I went back to my same size or smaller." In urging readers not to measure themselves by their scales, nor to count calories or diet or fret over their weight, Bevere's message—like Shamblin's, which also emphasizes her ease with pregnancy—reassures them that this path of nonresistance is the path to their perfect body. "God has been faithful to keep me at that weight independent of diet and exercise," she says. "I have trusted Him to watch over my weight as long as I keep food in the proper place." Ideal womanhood comes not through giving in to "brazen cultural influences" (which are, again, what Bevere considers the root of women's body obsessions) but through perfect surrender to God, which ends the weight struggle and also produces perfect bodies.[33]

While these juxtaposed types of womanhood—one sanctioned, the other deplored—were inscribed in the written word of the devotional diet literature and its visual accompaniments, they were sustained even more vividly by means of the diet groups and programs that arose to embody these diet principles. Though men attended these Christian counterparts to national weight-watcher programs, the founders, leaders, and majority of participants were in every case women. Carol Showalter's 1977 book, 3D, presented overeating as an exclusively female problem and women were the sole constituents of her devotional diet organization. Her husband, Bill, pastor of the church in which her local group met, inhabited her narrative as the stern sage who reproved her when she disobeyed God's will for the program and who thereby merited the real praise (after God) for the group's success.[34] Like Showalter, Coyle and her frequent coauthor, Marie Chapian, wrote of overeating as primarily a female problem; and the vast majority of their textual and visual examples cited overweight homemakers who were selfish, unhappy, and undisciplined. In their first joint effort, Free to Be Thin (1979), every one of the fifteen "before and after" photographs of Overeaters Victorious participants was female. The final words of their text quoted scripture from the Song of Solomon, as they noted Jesus' love for those who overcame the evils of fallen womanhood to embody pure Christian femininity: "We will all of us hear Him say one day: Behold, you are beautiful, my love, Behold, you are beautiful! . . . I will hie me to the mountain of myrrh and the hill of frankincense. You are all fair, my love; there is no flaw in you."[35]

Neither was there any perceptible flaw in the visual images of femininity purveyed by First Place. Though men have been welcome in these gatherings, as they have been in other programs, the main participants have by far been women, some medically obese but most hoping to lose only 10–20 pounds in order to achieve the standard their leaders have set before them. The women's testimonies follow the script of the First Place founders— transformation through weight loss—as they affirm to themselves and to outsiders their belief that, in one woman's words, God "want[s] my body to glorify Him as a disciplined believer." As the testimonies, promotional materials, and visual images from this and other evangelical diet programs reveal, slimness has acted as a crucial marker not simply of physical health or superior religious health but, more important, of true Christian womanhood.

While Shamblin's Weigh Down program appears to have drawn a higher percentage of men than previous programs, the vast majority of those who attend local Weigh Down meetings and larger conventions are women, as apparently are the majority of Shamblin's reading audience. One of Shamblin's key themes, in writing and in her public speech, is the principle of thoroughgoing submission to higher authorities, most commonly illustrated by wifely surrender to a husband's authority and submission of employees to their employers. "If you can't submit to your boss that you do see," she notes, "you can't submit to God, whom you don't see." The link between this model of obedience and her seemingly more generous plan of liberation from food compulsions is in her overriding premise that one cannot serve two masters without loving the one and hating the other. Thus: "You are either losing weight or not. This lets you know who you obey." And, "What wonderful news: as you love God, you will not be able to bow down to the brownies! It will be repulsive to eat the second half of the hamburger. You will despise worshipping the food. You cannot serve both God and someone or something else, therefore, the Promised Land is in sight— you will lose weight!"[36]

And what more might God want with women's bodies? Throughout female-authored Christian diet texts and the programs that have been founded and largely attended by women, the image of God as a divine lover or husband has served as a powerful motivational tool to compel women to get thin. Shamblin's method, especially, has been to entice followers not simply with weight loss but also with holy romance. Echoing Chapian and Coyle's usage of the Song of Solomon and Kreml's promise of the joys derived from being "slim for Him," Shamblin's second diet book, *Rise Above* (2000), promised a kind of erotic fulfillment from pleasing God, consistently described as handsome and charming, "the best-looking and most-loving and richest Husband of all times." The Lord is "not a wimpy lover," in her words, but "a passionate, jealous God," the "Hero we have all been dreaming of," the "passionate pursuer of our hearts," "my Knight in shining armor," "your first, honeymoon-passionate love." Judgment Day is "romantically delightful," an occasion for the bride to meet her groom. "I almost lose my breath when I think He is trying to get my attention now. . . . I have a crush on the Father, and this is what it looks like: I dress for Him and say, 'God, do you like this outfit?' . . . I look forward to a rendezvous with God. . . . I can't take my eyes off Him now." The pleasure of Shamblin's encounters with God seems literally orgasmic. One night, she writes, she dreamed of blowing God a kiss and feeling his response: "All I can describe to you is that it was . . . a head-to-toe tingling sensation and electrifying sensation that did not stop—unlike anything I have ever felt. It was so powerful that I woke up—crying—for I had experienced something that at the time I felt that I should never, ever share with anyone, for it was between me and God." Following this experience she wrote her song "Heaven's Kiss."[37]

Even authors who may not consider themselves part of the "Christian diet" genre regularly write about the religious importance of body image. In the fall of 2003, the mother-daughter team of Cynthia Culp Allen and Charity Allen Winters published *The Beautiful Balance for Body and Soul*. The ad copy for the book yet again targeted women's fears: "Would you wrap a priceless gift in a dingy grocery bag? Probably not. So why represent Jesus to others without looking confident, put together, and beautifully appealing—inside and out?" The book promised a " 'miracle make-over' that includes lips, eyes, skin, fashion, nails, perfume, accessories, hair, and more." Scriptural passages correlated with each physical beauty tip, illustrating God's teachings about female character and beauty. Allen, a licensed cosmetologist and beauty consultant, wrote of wanting readers to learn how "to know [Jesus] as Savior and Lord, to reflect His beauty, and to experience His healthy balance for their lives," citing Southern Baptist leaders Charles Stanley and Kay Arthur as her chief spiritual mentors. Advertising Winters as a professional model, actress, recording artist, and national speaker, the book promised that "Readers will learn to emphasize their good qualities and de-emphasize or improve problem areas—both body and soul—so that they feel beautiful and radiate beauty too."[38]

Yet as one recent publication (1998) suggests, some evangelicals may be entering a period of self-scrutiny. It is a late offering from Neva Coyle, the formerly obese author of several best-selling Christian diet books and founder of Overeaters Victorious. Some years after earning renown as the model for successful Christian dieting, Coyle gained back all the 100+ pounds she had so famously lost. Because she was still working in the Christian weight-loss industry, traveling around the country giving seminars and publicizing her books, her weight gain was public and deeply humiliating to her. She struggled despondently with her mortification and sense of failure until she finally came to believe that God loved her even as an overweight woman and that she should accept herself that way. And then, she writes, she got angry.

> Angry that I had been so unmerciful and shallow with myself and other large Christians. Angry that no one had guided me differently when I made decisions that risked my life and health in order to be slender. Angry that it had taken me so long and had cost me so much to finally realize that one reasonable alternative to weight management was healthy management of my large body. Angry that I had never before considered that one perfectly legitimate solution to my weight struggle was to focus not on the weight but on ending the struggle.[39]

Feeling *Loved on a Grander Scale*—the title of her new account—Coyle sought to undo the damage she had done before as one of this era's most influential purveyors of Christian dieting, to free women and men from the captivity to "fitness" that religious Americans have done so much to create.

However sincere, well intentioned, and penitent, Coyle stood rather forlorn. "I'm kind of a lone voice out there," she remarked in my 2001 interview with her. "It's not a real fun place to be. It's quite lonely at times. Especially when I've seen some of the leaders that were so active in Overeaters Victorious who really walked through at least the beginning part of this journey with me, and then to have them one by one just say, 'Ah, I can't go that way. I've got to go get thin,' and run off to [other Christian diet programs]." After she found the courage to make the videotape *Fit For a King*, an exercise video for large women, she received an angry phone call at 5:30 one morning from a stranger who told Coyle she had ruined the woman's entire weekend. "It was just like an intruder coming into my home," Coyle recalled. She further related stories of encounters with women who treated her with pity and contempt. Once, at a weekend retreat featuring Coyle as the main speaker, a woman threw herself to her knees, weeping to see this icon's enlarged form. Another time, when Coyle was slated to speak at a Christian event, "the lady that invited me said, 'I thought you'd be different. I thought you'd be younger and I thought you'd be thinner.' Just said it to me before I was supposed to speak. It was hard enough to forgive myself for not being able to maintain [my weight loss]." The indignities continue: *Loved on a Grander Scale* remained in print only a year, and media coverage was scarce to nonexistent. When called upon to comment on Shamblin's program by the producers of *Religion and Ethics Newsweekly*, aired on PBS, Coyle found her views got short shrift.

As in the fat liberation movement whose language Coyle echoes—the problem is not being fat, but rather society's hating people for being fat—

media attention is sparse, typically rendering the activists' radical message as scandalous, disagreeable, and pathetic: spawned by desperation, fueled by petulance, and destined for failure.[40] Compared to this disparaging portrayal, it is hardly to be wondered why the model of true Christian womanhood promoted by Shamblin and the Christian fitness industry more generally— slim, adorable, chaste and yet safely erotic—appears far more alluring to vast sectors of religious women. But what about those whom it casts in an unfavorable light or altogether excludes?

THE POWER OF PERFECTION: PURIFIED BODIES AND RACIALIZED WORLDS

Hillel Schwartz has illustrated many time-honored ways in which successful slimming programs have linked themselves to higher ends than personal fitness. As he notes in his cultural history of the American obsession with fat, the 1970s were a decade when "appetite and apocalypse" especially mixed, yet this was no new grouping. The concurrence of diet mania and the fear of global catastrophe could be read back for decades (if not centuries), as could its flip side: bodily regimen as a rapturous pathway to heaven.[41] Plainly apparent to Schwartz, and to observers of bodily preoccupations in many other times and places, is the fact that the quest for a particular kind of body is no merely individual matter but holds broad social and cultural implications. For many American Christians living in the latter half of the twentieth century, the pursuit of thinness has served numerous ends, from refiguring notions of sin and redemption to shoring up the bounds of sacred femininity to preparing for the apocalyptic return of Christ. All have functioned, in some way, to partition the world into stark categories of good and evil, as thin Christians stride forth to model virtue while fat ones languish somewhere in the drab purgatory of disobedience. The law of thinness, from Shedd to Shamblin, has carried with it the promise of personal purification— and, with that promise, hope of sanitizing a sinful, fallen world.

But there remains yet another and more sinister way in which weight watching has served to purify the world. Close observation of the popular texts and programs that comprise the Christian diet culture, along with insights gleaned from studies of the broader, "secular" American fitness culture, clarifies its central role in the reproduction and naturalization of a racialized ideal of whiteness, purged of the excesses associated with nonwhite cultures. The feminist philosopher Susan Bordo has written cogently about the disciplinary power of beauty practices, along with the images that legitimate and encourage them, and she includes dieting in her categorization of "practices that do not merely transform but *normalize* the subject." Looking back to the last third of the twentieth century, Bordo argues, "An increasingly universal equation of slenderness with beauty and success has rendered the competing claims of cultural diversity even feebler. Men who were teenagers from the mid-seventies on, whatever their ethnic roots or economic class, are likely to view long, slim legs, a flat stomach, and a firm rear end as essentials of female beauty."[42] That this particular formation of slenderness is rooted in Victorian images of Christian womanhood, and that its increasing severity is traceable in later formations of Christian culture, are not points of interest to Bordo, nor is religion's role in naturalizing late twentieth-century racial hierarchies of beauty. Careful consideration of Christian diet culture reveals, however, that along with being an essential component of femininity (and, though to a more variable degree, of masculinity as well), thinness has been a vital religious marker of race, even as race has been central to the discursive production of true Christian womanhood.

Signs abound in the literature of Christian fitness that its presumed audience has been white. Particularly in the formative decades of the devotional diet culture (the 1950s through the 1970s), the frequent cartoons, photographs, and "before and after" images invariably depicted white people, and the stories filling the pages did likewise. Indeed, the whiteness of these stories was made more obvious by the occasional nonwhite reference, the use of (usually) an African American figure in such a way as to indicate that no such readers were a part of the intended audience. For instance, Shedd, who was fond of telling anecdotes, included this one in *Pray Your Weight Away:* "When someone inquired of the peaceful colored woman how she got that way, she replied, 'When I works I works, and when I sits I sits loose.'" Elsewhere, in an apparent attempt at black dialect, he wrote breezily, "All God's chillun got woes these days."[43] Victor Kane quoted Joel Chandler Harris, the compiler of the well-known Uncle Remus stories in African American dialect, on fat and overeating: "Watch out w'en you'er gittin all you want. Fattenin' hogs ain't in luck!"[44] Certainly these references were hardly so blatantly racist as some passages in other, nonreligious texts on body and diet of the period: In a chapter vividly titled "Is it true that savages are never constipated?" for instance, the physician J. H. Montague wrote, "One has but to go to the moving picture theater and see travel pictures showing Darkest Africa in order to realize what a raw fruit and vegetable diet can do to you. If your ambition is to emulate the pot-bellied duskies who pop out from the bushes in these films, of course the answer is, stick to raw fruits and vegetables."[45] But the Shedd story of the "peaceful colored woman" and others like it, along with the (purportedly) comical employment of dialects other than white English grammar, begin to reveal how starkly racialized this Christian doctrine of slimness really was.

Inevitably, this racialized discourse around thinness likewise summoned an interconnected taxonomy of social class. Predictable stories of indigent or ignorant whites (rural mountain folk, mostly) made the rounds, sometimes to illustrate their failure to uphold acceptable standards of whiteness or else to impart some crucial lesson to their more sophisticated brethren. Kane adopted a typical southern preacher's style when he told of "that unknown woman from the Kentucky hills [who] remarked, upon enrolling her child at Berea College, 'Hits a lot worse to be soul hungry than body hungry.' "[46] Those whose syntax did not measure up to that of the cultured middle classes might make for touching narrative fodder, but they were clearly not part of the reading audience sought by Christian diet writers. Anne Ortlund, the blonde writer of *Disciplines of the Beautiful Woman*, who cheerily recounted spending over an hour a day on her looks, reported, "Before Laney the maid, I allowed only forty-five minutes a day and didn't exercise at night; that left me time to keep the clothes washed, ironed, dry cleaned, and mended." Though this mention of Laney reveals little, the details that emerge about Ortlund's later lifestyle—her Mediterranean cruise, her regular manicures, her Hawaiian vacations, not to mention the sixty-plus minutes she daily devoted to her beauty routine—clearly disclosed her own affluence, which she inferred to be a divine gift. "Don't think the moral of this story is that every woman who serves Christ gets a trip to Hawaii and a maid," she cautions her readers. "I only know that when we work in obedience to him, saying yes unreservedly before we see how, he will make it right. He will make it up to us in a thousand secret, delightful ways."[47]

Mostly, nonwhite and non-middle-class voices and bodies were simply excluded from the texts altogether, relegated only to the occasional talk of "the poor" who required white benevolence. Again, Ortlund's typical representation to her female readers is worth citing at length:

> The world is so needy! All around the globe are women who have so little! And yet they are just as feminine as we are, with the same longings to be pretty. I have bent down and stooped into a thatched hut deep in the jungles of South America and seen a cotton print dress hanging inside, the joy of that little primitive, pudding-bag-shaped woman. Someone she will never see had parted with it, and through missionaries bearing the love of Jesus, it came to her.[48]

"Primitive" others were not expected to be slim; they were plump and dark, hence distinguishable from this literature's writers and likely readers. The white middle class, by contrast, both could and should live up to the model of Christian perfection that (its members knew) God had laid out for them. In ways both explicit and implicit, white middle-class Christian women and men exchanged ideas about how to uphold their image in the world, to sustain their rightful place at the top of the racialized class hierarchy embedded in American society and the Anglo-American Christian tradition.

To say that white people were writing about body size to other white people, rather than those they considered nonwhites, seems in a sense obvious. Until very recently, African Americans and various other nonwhite ethnic groups living in the United States sustained fewer taboos against fat. The cultural critic bell hooks is one of many who have noted that for black women, "being overweight does not carry the stigma of unattractiveness, or sexual undesirability, that is the norm in white society."[49] While rates of eating disorders among African American girls and women have risen in recent years, their incidence still appears to be far lower than among white females.[50] Models of femininity presented in popular African American women's magazines such as *Essence* and *Heart and Soul*, meanwhile, retain a broader spectrum of body sizes than their white-dominated counterparts, while 90 percent of respondents in a 2001 *Essence* survey agreed that black women and white women had different views of body image. "Sisters believe that our community's preference for fuller, more voluptuous shapes has survived the larger society's brainwashing. Or at least that it should," the survey concluded.[51] Extreme thinness has been thought to be predominantly a white ideal, even as other groups have begun to laud or imitate it in what the social historian Roberta Pollack Seid ironically dubs "the democratization of physical ideals": "A well-bred person had to be slender, for a fat body was an uncivilized body. And, as long as the faith prevailed that people could control their body size, slenderness seemed a preeminently democratic value, consonant with America's cherished self-help ideology."[52] To acknowledge, then, that most diet books in modern times have been written both by and for a particular class of citizens, requires no great leap.

White Americans, moreover, have actively promoted cultural associations between black bodies and corpulence. "The widespread conflation of African American female bodies and fat," writes Doris Witt in her book *Black Hunger: Food and the Politics of U.S. Identity*, is "surely a function of the psychic needs of the dominant white society." In compiling diverse forms of evidence to support her argument, Witt cites the experience of the African American college student Retha Powers with food and dieting obsessions, and Powers's own critique of the proto-racism embedded in the assumption that "fat is more acceptable in the black community" than in the white. Examples from literary and popular culture demonstrate the many ways in which women of color have long worked to disrupt the predominantly white symbolizations of black bodies and rescript them for new ends; nonetheless, Witt argues, it remains the case that African American women, in particular, have "always been 'presences' in discourses about food and U.S. identities, particularly in specular form as the naturalized fat body."[53]

Yet such analyses have rarely remarked on religion's role in constructing and sustaining this ideal in a way that—intentionally or not—shored up the American social order. And no wonder: no devotional diet book, to my knowledge, has ever claimed outright to be directed toward an all-white readership or even deliberately treated race at all. Most Christian fitness authors would undoubtedly profess genuine shock at the idea that their teachings had anything whatsoever to do with class or race, perhaps responding that a healthy standard of thinness is one that should be sought by all people of whatever background, skin color, or economic level. But, as historians of science among others have dramatically revealed, physiological knowledge is never purely neutral but always ideological, helping to shore up other forms of social knowledge.[54] To uncover the role of race in Christian diet culture, then, is not unlike deciphering a coded language, which leaves out the most important details because they are so true and obvious that few think to articulate them. One way to unveil these hidden racial presuppositions is to analyze the core assumptions that twentieth-century Christian writers (and many of their non-Christian counterparts) have shared about large-bodied women.

Joan Cavanaugh's *More of Jesus, Less of Me* put it succinctly: "Being fat is basically a sign that something is seriously wrong. It is a big cover-up and when we get serious about losing our cover, we will need a big exposure. We will need to admit that we need help, and we will have to expose our hidden faults to the healing power of God." Christian diet literature then and later was steeped in psychological explanations: a woman's bulk revealed her as a binge-eater who was depressed, ashamed, angry, or unloved. Overeaters—and sizeable women were always presumed to be gluttonous overeaters—had personal problems with parents, spouses, or children, and they could not begin to eat normally until they faced up to the feelings and emotions that triggered uncontrolled eating. Diet writers thus took on the role of therapists as much as nutritionists, pleading with their audience to look deep within and discover the root suffering that made them eat sinfully and get fat. In terms that apparently made sense in their own lives, writers such as Cavanaugh could attribute binge eating to the attempt to bury hurts "under a layer of fat" or even to a kind of suicidal urge for self-destruction. Looking back to her own binge-filled childhood, she recalled, "It was my heart that was hungry, but all I could think to do was feed my face."[55]

However true such accounts may be to writers' personal experience and to that of many readers who purchased their books, they have acknowledged neither cultural nor socioeconomic reasons for differently sized bodies and so tell only a partial narrative. Census Bureau data, along with figures obtained by the National Center for Health Statistics, have long shown weight to be significantly affected by both race and class, especially for women. Data from the 1997 National Health Interview Survey showed black women to have the highest prevalence of overweight (64.5 percent), with Hispanic women next (56.8 percent), then white women (43.0 percent), and Asian/Pacific Islander women (25.2 percent). Black women, moreover, were nearly twice as likely as white women—and more than five times as likely as Asian/Pacific Islander women—to be obese. Educational attainment was similarly a factor in being overweight, especially for women: whereas 60 percent of women without high school degrees and 49 percent of high school graduates were definably overweight, that figure dropped to 29 percent of women with postgraduate college degrees. An even more dismal report issued in December 2001 by the former U.S. surgeon general David Satcher observed that 69 percent of non-Hispanic black women were overweight or obese and found that variables of race, class, and gender were equally significant in terms of both diet and exercise: "Physical inactivity is more prevalent among women than men, among blacks and Hispanics than whites, among older than younger adults, and among the less affluent than the more affluent."[56]

It has been pointed out numerous times that, in prosperous America at least, it takes money to be thin. For most, exercise and fitness regimens generally require both leisure time and a certain outlay of cash to purchase proper clothing, gym memberships, equipment such as weights or machines, and other accoutrements. Eating nutritiously, with an eye to calories and fat (among other things), is expensive, entailing the purchase of costly food items such as fresh fruits and vegetables, healthy meats or vegetarian substitutes, wholesome grains such as brown rice, and whole-wheat bread products. For those who are poor and who live someplace other than a farm, such foodstuffs are usually impossible luxuries. Their diet consists much more of starchy foods and fatty meats, a diet that, when combined with deficient amounts of leisure time and disposable income, greatly heightens the chances of obesity.[57] For middle-class African American women, meanwhile, the cultural pressures against weight watching can be severe, driving them to ignore the advice of their own physicians so as not to seem to be rejecting the food traditions of their elders or capitulating to body standards forged by whites.

Christian diet authors have not acknowledged these socioeconomic reasons for obesity or written about the structural realities that help observers predict the most obese segments of the American population. Rather, excess weight has been presumed to be always and everywhere a psychological problem. Even where economic, class, or cultural realities have been acknowledged—Frances Hunter described her own compulsive food habits as stemming from a childhood of deprivation and lack of good food, while T. D. Jakes attributed his weight gain to southern soul foods such as sweet potato pie, fried chicken, and barbecue ribs—such factors have not been placed in a larger social context. Somehow, *all* fat people have been seen as emotionally wounded. With proper doses of information and self-love, it would seem, any ostensibly miserable fat person could begin the hopeful journey toward thinness and discover a whole new, joyous life in the slimming process.

While it is impossible to say whether the denial of cultural and structural factors in national obesity rates is deliberate or merely uninformed, the result is the same and lends credence to bell hooks's point that "by perpetuating and upholding domination, society invests, so to speak, in the ill health of certain groups, all the better to oppress and exploit them." Putting it in even stronger terms, hooks argues, "Within white-supremacist capitalist patriarchal culture, black people are not supposed to be 'well.' This culture makes wellness a white luxury."[58] Confronting this widespread attitude in his damning indictment of American apathy toward the class-based realities of fat and poor health, the journalist Greg Critser acidly observes: "[W]hat do the fat, darker, exploited poor, with their unbridled primal appetites, have to offer us but a chance for we diet- and shape-conscious folk to live vicariously? . . . [F]at people do not threaten our way of life; their angers entombed in flesh, they are slowed, they are softened, they are *fed.*"[59] That most middle-class Americans have refused to face or be angered by these inequalities is lamentable, if unsurprising. That so many Christians, supposedly bound by their convictions to help the needy, have remained equally silent or willfully ignorant might well seem scandalous.[60]

Whether Christian fitness culture should be called "racist" is a thorny question. I would wager that no writer cited here would have ever asserted that his or her audience was necessarily restricted to whites. Nor has any writer, to my knowledge, ever published blunt tributes to fair-skinned bodies above all others or suggested that dark-skinned flesh is biologically unsuited for the slender beauty epitomized as God's ideal. Even T. D. Jakes, who himself is African American, recounted his own father's early demise from obesity-related kidney failure without mentioning race; moreover, Jakes counseled his readers to follow his own example for losing weight by purchasing a treadmill or joining a health club, presuming these to be attainable goals for what must be a fairly affluent readership.[61]

But if racism is a category based on intentional forms of exclusion, other less deliberate processes of racialization ("racialism")—such as those embedded in visual representations of holy womanhood—also have undeniably powerful consequences, even when authors have made conscious attempts at inclusion. One of the Christian beauty books mentioned earlier, *The Inside-Out Beauty Book*, repeatedly insisted that any woman, "whatever her race or ethnic origin," could be beautiful: "[B]eauty has absolutely no racial or ethnic bounds. God has not limited body beauty to any one group of people—and He never will. . . . *Since we are all God's children, our racial color never limits our potential for beauty, either inner or outer.*" Writing purposefully to include women who were "black, Oriental, American Indian, and East Indian" as well as "Caucasian," the authors urged their readers to ask themselves whether they had ever detected "even a subtle sense of prejudice" when seeing a nonwhite model on television. They included makeup and hair tips for women of various races and worked earnestly to be inclusive. At the same time, however, they upheld an unmistakably white image as their model beautiful woman, a practice even more apparent in the Christian diet literature (excepting Jakes).[62] Nonwhite bodies were beautiful, then, just to the degree that they approximated the lean, white ideal.

Promotional images of Christian women in white-owned publications such as *Today's Christian Woman* supply additional evidence of the racialized character of ideal evangelical femininity, as well as the disparate exemplars presented for nonwhite women. Issues published in the growth period of Christian fitness culture vividly present a more restricted set of body images for white women than for women of color, while yet managing to associate thinness with goodness just as strongly among the latter. White women featured on the magazine's cover, feature articles, and advertisements were and continue to be almost invariably thin, and articles featuring discussions of weight loss and fitness tips are virtually always illustrated with cartoons or photographs of white women. Women of color, who are far less represented in the magazine generally, are frequently thin, particularly cover models such as the conservative activist Star Parker. Often enough, however, black women are pictured as heavier than the white ideal, sometimes extensively so, as with the dramatic feature story "Hooked on Crack" (May–June 2000). While heaviness may coexist with Christian maturity for

17. "A Beauty Composite,"
from Betty Lougaris Soldo
and Mary Drahos, *Inside-
Out Beauty Book*, 167.

women of color, it is more closely identified with deviance, eroticism, or
criminality.

There are varied ways to read these contrasting, even incongruous
images: one might assume that black women are less anxious about thinness
than white women; or, given that the staff of the magazine is overwhelm-
ingly white, one might as easily surmise that no one expects the strict standards for white femininity to fit African American females. Inclusion of a
few large women of color, amid repetitions of very thin white women, may
be a very plain (if subconscious) comment about racial discrepancy that
stereotypes women of color as unable or unwilling to achieve the same body
type as their white counterparts. One could, of course, endlessly multiply
similar visual examples across the material culture of popular American
Christianity.

These images may seem so natural to *Today's Christian Woman* readers
because they not only mirror the recent "multicultural" turn in American
evangelicalism that professes to celebrate cultural differences across racial
and ethnic lines but also disclose older trajectories and associations. The
British film theorist Richard Dyer, who has analyzed representations of

18. Star Parker, from cover of
Today's Christian Woman,
July–August 1997 (photo
by Bill Bilsley).

whiteness in modern western culture, persuasively contends that whiteness and white embodiment have been constituted by the history of Christianity, "founded on the idea—paradoxical, unfathomable, profoundly mysterious—of incarnation, of being that is in the body yet not of it. This provides a compelling cosmology, as well as a vivid imagery and set of narrative tropes, that survive as characteristics of Western culture." The purity of the ethereal spirit, so celebrated in Christian theology and practice, has persistently been constructed against the filth of the corporeal body, an opposition upon which the categories of race (as well as those of gender) have been assembled. Hence, writes Dyer, "Black people can be reduced (in white culture) to their bodies and thus to race, but white people are something else that is realized in and yet is not reducible to the corporeal. . . . The white spirit organizes white flesh and in turn non-white flesh and other material matters: it has *enterprise.*" [63] Even in a popular Christian culture that no longer seeks to transcend the body—that seeks, instead, to create perfect bodies as reflecting the spirits within—nonwhite flesh retains its accustomed subordinate status and lowered expectations of purity. The many racialized images of black (and Asian) children, splashed about in these publications as beneficiaries of white mission work or charitable giving, illustrate but one way that older, imperializing racial hierarchies remain intact.

As to the ongoing class dimensions of Christian fitness culture, consider Shamblin's basic rule of thumb: eat only half of the food in front of you at any given time, and throw the rest away. She gives no thought to waste or

19. "Hooked on Crack," from *Today's Christian Woman*, May–June 2000 (photo by Kelly Culpepper).

to problems of poverty, inequity, and starvation, and one might well imagine how her rhapsodies to hunger would sound to many in the developing world: "If you would get hungry daily, you would find that love would grow and *love* will keep you alive, not the food. Love between you and God will keep your heart beating." The pleasures of hunger, in her case, always preface the pleasures of eating: "the truly empty, gnawing, burning sensation that feels so good, so right! I love to get to a growl and then get what I really love to eat. How fun! Greed and impatience are so juvenile and insulting to this incredibly good Father of ours." Shamblin does not acknowledge the exclusiveness of this pleasure, but then prosperity theologies have never been especially attentive to fiscal realities that refute their worldviews.[64]

On the one hand, Shamblin is a promoter of highly processed products that are decidedly middlebrow and widely accessible to people of diverse incomes, at least in the United States. God "created Fritos and dip for our enjoyment," Shamblin writes in *Rise Above*, while typical examples from her own food forays include McDonald's hamburgers and fries, candy bars, movie popcorn, and ice cream sundaes: standard American fare, especially on a limited budget. On the other, visual clues to her own standard of living—depicted in the published photographs of her mansion in Nashville, high-priced clothes, sleekly groomed hair, and so forth—are but whispered indications of the economic benchmarks she takes for granted. More than once in *Rise Above* she evokes devastation over a broken fingernail or a wardrobe choice gone awry.

God is cheerfully represented as the "ultimate shopper" who delights in the role of consultant regarding clothes and interior decorating; he also "fixes roof leaks without anyone's help" and is "a mechanic . . . a financier, He's been known to pay rent, and He can mysteriously place ten dollars in your pocket." Husband, mechanic, roofer, interior decorator, CEO, clothing consultant, party coordinator, entertainer, chef, physician: God is both master and partner, teaming up to preserve these sumptuous environs—a 9,000-square-foot antebellum home that Shamblin and her husband bought for $2.3 million in 1996—in an updated and intriguingly feminized version of the gospel of wealth. While the appeal of this plot line may seem apparent, whatever the class status of its American readers, the particular details of Shamblin's life are little more than a voyeuristic, romantic fantasy for the vast numbers of her audience who live more modestly.[65]

Whatever inclusive intentions individual Christian fitness authors may have had, texts such as those analyzed here have played a critical role in the reproduction of both racial ideology and class arrangements in the United States. And in some sense this outcome has been a measured rejection of those people deemed to belong to the American lower class. Elite Protestant attitudes toward the poor have ranged from benign goodwill to puzzled neglect to outright hostility; but even the best intentioned attempts at benevolence have always risked condescension, and few, if any, have made serious inroads on the "us/them" distinctions. Many Christians naturally shore up the boundaries of American thinness culture because they believe in the social distinctions entailed by this procedure; indeed, Protestant Christians helped establish these distinctions in the first place. The history of Christianity in America cannot be separated from histories of whiteness and race. The spiritually meaningful intentions for slimming expressed by diet writers—getting obedient, looking good in order to serve as a witness to God's transformative power, gaining the strength and stamina to live a full Christian life, all of which could be celebrated by Jakes no less than white fitness writers—fail to express some of the less munificent motives and outcomes of this pursuit. After all, one of the many messages evoked by the slender, white body of an American female has long been one of professed superiority to other bodies that are "out of bounds."[66] Such superiority remains short-lived and contingent, however, since one's body might always be unfavorably compared to another, thinner body—or one's spiritual maturity reduced to paltry dimensions by the religious fervor of another.

As growing numbers of African American Christians participate in America's devotional diet culture, these fabrications may be subverted or turned to new ends. Shamblin's Weigh Down diet has been somewhat successful in appealing to nonwhite women, judging by the many African American participants who have been featured on video segments and photographs, while Jakes's forays into the Christian fitness arena have undoubtedly had an increasing impact among African American women as well. Growing numbers of predominantly black churches, meanwhile, are participating in programs such as the Baltimore-based Community Health Awareness and Monitoring Program (CHAMP), which focuses specifically on hypertension and weight loss among black church members; the Church Health Education Resource Union Believers (CHERUB), a Maryland church coalition promoting healthy diet and physical activity through newsletters, pulpit messages, classes, and health assessments; the North Carolina-based Partnership to Reach African Americans to Increase Smart Eating (PRAISE!), a church-based nutrition intervention program funded by the National Cancer Institute; and REACH 2010: At the Heart of New Orleans, a church-based project funded by the Centers for Disease Control and Prevention to eliminate the disparities in cardiovascular diseases that face black women. It will be extremely interesting in future to compare these emergent agendas with their chiefly white counterparts.

Worth noting again here is the work of Dr. Jawanza Kunjufu, a black Christian psychologist in Chicago whose writings on health hark back as much to Elijah Muhammad and the Nation of Islam as to the wider Christian diet culture now surrounding him. In his book *Satan, I'm Taking Back My Health!* (2000), Kunjufu urges readers to adopt a strict vegetarian diet while confronting directly what his final chapter calls "the health legacy of slavery and racism": "During slavery, African Americans were forced to eat the worst food available. Pork was used at every meal, and every part of the pig was used, including the guts, which are called 'chitlins.' It was during this era that African Americans were forced to be as creative as they could with the worst food provided." The soul food diet that resulted from these harsh conditions, writes Kunjufu, is killing the souls of black Americans.[67] Surely the intent of such varied initiatives to reduce the health burdens faced by people of color is exemplary; still, it may prove difficult to keep these general health goals isolated from devotion to insidious body ideals and associations. Health and beauty have rarely been separable in white Christianity, where extreme thinness remains the highest standard for women and, as such, a cause for extreme self-loathing among those who fail to achieve it.

Blending Christian discipline with therapeutic ideals, the Christian diet industry has helped to forge a powerful mode of dealing with human embodiment, venerating the body's religious significance on the one hand and on the other championing modern forms of fleshly self-scrutiny, perfectibility, and exclusivity that would bewilder many of their Christian forebears. As with Christians in earlier periods, from Sylvester Graham to Father Divine, the diet culture has held out body salvation as the goal, but it is a version of paradise concocted from very different ingredients (lower-calorie ones, to be sure). Moreover, whereas Divine's whole platform sought to overcome earthly distinctions of class and race, purveyors of Christian diet programs have intensified these distinctions, however unwittingly. The failure in recent times to consider food habits in any other than psychological terms; the refusal to ponder either the role of culture in promoting divergent beauty standards in different communities or the socioeconomic conditions that have created the problem of obesity as increasingly a dilemma of the American poor; and the solipsistic celebration of slender bodies as somehow epitomizing divinely ordained beauty have worked seamlessly together to uphold a version of Christianity that not only is deeply gendered but also profoundly aids in bolstering hierarchies of supposed ethnic superiority. Primitivized, eroticized, and excluded, fat persons have become ever more emphatic symbols of peril and filth, the weight of a sinful world that must be purged from Christianity to make way for an army of born-again bodies.

Epilogue

Bodies in Crisis?

From Cotton Mather to Sylvester Graham, Samuel Wells to Elizabeth Towne, Bernarr Macfadden to Father Divine, Charlie Shedd to Gwen Shamblin, American Christians and their metaphysical heirs have unsettled, if not given the lie to, the putative legacy of body-spirit dualism bequeathed by their tradition. While speaking in disparate voices as to the particular techniques and aims most suitable for keeping the body in check, disciples have concurrently verified a basic religious obligation to cultivate correct bodily practice and create a proper *looking* body. Even Father Divine, who of all the individuals analyzed in this book did the most to counter the ideals of slimness and abstemious eating, controlled the dietary and sexual practice of his followers and believed that the body held the key to redemption; in fact, he insisted most vociferously upon incarnation as the core of true religion while benefiting heartily from his followers' worship of his flesh. At times men led the pursuit of bodily perfection and at other times women did, many decisively motivated by concerns about sex and racial classifications and most invoking motifs of perfection, purification, freedom, and power. Notwithstanding the very real gender differences over the broad course of the nineteenth and twentieth centuries, the doctrine of body salvation has increasingly held sway for all who see themselves made—and made fit—in the image of God.

The rich mélange of prescriptive texts and personal narratives analyzed in the foregoing chapters invites review of some near-sacrosanct presumptions about bodily discipline. Male-authored accounts promoting appetite restraint, for instance, challenge the entrenched supposition that men pay the body little mind while women work out deep feelings of grief and rage at the social order on the material of their bodies.[1] Exploring the ways in which men have made their bodies matter—whether through fasting, sex-

20. "In His Own Image,"
from Fran Carlton, *A Time
For Fitness,* 78.

ual control, bodybuilding, or other means—should also aid in upending the
stubborn categorical equation of female with body and nature, a triad
opposed to the similarly intermeshed abstractions of male, intellect, and
culture. For though the quest to transform self and world by controlling
dietary and sexual appetites has been pursued by both sexes in recent
American history, during periods such as the Progressive Era it has been
trumpeted with especial ardor by men. Finally, this chronicle should lay to
rest any characterization of American body history as an obvious secularization narrative—a nineteenth-century mutation from religious fasting
to secular dieting, in Brumberg's formulation—by clarifying some of the
explicitly religious meanings attached to bodily discipline by its therapeutic
advocates into the twenty-first century. Exploring these historical variations of austerity may, in short, begin to expand our historical sense of the
multivalent meanings, gendered and otherwise, of bodily discipline.

It turns out, then, that American culture's own purportedly secular
doctrine of the perfectible body is deeply indebted to currents that have
perceived the body as essential for pushing the soul along the path to redemption. Yet though particular religious forms and formulators hold
accountability for modern body crises—shoring up the somatic ideals of the
wider consumer culture—they have hardly been the sole perpetrators. How

and why the obsession with thinness has been sustained and fortified beyond the bounds of American religion is not the explicit subject of this book, but it is surely an essential subtext with vast implications for understanding the repressive body ideologies of our time. One of my aims has been to demonstrate what fans of Oprah Winfrey's spiritual-material fitness pursuits already know: that there is no tidy line between so-called religious and so-called secular prescriptive norms pertaining to the body. Even when persons have espoused such a distinction—some Protestants arguing that slimness should be an explicitly pious goal because it reflects God's glory, for instance—they have vigorously advocated the worldly benefits of a thin body, including health, beauty, love, and prestige. That one must painstakingly read this literature and the material culture of Christian diet programs to interpret the subtler inducements to slimness (those relating to social status or to anxieties about sin and appetite) hardly suggests that these meanings are peripheral for lay consumers of Christian culture. Patrons' hungry consumption of fitness products paradoxically reveals the hope of overcoming all earthly hungers, redirecting bodily desire toward intimate relationship with God.

Just as the health reform movements of the nineteenth century fed on evangelical Protestantism, so later developments in American fitness culture absorbed successive currents in American religion, most notably New Thought and its multiple offshoots (including its coupling with evangelicalism). Powerfully concerned with both emotional and physical healing, New Thought teachers asserted that mind controlled matter, then turned this doctrine on its head to proclaim matter as the key to all progress. Bodies, once relegated to instrumental status in God's cosmological scheme (at least in the Protestant mind), came to seem deeply weighted with devotional significance. Christian writers such as those examined in this book intensified the priority placed on personal appearance, especially for women. While some challenged these values, it is virtually impossible to imagine a voice like the later Neva Coyle's that advocates the liberation and lovability of fat bodies, able to rise to any level of success at the turn of the twenty-first century. Oprah may come closest, yet she perennially battles her own weight gains and wins her audience's devotion for never giving up. The emulators of Bernarr Macfadden and Alice Long have won the day.

Or perhaps the victory belongs as much to those modeling themselves more deliberately after Calvin, Wesley, and Finney: the devotional fasters. The recent resurgence of fasting as a sacred practice, both public and private, has been prominently featured in the media. From Jerry Falwell and Pat Robertson to Bill Bright, Franklin Graham, and Anne Graham Lotz, evangelicals are fasting for repentance and revival on a scale not visible since the eighteenth century. Books progressively leap off the presses from Christian authors who commend public and private fasting as instrumental for deepening their spirituality, gaining God's favor, and strengthening prayer. Web sites such as www.fastforbush.com urge cyber-audiences to pray for President George W. Bush, the presidential cabinet, and the full array of policies promoted by the Bush administration. The conservative Catholic Steve Habisohn founded a group called e5 men, named for Ephesians 5:25 ("Husbands, love your wives, as Christ loved the church and gave himself up for her"), whose members commit to a monthly 24-hour fast that creates a "fortress of flesh that protects the woman you love" for the purpose of recapturing men's headship over women within the home.[2] It is no secret that most of those promoting this type of fasting power worship the same masculinist image of God depicted by the political right.

"Fasting is the foundry in which we are purified," writes the health minister Lee Bueno-Aguer, founder of Born Again Body, Inc. "Its fires refine our faith; its flames separate the base impurities from our true character in Christ; its hot blasts purify our hearts. . . . Fasting produces a work of art—the tempered, selfless Christian—that can be created through no other process of refinement." More important, she continues, "Once we accept and practice fasting as a Christian duty, rewards will surely follow. The power of food will be exchanged for the miracle-working power of the fast." Abstinence is, in other words, once again acquiring merit as a tool for getting precisely what the praying faster wants, even as it is couched in terms of humility. "We may fast when prayer is not enough to receive the answers we need," Jerry Falwell contends, as when he underwent two forty-day fasts within three months to save the faltering Liberty University he had founded in Virginia: "then God gave the University $27 million dollars and other things necessary to stave off bankruptcy and loss of accreditation."[3]

The most successful literary patterns in this genre, not surprisingly, combine a devotional emphasis upon self-denial with arguments for the health benefits and pleasures of fasting. Graphic teachings about internal filth and cleansing, colon detoxification, and longevity mix readily with assurances about the other tangible results to be obtained via fasting, from spiritual maturity and divine approval to physical vitality and material wealth. In this sense, current fasting practice plainly combines older Christian forms of abstinence with New Thought influences, all the while remaining in close sympathy with contemporary diet and fitness culture. This mixing has been going on for some time, as we've seen: recall the Christian literary critic William Mueller's 1958 depiction of his fat-hating, carrot-juice-swilling

Presbyterian mother, whose portraits of John Calvin and Bernarr Macfadden hung above her dressing table in paired consecration. Abstemious eating has long been performed from a mix of sacred and mundane intentions, brought together in the claim of some Protestants that God favors fitness over sickliness, healthy Christians above their ill or flaccid brethren—hence the long history of Protestant puzzlement and intolerance greeting Catholic consecrations of pain and suffering. Evangelical fasting enthusiasts who claim to be repossessing an older sacred regimen are noting only part of the story since it is clear by now that the social, cultural, and political currents of the twentieth century profoundly shaped modern-day asceticisms.

Just as forms of devotional dieting and weight loss have shown themselves to signal a desire for particular kinds of intimate connections, so do restyled types of fasting point toward relational ends. Fasters restrain their eating for the sake of an other, whether a partner, a collectivity, a nation, or a divine authority. Intentional abstinence signifies submission to those whom one wishes to please and to influence; it is a means of marking obedience and sacrifice in order to conciliate anger or to stave off disapproval and abandonment. Those who show themselves keen and able to control physical appetites for the sake of higher ends receive rewards of honor and belongingness. Fasting purportedly heals ruptures and restores even as it transforms patterns of affection, identification, and esteem. Habisohn notes, for instance, "E5 men gives Christian men the opportunity to make a true, unselfish gift to their wives: eating only bread and water for one day is a selfless act that can bring grace, spiritual healing, and growth to their wife, or to their future bride if they're single. . . . The idea is that if the husband is healed, the wife will soon follow. If he was more kind, gentle, and patient, if he thought of her more often, she would be glad to respond in kind."[4] While contemporary fasters surely restrain their bodily appetites for sundry and complex ends, promises of relationship loom large among these.

But fasting is hardly the only or most visible corporeally oriented practice in which American Protestants engage at the turn of the twenty-first century. Indeed, some of the most interesting recent developments in Christian popular culture pertain to more innovative somatic applications: newly fashionable procedures for expressing religious convictions upon the body. Tattoos, once reviled by mainstream Anglo-Americans as seedy, low-class, and even satanic, now enjoy a refurbished reputation and are all the rage among growing segments of evangelical youth culture. Groups such as the Christian Tattoo Association support hundreds of tattoo artists across the country who decorate (or "ink") the bodies of countless more men and women with crosses and crucifixes, images of Jesus' face and muscle-bound physique, and sayings such as "He died for us." Body piercing, likewise, has gained an upward following among evangelical teens and young adults, who willingly endure epidermal incisions and puncturings upon body parts seen and unseen. While marking and piercing practices are by no means new, only recently in a U.S. context have they come to seem stylishly mainstream (and thus passé to older representatives of rebel tattoo culture).

Religious purveyors of both forms of body art praise different aspects of marking the body with holes and ink: it is a language variously perceived as evangelization, unification (via pain) with Christ's suffering on the cross, a rite of passage into adulthood, or simply a permanent sign of an intense physical or religious experience.[5] Whatever its meaning(s) for the individuals who pursue such bodily modifications, there is growing support within contemporary evangelicalism that setting apart the self as conspicuously Christian means more than simply sporting a gospel themed T-shirt or WWJD ("What Would Jesus Do?") wristband; rather, the inscription should be written in "eternal ink," proclaiming a permanent spiritual as well as corporeal transformation in the bearer.[6] This concern with reshaping the body for sincere religious objectives echoes resoundingly into the long reaches of Christian history. Self-styled alternative body artists insist that literally branding the body signals a maverick authenticity far more than either clothing or, for that matter, perfectly aerobicized bodies, those symbols of conformity and capitulation to prescribed social norms. Yet the more popular such practices become, the greater the need to find new ones, to signal simultaneously one's supreme individuality above the copycat masses *and* one's relationship to a community of likeminded cultural dissenters. Body art signifies a choice of interpersonal relationships no less than dieting or fasting.

The logical endpoint of contemporary Christians' quest for authentic individuality and belonging is hard to fathom. Not surprisingly, the trend in the wider non-Christian world of "fleshworks" is toward more rare and extreme procedures, including the subcutaneous implantation of beads, rings, crosses, and transdermal spikes; cautery-scalpel branding (via hollow or keloid scarification); dermal punching (think of a hole-puncher for the skin); and such anatomical mutations as tongue splitting, ear reshaping (forging angles out of cartilaginous curves, for instance, to resemble a cat's or a Star Trek figure's), waist-resculpting corsetry, and genital modifications that include elaborate penile subincisions and implantation of stainless steel rods along the contour of the shaft. As body parts are increasingly restructured and embedded with synthetic metals, enthusiasts seek a thoroughgoing makeover of the self into living sculpture or cyborg, generating in one devotee's words a "complete alteration and evolution of the body."[7] That vision doubtless strikes many religious persons as anathema, but only time will tell how future generations may feel.

Even while appropriating ink and metal customizations for devotional ends, Protestants have given ongoing, vigorous attention to sexual discipline, inspiring myriad campaigns for adolescent (and general premarital) chastity. This emphasis is a stark reminder of the distance between the earnest Christian tattoo culture and its more nonchalant, sexually explicit counterparts, yet chastity also harmonizes expediently with the more controversial appropriations of inking and piercing. Amplifying their zeal, some young men have even pierced their own penises as an unfailing, painful token—"definitely a reminder," in one young man's deadpan affirmation—of their religiously inspired commitment to postpone sexual intercourse until marriage.[8] More often, young unmarrieds—hundreds of thousands of them, in fact—have signed abstinence pledge cards from groups such as the Southern Baptist–sponsored True Love Waits and have discussed in devastating and poignant detail their struggles with sexual desire and self-denial in teen magazines such as *Brio* and *Breakaway* (evangelical magazines for adolescent girls and boys, respectively). Or they have gyrated in outdoor and convention hall chastity extravaganzas and Christian rock music festivals, where the pursuit of so-called clean (nonsexual) fun is a ubiquitous theme. Like food abstinence, sexual abstinence appeals to potential recruits through the promise of improving relationships, a promise spelled out by the True Love Waits campaign pledge: "Believing that true love waits, I make a commitment to God, myself, my family, my friends, my future mate, and my future children to a lifetime of purity including sexual abstinence from this day until the day I enter a biblical marriage relationship." Choosing to have sexual relations outside marriage, in turn, violates those present and future relationships and so leaves the piteous sinner in bad company, if not starkly alone.[9]

Young people, including children, in Christian culture also continue to struggle with eating disorders such as anorexia and bulimia at rates little different from the general American teen population's. The pressure to be thin and beautiful may be even greater for teens in the devotional world for the same reasons it is so considerable among their older female counterparts: the duty to serve as a glowing witness to Christ's transformative power. Straddling the norms of "secular" youth culture and the intense bodily disciplines of American Protestantism, Christian teens are as crushingly preoccupied with bodily control as with the many symbolizations of embodiment that aid them in signaling spiritual intensity and authenticity. Many, looking to the adults surrounding them, will likely continue to feed on these corporeal obsessions for much or all of their lives, even as they profess a higher allegiance to spiritual growth as a more exalted focus for the human self than the mortal body. And why should anyone expect otherwise? The American preoccupation with perfect health, whether as a means of beauty, a sign of success, or a way to stave off the inevitability of death, is one that insistently translates itself into a universal mandate. Christian versions of this formula are part and parcel of the wider culture; indeed, they helped bring us to this point.

Some religious innovators, aware or not of religion's role in American body obsessions, have sought resources within religious traditions to help people of faith, usually women, heal from such fixations. Eating disorders have especially generated increasing attention in religious circles. Conservative evangelicals may purchase texts such as Deborah Newman's *Loving Your Body: Embracing Your True Beauty in Christ* (2002), sponsored by Dobson's Focus on the Family. The Remuda Ranch Center for Anorexia and Bulimia in Arizona advertises itself as a "Christ-centered, Biblically-based program" that, unlike secular programs, is dedicated to God's perfect and everlasting truth as a cure for eating disorders. Among Jews, "Rosh Hodesh: It's a Girl's Thing!" and "Body and Soul" are two programs that work to enhance the self-esteem and body image of Jewish girls. Congregations across the spectrum often offer educational forums on eating disorders, with titles such as "Caring for God's Temple."[10] One certified Christian counselor specializing in eating disorders told a student researcher, "When I am meeting with someone for the first time, I always start with the passage where Paul says that the body is a temple of the Holy Spirit. . . . We should treat our bodies with as much care and respect as they treated the temple in Old Testament times. Anything less would be to profane God. When we understand that because of Jesus' ultimate sacrifice God dwells in us by the Holy Spirit, it really transforms the way we think about and treat our bodies."[11]

Numerous religious persons, then, seem eager to reexamine their scriptures for messages of love and wholeness that may abet the healing process of food-obsessed young women. These efforts deserve commendation, and many undoubtedly provide a form of help for women and girls in need. Insofar as they fail to question the religious discourse that has assumed such an influential role in American body obsessions, however, it is difficult to view them as a vital counter to the much older story described in the previous pages. Conservative Christian programs seem especially intent on protecting their faith from any historical reading that could generate this type of criticism: Newman's *Loving Your Body*, for instance, repeatedly points to Satan and his worldly temptations as the chief cause of poor body image: "There is nothing Satan would enjoy more than getting women to feel ugly and useless in God's kingdom," she notes. "The world measures men and women by their looks, their talents, their money, and their power. God has a completely different measuring system. We aren't supposed to measure ourselves by other people. We should measure ourselves only by God's Word." Blaming poor body image on all that is ostensibly secular and therefore derived from Satan, Newman fails to acknowledge the longstanding Christian ambivalence toward flesh as a vital source of contemporary obsessions. (Interestingly enough, a Christian diet book by Amy Nappa, another Focus on the Family writer, appeared at the same time as Newman's text.) With this strained blindness suffusing religious self-help literature, it will take more than a few well-meaning counselors and curriculum writers to undo the body worship to which vaster parts of their tradition have succumbed.[12]

These multifarious versions of intense embodiment, from inking and piercing to the re-regulation of sexuality are, in an important sense, simply the latest installment in the Christian project of body reformation. Studies of American youth culture in every generation point out despairing individuals searching for fresh ways to become "real," to encounter the world in an authentic experience, to make the self—body, soul, or spirit, variously conceived—truly matter. And this authenticity is both the promise of Protestantism and its coercive power. The long-affirmed belief that one could detect the inner self by its fruits—such as love, joy, goodness, and temperance—has blurred into reliance on bodily signs. This shift was, to be sure, anticipated long ago, far earlier even than Johann Lavater's eighteenth-century Protestant system of physiognomy; yet the relentless modern faith in the corporeal indicators of character ought to concern any of us yearning for a culture that is more than skin-deep.

In the introduction I mentioned but did not elaborate on the crises that confront living bodies in the twenty-first century. What does it mean to suggest that living bodies are in crisis? And how could a study of religious prescription and practice possibly contribute to such an urgent situation, if true? Bodies, or at least particular groups of bodies, have confronted catastrophe during countless other historical moments: plagues, world wars, natural disasters, genocide, and imperialistic encounters stretch long into human history. In another important sense, bodies—diseased, maimed, tortured, starving, aging, beaten, exhausted, embattled, dying daily—are perennially in crisis. Such qualifications notwithstanding, ample signs point to a context-specific, late modern predicament. Bookshelves bulge with trendy accounts of body fixation, and one cannot read a U.S. newspaper or magazine without encountering evidence of the widespread cultural obsession—so familiar as to seem, at least in certain guises, virtually invisible—with human health, longevity, and what has been blandly termed wellness, all of which relate to medical and cultural prescriptions surrounding thinness. The American slender body ideal stands in glaring contrast to attitudes throughout much of the developing world that associate fat with beauty, wealth, and merit or divine blessing; and more than a few commentators have denounced global patterns of food scarcity that emaciate impoverished populations in parts of Africa and Asia at the same time that privileged Americans struggle to stay fashionably slim. U.S. officials may lament the appalling realities of world hunger, yet few actively seek to promote physical health or longevity for those peoples considered national enemies (even potential ones), excepting types of humanitarian aid that unfortunately foster dependence and servility. It is well known that many citizens in other countries believe Americans to be deeply indifferent, even contemptuous, toward foreign bodies. The ill health, life-shrinking poverty, and high death rates of such bodies, after all, bolster U.S. supremacy in both material and mythic ways.

World hunger seems a discordant context for situating Protestant American body fixations, and it would be as absurd to link them cursorily as to deny the many initiatives aimed at helping the poor and hungry across the globe. Nor is it fitting purely to scorn modern-day fitness pursuits as "luxury problems, the edgy blatherings of women who have the time, energy, and resources to actually worry about their thighs or their wardrobes or their relative levels of personal fulfillment." As Caroline Knapp lucidly observes, anxieties about desire—"feeding, experiencing pleasure, taking in, deserving"—do not generally constitute life-or-death issues for the affluent, but they reveal a great deal about our culture's mixed feelings toward freedom and abundance, particularly salient in "a world that's still deeply ambivalent about female power and that manages to whet appetite and shame it in equal measure."[13] Observers may justly wonder, nonetheless, at the paradoxes evident here. U.S. corporations have abetted the global proliferation of fast-food chains and the promotion of heavily sugared drinks and processed snack foods in developing world markets, transforming local eating patterns and increasing obesity rates overseas. As nutritionists and investigative journalists have corroborated, these types of products contribute in highly visible ways to the bodily suffering, illness, and poverty of expanding consumer populations.[14] It is ironic, to say the least, that at a time when the most educated, well-to-do Americans increasingly shun junk food in favor of presumably healthier choices (labeled "organic" or "natural"), the fast-food, soft drink, and also tobacco industries have achieved unprecedented levels of success among the poor, both in the United States and abroad.

Mounting attention to the close correlations between ill health and indigence does not generally include religion as a key factor, nor are observers, aiming for pragmatic solutions more than scholarly analysis, particularly attentive to the nuances of history. Again, however, one of the claims sustained in *Born Again Bodies* is that religion—as a strategic network of emotions, practices, and social alliances—has held a vital historical role in American body politics: a system making some bodies healthier, more beautiful, more powerful, and longer lived than others. While Christianity is by no means the only religious tradition able to contribute to such measures across space and time, Protestantism—as the tradition that has most comprehensively influenced the course of American history—takes center stage in this story. Like participants in assorted other religions, Christians carefully distinguish insiders from outsiders—the saved from the damned—and this concern with salvation plays itself out in numerous mundane ways, including (though by no means only) those covered in this book. Intense concentration upon particular kinds of bodywork on the part of many American Christians provides a new way to read the politics of our cultural history and the crucial role of gender as well as more tacit, ambiguous, and intricate taxonomies of race and social class. Christian body practices offer, in short, a model for tracking the ways that ordinary middle-class white bodies have been tutored in the obligatory hungers and subtle yet stringent regulations of consumer capitalism.

With the kind of paradox that matters of body and self so often breed, information technologies now signal an apparent shift toward "posthuman" selves, to exemplify ever more powerful tides of disembodiment. Have we become, as science fiction writers so long predicted, "data made flesh"? And if so, what happens to living bodies? In Katherine Hayles's formulation of the posthuman condition that she believes now characterizes our world, "there are no essential differences or absolute demarcations between bodily existence and computer simulation, cybernetic mechanism and biological organism, robot teleology and human goals." From this point of view, humans become information-gathering machines; the body is no more than "the original prosthesis we all learn to manipulate," erasing distinctions between real and synthetic, flesh and spirit. Hayles, like many other cultural critics, wrestles with the implications of this situation while endeavoring to frame a palatable course for the future. Her "nightmare is a culture inhabited by posthumans who regard their bodies as fashion accessories rather than the ground of being": the devaluation of fleshly humanity into the "powerful illusion" of disembodiment. I share Hayles's hope for ways of restoring the value of bodies without viewing them merely as components of larger nationalist projects of political power.[15]

There are no easy remedies—perhaps no remedies at all—to the conditions promoting modern body devotion: a series of widely divergent practices, from the humdrum to the harrowing, that religious, medical, and scientific means among others have made to seem natural, if not uniquely virtuous. Yet historical awareness is one antidote to careless valuations of particular bodily forms; realizing a new history may at least help participants think more deeply about the motivations behind their own sorts of embodied religion. Modern fitness may not be a "religion" in the scholarly sense, but it surely has dense and unavoidable religious roots. A robust alternative to flippant use of religious metaphors that evoke devotion to fitness culture—a habit of journalistic observers, scholars, and fitness leaders themselves—is scrutiny of the specific historical links that have aided the creation of this culture, which together argue for a particular Protestant-derived legacy for modern body devotions. Outside the explicitly religious diet and exercise groups, there remains very little that is demonstrably Christian about contemporary fitness culture, but this lack hardly renders it "secular" in any clear sense. However little they may realize their participation in a time-honored tradition of religious observance, more people than ever today are avidly pursuing a born-again body.

Notes

INTRODUCTION

1. "Fat People Don't Go To Heaven," *Globe,* November 21, 2000, 5; Shamblin quoted in Ianthe Jeanne Dugan, "Church Lady of Diet Weighs In on Trinity and Her Flock Flees," *Wall Street Journal,* October 30, 2000, A1, A18.

2. My thanks to Christine Whelan for this statistic and for reminding me that these books rarely get on national bestseller lists, which are biased against religious titles. Kenneth F. Ferraro, "Firm Believers? Religion, Body Weight, and Well-Being," *Review of Religious Research* 39, no. 3 (March 1998): 238.

3. See Joan Scott, "Feminism's History" (paper presented at the American Historical Association's annual meeting January 4, 2003), 14–15.

4. Robert A. Orsi, "The Gender of Religious Otherness" (keynote address at the Women and Twentieth-Century Protestantism Conference, Chicago, April 23–25, 1998); published online at www.wheaton.edu/isae/Women/Orsiessay99 .html; see also Orsi, *Thank You, St. Jude: Women's Devotion to the Patron Saint of Hopeless Causes* (New Haven: Yale University Press, 1996).

5. Rather than exclude the disabled, this worldview honors them for disciplining their bodies in ways available to them. Joni Eareckson Tada, the famed evangelical speaker who is a quadriplegic, has long been celebrated for her disciplined lifestyle, and she recurrently invokes the language of discipline in her own writing. Weigh Down Workshop books and videotapes feature a multiple stroke victim in a wheelchair and praise her for her disciplined commitment to weight loss (she lost 110 pounds; see Gwen Shamblin, *Rise Above* [2000], 92). (NB: full publication data on Shamblin's titles and others I discuss in text are in the bibliography). One of my informants also noted proudly that her mentally retarded adult daughter was learning Weigh Down principles and losing weight. The point here is not that proponents only see physically ideal persons as saved, but rather that a particular form of discipline is both possible and required for people with varying levels of mobility.

6. William James, *The Varieties of Religious Experience,* reprinted in

William James, Writings 1902–1910, ed. Bruce Kuklick (New York: Literary Classics of the United States, 1987), 19n1.

7. Caroline Knapp, *Appetites: Why Women Want* (New York: Counterpoint, 2003), 32; Jana Evans Braziel and Kathleen Lebesco, eds., *Bodies Out of Bounds: Fatness and Transgression* (Berkeley: University of California Press, 2001). The literature that analyzes American attitudes toward fat is extensive; one influential source is Lisa Schoenfielder and Barb Wieser, eds., *Shadow on a Tightrope: Writings by Women on Fat Oppression* (Iowa City: Aunt Lute Book, 1983).

8. Scott, "Feminism's History," 11.

9. This explicit and unfashionable use of "ideology" invokes conceptual frameworks such as that of Slavoj Zizek, who describes a "generative matrix that regulates the relationship between visible and non-visible, between imaginable and non-imaginable, as well as the changes in this relationship." Zizek's model, influenced by Marxian social theory and psychoanalysis, proves useful for a number of reasons, including its refusal of easy distinctions between "religious" and "secular" as well as other entrenched binaries. See, for instance, Slavoj Zizek's introduction, "The Spectre of Ideology," in *Mapping Ideology*, ed. Slavoj Zizek (London: Verso Books, 1994).

10. Several useful, scholarly informed texts explore Christianity for positive resources of this kind; see especially Stephanie Paulsell, *Honoring the Body: Meditations on a Christian Practice* (San Francisco: Jossey-Bass, 2002).

11. Ray Kybartas, *Fitness Is Religion: Keep the Faith* (New York: Simon and Schuster, 1997).

12. Witness a smattering of recent titles: *Beyond the Food Game: A Spiritual and Psychological Approach to Healing Emotional Eating* (1993); *Love Yourself Thin: The Revolutionary Spiritual Approach to Weight Loss* (1997); *Feeding the Body, Nourishing the Soul: Essentials of Eating for Physical, Emotional, and Spiritual Well-Being* (1997); and *Thin through the Power of Spirit: Creating Paradise in Your Weight and World* (2000).

13. See, most notably, Laura Fraser, *Losing It: America's Obsession with Weight and the Industry That Feeds on It* (New York: E. P. Dutton, 1997); Michelle Mary Lelwica, *Starving for Salvation: The Spiritual Dimensions of Eating Problems among American Girls and Women* (New York: Oxford University Press, 1999); and Hillel Schwartz, *Never Satisfied: A Cultural History of Diets, Fantasies, and Fat* (New York: Free Press, 1986).

14. The most influential source for Europeanists remains Caroline Walker Bynum, *Holy Feast and Holy Fast: The Religious Significance of Food to Medieval Women* (Berkeley: University of California Press, 1987). Spurred by Bynum's pioneering inspiration, the literature has since burgeoned. On the American side, a book that takes up the subject of food in Protestant church life is Daniel Sack, *Whitebread Protestants: Food and Religion in American Culture* (New York: St. Martin's Press, 2000).

15. See Bryan S. Turner, "The Body in Western Society," in *Religion and the Body*, ed. Sarah Coakley (Cambridge: Cambridge University Press, 1997), 38.

16. Joan Jacobs Brumberg, *Fasting Girls: The History of Anorexia Nervosa*

(Cambridge, MA: Harvard University Press, 1988); Schwartz, *Never Satisfied;* Peter N. Stearns, *Fat History: Bodies and Beauty in the Modern West* (New York: New York University Press, 1997).

17. Stearns, *Fat History*, 243.

18. Here my argument diverges from that of the theologian Michelle Lelwica, who argues that dieting comprises a "secularized soteriology" for many girls and women in the United States, and that the female struggle to reduce appetite and body weight is essentially a sign of "spiritual hungers—desires for a sense of meaning and wholeness" (Lelwica, *Starving for Salvation,* 37, 7). Lelwica's concerns are chiefly normative, with the aim of constructing a viable path to holistic well-being for eating-disordered girls and women, instead of tracing precise routings of historical change and continuity between religious piety and bodily disciplines.

An interesting and ambitious attempt at interpreting "secular" fitness culture in light of religion can be found in Philip A. Mellor and Chris Shilling, *Re-forming the Body: Religion, Community, and Modernity* (London: Sage Publications, 1997).

19. Rebecca Arnold, *Fashion, Desire, and Anxiety: Image and Morality in the 20th Century* (New Brunswick, NJ: Rutgers University Press, 2001), 89, 125. Critical assessments of the fashion industry and advertising more broadly are numerous; in this context, see especially Susan Bordo, *Twilight Zones: The Hidden Life of Cultural Images from Plato to O. J.* (Berkeley: University of California Press, 1997).

20. A representative recent account that presumes such an American loathing of the flesh, stemming from early American Protestants, is Tracy Fessenden, Nicholas F. Radel, and Magdalena J. Zaborowska, eds., *The Puritan Origins of American Sex: Religion, Sexuality, and National Identity in American Literature* (New York: Routledge, 2001). Works that trace out the history of American obscenity laws, sexual regulation, and the control of vice generally rely on this trope of repressive religion.

21. Alice M. Long, *My Lady Beautiful* (1908), 92–93, quoted in Schwartz, *Never Satisfied,* 108. Schwartz makes this larger point about physiological and psychological resonances in that section.

1. GLUTTONS FOR REGIMEN

1. Caroline Walker Bynum, *The Resurrection of the Body in Western Christianity, 200–1336* (New York: Columbia University Press, 1995), 266. Bynum summarizes, "In the late fourth and early fifth centuries when Gregory of Nyssa, Jerome, and Augustine wrote of resurrection, ascetic notions of bodily discipline and the growing popularity of the cult of relics suggested that the body expressed self. The controlled, lightened, and hardened bodies of hermits and holy virgins were understood to move during life toward the subtlety and impassibility they would have in paradise" (200).

2. Classic historical summaries of Christian fasting include Rudolph Ars-

besmann, "Fasting and Prophecy in Pagan and Christian Antiquity," *Traditio* 7 (1949–51): 1–71; and A. J. Maclean, "Fasting (Christian)," in *Encyclopaedia of Religion and Ethics,* ed. James Hastings et al. (Edinburgh: T. and T. Clark, 1937), 5: 765–71. Later studies relevant to the study of lived religion include Caroline Walker Bynum, *Holy Feast and Holy Fast: The Religious Significance of Food to Medieval Women* (Berkeley: University of California Press, 1987); Teresa M. Shaw, *The Burden of the Flesh: Fasting and Sexuality in Early Christianity* (Minneapolis: Fortress Press, 1998); and Charles E. Hambrick-Stowe, *The Practice of Piety: Puritan Devotional Disciplines in Seventeenth-Century New England* (Chapel Hill: University of North Carolina Press, 1982). See also Rudolph M. Bell, *Holy Anorexia* (Chicago: University of Chicago Press, 1985); Veronika Grimm, *From Feasting to Fasting, the Evolution of a Sin: Attitudes to Food in Late Antiquity* (London: Routledge, 1996); and Walter Vandereycken and Ron van Deth, *From Fasting Saints to Anorexic Girls: The History of Self-Starvation* (New York: New York University Press, 1994 [published in Germany as *Hungerkünstler, Fastenwunder, Magersucht: eine Kulturgeschicte der Essstörungen,* 1990]). On Catherine of Siena, see especially Bynum, *Holy Feast and Holy Fast,* 42 and passim.

3. The broader literature on food patterns is vast, but worth noting is a book on dietary advice in Renaissance Europe: Ken Albala, *Eating Right in the Renaissance* (Berkeley: University of California Press, 2002).

4. Peter Brown, *The Body and Society: Men, Women and Sexual Renunciation in Early Christianity* (New York: Columbia University Press, 1988), 32.

5. Henry Holland, *The Christian Exercise of Fasting, Private and Publicke* (London: Printed by Widow Orwin for William Young, 1596); George Buddle, *A Short and Plaine Discourse Fully Containing the Whole Doctrine of Evangelicall Fastes* (London: Printed for Mathew Law, 1609).

6. Philip A. Mellor and Chris Shilling, *Re-forming the Body: Religion, Community, and Modernity* (London: Sage Publications, 1997).

7. Holland, *Christian Exercise of Fasting,* 4–8.

8. Holland, *Christian Exercise of Fasting,* 17–43, 70, 92.

9. Buddle, *Short and Plaine Discourse,* 32, 35, 36.

10. Holland, *Christian Exercise of Fasting,* A2, 103.

11. Holland, *Christian Exercise of Fasting,* A1; Jeremy Taylor, *The Rule and Exercises of Holy Living* (1650; reprint, Oxford: Clarendon Press, 1989), 204.

12. John Calvin, *Institutes* (1536), 4:12, 14, 15, cited in H. F. Jacobson, "Fasting, in the Christian Church," *Religious Encyclopædia, or Dictionary of Biblical, Historical, Doctrinal, and Practical Theology,* ed. Philip Schaff (New York: Christian Literature, 1889), 1:800. As the English Puritan movement became increasingly unified in the 1620s and 1630s, for instance, fasting was an important part of the unauthorized gatherings these dissenters convened to atone for public sins and beseech God on behalf of their misfortunes. Besides their spiritual uses in advancing personal and communal godliness, these conventicles also served as forums wherein religious and state authorities were criticized. Buddle's earlier charge that it was "Anabaptisticall" ("odious both to God and

good men") for an individual to proclaim or set up a public fast was undoubtedly fueled by rebellious developments of this kind. See Stephen Foster, "New England and the Challenge of Heresy, 1630 to 1660: The Puritan Crisis in Transatlantic Perspective," *William and Mary Quarterly* 38, no. 4 (1981): 626, 627; Buddle, *Short and Plaine Discourse*, 33. See also Stephen Foster, *The Long Argument: English Puritanism and the Shaping of New England Culture, 1570–1700* (Chapel Hill: University of North Carolina Press, 1991); and James Eric Hazell, "Triumph of Humility: The Puritan Fast Day, 1570–1740" (PhD diss., University of Maryland, 1997).

13. Thomas Thacher, "A Fast of Gods chusing. . . ." (1678), 9, cited in Hazell, "Triumph," 12; David D. Hall, *Worlds of Wonder, Days of Judgment: Popular Religious Belief in Early New England* (Cambridge, MA: Harvard University Press, 1990), 171; Thomas Cartwright, *Holy Exercise of a True Fast* (1580), 135–36, cited in Hazell, "Triumph," 42. The structure of fast days is elaborated in William DeLoss Love, *Fast and Thanksgiving Days of New England* (Boston: Houghton Mifflin, 1895); and in Hazell, "Triumph," chap. 6; Hazell's dissertation is the most detailed study of Puritan fasting practices to date.

14. Cartwright, *Holy Exercise of a True Fast*, 135, cited in Hazell, "Triumph," 51.

15. After 1660, notes Hall, tensions over fasting increased, as issues like the halfway covenant led to disputes between the Massachusetts General Court and the ministers. In fact, civil authorities blamed a drought occurring around the time of the halfway covenant's adoption on the church leaders who recommended this innovation, whereupon indignant clerics responded by pointing to the rains that fell in response to their fast (Hall, *Worlds of Wonder*, 171–72).

16. Love, *Fast and Thanksgiving Days*, 234–36; Hazell, "Triumph," 284–85. Hazell's primary argument is that Puritan fasting dramatically combined humility and aggression. In sketching the fast in Puritan England, he writes, "Although fasts were days of humiliation they could be both aggressive and subversive. By defining certain practices of the established church as sins in need of repenting, Puritans used fasting to condemn ecclesiastical policy, and the particular type of reforming needed to soothe God's anger rather closely resembled their own program. As Puritans gained strength in Parliament, and eventually during the Civil Wars, they continued to use fasting assertively, to articulate and promote their agenda" ("Triumph," 20).

17. Michael MacDonald writes extensively of healing fasts among English Puritans and their descendants; see MacDonald, "Religion, Social Change, and Psychological Healing in England, 1600–1800," in *The Church and Healing*, ed. W. J. Sheils (Oxford: Basil Blackwell, 1982), 101–26 (reference to the Surey Demoniack on 108–9); Hall, *Worlds of Wonder*, 203, 192.

18. Charles Wallace further analyzes the dietary restraint of the Oxford Holy Club, and of Wesley's own emphasis on diet; see Wallace, "Simple and Recollected: John Wesley's Life-Style," *Religion in Life* 46 (Summer 1977): 198–212.

19. "Fasting," in *Encyclopedia of World Methodism*, ed. Nolan B. Harmon (Nashville: United Methodist Publishing House, 1974), 1:832.

20. These verses (Matt. 6:16–18 [KJV]) read, "Moreover, when ye fast, be not as the hypocrites, of a sad countenance; for they disfigure their faces, that they may appear unto men to fast. Verily I say unto you, They have their reward. But thou, when thou fastest, anoint thy head, and wash thy face; That thou appear not unto men to fast, but unto thy Father which is in secret; and thy Father, which seeth in secret, shall reward thee openly." Entitled "Upon Our Lord's Sermon on the Mount: Discourse the Seventh," the sermon is reprinted in *Works of John Wesley*, ed. Albert C. Outler (Nashville: Abingdon Press, 1984), 1:608, 609. Here and in all subsequent quotations, emphasis is in original text unless otherwise noted.

21. Early modern fasting shifted in practice and meaning from its late medieval form, when the extravagance of food abstinence was not infrequently extolled as a sign of sanctity. Erased from Protestant fasting, at least in its commonplace forms, were accompanying visions of blood and milk pouring out from the orifices of the pious body. Absent too were the accounts once told of mystics drinking pus from the sores of lepers, exhibiting the wounds of Christ in stigmatic bleedings, lactating mysteriously, or exuding aromas and healing fluids even in death. See Susan Juster, "Mystical Pregnancy and Holy Bleeding: Visionary Experience in Early Modern Britain and America," *William and Mary Quarterly* 57, no. 2 (April 2000): 249–88. Juster's focus on the extremes of evangelical experience, however riveting, nonetheless lends undue credence to the chestnut of Protestantism as a thoroughly disembodied tradition, its leaders conspiring to eradicate both pleasure and pain in an attempt to rely solely on the cool, rational mind.

22. Leigh Eric Schmidt, *Holy Fairs: Scottish Communions and American Revivals in the Early Modern Period* (Princeton: Princeton University Press, 1989), 77, 78; Schmidt quotes "holy Revenge" from John Willison, *A Sacramental Catechism, or A Familiar Instructor for Young Communicants* (1720; Edinburgh: Samuel Willison, 1756), 178.

23. James Hargreaves, *An Address to Christians on the Propriety of Religious Fasts* (London: Wightman and Cramp, 1828), 40, 39, 56, 58.

24. "Progress of Religion in the United States," *Congregational Magazine*, n.s., 11, no. 47 (November 1828): 611.

25. W. C. Walton, *Preparation for Special Efforts to Promote the Work of God* (Hartford: Andrus and Judd, 1833), 26.

26. "I see no ground, in any of the teachings or practices of Christ, for abstaining from food, unless the appetite is impaired. When Christ had fasted forty days, it is said that he became an hungered, and did eat; plainly implying that during the period of fasting, he had not been an hungered" (Amariah Brigham, *Observations on the Influence of Religion Upon the Health and Physical Welfare of Mankind* [1835; reprint, New York: Arno Press, 1973], 106–7).

27. See John B. Boles, *The Great Revival: Beginnings of the Bible Belt* (Lexington: University Press of Kentucky, 1996), esp. 31–34, 51, 147.

28. See Garth M. Rosell and Richard A. G. Dupuis, eds., *The Memoirs of*

Charles G. Finney (1876; Grand Rapids, MI: Zondervan Publishing House, 1989), 391, 39.

29. Dan. 9:3, the verse Samuel Miller used as source for his sermons, reads, "And I set my face unto the Lord God, to seek by prayer and supplication with fasting."

30. Samuel Miller, "The Duty, the Benefits, and the Proper Method of Religious Fasting," *The National Preacher* 5, no. 10 (March 1831): 152, where he also united fasting with the aims of charity, encouraging Christians to fast for the sake of feeding and missionizing the poor.

31. Ronald Hogeland, "Charles Hodge, the Association of Gentlemen and Ornamental Womanhood," *Journal of Presbyterian History* 53 (Fall 1975): 251, cited in Margaret Lamberts Bendroth, *Fundamentalism and Gender, 1875 to the Present* (New Haven: Yale University Press, 1993), 35.

32. Miller, "Religious Fasting," 158, 159.

33. See *The Power of Faith, Exemplified in the Life and Writings of the Late Mrs. Isabella Graham* (New York: American Tract Society, 1843), 297, 316, 315, 335, 336.

34. Woodbury M. Fernald, ed., *Memoirs and Reminiscences of the Late Prof. George Bush* (Boston: Otis Clapp, 1860), 49, 51.

35. Elizabeth Prentiss, *Stepping Heavenward* (1869; reprint, Sterling, VA: GAM Publications, 1993), 264–65, 305. Roman Catholics and Episcopalians, of course, continued to advocate for fasting during Lent and on Fridays; Episcopal leaders also urged fasting on Ember Days. Other defenses of fasting appeared during the Civil War but entailed a different genre.

36. George Miller Beard, *Eating and Drinking: A Popular Manual of Food and Diet in Health and Disease* (New York: G. P. Putnam and Sons, 1871), iv, 7, 124, 125, 8. Beard's concern was echoed in other quarters; an 1880 diatribe against mysticism and asceticism spoke scathingly: "An every-day observation proves the demoralizing tendency of asceticism. Every man is harsher, more severe, less obliging when hungry than when satisfied,—a truth which extends to the very beasts. . . . Now the ascetic not merely practices a vice, but, unlike the sensualist, he even glories in it and pronounces it a virtue" (Frank Fernseed, "Mysticism and Asceticism," *Journal of Science* 17 [November 1880]: 699–700).

37. "The Human Body as Related to Sanctification," *Princeton Review* 34, no. 1 (January 1862): 101, 102, 103.

38. *Fasting: In Theory and Practice* (New York: G. F. Nesbitt, 1875). Accounts of intense and frequent fasting are also found in accounts of missionized Christians in other parts of the world. See, for instance, Mrs. Howard Taylor, *Pastor Hsi (of North China): One of China's Christians,* 5th ed. (London: Morgan and Scott for the China Inland Mission, 1904).

39. *Doctrine and Covenants* 88:76 (cited in the *Encyclopedia of Mormonism* [New York: Macmillan, 1992]).

40. See *Doctrine and Covenants* 59:14; and from the *Book of Mormon,* Alma 5:46, Alma 17:3, and Mosiah 27:22–23.

41. Phoebe Palmer, ed., *Pioneer Experiences, or The Gift of Power Received By Faith* (1868; New York: Garland, 1984), 18, 34, 110, 111, 180, 322.

42. Taylor, *Holy Living*, 203; section on temperance, 64–72.

43. William Law, *A Serious Call to a Devout and Holy Life* (1728; London: J. M. Dent and Sons, 1906), 78.

44. Howard Malcolm, the editor of an 1835 edition published in Boston, wrote in his introduction that as of his writing, eighteen editions had "already been printed in this country beside a still larger number in England."

45. Ken Albala explains this change in his chapter, "The Emergence of Fat as Sin in Dietary Literature of the Pre-Modern Era," in *Cultures of the Abdomen: Dietetics, Digestion, and Obesity in the Modern World*, ed. Christopher E. Forth and Ana Carden-Coyne (Palgrave Press, forthcoming).

46. Luigi Cornaro, *The Art of Living Long; A New and Improved English Version of the Treatise of the Celebrated Venetian Centenarian, Louis Cornaro, with Essays by Joseph Addison, Lord Bacon, and Sir William Temple* (Milwaukee, W.F. Butler, 1903). Sundry editions of Cornaro's text, including this one, continued to be available for purchase as late as spring 2004 from Kessinger Publications.

47. On Cheyne's mystical readings, see Anita Guerrini, "The Hungry Soul: George Cheyne and the Construction of Femininity," *Eighteenth-Century Studies* 32, no. 3 (1999): 282 and passim; Guerrini, *Obesity and Depression in the Enlightenment: The Life and Times of George Cheyne* (Norman: University of Oklahoma Press, 2000).

48. Cheyne's weight has long been referred to in American circles as 450 pounds; but as one critic notes, the definition of the English stone has varied over time. If in Cheyne's time it was still considered 8 pounds (as noted in a 1674 source cited in the *Oxford English Dictionary*), Cheyne would have been closer to 256 pounds. See Bernadine Z. Paulshock, review *of Obesity and Depression in the Enlightenment: The Life and Times of George Cheyne, Journal of the American Medical Association* 284, no. 10 (2000): 1305.

49. Guerrini, "The Hungry Soul," 280.

50. Letter, Whitefield papers, Methodist Archive, John Rylands Library, University of Manchester, cited in David E. Shuttleton, "Methodism and Dr. George Cheyne's 'More Enlightening Principles,'" in *Medicine in the Enlightenment*, ed. Roy Porter (Amsterdam: Rodopi, 1995), 321. Much of this discussion of Cheyne's influence on Whitefield and Wesley draws on Shuttleton's work. E. Brooks Holifield also briefly discusses Cheyne's influence on Wesley in *Health and Medicine in the Methodist Tradition: Journey Toward Wholeness* (New York: Crossroads Publishing, 1986), 32, 35.

51. Cited in Wallace, "Simple and Recollected," 202.

52. Richard Graves, *The Spiritual Quixote, or the Summer's Ramble of Mr. Geoffrey Wildgoose* (1773), cited in Shuttleton, "Methodism and Dr. Cheyne," 319 and passim.

53. "Upon Our Lord's Sermon on the Mount," in Outler, *Wesley*, 608, 599; Jesse Lee, *Practical Piety: The Substance of a Sermon Preached at a Watch-*

Night Held in Johnston, Delaware State, on Nov. 18th, 1785 (Baltimore: John Hagerty, 1814), 8.

54. *The Immortal Mentor, or Man's Unerring Guide to a Healthy, Wealthy, and Long Life, in Three Parts by Dr. Cornaro, Dr. Franklin, and Dr. Scott* (Philadelphia: Printed for the Rev. Mason L. Weems, by Francis and Robert Bailey, 1796).

55. *Discourses on a Sober and Temperate Life, by Lewis Cornaro, A Noble Venitian* [sic], *with an Introduction and Notes by Sylvester Graham* (New York: Day, 1833), xiii; Guerrini, *Obesity and Depression,* 118.

56. Benjamin Rush, *Sermons to Gentlemen Upon Temperance and Exercise* (Philadelphia: John Dunlap, 1772), 10, 11, 16.

57. James C. Whorton, *Crusaders for Fitness: The History of American Health Reformers* (Princeton: Princeton University Press, 1982), 54; Robert H. Abzug, *Cosmos Crumbling: American Reform and the Religious Imagination* (New York: Oxford University Press, 1994), 163–64. This emphasis on simplicity also drove the diet of Henry David Thoreau at Walden Pond; see Stephen Adams and Barbara Adams, "Thoreau's Diet At Walden," in *Studies in the American Renaissance,* ed. Joel Myerson (Charlottesville: University Press of Virginia, 1990), 243–60.

58. Joseph H. Jones, *The Influence of Physical Causes on Religious Experience* (Philadelphia: William S. Martien, 1846), 94, 95.

59. Horace Bushnell, *Christian Nurture* (1860; New Haven: Yale University Press, 1916), 234, 195, 233. I am indebted to a lecture by Richard Lyman Bushman on Bushnell and taste (during a conference on religion and the senses, at Princeton in May 1999), for spurring me to explore these bodily concerns in *Christian Nurture.*

60. Thomas Wentworth Higginson, "Saints and Their Bodies," *Atlantic Monthly,* March 1858, 583, 582, 585–86.

61. Martin Luther, "A Sermon on the Estate of Marriage," in *Luther's Works,* ed. James Atkinson (Philadelphia: Fortress Press, 1966), 44:9, cited in Erik R. Seeman, " 'It Is Better to Marry Than to Burn': Anglo-American Attitudes Toward Celibacy, 1600–1800," *Journal of Family History* 24, no. 4 (October 1999): 399.

62. Seeman, "It Is Better," 401. The ideas in this and the following paragraph have been influenced by Seeman's work; on celibacy and Reformed ministers' wariness toward the body, see also Erik R. Seeman, "Sarah Prentice and the Immortalists: Sexuality, Piety, and the Body in Eighteenth-Century New England," in *Sex and Sexuality in Early America,* ed. Merril D. Smith (New York: New York University Press, 1998), 116–31.

63. Thomas A. Foster, "Deficient Husbands: Manhood, Sexual Incapacity, and Male Marital Sexuality in Seventeenth-Century New England," *William and Mary Quarterly* 56, no. 4 (October 1999): 724.

64. Else K. Hambleton, "The World Filled with a Generation of Bastards: Pregnant Brides and Unwed Mothers in Seventeenth-Century Massachusetts" (PhD diss., University of Massachusetts, 2000), 11–12, cited in Samira Mehta,

"The Ellinwood Divorce and the Embodiment of Marital Ideals" (paper presented as a research project for HDS 2379, Harvard Divinity School, January 2003), 3. I am grateful to Mehta for introducing me to Hambleton's work and sharing other sources with me.

65. T. Foster, "Deficient Husbands," 729, 728; Mehta, "The Ellinwood Divorce"; Cotton Mather, *Ornaments for the Daughters of Zion* (Cambridge, MA: S. Green and B. Green, 1692), 77, cited in Seeman, "It Is Better," 405.

66. Hambleton, "Pregnant Brides," 339, 340, 342.

67. Nicholas F. Radel, "A Sodom Within: Historicizing Puritan Homoerotics in the Diary of Michael Wigglesworth," in *The Puritan Origins of American Sex: Religion, Sexuality, and National Identity in American Literature*, ed. Tracy Fessenden, Nicholas F. Radel, and Magdalena J. Zaborowska (New York: Routledge, 2001), 42; Wigglesworth citation is from *The Diary of Michael Wigglesworth, 1653–1657*, ed. Edmund S. Morgan (Gloucester, MA: Peter Smith, 1970), 31, 9.

68. Jodi Schorb, "Uncleanliness Is Next to Godliness: Sexuality, Salvation, and the Early American Woman's Execution Narrative," in *Puritan Origins of American Sex*, 72–92.

69. Ed Ingebretsen, "Wigglesworth, Mather, Starr: Witch-Hunts and General Wickedness in Public," in *Puritan Origins of American Sex*, 36.

70. In his work on nineteenth-century antimasturbation campaigns, Russ Castronovo argues that "modernity is typified by an obsessive injunction to confess, study, and speak openly about sex in ways that are neither strictly repressive nor puritanical" (Castronovo, "Enslaving Passions: White Male Sexuality and the Evasion of Race," in *Puritan Origins of American Sex*, 145).

71. William G. McLoughlin, *Diary of Isaac Backus*, 294, quoted in Seeman, "Sarah Prentice and the Immortalists," 121.

72. Seeman, "It Is Better," 410. Seeman speculates on Prentice and the Immortalists' beliefs about celibacy in "Sarah Prentice and the Immortalists," 120. The evidence is much stronger, however, on the Shakers.

73. Historians such as Lawrence Foster and Robert Fogarty have written extensively on radical communitarian movements, particularly those that were prominent during the fervid 1830s and 1840s, along with the attraction they held for some antebellum Americans who sought an alternative to conventional marriage and sex-role relationships. See three works by Lawrence Foster, *Religion and Sexuality: Three American Communal Experiments of the Nineteenth Century* (New York: Oxford University Press, 1981); *Women, Family, and Utopia: Communal Experiments of the Shakers, the Oneida Community, and the Mormons* (Syracuse, NY: Syracuse University Press, 1991); and *Free Love in Utopia: John Humphrey Noyes and the Origin of the Oneida Community* (Urbana: University of Illinois Press, 2001); see also two works by Robert S. Fogarty, *All Things New: American Communes and Utopian Movements 1860–1914* (Chicago: University of Chicago Press, 1990); and *Dictionary of American Communal and Utopian History* (Westport, CT: Greenwood Press, 1980). More focused studies are cited below.

74. Jean M. Humez, ed., *Mother's First-Born Daughters: Early Shaker Writings on Women and Religion* (Bloomington: Indiana University Press, 1993), xvi. Given this segregated world, it is not surprising that Shakerism, whose numbers peaked in the mid-nineteenth century, fostered intimacy and affection among women and that the society's leaders had to issue warnings against "special friendships" that could presumably threaten wider communal bonds; see Rosemary D. Gooden, " 'In the Bonds of True Love and Friendship': Some Meanings of 'Gospel Affection' and 'Gospel Union' in Shaker Sisters' Letters and Poems," in *Women in Spiritual and Communitarian Societies in the United States*, ed. Wendy E. Chmielewski, Louis J. Kern, and Marlyn Klee-Hartzell (Syracuse, NY: Syracuse University Press, 1993), 104–13. The authoritative history of Shakers in America is Stephen J. Stein, *The Shaker Experience in America: A History of the United Society of Believers* (New Haven: Yale University Press, 1992).

75. Suzanne Thurman, "The Seat of Sin, the Site of Salvation: The Shaker Body and the Nineteenth-Century American Imagination," *Nineteenth-Century Studies* 15 (2001): 3, 6.

76. Thurman, "The Seat of Sin," 7. Catholic nuns' bodies were often seen as deviant for the same reason; see Jenny Franchot, *Roads to Rome: The Antebellum Protestant Encounter with Catholicism* (Berkeley: University of California Press, 1994).

77. These passages are cited in Humez, *Mother's First-Born Daughters*, 221–22, and I am using Humez's analysis to ground this discussion.

78. Louis J. Kern, *An Ordered Love: Sex Roles and Sexuality in Victorian Utopias—The Shakers, the Mormons, and the Oneida Community* (Chapel Hill: University of North Carolina Press, 1981), 87ff; Stein, *Shaker Experience*, 96.

79. Hilda Herrick Noyes, interview with R. D. Dickinson, September 1926, from archives of the Kinsey Institute for Research in Sex, Gender, and Reproduction, Indiana University, Bloomington, cited in Spencer Klaw, *Without Sin: The Life and Death of the Oneida Community* (New York: Penguin Books, 1993), 178.

80. John Humphrey Noyes, "Male Continence" (Oneida, NY: Office of Oneida Circular, 1872), 16, reprinted in Charles Rosenberg and Carroll Smith-Rosenberg, eds., *Sexual Indulgence and Denial: Variations on Continence* (New York: Arno Press, 1974).

81. Robert S. Fogarty, ed., *Desire and Duty at Oneida: Tirzah Miller's Intimate Memoir* (Bloomington: Indiana University Press, 2000), 99.

82. Fogarty, *Miller's Intimate Memoir*, 135, 136.

83. Fogarty, *Miller's Intimate Memoir*, 60, 23.

84. Jonathan Edwards, *A Treatise Concerning Religious Affections* (1746); reprinted in *The Works of Jonathan Edwards*, ed. John E. Smith (New Haven: Yale University Press, 1959, 1987), 2:98.

85. Johann Caspar Lavater, *Essays on Physiognomy; for the Promotion of the Knowledge and the Love of Mankind*, trans. Thomas Holcroft, 2d ed. (London, 1804), 16–17.

86. Unlike physiognomy, early phrenology generally limited its analysis to anatomical bumps on the skull; Lavater's physiognomy, with its attention to the countenance and insistence upon the revelatory power of all human body parts, was much broader, as were later, Americanized versions of phrenology. Sources on phrenology are sketchy and of mixed quality; see Madeleine B. Stern, *Heads and Headlines: The Phrenological Fowlers* (Norman: University of Oklahoma Press, 1971); Roger Cooter, *The Cultural Meaning of Popular Science: Phrenology and the Organization of Consent in Nineteenth-Century Britain* (Cambridge: Cambridge University Press, 1984); and Charles Colbert, *A Measure of Perfection: Phrenology and the Fine Arts in America* (Chapel Hill: University of North Carolina Press, 1997). Abzug contextualizes phrenology among related reform movements of the nineteenth century in *Cosmos Crumbling,* 163–82.

87. Literary examples are taken from Stern, *Heads and Headlines,* xiv–xv; on the Fowlers' Americanization of phrenology, see 34–35 and passim. Cooter, writing of British phrenology, acidly disparages the Fowlers for draining the intellectual life from older versions of phrenology with their "cheap publications" and "nonintellectualist, healthean-watered, fruity, and farinaceous" tone (*Cultural Meaning of Popular Science,* 156).

88. Orson Squire Fowler, "Phrenology of Moses A. Cartland" (1839), Cartland Family papers (series 5, container 675), Houghton Library, Harvard University.

89. On Swedenborg's influence on phrenology, see Colbert, *A Measure of Perfection,* 30–33 and passim. An intriguing, if sketchy, treatment of Swedenborg's broader influence upon American religion and culture in the nineteenth century is found in Eugene Taylor, *Shadow Culture: Psychology and Spirituality in America* (Washington, DC: Counterpoint, 1999), 61–97; see also Leigh Eric Schmidt, *Hearing Things: Religion, Illusion, and the American Enlightenment* (Cambridge, MA: Harvard University Press, 2000), 221–30 and passim; and Ann Taves, *Fits, Trances, and Visions: Experiencing Religion and Explaining Experience from Wesley to James* (Princeton: Princeton University Press, 1999), esp. chap. 4.

90. The most comprehensive history of nineteenth-century health reform, for instance, fails to reckon with phrenology's social impact, instead disdaining it (to a greater degree than other health reform initiatives) as "pseudoscience" that was "vulgarized, being reduced in many hands to a type of fortune telling" (Whorton, *Crusaders for Fitness,* 124). In *A Measure of Perfection,* Colbert delineates phrenology's saturation of the fine arts.

91. Nelson Sizer, *Forty Years in Phrenology* (1882), 97, 385, quoted in Michael Sappol, *A Traffic of Dead Bodies: Anatomy and Embodied Social Identity in Nineteenth-Century America* (Princeton: Princeton University Press, 2002), 174–75. Sappol's excellent treatment of popular nineteenth-century anatomy lends further credence to the growing American belief in body-soul correspondences.

92. Ernest von Feuchtersleben, *The Dietetics of the Soul,* 7th German ed. (New York: C. S. Francis, 1854), 43, 161, 168–69.

93. John B. DeMotte, *The Secret of Character Building* (1892), 64–65.

94. DeMotte, *Secret of Character Building,* 65.

95. DeMotte, *Secret of Character Building,* 110.

96. As Jennifer Terry and Jacqueline Urla have noted in studying how categories of difference are produced, "The somatic territorializing of deviance, since the nineteenth century, has been part and parcel of a larger effort to organize social relations according to categories denoting normality versus aberration, health versus pathology, and national security versus social danger" (Terry and Urla, eds., introduction to *Deviant Bodies: Critical Perspectives on Difference in Science and Popular Culture* [Bloomington: Indiana University Press, 1995], 1).

97. "The Best Indian," *American Phrenological Journal* 41, no. 1 (January 1865): 7.

98. Letter titled "Young America," *American Phrenological Journal* 41, no. 1 (January 1865): 32.

99. Samuel R. Wells, *How to Read Character: A New Illustrated Hand-Book of Phrenology and Physiognomy for Students and Examiners; with a Descriptive Chart* (New York, 1870), vii, viii.

100. "The Head, Face, and Expression," 106, 109–10, notebook 2, box 1, folder 4, Hattie A. Harlow collection, Radcliffe Institute for Advanced Study, Schlesinger Library, Harvard University.

101. "Head, Face, and Expression," 27 and passim.

102. Notebook "Personal Culture, etc.," box 1, folder 7, Harlow collection 11, 2, 5–6.

103. See Cooter, *Popular Science,* 123.

104. Colbert, *A Measure of Perfection,* 33–34.

2. SCULPTORS OF OUR OWN EXTERIOR

1. William Walker Atkinson, *Human Nature* (1910). Although his well-known chronicle of the movement was not yet published, Atkinson was well traveled and highly respected in New Thought circles, having served as associate editor of *New Thought* magazine; see his *New Thought, Its History and Principles, or The Message of the New Thought: A Condensed History of Its Real Origin with Statement of Its Basic Principles and True Aims* (Holyoke, MA: Elizabeth Towne, 1915). He was also a noted popularizer of Hinduism, writing a dozen or so books under the pseudonym of Yogi Ramacharaka. Other early twentieth-century books invoked this tradition of New Thought physiognomy, from Susanna Cocroft, *Character as Expressed in the Body* (1915), to David Van Bush, *Character Analysis* (1923), among others.

2. Among others, see Peter N. Stearns, *Fat History: Bodies and Beauty in the Modern West* (New York: New York University Press, 1997); and Hillel Schwartz, *Never Satisfied: A Cultural History of Diets, Fantasies, and Fat* (New York: Free Press, 1986).

3. Albert B. Olston, *Mind Power and Privileges* (New York: Thomas Y. Crowell, 1902), 212.

4. Letter to a patient, 1854, *The Quimby Manuscripts*, ed. Horatio W. Dresser (New York: Thomas Y. Crowell, 1921), 112; letter to a patient, Nov. 4, 1856, 74. Catherine L. Albanese analyzes Quimby's "ambiguity that dissolves into a total mixing of models" regarding mind and matter (Albanese, *Nature Religion in America: From the Algonkian Indians to the New Age* [Chicago: University of Chicago Press, 1990], 112 and passim). This notion of fluids was, of course, indebted to theories of animal magnetism; see Taves, *Fits, Trances, and Visions.*

5. *Quimby Manuscripts,* 112, 113.

6. *Quimby Manuscripts,* 113, 114.

7. The water applications are mentioned in Stephen Gottschalk, *The Emergence of Christian Science in American Religious Life* (Berkeley: University of California Press, 1973), 105.

8. This patient's wife was also invited to benefit from Quimby's distant mind cure: "Tell your wife to sit down and give her attention and I will affect her in the same way. Please take a little water when you are sitting, say about 9 o'clock in the evening" *(Quimby Manuscripts,* 114–15).

9. Mary Baker Eddy, *Science and Health* (1906 ed.), 277, quoted in Alan Anderson, "Contrasting Strains of Metaphysical Idealism Contributing to New Thought," Monograph no. 1, Society for the Study of Metaphysical Religion (1991), 17, www.websyte.com/alan/contrast.htm (accessed 2 Nov 2000).

10. Mary Baker Glover [later Eddy], *Science and Health* (Boston: Christian Science Publishing, 1875), 32.

11. *Science and Health* (1875), 214–15 (apparently this material was excised from the book's later editions, making Eddy into more of a pure antimaterialist than evidenced by her original writings), 347, 344.

12. *Science and Health* (1875), 404, 434–35.

13. *Science and Health* (1875), 191, 341–42.

14. *Science and Health* (1875), 189–90. The passage is also cited in Gillian Gill, *Mary Baker Eddy* (Reading, MA: Perseus Books, 1998), 47. In later editions of *Science and Health,* Eddy would rewrite this incident in the third person; see *Science and Health with Key to the Scriptures* (Boston: First Church of Christ, Scientist, 1994), 221–22.

15. Gill, *Eddy,* 392; Mary Baker Eddy to Pamelia [*sic*] J. Leonard, March 22, 1900 (Mary Baker Eddy Library for the Betterment of Humanity, accession no. L07955). But see the letter of her secretary, William Rathvon, to Peter Baggerly in 1909, just months prior to her death: "Personally she [Eddy] gives little thought to eating except to heed Paul's directions as expressed in 1 Cor. 10–31" (accession no. L18433).

16. Mark Twain's loathing for what he considered Eddy's unforgivable greed and love of commercialism is evident in many parts of that text, originally published as a series of magazine articles (Twain, *Christian Science, with Notes Containing Corrections to Date* [New York: Harper and Brothers, 1907]).

17. Eddy to Caroline W. Frame, February 19, 1901 (accession no. L08560); Eddy to Carrie E. Smith, June 18, 1907 (accession no. L13515).

18. Eddy to Augusta E. Stetson, November 3, 1893 (accession no. V01263); Eddy to James T. White, October 13, 1897 (accession no. L02547); Eddy to Sarah T. Winslow, October 26, 1899 (accession no. L11310); Eddy to James A. Neal, January 28, 1901 (accession no. V01813); Eddy to James A. Neal, January 31, 1901 (accession no. L03561); Eddy to D. E. Fultz, June 13, 1901 (accession no. L14269); Eddy to D. E. Fultz, July 22, 1901 (accession no. V01856); Eddy to Willis G. C. Kimball, August 2, 1902 (accession no. L08091); Eddy to Emilie Hergenroeder, February 4, 1904 (accession no. V00508).

19. Eddy, *Science and Health* (1994), 162, 242, 382.

20. On physical beauty being despised, see *Science and Health* (1994), 57, 247, 383; also "We need a clean body and a clean mind,—a body rendered pure by Mind as well as washed by water. One says: 'I take good care of my body.' To do this, the pure and exalting influence of the divine Mind on the body is requisite, and the Christian Scientist takes the best care of his body when he leaves it most out of his thought, and, like the Apostle Paul, is 'willing rather to be absent from the body, and to be present with the Lord.' "

21. *Science and Health* (1994), 272, 57 (in the original 1875 edition this passage read, "Virtue is the basis of civilization and progress; without it there is no true foundation to society. Owing to the shocking depravity of mankind, chastity is looked at suspiciously" [314]), 405.

22. Anderson, "Contrasting Strains."

23. Margaret Fowler Dunaway papers, box 2, folder 41, Radcliffe Institute for Advanced Study, Schlesinger Library, Harvard University.

24. Barbara Wilson, *Blue Windows: A Christian Science Childhood* (New York: Picador, 1997), 70, 71, 146.

25. Thomas Simmons, *The Unseen Shore: Memories of a Christian Science Childhood* (Boston: Beacon Press, 1991), 4–5, 140, 141, 140.

26. Simmons, *Unseen Shore*, 101–2.

27. For a brief biographical sketch of Gestefeld, see Beryl Satter, *Each Mind a Kingdom: American Women, Sexual Purity, and the New Thought Movement, 1875–1920* (Berkeley: University of California Press, 1999), 126–27; Charles Samuel Braden also writes extensively about her in *Spirits in Rebellion: The Rise and Development of New Thought* (Dallas: Southern Methodist University Press, 1963). Recent dissertations on the New Thought movement also discuss Gestefeld, notably Ferriss Clay Bailey, " 'Preachers Without Pulpits': New Thought and the Rise of Therapeutic Self-Help in Progressive Era America" (PhD diss., Vanderbilt University, 1999); see also Bailey's entry on Gestefeld in the *American National Biography*. An obituary of Gestefeld appeared in the *New York Times*, October 25, 1921, 17.

28. Ursula N. Gestefeld, *How We Master Our Fate* (New York: Alliance Publishing, 1899), 108.

29. Gestefeld, *How We Master Our Fate*, 50, 55, 107.

30. Gestefeld, *How We Master Our Fate*, 55, 56.

31. Satter's book *Each Mind a Kingdom*, the first in-depth scholarly treatment of the New Thought movement since Gail Thain Parker's *Mind Cure in*

New England (1973), is very useful for depicting this highly influential yet understudied movement, although I think her depiction of an overriding fixation with gender roles is somewhat restrictive. A nuanced study of a related contemporary movement is Joy Dixon, *Divine Feminine: Theosophy and Feminism in England* (Baltimore: Johns Hopkins University Press, 2001).

32. Gestefeld, *How We Master Our Fate,* 102, 44.

33. A venerable literature charts this anxiety in America. While the lineage I have in mind is akin to that traced elsewhere (e.g., Karen Halttunen, *Confidence Men and Painted Women: A Study of Middle-Class Culture in America, 1830–1870* [New Haven: Yale University Press, 1982]), I am more interested in the explicit discourses of health that stoked this anxiety before attempting to relieve or profit from it.

34. Gestefeld, *How We Master Our Fate,* 68, 61, 68, 69.

35. Atkinson, *New Thought,* 19; Eva Martin, *Prentice Mulford: "New Thought" Pioneer* (London: William Rider and Son, 1921), 7, 66. Rider and Son also published Mulford's essays in England. In midcentury, a California publisher issued *Prentice Mulford's Story,* complete with illustrations by Frederic Remington (Oakland, CA: Biobooks, 1953).

36. Prentice Mulford, "The Material Mind Versus the Spiritual Mind," in *The Gift of the Spirit* (1908), 101.

37. "It Was Prentice Mulford: Sheepshead Bay Mystery Was Solved Yesterday," *New York Times,* June 1, 1891, 1.

38. Quoted in Martin, *Prentice Mulford,* 55.

39. Mulford, "Immortality in the Flesh," in *Gift of the Spirit,* 158, 168. Mulford compared the effects of human craving for physicality to the work performed by disease or sickness, the purpose of which was to reconstruct the physical body. Though simultaneous with the reconstruction of the spirit, the ultimate aim was the prevention of physical " 'ageing,' shrivelling, weakening," and death (159). So body-oriented was Mulford that Martin, his theosophist biographer, had to warn readers, "It is on points such as this that Mulford parts company with the more deeply mystical schools of thought, for he is so immersed at times, in the task of making the best of this life, and getting the best out of it, that he is apt to forget that the true life of the spirit in man is not here—though temporarily focused in this world—but in those dwellings 'not made with hands, eternal in the heavens'" (Martin, *Prentice Mulford,* 61–62).

40. Mulford, "Immortality in the Flesh," 169. Some of Mulford's thinking on immortality resembles Mary Baker Eddy's early writings that lingered wistfully on the possibility of eternal youth and beauty (1875 version; these were excised from later editions of *Science and Health*).

41. Mulford, "Immortality in the Flesh," 170.

42. Prentice Mulford, "Grace Before Meat, or The Science of Eating," in *Essays of Prentice Mulford* (1890), 38.

43. Mulford, "Grace Before Meat," 39, 40, 41.

44. Mulford, "Grace Before Meat," 41, 42, 43.

45. Mulford, "Regeneration, or Being Born Again," in *Gift of the Spirit,* 181.

46. Mulford, "Re-embodiment Universal in Nature," in *Gift of the Spirit*, 199–200, 201–2.

47. Like Gestefeld and Mulford, other New Thought figures distinguished between the spiritual and the natural body. Annie Payson Call (1853–1940)—a later, more prolific, and more widely read author than either Gestefeld or Mulford—used science to defend not simply the theory of correspondence but an identifiable unification of these two bodies made apparent in the human nervous system. While for Call, spiritual advancement remained the highest end of human living, the physical was, in every way, the essential foundation for such growth, and she focused at length on care of the physical body, particularly in such New Thought classics as *Power through Repose* (1891) and *As a Matter of Course* (1894).

48. See Bradford J. M. Verter, "Dark Star Rising: The Emergence of Modern Occultism, 1800–1950" (PhD diss., Princeton University, 1997).

49. There are innumerable sources available on this subject; one recent treatment is Michael Edward Melody and Linda M. Peterson, *Teaching America about Sex: Marriage Guides and Sex Manuals from the Late Victorians to Dr. Ruth* (New York: New York University Press, 1999).

50. Further biographical information on Stockham is available in Satter, *Each Mind a Kingdom,* 134–38 and passim.

51. Alice B. Stockham, *Tokology* (1902), 349–50.

52. Alice B. Stockham, *Karezza* (1903), reprinted in Charles Rosenberg and Carroll Smith-Rosenberg, eds., *Sexual Indulgence and Denial: Variations on Continence* (New York: Arno Press, 1974), vii, 18, 24, 25, 25–26. Stockham had some knowledge of Indian tantric writings, and her book has gained contemporary status as an underground classic among American enthusiasts of tantric sexual practice, for whom she seems to represent a kind of early feminist sex guru.

53. Stockham, *Karezza,* 26, 27, 29.

54. Stockham, *Karezza,* 38, 39, 41, 43, 46.

55. Stockham, *Karezza,* 57, 62, 64–65, 66, 74.

56. Ida C. Craddock, *The Wedding Night,* 3d ed. (New York, 1902), 9, 8–9, 5. Besides her writings on sex, Craddock was also the author of *Primary Phonography: An Introduction to Isaac Pitman's System of Phonetic Shorthand; with a Series of Original Exercises* (Philadelphia, 1882; revised in 1884 and 1892). Craddock has escaped the notice of most historians; an essay that treats her life and work is Shirley J. Burton, "Obscene, Lewd, and Lascivious: Ida Craddock and the Criminally Obscene Women of Chicago, 1873–1913," *Michigan Historical Review* 19, no. 1 (Spring 1993): 1–16.

57. Craddock, cited in Burton, "Obscene, Lewd, and Lascivious," 1.

58. "Pantherapeutic" appeared in one of the journal's titles: the *Chicago Clinic and Pantherapeutic Journal* (originally the *Chicago Clinic and Pure Water Journal*).

59. Craddock, cited in Burton, "Obscene, Lewd, and Lascivious," 5.

60. Craddock, *Wedding Night,* 6, 5, 7, 11, 12, 13. Craddock's title-page moniker was "Pastor of the Church of Yoga."

61. Albert Chavannes, *Magnetation* (1898), 2, 8, 19, 24.

62. Albert Chavannes to Ida Craddock, August 27, 1899, collection 18, Ida Craddock collection, Morris Library, Southern Illinois University at Carbondale.

63. Craddock, *Wedding Night*, 24; Chavannes, *Magnetation*, 37, 40.

64. Ralph Waldo Trine, *In Tune with the Infinite* (1897), 16, 18.

65. Trine, *In Tune with the Infinite*, 121–22.

66. Trine, *In Tune with the Infinite*, 219.

67. Quoted in Thomas E. Witherspoon, *Myrtle Fillmore: Mother of Unity* (Unity Village, MO: Unity Books, 1977), 206, 212.

68. Charles Fillmore, "As to Meat Eating," *Unity* 14, no. 4 (October 1903): 195, 198–99.

69. Charles Fillmore, *Keep a True Lent* (1953), 140.

70. Quoted in Witherspoon, *Myrtle Fillmore*, 214. Hauser's book *Look Younger, Live Longer*, for instance, sold more than 450,000 hardcover copies in a short span of years; according to best-seller lists, it was the number three best-selling nonfiction book of 1950 and number one for 1951. Though some of Hauser's findings were excoriated by the Food and Drug Administration, he was one of the period's most popular food and diet writers.

71. *Letters of Myrtle Fillmore*, 87; Witherspoon, *Myrtle Fillmore*, 270; James Dillet Freeman, *The Household of Faith: The Story of Unity* (Lee's Summit, MO: Unity School of Christianity, 1951), 144, 132.

72. Most breatharian groups appear inspired by the Hindu saddhas or holy men who have supposedly lived without eating; examples from this genre include Viktoras Kulvinskas, *Survival into the 21st Century: Planetary Healers Manual* (Woodstock Valley, CT: Omangod Press, 1975); and Jasmuheen, *Living on Light: The Source of Nourishment for the New Millennium* (Burgrain, Germany: KOHA-Verlag, 1998). The Breatharian Institute of America is located in Carson City, Nevada, or online at www.breatharian.com/index.htm. Various other sources, including chat groups, are available on the Internet.

73. Satter, *Each Mind a Kingdom*, 326n52.

74. Elizabeth Towne, *Practical Methods* (1904), 47–48, 46.

75. Towne, *Practical Methods*, 113, 114–15, 113.

76. Towne, *Practical Methods*, 48, 49.

77. Towne, *Practical Methods*, 60, 76.

78. Alice M. Long, *My Lady Beautiful* (1908), 19–20, 126, 167, 156, 180; Towne, *Practical Methods*, 154. Another important writer in this vein was Susanna Cocroft, the New Thought author of books such as *Character as Expressed in the Body* (1912), and *Beauty a Duty* (1915).

79. Sydney B. Flower, *New Thought System of Physical Culture and Beauty Culture* (1921), 7, 10.

80. Flower, *Physical Culture*, 11, 12, 13.

81. Flower, *Physical Culture*, 46, 50, 51.

82. Flower, *Physical Culture*, 37, 43, 44.

83. Flower, *Physical Culture*, 84, 86.

84. Flower, *Physical Culture*, 86.
85. Sydney B. Flower, *New Thought System of Dietetics* (1921), 5, 7–8, 9–10.
86. David Van Bush, *What to Eat* (1922), 33.

3. MINDING THE BODY

1. Letter of July 29, 1907, quoted in Irving James Eales, *Healthology*, 87. Low's postfasting feats were also recorded by Elizabeth Towne, introduction to Wallace D. Wattles, *Health through New Thought and Fasting* (1907); and Hereward Carrington, *Vitality, Fasting, and Nutrition*, 382–83. See also James C. Whorton, *Crusaders for Fitness: The History of American Health Reformers* (Princeton: Princeton University Press, 1982), 268.

2. Billy Sunday, "Positive vs. Negative Religion," quoted in Margaret Lamberts Bendroth, *Fundamentalism and Gender, 1875 to the Present* (New Haven: Yale University Press, 1993), 24; Bruce Barton, *The Man Nobody Knows* (Indianapolis: Bobbs-Merrill, 1925); Upton Sinclair and Michael William, *Good Health and How we Won It* (1909), 11–12. The broader context of muscular Christianity during this era is detailed in Cliff Putney, *Muscular Christianity: Manhood and Sports in Protestant America, 1880–1920* (Cambridge, MA: Harvard University Press, 2001). On muscular interpretations of Jesus, see Stephen Prothero, *American Jesus: How the Son of God Became a National Icon* (New York: Farrar, Straus and Giroux, 2003); and Richard Wightman Fox, *Jesus in America: Personal Savior, Cultural Hero, National Obsession* (San Francisco: Harper San Francisco, 2004).

Those historians who have highlighted fasting in this period have been preoccupied with historicizing modern dietary obsessions that disproportionately afflict women and so have focused on a series of notorious cases of prolonged abstinence, concentrated among young women in nineteenth-century Britain and America, which later medical historians have interpreted as prefiguring contemporary eating disorders. See Joan Jacobs Brumberg, *Fasting Girls: The History of Anorexia Nervosa* (Cambridge, MA: Harvard University Press, 1988); these cases also earn extensive attention in Walter Vandereycken and Ron van Deth, *From Fasting Saints to Anorexic Girls: The History of Self-Starvation* (New York: New York University Press, 1994). Appropriations of this historical narrative saturate the clinical literature on this subject; for instance, Jules R. Bemporad, "Self-Starvation through the Ages: Reflections on the Pre-History of Anorexia Nervosa," *International Journal of Eating Disorders* 19 (April 1996): 217–37.

3. The sex ratio of this literature's readership, and that of ordinary practitioners, is much less clear. Charles Courtney Haskell printed over a hundred pages of letters and testimonies that he had allegedly received from converts to fasting. If his numbers are proportional, many more men than women were drawn to the gospel of fasting, although there was no shortage of women in his pages either (*Perfect Health* [1901], 106–209). The reception of these texts—

and of the practice of fasting more generally—is difficult to grasp, making pur-veyors much easier to analyze than consumers of the message.

4. Brumberg traces this history; see *Fasting Girls*, 101–25. She notes that up through the 1930s, American doctors used the terms "hysterical anorexia" and "anorexia nervosa" almost interchangeably (110).

5. Edward Hooker Dewey, *The True Science of Living* (1899), 242, 244, 306, 309, 241, 243. Alcott had similarly noted that Sunday dinners were "immoral, unchristian, and—to coin a term—unrepublican" (William Andrus Alcott, "Sunday Dinners," in *The Moral Reformer and Teacher on the Human Consti-tution* [1835], 1:23, cited in Robert H. Abzug, *Cosmos Crumbling: American Reform and the Religious Imagination* [New York: Oxford University Press, 1994], 171).

6. Dewey, *True Science of Living*, 213, 120.

7. Dewey, *True Science of Living*, 47, 52.

8. George Frederick Pentecost, introduction to *True Science of Living*, 4.

9. Haskell, *Perfect Health*, 12, 79, 32, 33, 34, 40.

10. Haskell, *Perfect Health*, 100. The biblical quote is from 1 Corinthians 9:27.

11. Bernarr Macfadden and Felix Oswald, *Fasting—Hydropathy—Exercise* (1900), 11. The struggle between nature and civilization was of enormous inter-est to Macfadden. His fascination with photographic images of "primitives" such as Africans and Asians is especially evident in the many revised editions of the *Encyclopedia of Health and Physical Culture*; as in 1925, see 5:1926–32.

12. Macfadden and Oswald, *Fasting—Hydropathy—Exercise*, 11, 12, 53. *Superb Virility of Manhood* was the title of Macfadden's later work (1904), but the concern for manhood was everywhere apparent in his writing.

13. Macfadden and Oswald, *Fasting—Hydrotherapy—Exercise*, 62, 64.

14. Macfadden, ed., *Encyclopedia*, 1:146.

15. Alice M. Long, *My Lady Beautiful* (1908), 89, 90, 87.

16. Linda Burfield Hazzard, *Fasting for the Cure of Disease* (1910), 45, 47. See also Julia Seton, *The Short Cut—Regeneration through Fasting* (1929). The series of events surrounding Hazzard's prison sentence is described in William R. Hunt, *Body Love: The Amazing Career of Bernarr Macfadden* (Bowling Green, OH: Bowling Green State University Popular Press, 1989), 61–63.

17. Eales, *Healthology*, 200.

18. Edward Earle Purinton, *The Philosophy of Fasting* (1906), 40.

19. Haskell, letters of May 15, 25, and 27, 1905, quoted in J. Austin Shaw, *The Best Thing in the World*, 94, 103, 105. The story of Mollie Fancher, the "Brooklyn Enigma," is recounted in Brumberg, *Fasting Girls*, 77–91. See also Hillel Schwartz, *Never Satisfied: A Cultural History of Diets, Fantasies, and Fat* (New York: Free Press, 1986), 115–19 and passim; Jane Shaw, "Religious Expe-rience and the Formation of the Early Enlightenment Self," in *Rewriting the Self: Histories from the Renaissance to the Present*, ed. Roy Porter (London: Routledge, 1997), 61–71. Charges of fraud accompanied most of these fasting

girls, whom critics presumed to be sneaking food for survival; such presumptions were occasionally proven and the girls discredited.

20. Wallace D. Wattles, *Health through New Thought and Fasting* (1907), 7, 8, 15–16, 55. The penultimate chapter is entitled "New Light on Immortality" (82–87).

21. Beryl Satter, *Each Mind a Kingdom: American Women, Sexual Purity, and the New Thought Movement, 1875–1920* (Berkeley: University of California Press, 1999), 13–18 and passim. Gail Bederman anticipated this argument in her discussion of the contest between the ideals of "manliness" and those of "masculinity" in the 1890s (Bederman, *Manliness and Civilization: A Cultural History of Gender and Race in the United States, 1880–1917* [Chicago: University of Chicago Press, 1995], esp. 18–20).

22. Seton, *Short Cut*, 14.

23. Edward Earle Purinton, *The Purinton Foundation Course in Personal Efficiency* (New York: Independent Corporation, 1918), lesson 7, part 2, 13–28.

24. Wattles quoted William James to point out that "disciples of asceticism can reach very high levels of freedom and power of will" (*Health*, 56), referring to James's 1907 essay, "The Energies of Man," originally the presidential address delivered to the American Philosophical Association reprinted in the *Philosophical Review* (January 1907) and, under the title "The Powers of Men," in the *American Magazine* (October 1907). In this essay James enthusiastically described the experience of a friend with "Hatha Yoga," in which, through fasting, breathing exercises, and "posture-gymnastics," the man seemed to have "succeeded in waking up deeper and deeper levels of will and moral and intellectual power in himself, and to have escaped from a decidedly menacing brain-condition of the 'circular' type, from which he had suffered for years." James even mentioned Edward Hooker Dewey's no-breakfast plan and the fasting disciples using this "ascetic idea" who achieved success. The *American Magazine* version of James's essay is reprinted in John J. McDermott, ed., *The Writings of William James: A Comprehensive Edition* (Chicago: University of Chicago Press, 1977), 679, 680.

25. Robert Baille Pearson, *Fasting and Man's Correct Diet* (1921), 16, 18.

26. Pearson, *Fasting*, 44, 45, 47. In the second quote, Pearson directly quotes Horace Fletcher, *The A.B.–Z. of Our Own Nutrition*, 11. James C. Whorton recounts the modern history of excremental obsessions in *Inner Hygiene: Constipation and the Pursuit of Health in Modern Society* (New York: Oxford University Press, 2000).

27. Quoted in "Sewers and Wastewater Treatment," in *History of Public Works in the United States, 1776–1976*, ed. Ellis L. Armstrong (Chicago: American Public Works Association, 1976), 401.

28. Alain Corbin, *The Foul and the Fragrant: Odor and the French Social Imagination*, trans. Miriam L. Kochan (Cambridge, MA: Harvard University Press, 1986); Peter Stallybrass and Allon White, *The Politics and Poetics of Transgression* (Ithaca: Cornell University Press, 1986), esp. 139–40. See also Mary Douglas, *Purity and Danger: An Analysis of Concepts of Pollution and*

Taboo (London: Routledge and Kegan Paul, 1966). T. J. Jackson Lears has noted the early twentieth-century obsession with odor, attributing it to "the coming of an urban society and the increase in person-to-person contact" (Lears, *Fables of Abundance: A Cultural History of Advertising in America* [New York: Basic Books, 1994], 171).

29. Hereward Carrington, *Vitality, Fasting, and Nutrition* (1908), 60. A mesmerizing, if cheeky, treatment of these entwined impulses of fascination and repulsion toward human waste is Dan Sabbath and Mandel Hall, *End Product: The First Taboo* (New York: Urizen Books, 1977).

30. A. B. Jamison, *Intestinal Ills* (1901), 36–37, quoted in Carrington, *Vitality, Fasting, and Nutrition,* 407.

31. Carrington, *Vitality,* 407, 63.

32. Macfadden, *Encyclopedia,* 5:1929–30.

33. Macfadden, *Encyclopedia,* 1:401. On the various discourses of race and eugenic theory popular during this period, see Matthew Frye Jacobson, *Whiteness of a Different Color: European Immigrants and the Alchemy of Race* (Cambridge, MA: Harvard University Press, 1998), esp. 75–90.

34. William S. Sadler, *Race Decadence: An Examination of the Causes of Racial Degeneracy in the United States* (Chicago: A. C. McClurg, 1922), 404–8, 205; Sadler's dietary plan is summarized on 186–88.

35. See Bederman, *Manliness and Civilization,* esp. 16–20.

36. Very little work has been done on Sheldon, most of it by historians of science and medicine who interpret him as a quack figure singlehandedly responsible for destroying the mid-twentieth-century promise of holistic medicine. See, for instance, Sarah W. Tracy, "An Evolving Science of Man: The Transformation and Demise of American Constitutional Medicine, 1920–1950," in *Greater Than the Parts: Holism in Biomedicine, 1920–1950,* ed. Christopher Lawrence and George Weisz (New York: Oxford University Press, 1998), 161–88; Tracy has also written Sheldon's entry for the *American National Biography,* which contains a useful albeit partial bibliography. The art historian George L. Hersey usefully contextualizes Sheldon in the Euro-American traditions of physiognomy and physical anthropology; see Hersey, *The Evolution of Allure: Sexual Selection From the Medici Venus to the Incredible Hulk* (Cambridge, MA: MIT Press, 1996), 90–100. While finishing this manuscript, I also discovered Patricia Vertinsky, "Embodying Normalcy: Anthropometry and the Long Arm of William H. Sheldon's Somatyping Project," *Journal of Sport History* 29, 1 (spring 2002): 95–133. The most thoroughly researched source on Sheldon, where he is interpreted as an American cultural modernist, is Stephen H. Gatlin, "William H. Sheldon and the Culture of the Somatotype" (PhD diss., Virginia Polytechnic Institute and State University, 1997).

37. William Herbert Sheldon, *The Varieties of Human Physique* (1940), xi.

38. William Herbert Sheldon, *Prometheus Revisited* (1975), 248 and passim.

39. Earnest A. Hooton, *The American Criminal: An Anthropological Study* (Cambridge, MA: Harvard University Press, 1939), 309; William H. Sheldon, Emil M. Hartl, and Eugene McDermott, *Varieties of Delinquent Youth,* dedica-

tion page; both works are cited in Nicole Hahn Rafter, *Creating Born Criminals* (Urbana: University of Illinois Press, 1997), 211. Gatlin, "William H. Sheldon," 6, 7, 91, 7.

40. David Yosifon and Peter N. Stearns, "The Rise and Fall of American Posture," *American Historical Review* 103, no. 4 (October 1998): 1057–95; see also Ron Rosenbaum, "The Great Ivy League Nude Posture Photo Scandal," *New York Times Sunday Magazine*, January 15, 1995.

41. Sheldon, *Varieties of Human Physique*, 12; Rosenbaum, "Photo Scandal." Two follow-up stories tell later chapters in this story: "Nude Photos Are Sealed At Smithsonian," *New York Times*, January 21, 1995, 11; and "Nude Photos of Yale Graduates Are Shredded," *New York Times*, January 29, 1995, 16.

42. Sheldon et al., *Varieties of Delinquent Youth*, 2:687, 600, 569.

43. Heath and J. E. Lindsay Carter, *Somatotyping—Development and Applications* (Cambridge: Cambridge University Press, 1990), 3–15; Gatlin, "William H. Sheldon."

44. Tracy, "Transformation and Demise," 187n58; *Cosmopolitan* published quizzes about how to understand your husband on the basis of somatotype, mentioned in Rosenbaum, "Photo Scandal."

45. Gatlin, "William H. Sheldon," 209, 214; see Sheldon et al., *Varieties of Delinquent Youth*, 2:513, 435. That book is filled with racialized and sexualized descriptions of delinquent men such as, "He has a paranoid Irish eye in a massive Jewish face" (565), or "throws like a girl" (617), as well as with reports of alcoholic fathers and promiscuous (or occasionally "mannish") mothers (654).

46. Rosenbaum, "Photo Scandal."

47. Sheldon, *Psychology and the Promethean Will* (1936), 60, 47.

48. Letter from Aldous to Julian Huxley (1937), in Grover Smith, ed., *Letters of Aldous Huxley* (London: Chatto and Windus, 1969), 428, cited in Gatlin, "William H. Sheldon," 13. Letter from Huxley to Grace Hubble (1944), in Smith, *Letters*, 505, cited in Gatlin, "William H. Sheldon," 14.

49. Sheldon, *Psychology and the Promethean Will*, 201, 202, 203, 204, 205. Sheldon emphasized, "*Under no circumstances should a human child ever be born in a city, or allowed to spend any of the growing years within reach of the urban influence.* This handicap is too much for any mind to overcome, and I do not understand how those individuals who had to spend their earliest conscious years near the environs of massed population, ever succeed in living at all, beyond the period of sexual interest" (205).

50. Sheldon, *Psychology and the Promethean Will*, 63–64, 66.

51. Sheldon, *Varieties of Human Physique*, 192, 191; Sheldon, *Varieties of Temperament*, 33.

52. For titles, see various issues of *New Day:* December 16, 1937, 4 (this headline is repeated elsewhere); January 20, 1938, 27; January 6, 1938, 22; May 19, 1938, 19; October 19, 1939, 106; and June 22, 1939, 27. Unless otherwise stated, documents cited here and throughout this chapter are original Peace Mission movement periodicals, available on microfilm at the Schomberg Center for Research in Black Culture in New York. The Peace Mission has also repub-

lished a lot of its historical material on the Internet, and, as noted, I have occasionally used Web sources as well.

53. The two most useful scholarly monographs on Father Divine are Jill Watts, *God, Harlem U.S.A.: The Father Divine Story* (Berkeley: University of California Press, 1992), and Robert Weisbrot, *Father Divine and the Struggle for Racial Equality* (Urbana: University of Illinois Press, 1983). A somewhat dated but still useful source is Kenneth E. Burnham, *God Comes to America: Father Divine and the Peace Mission Movement* (Boston: Lambeth Press, 1979).

54. Watts, *God, Harlem*, 142; Weisbrot, *Father Divine*, 69. Watts bases her estimate on circulation of the *Spoken Word*, while Weisbrot includes in his greater number those thousands who attended Divine's communion banquets, defended him against his accusers, or simply admired his work on racial equality.

55. Mother Divine led the group into the twenty-first century at Woodmont, where a place is always set for Father Divine at the festive table. The Peace Mission movement maintained a Web site, www.libertynet.org/fdipmm. Leonard Primiano has extensively studied the contemporary movement and is working on a documentary film.

56. This term is from Arthur Huff Fauset's book, *Black Gods of the Metropolis: Negro Religious Cults of the Urban North* (Philadelphia: University of Pennsylvania Press, 1944).

57. On this point, see Judith Weisenfeld, "We Have Been Believers: Patterns of African-American Women's Religiosity," in *This Far By Faith: Readings in African-American Women's Religious Biography*, ed. Judith Weisenfeld and Richard Newman (New York: Routledge, 1996), 9–10. The most complete attempt to trace Father Divine's relationship to New Thought is Ronald Moran White, "New Thought Influences on Father Divine" (master's thesis, Miami University, Oxford, Ohio, 1980); I am grateful to Catherine Albanese for this citation and to Peter W. Williams for making this valuable manuscript available to me. White's findings have also influenced the account of Father Divine in Catherine L. Albanese, *America: Religions and Religion*, 3d ed. (Belmont, CA: Wadsworth Publishing, 1999), 207–8. Watts extends this investigation briefly in *God, Harlem*, esp. 21–25; while Beryl Satter has further discussed the influence of New Thought upon Divine as well as on Marcus Garvey in Satter, "Marcus Garvey, Father Divine and the Gender Politics of Race Difference and Race Neutrality," *American Quarterly* 48, no.1 (1996): 43–76. Also, as Satter's endnotes indicate, Robert A. Hill, director of the Marcus Garvey and Universal Negro Improvement Association papers project at the University of California, Los Angeles, has frequently noted the influence of New Thought on Garvey; see Robert A. Hill and Barbara Bair, eds., *Marcus Garvey: Life and Lessons* (Berkeley: University of California Press, 1987), 7, 149, 275; personal correspondence with Hill, November 9, 1999.

58. Satter reads Father Divine (erroneously, in my view) as having denied the body, because of his emphasis on celibacy. In her words, "Divine's answer to segregation and racism was to deny the body altogether—both the racialized

and the sexualized body. . . . It was Divine's firm belief that the human body had been transcended that enabled Divine's followers to battle segregation and to live in racially integrated groups; black and white together was the ultimate symbol that the human body itself no longer reigned" (Satter, "Marcus Garvey, Father Divine," 55). This chapter claims that the concrete reality of the human body was, rather, crucial for Divine and his followers.

59. Watts, *God, Harlem*, 190n24. Here Watts disagrees with White's argument, in "New Thought Influences on Father Divine," that Divine's teachings were most heavily influenced by the New Thought writers Robert Collier and Baird Spalding.

60. Fillmore, *Keep a True Lent*, 22, 19, 20. This posthumous collection of Fillmore's writings compiled *Unity* articles and excerpts from other books by Fillmore published years earlier.

61. Message delivered June 26, 1942; republished online, "I Have Established the Perfection of a Feast for the Children of Men," www.libertynet.org/fdipmm/worddrtv/42062617.html, 3.

62. Earl Wilson, "Hahn'tchuglad?" *Negro Digest* 2, no. 5 (March 1944): 61–63; condensed from the *New York Post*, January 3, 1944. See also Sid Hantman, "No Food Shortage for 'God,'" *Negro Digest* 4, no.12 (October 1946): 25–26; and the somewhat less hostile article by Edwin A. Lahey, "Peace! It's Still Wonderful," *Negro Digest* 2, no. 7 (May 1944): 27–30. About the gentlest description of the movement was Gunnar Myrdal's report of "this bizarre sect" in Myrdal, *An American Dilemma: The Negro Problem and Modern Democracy* (New York: Harper and Brothers, 1944), 871n; see the report commissioned by Myrdal and authored by Guion G. Johnson and Guy B. Johnson, "The Church and the Race Problem in the United States," in *Carnegie-Myrdal Study of the Negro in America Research Memoranda Collection, 1935–1948*, Schomberg Center microfilm reels (roll 7), especially appendices C and D on Father Divine's movement.

63. Charles Samuel Braden, *These Also Believe: A Study of Modern American Cults and Minority Religious Movements* (New York: Macmillan, 1956), 45, 28.

64. *New Day*, October 26, 1939, 86.

65. Quoted in Burnham, *God Comes to America*, 133.

66. Message from August 11, 1936, printed in *New Day* August 27, 1936, 3.

67. Message from August 2, 1936, printed in *New Day* August 13, 1936, 3.

68. *New Day*, November 23, 1939, 24; see also 48.

69. Message from October 20, 1937, printed in *New Day* October 28, 1937, 25.

70. No evidence ever emerged to support the latter claim. Even Sara Harris, who seemed obsessed with Divine's sex appeal and the public displays of orgasmic ecstasy he could generate simply by glancing at one of his female followers, admitted that the notion of Divine carrying on in secret with his harem of virgins (including his own wife) was virtually unimaginable (Sara Harris, with the assistance of Harriet Crittenden, *Father Divine: Holy Husband* [Garden City, NY: Doubleday, 1953]).

71. Hadley's report was printed in the *Suffolk County News,* April 25, 1930, 1, 7 (quotes) and is also cited in Watts, *God, Harlem,* 64–68.

72. Watts, *God, Harlem,* 2.

73. The *Montgomery County Sentinel,* recounting Nancy Baker's death in 1897, called her "without a doubt the largest woman in the county, if not the state" (May 28, 1897, 3, cited in Watts, *God, Harlem,* 12).

74. Horace Cayton and St. Clair Drake described her as "elderly, corpulent, dark-skinned and maternal," writing that she was "the mother image of the drifting black masses" (Cayton and Drake, *Black Metropolis: A Study of Negro Life in a Northern City* [New York: Harcourt Brace, 1945], 643, quoted in Wallace Best, "'The Spirit of the Holy Ghost Is a Male Spirit': African-American Preaching Women and the Paradox of Gender Normativity" (paper presented at Women and Religion in the African Diaspora conference, April 25, 2004), 22.

75. Notably, Divine's second wife, whom he married in 1946 (Peninniah died in 1943), was thin. Half a century later, as she presided over the Peace Mission movement from the Woodmont estate in Gladwyne, Pennsylvania, Mother Divine was reported to live a health-conscious life, exercising and presiding over a very different menu than that of her husband years before. According to Watts, the communion banquet offerings centered on "natural foods, poultry, vegetables, and tofu," which "reflected her concern with health and nutrition" (Watts, *God, Harlem,* 177).

76. *New Day,* June 29, 1939, 42; *New Day,* October 26, 1939, 45.

77. *New Day,* November 23, 1939, 56; and December 30, 1937, 8.

78. Message delivered June 1, 1941; republished online, "The Festive Board that Extends around the World," www.libertynet.org/fdipmm/wrddrtv2/621117ar .html, 8, 9.

79. *New Day,* August 3, 1939, 60; and October 19, 1939, 106.

80. *New Day,* August 3, 1939, 60.

81. *New Day,* November 30, 1939, 29.

82. *New Day,* November 30, 1939, 43; see also the issue of October 6, 1945, 8 (cited in Braden, *These Also Believe,* 64–65); July 14, 1938, 20; and July 14, 1938, 20.

83. *New Day,* July 14, 1938, 40, 41.

84. See *New Day,* July 20, 1939, 67–69.

85. *New Day,* August 10, 1939, 55.

86. Cited in Watts, *God, Harlem,* 12.

87. Cited in Watts, *God, Harlem,* 168.

88. Song cited in Braden, *These Also Believe,* 19–20.

89. Elijah Muhammad, *How to Eat to Live,* book no. 2 (Chicago: Muhammad's Temple of Islam no. 2, 1972), 7, 11, 14, 39. "Before the white man was made," he wrote, "the Black man was known to live approximately a thousand years. He ate the right food and ate it at the right time" (17).

90. Muhammad, *How to Eat to Live,* 41, 42.

91. Farrakhan cited in Doris Witt, *Black Hunger: Food and the Politics of U.S. Identity* (New York: Oxford University Press, 1999), 113; Louis Farrakhan,

"Exercise to Stay Alive! The War Against Obesity (Fat), Part Three," *The Final Call*, August 19, 1991, 28.

92. Muhammad, *How to Eat to Live*, 93.

93. Witt, *Black Hunger*, 113. Witt's analysis of the comedian-turned-natural foods activist Dick Gregory, who was similarly obsessed with bodily purification and fasting while yet writing in a different vein, is also instructive (126–51).

94. Muhammad, *How to Eat to Live*, 81.

95. Jawanza Kunjufu, *Satan, I'm Taking Back My Health!* (2000), 1, 4.

4. PRAY THE WEIGHT AWAY

1. Hillel Schwartz, *Never Satisfied: A Cultural History of Diets, Fantasies, and Fat* (New York: Free Press, 1986), 308–10; Mary Louise Bringle, *The God of Thinness: Gluttony and Other Weighty Matters* (Nashville: Abingdon Press, 1972), 13–14, 116–17, 119, and passim; Michelle Mary Lelwica, *Starving for Salvation: The Spiritual Dimensions of Eating Problems among American Girls and Women* (New York: Oxford University Press, 1999), 75–77.

2. On postwar American Catholic patterns of devotionalism, see Robert A. Orsi, *Thank You, St. Jude: Women's Devotion to the Patron Saint of Hopeless Causes* (New Haven: Yale University Press, 1996).

3. Deborah Pierce, *I Prayed Myself Slim* (1960), 13.

4. Pierce, *I Prayed Myself Slim*, 109, 108.

5. Charlie Shedd, *Pray Your Weight Away* (1957), 11–12, 14, 12.

6. William R. Mueller, "Of Obesity and Election," *Christian Century*, November 26, 1958, 1366–68.

7. Gerald Weales, "A Family that Prays Together Weighs Together," *New Republic*, March 25, 1957, 19–20.

8. James C. Whorton, *Inner Hygiene: Constipation and the Pursuit of Health in Modern Society* (New York: Oxford University Press, 2000), 242–44. Whorton rightly notes that "the theory of self-poisoning from the gut did continue to thrive in the world of alternative medicine and holistic health. 'Detoxification' of the body through the use of herbal laxatives, colonic irrigations, and other 'natural' remedies was, in fact, embraced by the New Age counterculture of the last third of the century as the cornerstone of physical purity" (244).

9. J. Carter Swaim, "Temperance or Self-Control?" *Religion and Health* 6, no. 2 (March 1957): 32–36. On the postwar rise in weight consciousness, see Schwartz, *Never Satisfied*. Elizabeth Sharon Hayenga has meticulously studied popular diet literature between 1940 and 1987, in "Dieting through the Decades: A Comparative Study of Weight Reduction in America as Depicted in Popular Literature and Books from 1940 to the late 1980s" (PhD diss., University of Minnesota, 1988). As Hayenga argues, "Prior to the forties, excess weight was generally attributed to organic failure—usually the thyroid. The newly articulated and widely publicized causal relationship between eating and fat legitimized dieting as the accepted way of controlling weight and set the stage for widespread dieting in America. What followed were decades of exponential

growth in all aspect[s] of the 'diet' business and an escalating cultural obsession with being thin" (2).

10. Shedd, *Pray Your Weight Away*, 12.

11. Pierce, *I Prayed Myself Slim*, 101, 107.

12. Shedd, *Pray Your Weight Away*, 42–48, 14, 15, 40.

13. Pierce, *I Prayed Myself Slim*, 112.

14. Shedd, *Pray Your Weight Away*, 16, 18. The Charlie Shedd Institute of Clinical Theology, based at the Psychological Studies institute in Atlanta, Georgia, proudly notes one of Shedd's major accomplishments as "being the originator of the 'Christian' weight-loss movement" (www.psi-atl.edu/frm_ict_main.htm [accessed 4 Jan 2001]). I thank Shedd for our interview on this subject and for his permission to reprint these early "before and after" photographs. In 2003 he published his forty-first book, *I'm Odd, Thank You God*.

15. LaLanne quoted in Schwartz, *Never Satisfied*, 233; and Bringle, *God of Thinness*, 99.

16. Shedd, *Pray Your Weight Away*, 19.

17. Shedd, *Pray Your Weight Away*, 90, 40.

18. Shedd interview, January 12, 2001.

19. H. Victor Kane, *Devotions for Dieters* (1967), 7, 21–22, 17.

20. Kane, *Devotions for Dieters*, 16–17.

21. Kane, *Devotions for Dieters*, 39; Frances G. Hunter, *God's Answer to Fat* (1975), 100; Betty Lougaris Soldo and Mary Drahos, *The Inside-Out Beauty Book* (1978), 39; see also Roger F. Campbell, *Weight!* ([1976] 1999), 45–47.

22. Shedd, *Letters to Karen: On Keeping Love in Marriage* (Nashville: Abingdon Press, 1965); *Letters to Philip: On How to Treat a Woman* (New York: Doubleday, 1968); *The Fat Is in Your Head*. Information on *Fat Is in Your Head* comes from the official publication of the Christian Booksellers Association, *Bookstore Journal* 8, no. 8 (October 1975): 80; and 9, no. 2 (February 1976): 127. In another issue, Shedd's book was noted to have twice been the third best-selling book on the National Religious Bestsellers list: in 1973 and 1975 (*Bookstore Journal* 8, no. 1 [January 1975]: 98).

23. Sales figures obtained from *Bookstore Journal* 12, no. 2 (February 1979): 22. Previous issues of *Bookstore Journal* (from July to December 1978) list Lovett's book on the National Religious Bestsellers paperback list.

24. A list of books appeared in *Booksellers Journal* 9, no. 7 (July–August 1976): 132. Sales figures from *Bookstore Journal* 12, no. 2 (February 1979): 22; and from Neva Coyle. Beginning in 1982, Chistians could also purchase the "Funtastic Fitness Game," a conventional board game with "non-threatening insights" such as "Smile, God loves YOU! ADVANCE TO YOUR SCALES!" (Kirkland, WA: Marlan Products, 1982).

25. Pierce, *I Prayed Myself Slim*, 124–27. Laura Fraser analyzes a variety of programs and diet companies in *Losing It: America's Obsession with Weight and the Industry That Feeds on It* (New York: E. P. Dutton, 1997) and lists their founding dates on 155.

26. Ron Enroth, "All Isn't Well in a Popular Christian Diet Program," *Chris-*

tianity Today, April 9, 1982, 54–58. Enroth was particularly concerned about 3D's connection with the Community of Jesus, which he believed to be a cult.

27. Interview with Julie Morris, August 16, 2002.

28. Interview with Margie Hesson, February 13, 2003. From "Body and Soul Program Guide—Getting Started" (Nashville: Abingdon Press, 1995), 1. This guide, and other Body and Soul materials, recognize that many facilitators and participants will want foremost to lose weight; the guide assures them, "If you are overweight now you probably *will* lose weight." To participants, leaders should "*Stress that the first ten weeks is a basic introduction to healthful, disciplined living. Once we have learned these basics, the following weeks will have a stronger emphasis on weight loss, although the primary purpose is still to learn good habits that will last a lifetime.*" The participants' materials, in fact, focus tremendous attention on weight loss and include various fat gram counters, food diaries, and the like.

29. The story of First Place's founding is recounted in Carole Lewis, *Choosing to Change* (1996), 7–17; testimonial quote on 89. Interview with First Place participants, August 12, 2002.

30. *Good Housekeeping,* February 1998, 26; Rebecca Mead, "Slim for Him," *New Yorker,* January 15, 2001, 48–56. Shamblin cited in Christine Arpe Gang, "God and Waistline: Church Diets Feed the Soul, Trim the Fat," *Commercial Appeal* (Memphis), October 18, 1994, 1C. The earliest newspaper article I found on the Weigh Down diet is Gang's piece in the *Commercial Appeal* (January 30, 1991), where she described Weigh Down as a business, with no religious orientation mentioned. A second mention of Shamblin, from the *Commercial Appeal* in April 1991, likewise made no mention of religion. Few newspaper sources appeared again until 1994, when Shamblin's religious message was quite apparent (www.lexis-nexis.com [accessed 26 Apr 2001]). Statistics obtained from the official Weigh Down Web site, www.weighdown.com/home.htm (accessed 11 Jan 2001). Statistics from Gang, "God and Waistline."

31. Shamblin's clothes size appeared on Weigh Down's Web site under the question "Who is Gwen Shamblin?", www.wdworkshop.com/wdw/wdwfaq .asp#Q1 (accessed 22 Jan 2001). Shamblin quoted in Mary Lou Aguirre, "Dieters, the Lord Can Help," *Fresno Bee,* August 16, 1994, D1. Hazzard, *Fasting for the Cure of Disease,* 3.

32. George H. Malkmus, with Michael Dye, *God's Way to Ultimate Health* (1995), 30. Besides Malkmus, these include Baker, Dorian, Swope, Russell, and Kunjufu. All but Russell advocate a completely vegetarian diet. Don Colbert, a physician trained at Oral Roberts University School of Medicine, also authored *Toxic Relief,* a book on fasting.

33. http://www.faithfullyfit.com/Merchant2/merchant.mvc?Screen=CTGY &Store_Code=CAR&Category_Code=V.

34. Obtained from First Place Web site, www.firstplace.org/NEWLAYOUT/ HTML/FAQ.htm#Are there statistics showing how much weight your members have lost?? (accessed 23 Jan 2001). Obtained from Weigh Down Workshop Web site, www.wdworkshop.com/wdw/wdwfaq.asp#Q9 (accessed 23 Jan 2001).

Incidentally, a Christian researcher has attempted to compare these plans on both practical and religious grounds; see Maria C. Appelzoller, "A Critical Assessment of Christian Diet Plans, Related Literature, and Biblical References" (PhD diss., Trinity Theological Seminary, 2003).

35. Dan R. Dick, *Devotions for Dieters* (1989), 1; Mab Graff Hoover, *God Even Likes My Pantry* (1983), 9, 62; Hunter, *God's Answer to Fat,* 22.

36. Hoover, *God Even Likes My Pantry,* 96; Marie Chapian and Neva Coyle, *Free to Be Thin* (1979), 21.

37. Haydn Gilmore, *Jog for Your Life* (1974), 149.

38. T. D. Jakes, *Lay Aside the Weight* (1997), 27.

39. Kenneth F. Ferraro, "Firm Believers? Religion, Body Weight, and Well-Being," *Review of Religious Research* 39, no. 3 (March 1998): 238.

40. Shirley Cook, *Diary of a FAT Housewife* (1977), 15.

41. Shamblin, *Rise Above,* 130. E-mail from Shamblin to the Weigh Down Workshop weekly e-mail list, "September 11th, TRAGEDY . . . a wake-up call!" (sent 11 September 2001, 9:05 PM).

42. Patricia B. Kreml, *Slim for Him* (1978), 4, 117, 134–35.

43. Schwartz, *Never Satisfied,* 313.

44. Sales statistics from Ray Walters, "Paperback Talk," *New York Times Book Reviews,* April 6, 1980, 27. Hal Lindsey, with C. C. Carlson, *The Late Great Planet Earth* (1970; New York, Zondervan Publishing House, 1977), 130. Likewise, another author wrote, "The coming resurrection reveals divine regard for our bodies. Christ was resurrected bodily from the grave, just as we shall be at His coming. When that day arrives our bodies will be perfect without the aid of diets or doctors. Till then, count calories" (Campbell, *Weight!* 14).

45. Dee Brestin and Peggy Johnston, *The Joy of Eating Right* (1993), 17. For charts and graphs, see 104–11.

46. Pamela Snyder, *A Life Styled by God* (1985), back cover. Pamela M. Smith, *Food for Life* (1997), 224.

47. Smith, *Food for Life,* 224, 188, 205, 212, 176.

48. David L. Meinz, *Eating by the Book* (1999), xiii, 4, 42, 235. The runners-at-sunrise photo is remarkably similar to a photograph on the dust jacket of Kenneth Cooper's *Faith-Based Fitness* (1995), also published by Thomas Nelson.

49. Smith, *Food for Life,* 224, 210, 213.

50. Interview with Rebecca, February 21, 2003.

51. Interview with Anna, August 16, 2002.

52. Interview with Rita, August 15, 2002. Interview with Joe, August 21, 2002. Interview with Angela, August 22, 2001.

53. Interview with Tish, February 18, 2003.

54. Quotations are from group interview with First Place participants, August 12, 2002.

55. E-mail correspondence with Andrea, February 13, 2003.

56. Like Malkmus's Hallelujah diet, Scott's plan relies on Genesis 1:29.

57. John A. Widtsoe and Leah D. Widtsoe, *The Word of Wisdom* (1937), 20, 235–36; the authors summarize this code of health on 246–50.

58. Earl F. Updike, *The Mormon Diet* (1991), 14–15, 17; Chris Rucker, *Seventh-Day Diet* (2002 ed.), 225; Ethel C. Updike, Dorothy E. Smith, and Earl F. Updike, *The Mormon Diet Cookbook* (1992), 23–24. Heinerman's treatise is also relevant (see bibliography).

59. Colleen Bernhard, *He Did Deliver Me from Bondage* (1994), ii. Colleen H. (Heart t' Heart discussion group on Food Addiction, www.heart-t-heart.org/forum/display_message.asp?mid = 65 [accessed 3 Mar 2002]). In this same posting, Harrison sounds a lot like Shamblin in her idea that repentance for sin is not enough but that dieters must strive to move beyond sin altogether: "To have NO MORE DISPOSITION TO EAT THAT STUFF—whatever it is. (For me it's excess food in general and especially and particularly junk-carbs.) I have not more disposition to do that 'evil' in my life. My desires have been changed, as if someone has gone into my neuro-pathways and brain chemistry and flipped a switch." See www.heart-t-heart.org.

60. Heart t' Heart discussion group on food addiction, www.heart-t-heart .org/forum/display_forum.asp (April 2002).

61. E-mail correspondence with Lynn, February 12, 2003.

62. Interview with Jill, February 24, 2003.

63. In my extensive search to locate such a book, I sent this e-mail message to a prominent Catholic bookseller on the Internet: "I would be interested to learn of any diet, nutrition, fitness, or weight loss books you know of that are written from a Catholic perspective. Can you help me?" He responded tersely: "None. Maybe u are the one who could write the books but u would probably not sell more than 1 copy and u would be the buyer. No market for such a book" (e-mail from John R. Walsh, www.Catholicbook.com, 18 January 2001). Orsi notes the publication, sometime around 1940, of a Franciscan-authored pamphlet on diet, "Easy Exercise Routine Re-Makes Your Figure" (*Thank You, St. Jude*, 15).

64. William Pauley, as told to Jack Houston, "Mister Before and After," *Power Life*, April 23, 1967, 4–6.

65. Interview with Alicia, February 25, 2003.

66. Regnum Christi is an association supported by the Vatican that promotes vocations within the church; it includes men and women and is affiliated with the priestly order, the Legion of Christ. These conservative groups are controversial among Catholics and are banned in some U.S. dioceses. Alicia's depiction of her attempted recruitment is anecdotal, and I have not attempted to research the group further.

67. When one fitness expert devised a workout for Catholic nuns in New York, the response was so enthusiastic that she turned the workout into a book, *Changing Habits: The Sisters' Workout*. Aimed at older nuns, overburdened and unable to retire because so few younger women were becoming sisters, this workout appealed because of its emphasis on stress reduction and health, not thinness and beauty (Larry Fine, "Nuns Told to Shape Up," Reuters, April 30, 2003, http://story.news.yahoo.com/news?tmpl = story&cid = 856&ncid = 856&e = 2&u = /nm/20030501/od_uk_nm/oukoe_life_nuns [accessed 2 May 2003]).

68. See www.lightweigh.com/story.htm. The church bulletin ad is from

the All Saints Catholic Newman Center at Arizona State University, www
.newman-asu.org.

69. Interview with Suzanne Fowler, March 11, 2003.

70. Moshe Goldberger, *Watching Your Weight—the Torah Way: A Diet
That Will Change Your Life!* (Staten Island, NY, 1989), 5, 9, 12, 21.

71. *Shvitz! My Yiddisheh Workout*, Workmen's Circle, 45 East 33rd Street,
New York, NY 10016; *Rise Like a Lion*, vol. 1: *Daily Exercises for Health and
Well-Being* (Smiloo Productions, 2001).

72. Interview with Debra, February 28, 2003.

73. In order, the texts I mention are Ronna Kabatznick, *The Zen of Eating:
Ancient Answers to Modern Weight Problems* (New York: Berkley Publishing
Group, 1998); Donald Altman, *Art of the Inner Meal: Eating as a Spiritual Path*
(San Francisco: HarperSan Francisco, 1999); Kareen Zebroff, *Beauty through
Yoga: Slim and Trim in 14 Days* (Seattle: Gordon Soules Book Publishers, 1989);
and the last, with its ad copy, is *The Yoga Mini Book for Weight Loss and Fitness*,
www.dwellinpossibility.com/yogminbookfo2.html.

74. Jere Longman, "A Running Club Is 100 Miles Outside of the Mainstream," *New York Times*, July 28, 1997, A1; Tizer's claim about sleep is on C7.
Another piece on the topic is Michael Finkel, "Running Like Hell," *Women's
Sports and Fitness*, November–December 1999. Interview with Julie, March 3,
2003.

75. Interview with Gauri, March 7, 2003.

76. Debbie Johnson, *Think Yourself Thin: The Visualization Technique That
Will Make You Lose Weight without Diet or Exercise* (New York: Hyperion,
1996); Richard and Mary-Alice Jafolla, *Nourishing the Life Force* (Unity Village,
MO: Unity Books, 1983), 68. Norris J. Chumley, *The Joy of Weight Loss* (2001);
Bob Greene and Oprah Winfrey, *Make the Connection: Ten Steps to a Better
Body and a Better Life* (New York: Hyperion, 1996); Colleen Zuck, Elaine
Meyer, and Jamie Wright, *Daily Word for Weight Loss* (2002).

77. *Christian Science Sentinel*, September 8, 1997. The cover reads, "Tired of
diets? Read how people normalized their weight without dieting," and the opening editorial notes that the authors in this special issue "offer some perspective
that permanently transformed how they were thinking about their bodies. And
that resulted in a change in weight" (3). In an article titled "How Changing My
Thoughts Led to a Change in My Weight," Judith H. Hedrick summarizes,
"Through prayer, by minding the things of Spirit (rather than the flesh), and
through temperance, I let go of the habits of daydreaming about food, craving
chocolate, and overeating and gained the spiritual understanding that brings satisfaction and peace. I felt the comfort we can all find in Christian Science. It
wasn't too long before I noticed my clothes were fitting again" (12). See also
David M. Wilson, "Overeating Can Be Checked," *Christian Science Sentinel*,
June 11, 1984, 1003–5.

78. Chapian and Coyle, *Free to Be Thin*, 17; Jan Christiansen, *More of Him, Less of Me* (1998), ix. Shamblin also used this formulation.

5. "DON'T EAT THAT"

1. Chapian and Coyle, *Free to Be Thin*, 27.

2. Pierce, *I Prayed Myself Slim*, 19. Chapian and Coyle, *Free to Be Thin*, 21, 31, 33.

3. Chapian and Coyle, *Free to Be Thin*, 107, 109, 115.

4. Chapian and Coyle, *Free to Be Thin*, 60, 64. This story comes from the first chapter of the Book of Daniel in the Hebrew Bible. Campbell's *Weight!* also mentioned Daniel's vegetarian diet, noting from scripture that, after eating this way for ten days Daniel and his friends were "fairer and fatter in flesh" than the others; Campbell then qualifies, "While at this time, 'fat flesh' is anything but our goal, the principle stands" (21). Other uses of this story include Edward Dumke, *The Serpent Beguiled Me*, chap. 6 (see esp. 72); Hunter, *God's Answer to Fat*, esp. 46–53; and Kane, *Devotions for Dieters*, 40–41.

5. Hoover, *God Even Likes My Pantry*, 20.

6. Hoover, *God Even Likes My Pantry*, 56.

7. Hoover, *God Even Likes My Pantry*, 24, 29–30, 26, 110. Shedd had depicted Paul in a rather different light: "The Bible is never explicit about Paul's 'thorn in the flesh.' Some scholars say it was epilepsy. . . . Others opt for poor eyesight. . . . [M]y guess is that he had a weight problem. I think he might have been a fatty just like us" (*Fat Is in Your Head*, 87; see also *Pray Your Weight Away*, 120).

8. Snyder, *A Life Styled by God*, 22.

9. Bruce T. Marshall, "The Theology of Eating," *Christian Century*, March 18, 1981, 301–2.

10. Dumke, *The Serpent Beguiled Me*, 109, 110, 82–85. Episcopal authors generally seem more positive about food than their evangelical counterparts. Kane had earlier assured his readers, "Jesus was not an ascetic. He loved to eat, in spite of the fact that he frequently fasted and attributed a part of his power to it. . . . We think of the Last Supper as a meager affair of bread and wine but it was not so. This symbolic meal, which ultimately became the Holy Communion, was really the aftermath of a farewell banquet arranged for Jesus and his friends." Yet just a few pages later, he divided food into three kinds, including a category that included "rich gravies, creamed sauces, and baked beans" and was "absolutely illegal" for the person concerned about his or her shape (Kane, *Devotions for Dieters*, 49–50, 54).

11. Hoover, *God Even Likes My Pantry*, 95, 96.

12. Zola Levitt, *How to Win at Losing* (1976), 83–84.

13. Chapian and Coyle, *Free to Be Thin*, 40.

14. George Malkmus, *Why Christians Get Sick* (1989), 34, 26, 72. The citation is from 1 Corinthians 3:17 (KJV).

15. Malkmus, *God's Way to Ultimate Health,* 217–18. Malkmus here reprinted passages from Lester Roloff's own work, presumably *Soul, Mind, and Body* (1967) and *Food, Fasting and Faith* (1960). Roloff was the influence for Malkmus's conversion to natural foods in 1976.

16. Shamblin, *Weigh Down Diet,* 149.

17. Shamblin, *Rise Above,* 196, 81.

18. E-mail correspondence, January 4, 2002. E-mail correspondence, January 3, 2002.

19. Dr. Daniel Harrell, "Gluttony, March 8, 2003," www.parkstreet.org/pulpit/dh03/dh030903.shtml (accessed 2 Apr 2003). *Re:Generation Quarterly,* founded in 1994, was a print and online journal that discussed contemporary Christian faith; the discussion thread on gluttony was available for public viewing at www.regenerator.com/conversations/showthread.php?s = b9b2d3edccc03e4550484a5fdf4ce167&threadid = 970 (accessed 2 Apr 2003).

20. Kreml, *Slim for Him,* 126.

21. Cook, *Diary of a FAT Housewife,* 120.

22. Soldo and Drahos, *Inside-Out Beauty Book,* 49.

23. Anne Ortlund, *Disciplines of the Beautiful Woman* (1984), 45, 44, 78.

24. "Recent Trends in Christian Bookselling Reflected in the National Religious Bestsellers," *Bookstore Journal* 8, no. 8 (October 1975): 80.

25. Cavanaugh, *More of Jesus, Less of Me,* 68, 69.

26. Shedd, *Fat Is in Your Head,* 26–27.

27. Shedd, *Fat Is in Your Head,* 64, 70, 71, 62.

28. Kreml, *Slim for Him,* 3. Kane, *Devotions for Dieters,* 25–26.

29. Cook, *Diary of a FAT Housewife,* 29–30, 39–40.

30. See, for instance, Jim Tear and Jan Houghton Lindsey, "Women: Their Special Problems and Their Role in Creating Fat Environments," in *Fed Up with Fat* (1978), 123–40.

31. Hunter, *God's Answer to Fat,* 22, 10; Cavanaugh, *More of Jesus, Less of Me,* 53.

32. Brestin and Johnston, *Joy of Eating Right,* 9.

33. Lisa Bevere, *You Are NOT What You Weigh* (1998), 29, 98, 99, 161. This path of nonresistance is strikingly different from Christian chastity writing directed to girls, where resistance is vital to maintaining the perfectly pure body; see Heather Hendershot, *Shaking the World for Jesus: Media and Conservative Evangelical Culture* (Chicago: University of Chicago Press, 2004). Another contrast with chastity literature pertains to the way in which boys are perceived unable to control their sexual drives, whereas in Christian diet literature, women are the ones seen as out of control (personal correspondence with Hendershot, September 2001).

34. Carol Showalter, *3D* (1997); for accounts of Bill's admonishments, see 32, 55, 61–62, 71–72, 73–75, 87–89, and 91.

35. Chapian and Coyle, *Free to Be Thin,* 179 (ellipsis in original).

36. Shamblin, *Rise Above,* 177, 129–30, 177.

37. Shamblin, *Rise Above*, 99, 135, 137, 305, 5, 165, 191–92, 317; her song "Heaven's Kiss," is on 319.

38. Ad copy and author information obtained from the authors' own Web site, where they call themselves the "Life Balance Ladies": http://lifebalanceladies .com/books/the-beautiful-balance.asp.

39. Neva Coyle, *Loved on a Grander Scale* (1998), 10.

40. Interview with Coyle, February 1, 2001. A transcript of this PBS profile is accessible online at www.pbs.org/wnet/religionandethics/week431/profile .html. The literature of fat activism is extensive; see especially Lisa Schoenfielder and Barb Wieser, eds., *Shadow on a Tightrope: Writings by Women on Fat Oppression* (Iowa City: Aunt Lute Books, 1983); and Shelley Bovey, *The Forbidden Body: Why Being Fat Is Not a Sin*, rev. ed. (New York: New York University Press, 1994).

41. Hillel Schwartz, *Never Satisfied: A Cultural History of Diets, Fantasies, and Fat* (New York: Free Press, 1986), 313.

42. Susan Bordo, *Unbearable Weight: Feminism, Western Culture, and the Body* (Berkeley: University of California Press, 1993), 254, 102. A number of commentators on the American obsession with body weight, including those who mention the Christian diet movement, treat the racialized discourse of American dieting at length. None, however, analyze this discourse as it occurs explicitly in Christian books and programs. Hence the specific religious underpinnings of idealized white femininity's racist dimensions remain overlooked. See, for instance, Bringle, *God of Thinness*, and Michelle Mary Lelwica, *Starving for Salvation: The Spiritual Dimensions of Eating Problems among American Girls and Women* (New York: Oxford University Press, 1999).

43. Shedd, *Pray Your Weight Away*, 131, 30.

44. Kane, *Devotions for Dieters*, 53; Kane refers to Joel Chandler Harris, *Uncle Remus, His Songs and His Sayings* (New York: D. Appleton, 1880), 177.

45. Montague, *How to Overcome Nervous and Other Forms of Constipation*, 130.

46. Kane, *Devotions for Dieters*, 61.

47. Ortlund, *Disciplines of the Beautiful Woman*, 46, 42. Laney the maid is "a dear woman, conscientious and capable, [who] has worked for me four half-days a week—shopping, running errands, cleaning and cooking, washing and ironing. She prays for me as she does it; she knows she's contributing to ministry; she brings me cups of tea or an encouraging word. The house shines, and my work load is exactly matched to my capacity" (41–42).

48. Ortlund, *Disciplines of the Beautiful Woman*, 47.

49. bell hooks, *Sisters of the Yam: Black Women and Self-Recovery* (Boston: South End Press, 1993), 71.

50. The sociologist Becky Thompson has questioned this truism, noting that African American eating disorders are way underreported because of the stigma of dieting in many African American communities. Shame, in Thompson's view, serves to silence women of color and others (such as lesbians) who don't fit the media profile of an anorexic woman; see Thompson, *A Hunger So Wide and So*

Deep: A Multiracial View of Women's Eating Problems (Minneapolis: University of Minnesota Press, 1997).

51. Ziba Kashef, "Mind Body: What We See in the Mirror," *Essence* 31, no. 12 (April 2001): 96.

52. Roberta Pollack Seid, *Never Too Thin: Why Women Are at War with Their Bodies* (New York: Prentice Hall, 1989), 225, 226.

53. Doris Witt, *Black Hunger: Food and the Politics of U.S. Identity* (New York: Oxford University Press, 1999), 189, 191; Retha Powers cited from her autobiographical essay, "Fat Is a Black Women's Issue," *Essence* October 1989, 75+.

54. See, for instance, Roger Cooter's argument about physiology as "live ideology": "Physiology viewed in this light, as inherently ideological, makes superfluous the distinction that is commonly entered into when referring to popular science—the distinction between 'science' and 'scientism,' or between what is 'real' and what is 'false' or 'ideological.'" While Cooter focuses his own analysis on early nineteenth-century physiology, his insights as to the ways in which physiology's popularizers abetted contemporary social (class) hierarchies are, of course, broadly applicable (Cooter, "The Power of the Body: The Early Nineteenth Century," in *Natural Order: Historical Studies of Scientific Culture*, ed. Barry Barnes and Steven Shapin [Beverly Hills: Sage Publications, 1979], 81).

55. Cavanaugh, *More of Jesus, Less of Me*, xi, 8, 24.

56. *Surgeon General's Report on Physical Activity and Health;* summary available on the Web site for the Centers for Disease Control and Prevention at www.cdc.gov/nccdphp/sgr/chapcon.htm (accessed 15 Feb 2001). The report defines as "overweight" those with a body-mass index (BMI—a calculation of height-weight ratios) between 25 and 29.9; the "obese" are those with a BMI of 30 or higher. Summarized, and illustrated by statistical tables, data on the prevalence of overweight and obesity among American adults are on the Web site of the National Center for Health Statistics at www.cdc.gov/nchs/products/pubs/pubd/hestats/3and4/overweight.htm (accessed 15 Feb 2001).

57. The journalist David Barboza documents this problem in "Rampant Obesity, a Debilitating Reality for the Urban Poor," *New York Times*, December 26, 2000, F5; this article is part of a larger *Times* series on obesity, available online at www.nytimes.com/obesity.

58. hooks, *Sisters of the Yam*, 70, 29.

59. Greg Critser, "Let Them Eat Fat: The Heavy Truths about American Obesity," *Harper's Magazine*, March 2000, 47. Critser notes the myopia toward the socioeconomic conditions of American obesity among writers such as Susie Orbach who, in her best-selling 1978 book, *Fat Is a Feminist Issue*, argued, "Fat is a social disease, and fat is a feminist issue. Fat is not about self-control or lack of will power. . . . It is a response to the inequality of the sexes (quoted on 45–46). See also Critser, *Fat Land: How Americans Became the Fattest People in the World* (Boston: Houghton Mifflin, 2003).

60. In recent years, a fairly extensive network of efforts has emerged from within black congregations to address matters of health and weight. See, for instance, J. S. Levin, "The Role of the Black Church in Community Medicine,"

Journal of the National Medical Association 76 (May 1984): 477–83; Emil Dean Peeler, "Black Preaching and Health Education" (DMin diss., Claremont School of Theology, Claremont, CA, 1992); and Jawanza Kunjufu, *Satan, I'm Taking Back My Health!* (2000). Another recent initiative is the National Cancer Institute–funded PRAISE! (Partnership to Reach African Americans to Increase Smart Eating) project, headquartered in the Nutrition Department of the University of North Carolina, Chapel Hill, and based in sixty predominantly black churches in eight North Carolina counties; see www.sph.unc.edu/nutr/Divisions/praise.htm (accessed 24 Jul 2001).

61. Jakes mentions race in relation to his father's story only when, describing the janitorial company his father built in Charleston, South Carolina, he remarks, "For a man of color to build a successful company at that time was quite a feat" (*Lay Aside the Weight*, 16).

62. Soldo and Drahos, *Inside-Out Beauty Book*, 15, 34, 103, 105, 117.

63. Richard Dyer, *White* (London: Routledge Press, 1997), 14–15.

64. Shamblin, *Rise Above*, 146, 151.

65. Shamblin, *Rise Above*, 265, 144–45; see also 321–22. On the purchase of Ashlawn, along with the Shamblins' subsequent building permit to add a $60,000 pool house, see Candy McCampbell, "You Could've Had It, for $2.3 million," *The Tennessean*, March 11, 1996, 1E; and "Building Permits," *The Tennessean*, July 1, 1997, 5W.

66. Jana Evans Braziel and Kathleen Lebesco, eds., *Bodies Out of Bounds: Fatness and Transgression* (Berkeley: University of California Press, 2001).

67. Kunjufu, *Satan, I'm Taking Back My Health!*, 155.

EPILOGUE

1. The only serious challenge to this view has come from treatments of male bodybuilding and other sports in which the primary goal is to attain bodily strength and muscularity. See, for instance, Harvey Green, *Fit for America: Health, Fitness, Sport, and American Society* (New York: Pantheon, 1986); Elliot J. Gorn, *The Manly Art: Bare-Knuckle Prize Fighting in America* (Ithaca: Cornell University Press, 1986); Donald J. Mrozek, *Sport and American Mentality, 1880–1910* (Knoxville: University of Tennessee Press, 1983); Elizabeth H. Pleck and Joseph H. Pleck, eds., *The American Man* (Englewood Cliffs, NJ: Prentice Hall, 1980), 24–25; and E. Anthony Rotundo, *American Manhood : Transformations in Masculinity from the Revolution to the Modern Era* (New York: Basic Books, 1993), 222–46.

2. Habisohn is also founder and president of the GIFT Foundation, a conservative Catholic apostolate that is anti-abortion, anti-contraception, and pro-chastity; for more on e5 men see R. Marie Griffith, "The Fasting Masters of the Twenty-First Century" (www.beliefnet.com/frameset.asp?pageLoc = /story/122/story_12233_1.html&boardID = 53017).

3. Lee Bueno-Aguer, *Fast Your Way to Health* (2001), 201, 202. Jerry Falwell and Elmer Towns, eds., *Fasting Can Change Your Life* (1998), 11.

4. Laura Sheahan, " 'Husbands Crucified': Men Take up the Cross for Their Wives" (interview with Steve Habisohn), www.beliefnet.com/story/122/story _12273_1.html.

5. See Donald E. Miller, Lori Jensen, and Richard W. Flory, "Marked for Jesus: Sacred Tattooing Among Evangelical GenXers," in *GenX Religion*, ed. Richard W. Flory and Donald E. Miller (New York: Routledge, 2000), 15–30; and Tom Beaudoin, *Virtual Faith: The Irreverent Spiritual Quest of Generation X* (San Francisco: Jossey-Bass, 1998). Beaudoin, himself a Generation X Christian whose body is pierced, has discussed piercings and tattoos further in the media; see his comments in Laurie Lattimore and Greg Warner, "Bearing the Mark," www.faithworks.com/articles/article%20archive/pierce.htm (accessed 26 Jul 2001). Another instructive piece, though less relevant to contemporary religion, is Susan Holtham, "Body Piercing in the West: A Sociological Inquiry," www.bme.freeq.com/pierce/bodypier.html (accessed 26 Jul 2001).

6. "Eternal Ink" is the name of the Christian Tattoo Association's online newsletter, www.xtat.org/newsletters/newsletters.htm (accessed 26 Jul 2001).

7. Jesse Jarrell, a client of the premier body artist Steve Haworth, quoted in Maureen Mercury, *Pagan Fleshworks: The Alchemy of Body Modification* (Rochester, VT: Park Street Press, 2000), 67. The literature on this topic is too extensive to detail here, but see especially Housk Randall and Ted Polhemus, *The Customized Body* (London: Serpent's Tail, 1996).

8. See the comments by twenty-five-year old Mike Gray, the son of a Baptist preacher in rural Texas: " 'I got the Prince Albert [pierced penis, named for the Victorian royal] for no good reason except I was not using it. Because of my faith and the fact I'm not married, I don't have sex.' The piercing is 'definitely a reminder of his Christian commitment' " (Greg Warner, "Stigma," www .faithworks.com/articles/article%20archive/pierce.htm [accessed 27 Jul 2001]). For non-Christian men immersed in the inking-piercing world of alternative culture, of course, the Prince Albert is thought to enhance, rather than curb, sexual pleasure.

9. On the evangelical chastity movement, see Heather Hendershot, "Virgins for Jesus: The Gender Politics of Therapeutic Christian Fundamentalist Media," in *Hop on Pop: The Pleasures and Politics of Popular Culture*, ed. Henry Jenkins, Tara McPherson, and Jane Shattuc (Durham, NC: Duke University Press, 1998); see also Hendershot, *Shaking the World for Jesus: Media and Conservative Evangelical Culture* (Chicago: University of Chicago Press, 2004). "True Love Waits" is the best known and probably largest of the national chastity campaigns, organized by Southern Baptists; see www.lifeway.com/tlw/. A 1996 event featured 340,000 pledge cards on display at the Georgia Dome while in 1999, 1,500 youth transported 100,000 cards across San Francisco's Golden Gate Bridge.

10. Deborah Newman, *Loving Your Body* (2002); Gregory L. Jantz, *Hope, Help, and Healing for Eating Disorders* ([1995] 2002); www.remuda-ranch.com; "Rosh Hodesh: It's a Girl's Thing!" comes from KOLOT: the Center for Jewish Women's and Gender Studies, Reconstructionist Rabbinical College, 1299

Church Road, Wyncote, PA 19095–1898 (thanks to Mindy Shapiro, project director, for corresponding with me); a prominent United Church of Christ church in New England sent out the following announcements to parishioners: "Faith Education Forum, Sunday, March 30th, 12:30pm: The Christian education committee invites everyone to 'Caring for God's Temple,' a workshop on eating disorders."

11. "Anne," quoted in Rebecca Hylander, "Starving and Saving the Body: Christianity as Cause and Cure of Eating Disorders" (senior thesis, Department of Religion, Princeton University, 2003), 74.

12. Newman, *Loving Your Body*, 34, 24; Amy Nappa, *The Low-Fat Lifestyle* (2002; Nappa has been a columnist for *Focus on the Family* magazine). Also relevant in this context is Os Guinness's scathingly titled book, *Fit Bodies, Fat Minds: Why Evangelicals Don't Think and What to Do about It* (Grand Rapids, MI: Baker Book House, 1994).

13. Caroline Knapp, *Appetites: Why Women Want* (New York: Counterpoint, 2003), 18, 19.

14. Marion Nestle, *Food Politics: How the Food Industry Influences Nutrition and Health* (Berkeley: University of California Press, 2002); Eric Schlosser, *Fast Food Nation: The Dark Side of the All-American Meal* (New York: Houghton Mifflin, 2001); Critser, *Fat Land*.

15. N. Katherine Hayles, *How We Became Posthuman: Virtual Bodies in Cybernetics, Literature, and Informatics* (Chicago: University of Chicago Press, 1999), 3, 47; for a related view of how bodies are being appropriated to political ends, see Brian Pronger, *Body Fascism: Salvation in the Technology of Physical Fitness* (Toronto: University of Toronto Press, 2002).

Primary Source Bibliography

NB: full citations of secondary sources are in the backnotes. Corrections and additions to this primary source list, split roughly at the mid-twentieth century, will be noted in any future editions of this book, as well as in the online version of this bibliography, www.princeton.edu/~griffith/BornAgainBodies .htm. I have not sought to include all editions of every published text.

SELECTED NEW THOUGHT-INSPIRED BOOKS ON DIET, BODY IMAGE, AND RELATED TOPICS

Atkinson, William Walker. *Human Nature: Its Inner States and Outer Forms.* Chicago, IL: Progress, 1910.

Barber, Edith M. *What Shall I Eat?* New York: Macmillan, 1933.

Bush, David Van. *What to Eat.* St. Louis, MO, 1922.

Bush, David Van, and W. Waugh. *Character Analysis: How to Read People at Sight.* St. Louis, MO: Lincoln Press, 1923.

Call, Annie Payson. *A Matter of Course.* Boston: Roberts Brothers, 1894.

———. *Power through Repose.* Boston: Roberts Brothers, 1892.

Carrington, Hereward. *Vitality, Fasting, and Nutrition.* New York: Rebman, 1908.

Chavannes, Albert. *Magnetation, and Its Relation to Health and Character.* Knoxville, TN, 1898.

———. *Mental Science, as a Guide to Health, Happiness, and Business Success.* Knoxville, TN, 1902.

Cocroft, Susanna. *Beauty a Duty: The Art of Keeping Young.* Chicago: Rand McNally, 1915.

———. *Character as Expressed in the Body.* Chicago: Physical Culture Extension Society, 1906.

DeMotte, John B. *The Secret of Character Building.* Chicago: S. C. Griggs, 1892.

Densmore, Emmet. *How Nature Cures.* London: Swan Sonnenschein; New York: Stillman, 1892.

Dewey, Edward Hooker, MD. *The No-Breakfast Plan and the Fasting-Cure.* London: L. N. Fowler, 1900.

———. *The True Science of Living: The New Gospel of Health.* Norwich, CT: Charles Courtney Haskell and Son, 1899.

Eales, Irving James. *Healthology.* London: L. N. Fowler, 1907.

Fillmore, Charles. *Keep a True Lent.* Unity Village, MO: Unity School of Christianity, 1953.

Fillmore, Myrtle. *Letters of Myrtle Fillmore.* Kansas City, MO: Unity School of Christianity, 1936.

Fitzgerald, O. P. *Sunset Views.* Nashville: Publishing House of the Methodist Episcopal Church, South, 1900.

Fletcher, Horace. *The A.B–Z. of Our Own Nutrition.* New York: F. A. Stokes, 1903.

———. *Glutton or Epicure?* New York: H. S. Stone, 1899.

Flower, Sydney B. *New Thought System of Dietetics.* Chicago: New Thought Book Department, 1921.

———. *New Thought System of Physical Culture and Beauty Culture.* Chicago: New Thought Book Department, 1921.

Haskell, Charles Courtney. *Perfect Health: How to Get It and How to Keep It, by One Who Has It.* Norwich, CT: Charles Courtney Haskell and Son, 1901.

Hauser, Bengamin Gayelord. *Food Science and Health.* New York: Tempo Books, 1930.

———. *Look Younger, Live Longer.* New York: Farrar, Straus, 1950.

Hay, William Howard. *Health Via Food.* East Aurora, NY: Sun-Diet Health Foundation, 1933.

Hazzard, Linda Burfield, MD. *Fasting for the Cure of Disease.* 2d ed. Seattle: Hazzard Publishing, 1910.

Herrick, Christine Terhune. *Lose Weight and Be Well: The Story of a Stout Woman Now Thin.* New York: Harper and Brothers, 1917.

Hoelzel, Frederick. *A Devotion to Nutrition.* New York: Vantage Press, 1954.

Long, Alice M. *My Lady Beautiful, or The Perfection of Womanhood.* Chicago: Progress, 1908.

Macfadden, Bernarr. *Fasting for Health: A Complete Guide on How, When and Why to Use the Fasting Culture.* New York, 1923.

———. *Macfadden's Encyclopedia of Physical Culture: A Work of Reference, Providing Complete Instructions for the Cure of All Diseases through Physcultopathy, with General Information on Natural Methods of Health-Building and a Description of the Anatomy and Physiology of the Human Body.* New York: Physical Culture Publishing, 1912.

———. *Superb Virility of Manhood: Giving the Causes and Simple Home Methods of Curing the Weaknesses of Men.* New York, 1904.

———. *Vitality Supreme.* New York: Physical Culture Publishing, 1915.

Macfadden, Bernarr, and Felix Oswald. *Fasting—Hydropathy—Exercise: Nature's Wonderful Remedies for the Cure of All Chronic and Acute Diseases.* New York: Physical Culture Publishing, 1900.

Mulford, Prentice. *The Gift of the Spirit: A Selection from the Essays of Prentice Mulford,* with preface and introduction by Arthur Edward Waite. London: William Rider and Son, 1908.

———. *Essays of Prentice Mulford: Your Forces, and How to Use Them.* Vols. 4–6. New York: F. J. Needham, 1890.

———. *Thoughts Are Things.* London: G. Bell and Sons, 1911.

Olsten, Albert. *Mind, Power and Privileges.* New York: Thomas Y. Crowell, 1902.

Pearson, Robert Baille. *Fasting and Man's Correct Diet.* Chicago, 1921.

Peters, Lulu Hunt. *Diet and Health with Key to the Calories.* Chicago: Reilly and Lee, 1918.

Purinton, Edward Earle. *The Philosophy of Fasting: A Message for Sufferers and Sinners.* New York: Benedict Lust, 1906.

———. *The Purinton Foundation Course in Personal Efficiency.* New York: Independent Corporation, 1918.

Seton, Julia. *The Short Cut—Regeneration through Fasting.* Chicago: Occult Publishing, 1929.

Shaw, J. Austin. *The Best Thing in the World, Good Health: How to Keep It for a Hundred Years.* Norwich, CT: Charles Courtney Haskell and Son, 1906.

Sheldon, William Herbert. *Prometheus Revisited: A Second Look at the Religious Function in Human Affairs, and a Proposal to Merge Religion with a Biologically Grounded Social Psychiatry.* Cambridge, MA: Schenkman Publishing, 1975.

———. *Psychology and the Promethean Will: A Constructive Study of the Acute Common Problem of Education, Medicine and Religion.* New York: Harper and Brothers, 1936.

———. *The Varieties of Human Physique: An Introduction to Constitutional Psychology.* New York: Harper and Brothers, 1940.

———. *The Varieties of Temperament: A Psychology of Constitutional Differences.* New York: Harper and Brothers, 1942.

Sheldon, William H[erbert], Emil M. Hartl, and Eugene McDermott. *Varieties of Delinquent Youth: An Introduction to Constitutional Psychiatry.* New York: Harper and Brothers, 1949.

Sinclair, Upton. *The Fasting Cure.* New York: Health Research, 1996. First published 1911 by W. Heinemann.

Sinclair, Upton, and Michael William. *Good Health and How We Won It, with an Account of the New Hygiene.* New York: F. A. Stokes, 1909.

Stockham, Alice B. *Karezza: Ethics of Marriage.* New and rev. ed. Chicago: Stockham Publishing, 1903.

———. *Tokology: A Book for Every Woman.* Chicago: Stockham Publishing, 1902.

Thompson, Vance. *Eat and Grow Thin: The Mahdah Menus.* New York: E. P. Dutton, 1914.

Towne, Elizabeth. *How to Use New Thought in Home Life.* London: L. N. Fowler, 1916.

———. *Practical Methods for Self Development: Spiritual—Mental—Physical.* Holyoke, MA: Elizabeth Towne, 1904.

Trine, Ralph Waldo. *In Tune with the Infinite, or Fullness of Peace, Power, and Plenty.* New York: Thomas Y. Crowell, 1897.

Wattles, Wallace D. *Health through New Thought and Fasting.* Holyoke, MA: Elizabeth Towne, 1907.

Welsh, Francis Gordon. *Can We Live Forever?* Chicago: Weldon Press, 1938.

White, Ellen. *Ministry of Healing.* Mountain View, CA: Pacific Press Publishing, 1905.

Whiting, Lilian. *The World Beautiful.* 1st–3d series. Boston: Little, Brown, 1907.

Winslow, Thyra S. *Think Yourself Thin.* New York, 1951.

SELECTED CHRISTIAN BOOKS ON DIET, BODY IMAGE, AND RELATED TOPICS

Allen, Cynthia Culp, and Charity Allen Winters. *The Beautiful Balance for Body and Soul.* Grand Rapids: Fleming H. Revell, 2003.

Anderson, Andy. *Fasting Changed My Life.* Nashville: Broadman Press, 1977.

Arterburn, Stephen, Mary Ehemann, and Vivian Lamphear. *Gentle Eating: Achieve Permanent Weight Loss through Gradual Life Changes.* Nashville: Thomas Nelson Publishers, 1994.

Baker, Elizabeth. *Does the Bible Teach Nutrition?* Mukilteo, WA: Winepress Publishing, 1997.

Baldinger O'Bannon, Kathleen, with Barry Richards. *God's Word for the Biblically-Inept.* Lancaster, PA: Starburst Publishers, 1999.

Barnes, Emilie. *Simply Dinner.* Eugene, OR: Harvest House Publishers, 1998.

Barnes, Emilie, and Sue Gregg. *The Busy Woman's Guide to Healthy Eating.* Eugene, OR: Harvest House Publishers, 2002.

Bernhard, Colleen [Colleen C. Harrison]. *He Did Deliver Me from Bondage: Using the Book of Mormon and the Principles of the Gospel of Jesus Christ as They Correlate with the Twelve-Step Program to Overcome Compulsive/ Addictive Behavior.* Orem, UT: Windhaven Publishing and Productions, 1994.

Bevere, Lisa. *You Are NOT What You Weigh: Escaping the Lie and Living the Truth.* Lake Mary, FL: Creation House, 1998.

Brestin, Dee, and Peggy Johnston. *The Joy of Eating Right: Spiritual and Nutritional Principles for Weight Control.* Wheaton, IL: Victor Books, 1993.

Bright, Bill. *Seven Basic Steps to Successful Fasting and Prayer.* Orlando, FL: New Life Publications, 1995.

Broer, Ted. *Maximum Energy.* Lake Mary, FL: Siloam Press, 1999.

Bryant, Anita, and Bob Green. *Running the Good Race.* Old Tappan, NJ: Fleming H. Revell, 1976.

Bueno-Aguer, Lee. *Fast Your Way to Health.* 1991. New Kensington, PA: Whitaker House, 2001.

Campbell, Roger F. *Thin, Trim, and Triumphant: How to Get God's Help in Losing Unwanted Pounds.* Wheaton, IL: Victor Books, 1989.

———. *Weight! A Better Way to Lose.* 3d ed. Grand Rapids, MI: Kregel Publications, 1999. First published 1976 by Victor Books.

Capon, Robert F. *The Supper of the Lamb.* Garden City, NY: Doubleday, 1969.

Carlton, Fran. *A Time for Fitness: A Daily Exercise Guide for the Christian.* Waco, TX: Word Books, 1976.

Cavanaugh, Joan, with Pat Forseth. *More of Jesus, Less of Me.* Plainfield, NJ: Logos International, 1976.

Chapian, Marie, and Neva Coyle. *Free to Be Thin.* Minneapolis: Bethany House, 1979.

Chatham, R. D. *Fasting: A Biblical-Historical Study.* South Plainfield, NJ: Bridge Publishing, 1987.

Christiansen, Jan. *Desert Morsels: A Journal with Encouraging Tidbits from My Journey on the Weigh Down Diet.* Lancaster, PA: Starburst Publishers, 2000.

———. *More of Him, Less of Me: My Personal Thoughts, Inspirations, and Meditations on the Weigh Down Diet.* Lancaster, PA: Starburst Publications, 1998.

Chumley, Norris J. *The Joy of Weight Loss: A Spiritual Guide to Easy Fitness.* New York: Lantern Books, 2001.

Cloninger, Claire, and Laura Barr. *Faithfully Fit: A 40-Day Devotional Plan to End the Yo-Yo Lifestyle of Chronic Dieting.* Dallas: Word Publishing, 1991.

Colbert, Don. *Toxic Relief.* Lake Mary, FL: Siloam Press, 2001.

———. *What Would Jesus Eat? The Ultimate Program for Eating Well, Feeling Great, and Living Longer.* Nashville: Thomas Nelson Publishers, 2002.

Cook, Shirley. *Diary of a FAT Housewife.* Denver: Accent Books, 1977.

———. *The Exodus Diet Plan.* Old Tappan, NJ: Fleming H. Revell, 1986.

Cooper, Kenneth H. *Faith-Based Fitness.* Nashville: Thomas Nelson Publishers, 1995.

———. *It's Better to Believe.* Nashville: Thomas Nelson Publishers, 1995.

Couey, Dick. *Happiness Is Being a Physically Fit Christian.* Nashville: Broadman Press, 1985.

Couey, Dick, and Tommy Yessick. *Fit to Serve Him Longer . . . and Better: A Physical Fitness and Nutrition Guide for Christians.* Nashville: LifeWay Press, 1998.

Coyle, Neva. *The All-New Free-to-be-Thin Lifestyle Plan.* Minneapolis: Bethany House, 1993.

———. *Free to Be Thin Cookbook.* Minneapolis: Bethany House, 1982.

———. *Free to Dream.* Minneapolis: Bethany House, 1990.

———. *Loved on a Grander Scale: Affirmation, Acceptance, and Hope for Women Who Struggle With Their Weight.* Ann Arbor, MI: Servant Publications, 1998.

———. *Overcoming the Dieting Dilemma: What to Do when the Diets Don't Do it.* Minneapolis: Bethany House, 1991.

Coyle, Neva, and Marie Chapian. *The All-New Free to Be Thin.* Minneapolis: Bethany House, 1993.

———. *There's More to Being Thin than Being Thin.* Minneapolis: Bethany House, 1984.

Demetre, Danna. *Scale Down: A Realistic Guide to Balancing Body, Soul, and Spirit.* Grand Rapids, MI: Fleming H. Revell, 2003.

Dick, Dan R. *Devotions for Dieters: A 365-Day Guide to a Lighter You!* Uhrichsville, OH: Barbour, 1989.

Dillinger, Jesse. *Reasonably Thin: The Spiritual Aspects of Over- and Under-eating.* Nashville: Thomas Nelson Publishers, 1998.

Dorian, Terry. *Health Begins in Him: Biblical Steps to Optimal Health and Nutrition.* Lafayette, LA: Huntington House Publishers, 1995.

———. *Total Health and Restoration: A 180-Day Journey.* Lake Mary, FL: Siloam Press, 2002.

Dumke, Edward J. *The Serpent Beguiled Me and I Ate: A Heavenly Diet for Saints and Sinners.* New York: Doubleday, 1986.

Evans, Debra. *The Christian Women's Guide to Personal Health Care.* Wheaton, IL: Crossway Books, 1998.

Falwell, Jerry, and Elmer Towns, eds. *Fasting Can Change Your Life.* Ventura, CA: Regal Books, 1998.

Fat-Burning Bible Diet. Lantana, FL: MicroMags, 2000.

Fit 4. *Fitness Member Workbook.* Nashville: LifeWay Press, 2000.

Fitzpatrick, Elyse. *Love to Eat, Hate to Eat: Breaking the Bondage of Destructive Eating Habits.* Eugene, OR: Harvest House Publishers, 1999.

Fletcher, Kingsley. *Prayer and Fasting.* New Kensington, PA: Whitaker House, 1992.

Gault-McNemee, Dorothy. *God's Diet.* New York: Three Rivers Press, 1995.

Gilmore, Haydin. *Jog for Your Life.* Grand Rapids, MI: Zondervan Publishing House, 1974.

Halliday, Judy Wardell, and Arthur Halliday. *Silent Hunger: A Biblical Approach to Overcoming Compulsive Eating and Overweight.* Grand Rapids, MI: Fleming H. Revell, 1994.

———. *Thin Again: A Biblical Approach to Food, Eating, and Weight Management.* 1994. Grand Rapids, MI: Baker Book House, 2002.

———. *Thin Within: A Grace-Oriented Approach to Permanent Weight Loss.* Nashville: W. Publishing Group, 2002. First published 1985 by Harmony Books.

Hammond, Beth. *Lord, Help Me! The Desperate Dieter.* St. Louis, MO: Concordia Publishing House, 1983.

Hampton, Diane. *The Diet Alternative.* New Kensington, PA: Whitaker House, 1984.

Hansen, Jane. *Where Hearts Are Shared Cookbook.* Ventura, CA: Regal Books, 2001.

Heinerman, John. *Joseph Smith and Natural Foods: A Treatise on Mormon Diet.*

Springville, UT: Bonneville Books, 2001. First published 1976 by Mountain Valley Publishers.

Heller, A. L. *Your Body His Temple.* Nashville: Thomas Nelson Publishers, 1981.

Hesson, Margie. *Body and Soul: A Disciplined Approach to a Healthy Lifestyle.* Units 1–5. Nashville: Abingdon Press, 1995–97.

Hesson, Margie, Millsaps Dye Jr., and Alice Weldon Perry. *Body and Soul: A Healthy Lifestyle Adventure.* Lake Junaluska, NC: SEJ Administrative Council, 1990.

Higgs, Liz Curtis. *One Size Fits All and Other Fables.* Nashville: Thomas Nelson Publishers, 1993.

Hill, Harold, with Irene Burk Harrell and Gretchen Black. *How to Flip Your Flab—Forever.* Plainfield, NJ: Logos International, 1979.

Hill, Lynn. *The Weigh to Win at Weight Loss Calendar.* Wheaton, IL: Victor Books, 1993.

Holmes, Marjorie. *God and Vitamins: How Exercise, Diet, and Faith Can Change Your Life.* New York: Doubleday, 1980.

Hoover, Mab Graff. *God Even Likes My Pantry: Meditations for Munchers.* Grand Rapids, MI: Zondervan Publishing House, 1983.

———. *God Still Loves My Kitchen.* Grand Rapids, MI: Zondervan Publishing House, 1981.

Hunter, Frances G. *God's Answer to Fat—Looose It.* Houston: Hunter Ministries, 1975.

If I Really Wanted to Lose Weight I Would. . . . Tulsa, OK: Honor Books, 2000.

Jakes, T. D. *Lay Aside the Weight: The Essential Companion to the Bestselling Book.* Grand Rapids, MI: Bethany House, 1998.

———. *Lay Aside the Weight: Take Control of It Before It Takes Control of You.* Tulsa: Albury Publishing, 1997.

———. *Lay Aside the Weight: Workbook/Journal.* Grand Rapids, MI: Bethany House, 1998.

Jantz, Gregory L. *Hope, Help and Healing for Eating Disorders.* Colorado Springs: Waterbrook Press, 2002. First published 1995 by Harold Shaw Publishers.

———. *21 Days to Eating Better.* Grand Rapids, MI: Zondervan Publishing House, 1998.

Johnson, Jan. *When Food Is Your Best Friend (and Worst Enemy): An Intimate Look at Eating from 12-Step and Christian Perspectives.* San Francisco: HarperCollins, 1993.

Johnson, Paul, with Larry Richards. *Spiritual Secrets to Physical Health.* Waco, TX: Word Books, 1987.

Kane, H. Victor. *Devotions for Dieters: A Spiritual Life for Calorie Counters, with a Touch of Irony, by a Fellow Sufferer.* Old Tappan, NJ: Spire Books, 1967.

Kellman, Ira A. *Power Living: Everybody's Health and Diet Book.* Shippensburg, PA: Treasure House, 1996.

Kingsbury, Karen. *The PRISM Weight Loss Program.* Sisters, OR: Multnomah Publishers, 1999.

Kirban, Salem. *How to Eat Your Way Back to Vibrant Health.* Irvine, CA: Harvest House Publishers, 1977.

———. *How to Keep Healthy and Happy by Fasting.* Huntingdon Valley, PA: Salem Kirban, 1976.

Kliewer, Evelyn. *Freedom from Fat.* Old Tappan, NJ: Fleming H. Revell, 1977.

Koch, Karl, and Joyce Heil. *God Knows You'd Like a New Body.* Notre Dame, IN: Sorin Books, 2001.

Kopp, Heather Harpham. *The Dieter's Prayer Book: Spiritual Power and Daily Encouragement.* Colorado Springs: Waterbrook Press, 2000.

Krafft, James. *Flab: The Answer Book.* Old Tappan, NJ: Fleming H. Revell, 1983.

Kreml, Patricia B. *Slim for Him.* Plainfield, NJ: Logos International, 1978.

Kunjufu, Jawanza. *Satan, I'm Taking Back My Health!* Chicago: African American Images, 2000.

Lerner, Ben. *Body by God: The Owner's Manual for Maximized Living.* Nashville: Thomas Nelson, 2003.

Levitt, Zola. *How to Win at Losing.* Wheaton, IL: Tyndale House Publishers, 1976.

Lewis, Carole. *Back on Track: A Sixteen-Week Challenge to Help You Reach Your Weight-Loss Goals.* Ventura, CA: Regal Books, 2003.

———. *Choosing to Change: The First Place Challenge.* Nashville: LifeWay Press, 1996.

———. *First Place: Lose Weight and Keep It Off Forever.* Ventura, CA: Gospel Light, 2001.

———, ed. *Today Is the First Day: Daily Encouragement on the Journey to Weight Loss and a Balanced Life.* Ventura, CA: Gospel Light, 2002.

Lewis, Carole, with W. Terry Whalin. *First Place: The Original Spiritually Based Weight Loss Plan for Whole Person Fitness.* Nashville: Broadman and Holman Publishers, 1998.

Little, Deidre. *Fit for Eternity: Balanced Living through Better Nutrition and Spiritual Health.* Minneapolis: Bethany House, 2002.

Lovett, C. S. *Help Lord—The Devil Wants Me Fat!* Baldwin Park, CA: Personal Christianity, 1977.

———. *Jesus Wants You Well!* Baldwin Park, CA: Personal Christianity, 1973.

———. *Jogging with Jesus.* Baldwin Park, CA: Personal Christianity, 1978.

Ludington, Aileen. *Feeling Fit: True Stories of People Who Turned Their Health Around.* Hagerstown, MD: Review and Herald Publishing Association, 1997.

McClure, Cynthia Rowland. *The Monster Within: Facing an Eating Disorder.* 1984. Grand Rapids, MI: Baker Book House, 2002.

McDaniels, Evelyn. *Loving More, Eating Less.* Laramie, WY: Jelm Mountain Press, 1988.

Malkmus, George H. *Why Christians Get Sick.* Eidson, TN: Hallelujah Acres Publishing, 1989.

Malkmus, George H., with Michael Dye. *God's Way to Ultimate Health: A*

Common Sense Guide for Eliminating Sickness through Nutrition. Shelby, NC: Hallelujah Acres Publishing, 1995.

Meinz, David L. *Eating by the Book.* Virginia Beach: Gilbert Press, 1999.

Meyer, Joyce. *Eat and Stay Thin: Simple, Spiritual, Satisfying Weight Control.* Tulsa, OK: Harrison House, 1999.

Minirth, Frank B., Paul Meier, Robert Hemfelt, Sharon Sneed, and Don Hawkins. *Love Hunger.* Nashville: Thomas Nelson Publishers, 1990.

Mintle, Linda. *Breaking Free from Anorexia and Bulimia: How to Find Healing from Destructive Eating Disorders.* Lake Mary, FL: Charisma House, 2002.

———. *Breaking Free from Compulsive Overeating: Steps to Overcome a Life-Controlling Habit.* Lake Mary, FL: Charisma House, 2002.

Morris, Julie. *Step Forward! Diet: Learn to Cast Your Cares on God—not the Refrigerator!* Nashville: Abingdon Press, 1999.

Mundy, Linus. *The Complete Guide to Prayer-Walking.* New York: Crossroads Publishing, 1997.

Murphey, Cecil B. *Devotions for Calorie Counters.* Old Tappan, NJ: Fleming H. Revell, 1982.

———. *Fitness: The Answer Book.* Old Tappan, NJ: Fleming H. Revell, 1983.

Nappa, Amy. *The Low-Fat Lifestyle: Optimum Health for Body, Soul and Spirit.* Colorado Springs: Waterbrook Press, 2002.

Naylor, Barbara. *The Basic Ingredient: The Becomer's Balanced Diet and Complete Weight Loss Program.* Wheaton, IL: Harold Shaw Publishers, 1978.

Newman, Deborah. *Loving Your Body: Embracing Your True Beauty in Christ.* Wheaton, IL: Tyndale House Publishers, 2002.

O'Mathuna, Donal, and Walt Larimore. *Alternative Medicine: The Christian Handbook.* Grand Rapids, MI: Zondervan Publishing House, 2001.

Omartian, Stormie. *Better Body Management: Practical Tips for a Lifetime of Health and Fitness.* Nashville: Sparrow Press, 1993.

———. *Greater Health God's Way: Seven Steps to Health, Youthfulness, and Vitality.* Chatsworth, CA: Sparrow Press, 1984.

———. *Greater Health God's Way: Seven Steps to Inner and Outer Beauty.* Eugene, OR: Harvest House Publishers, 1996.

O'Neil, Cherry Boone. *Starving for Attention.* New York: Continuum, 1982.

Ortlund, Anne. *Disciplines of the Beautiful Woman.* 1977. Waco, TX: Word Books, 1984.

Pierce, Deborah, as told to Frances Spatz Leighton. *I Prayed Myself Slim: The Prayer-Diet Book.* New York: Citadel Press, 1960.

Piper, John. *A Hunger for God: Desiring God through Fasting and Prayer.* Wheaton, IL: Crossway Books, 1997.

Ploeger, JoAnn. *Slim Living Day by Day.* Wheaton, IL: Tyndale House Publishers, 1977.

Prince, Dereck. *Shaping History through Prayer and Fasting.* Springdale, PA: Whitaker House, 1973.

Renwick, Ethel Hulbert. *Let's Try Real Food: A Practical Guide to Nutrition and Good Health.* Grand Rapids, MI: Zondervan Publishing House, 1976.

Rogers, Joyce. *The Bible's Seven Secrets to Healthy Eating.* Wheaton, IL: Crossway Books, 2001.

Rohrer, Virginia, and Norman B. Rohrer. *How to Eat Right and Feel Great.* Wheaton, IL: Tyndale House Publishers, 1977.

———. *Junk Food: The Answer Book.* Old Tappan, NJ: Fleming H. Revell, 1983.

Rubin, Jordan S. *The Maker's Diet: The 40-Day Health Experience That Will Change Your Life Forever.* Lake Mary, FL: Siloam, 2004.

Rucker, Chris. *The Seventh-Day Diet: A Practical Plan to Apply the Adventist Lifestyle to Live Longer, Healthier, and Slimmer in the 21st Century.* Nampa, ID: Pacific Press Publishing, 2002. Originally coauthored with Jan Hoffman and published as *The Seventh-Day Diet: How the "Healthiest People in America" Live Better, Longer, Slimmer—And How You Can Too* (New York: Random House, 1991).

Russell, Rex. *What the Bible Says about Healthy Living: Three Biblical Principles That Will Change Your Diet and Improve Your Health.* Ventura, CA: Regal Books, 1996.

Salter, Charles A. *Getting It Off, Keeping It Off: Following God's Plan for Weight Control and Health.* Old Tappan, NJ: Fleming H. Revell, 1988.

Sanna, Ellyn. *Dieting in Real Life: 101 Tips and Inspiration for a Healthier You.* Uhrichsville, OH: Barbour Books, 2003.

Scott, William D. *In The Beginning, God Said: Eat Raw Food: Genesis 1:29, a Closer Look.* Coeur d'Alene: North Idaho Publishing, 2000.

Shambach, Mandel Conger, with Evelyn Campbell. *The King's Diet.* Harrison, AK: New Leaf Press, 1979.

Shamblin, Gwen. *Rise Above: God Can Set You Free from Your Weight Problem Forever.* Nashville: Thomas Nelson Publishers, 2000.

———. *The Weigh Down Diet.* New York: Doubleday, 1997.

Shedd, Charlie W. *Devotions for Dieters.* Waco, TX: Word Books, 1983.

———. *The Fat Is in Your Head.* Waco, TX: Word Books, 1972.

———. *Pray Your Weight Away.* Philadelphia: J. B. Lippincott, 1957.

Shepherd, Sheri Rose. *Fit for Excellence: God's Design for Spiritual, Emotional, and Physical Health.* Lake Mary, FL: Creation House, 1998.

Showalter, Carol. *3D.* Orleans, MA: Rock Harbor Press, 1977.

———. *3D: Diet, Discipline, and Discipleship.* Brewster, MA: Paraclete Press, 2002.

———. *3D Member's Manual: Your Guide to a Christ-Centered Program.* Brewster, MA: Paraclete Press, 1998.

Smith, Pamela M. *Food for Life: Breaking Free from the Food Trap.* 1994. Lake Mary, FL: Creation House, 1997.

Sneed, Sharon. *The Love Hunger Action Plan: A Dynamic Lifetime Weight-Loss and Maintenance Program.* Nashville: Thomas Nelson Publishers, 1993.

Snyder, Pamela E. *A Life Styled by God: A Woman's Workshop on Spiritual Discipline for Weight Control.* Grand Rapids, MI: Zondervan Publishing House, 1985.

Soldo, Betty Lougaris, and Mary Drahos. *The Inside-Out Beauty Book: The*

Complete Beauty Manual for Body and Soul. Old Tappan, NJ: Fleming H. Revell, 1978.

Sweet, Leonard I. *The Jesus Prescription for a Healthy Life.* Nashville: Abingdon Press, 1996.

Swope, Mary Ruth. *Are You Sick and Tired [of Feeling Sick and Tired]? A Nutrition Sourcebook.* Springdale, PA: Whitaker House, 1984.

———. *Lifelong Health.* New Kensington, PA: Whitaker House, 1997.

Tear, Jim, and Jan Houghton Lindsey. *Fed Up with Fat.* Old Tappan, NJ: Fleming H. Revell, 1978.

Thomas, Ann. *God's Answer to Overeating: A Study of Scriptural Attitudes.* Aglow Bible Study no. 7. Edmonds, WA: Women's Aglow Fellowship, 1975.

Tirabassi, Becky. *Change Your Life: Achieve a Healthy Body, Heal Relationships and Connect with God.* New York: G. P. Putnam's Sons, 1999.

Tirabassi, Becky, and Candice Copeland-Brooks. *Thoroughly Fit: How to Make a Lifestyle Change in 90 Days.* Grand Rapids, MI: Zondervan Publishing House, 1993.

Towns, Elmer L. *Fasting for Spiritual Breakthrough: A Guide to Nine Biblical Fasts.* Ventura, CA: Regal Books, 1996.

Updike, Earl F. *The Miracle Diet: Easy Permanent Weight Loss: 14 Days to New Vigor and Health.* Phoenix: Best Possible Health, 1995.

———. *The Mormon Diet: A Word of Wisdom: 14 Days to New Vigor and Health.* Bayfield, CO: Best Possible Health, 1991. Distributed by Cedar Fort.

Updike, Ethel C., Dorothy E. Smith, and Earl F. Updike. *The Mormon Diet Cookbook: Easy Permanent Weight Loss.* Bayfield, CO: Best Possible Health, 1992. Distributed by Cedar Fort.

Wade, Jean G., and Helen Kooiman Hosier. *Eating Your Way to Good Health: The Bible, Food, and You.* Old Tappan, NJ: Fleming H. Revell, 1977.

Wallis, Arthur. *God's Chosen Fast.* Fort Washington, PA: Christian Literature Crusade, 1968.

Ware, Nathan M. *The B.I.B.L.E. Diet: Believing in Becoming Lighter Eaters.* Madison, IN: Mark Art Productions, 1990.

Washington, Loricea. *The Annointing: Prayer, Fasting, and the Spirit-Filled Diet.* Newport News, VA: Faith for Living Publishing, 1993.

Weaver, La Vita M. *Fit for God: The 8–Week Plan that Kicks the Devil OUT and Invites Health and Healing IN.* New York: Doubleday, 2004.

Widtsoe, John A., and Leah D. Widtsoe. *The Word of Wisdom: A Modern Interpretation.* [Salt Lake City:] Deseret Book, 1937.

Wise, Karen. *God Knows I Won't Be Fat Again.* Nashville: Thomas Nelson Publishers, 1978.

Zeolla, Gary F. *Creationist Diet.* Bloomington, IN: First Books Library, 2000.

Zuck, Colleen, Elaine Meyer, and Jamie Wright. *Daily Word for Weight Loss: Spiritual Guidance to Give You Courage in Your Journey.* Emmaus, PA: Rodale Press, 2002.

SELECTED WEB SITES FOR FURTHER RESEARCH

www.billyblanks.com (Tae Bo system developed by Billy Blanks)
www.faithfullyfit.com (Products for the Christian Aerobics Resource)
www.firstplace.org (First Place, founded in 1981)
www.hacres.com (Hallelujah Acres and the Hallelujah Diet)
www.lifeway.com/fit4/ (A wellness program sponsored by Lifeway Christian
Resources of the Southern Baptist Convention)
www.lightweigh.com (The Light Weigh, a Catholic program)
www.mybodyhistemple.com (Electronic books and a newsletter published by
Kenneth Loy)
www.rawhealth.net/jesusdiet.htm (Explanation of the "Essene Fruitarian Diet
practiced and advocated by Jesus Christ")
www.stepforwarddiet.com/home.htm (Christian twelve-step diet)
www.wdworkshop.com (Weigh Down Workshop)

Index

Page numbers in *italic* refer to figures.

Indexer: Patricia Deminna
Compositor: BookMatters, Berkeley
Text: 10/13 Sabon
Display: Sabon